Rico Isaacs is an Associate Professor of Politics at the University of Lincoln. His research interests lay at the intersection of authoritarianism, culture, and political theory in post-Soviet states with a particular focus on the Central Asian Republics. He writes regularly on Central Asian politics and culture and is the current serving editor of *Central Asian Survey*.

'A fresh and a much needed account on nation-building studies and on the alternative ways in which nationalist and national narratives emerge in the cultural realm of cinema. The book presents a very succinct and eloquent narration of the historical development of Kazakh cinema from the Soviet period to the most recent contemporary works. The analysis focuses on different perspectives and themes that films provide – from government-sponsored ideas of modernity and state efficiency, to Tengrism (one of the most beautifully written chapters in the book!) to the everyday struggles of simple citizens. All of the themes represent a particular understanding and depiction of the national character or national idea of Kazakhstani society.'

Diana T. Kudaibergenova, Lund University and
University of Cambridge

'An excellent book exploring the link between cinema and the development of nations and nationalism, using as a case study the post-Soviet republic of Kazakhstan. The book provides an important contribution to our understanding of the nature of nations and nationalism, feeding into the broader disciplinary domain of political studies. I think it could become a classic in its domain, and addresses some important questions in a time marked by an increasing interest (and relevance) towards issues related to nationalism and means of popular political communication.'

Filippo Menga, Marie Sklodowska-Curie Research Fellow,
University of Manchester

FILM AND IDENTITY IN KAZAKHSTAN

Soviet and Post-Soviet Culture in Central Asia

RICO ISAACS

BLOOMSBURY ACADEMIC
LONDON • NEW YORK • OXFORD • NEW DELHI • SYDNEY

BLOOMSBURY ACADEMIC
Bloomsbury Publishing Plc
50 Bedford Square, London, WC1B 3DP, UK
1385 Broadway, New York, NY 10018, USA
29 Earlsfort Terrace, Dublin 2, Ireland

BLOOMSBURY, BLOOMSBURY ACADEMIC and the Diana logo are trademarks of Bloomsbury Publishing Plc

First published in Great Britain by I.B. Tauris 2018
Paperback edition published by Bloomsbury Academic 2022

Copyright © Rico Isaacs, 2018

Rico Isaacs has asserted their right under the Copyright, Designs and Patents Act, 1988, to be identified as Author of this work.

For legal purposes the Acknowledgements on pp. xiii-xv constitute an extension of this copyright page.

All rights reserved. No part of this publication may be reproduced or transmitted in any form or by any means, electronic or mechanical, including photocopying, recording, or any information storage or retrieval system, without prior permission in writing from the publishers.

Bloomsbury Publishing Plc does not have any control over, or responsibility for, any third-party websites referred to or in this book. All internet addresses given in this book were correct at the time of going to press. The author and publisher regret any inconvenience caused if addresses have changed or sites have ceased to exist, but can accept no responsibility for any such changes.

A catalogue record for this book is available from the British Library.

A catalog record for this book is available from the Library of Congress.

ISBN: HB: 978-1-7845-3838-5
PB: 978-1-3502-5229-5
ePDF: 978-1-8386-0853-8
ePub: 978-1-8386-0852-1

Typeset in Garamond Three by OKS Prepress Services, Chennai, India

To find out more about our authors and books visit www.bloomsbury.com and sign up for our newsletters.

For Oscar, Reuben, Seren and Olivia

CONTENTS

Note on Transliteration x
List of Illustrations xi
Acknowledgements xiii

Introduction   From Constructed to Contested Nations:
Theorising and Analysing Nation and Cinema   1
   Nations as Constructed   3
   Nations as Contested and Multiple   6
   Enter Cinema: Nationalist Myth-making and Myth-breaking 11
   Multiple Nationalisms and National Identities in
      Kazakhstan   14
   Analytical Framework and Methods   19
   Structure of the Book   30

1. Kazakh Khanate to Kazakh Eli: Nation-building in
   Kazakhstan in Historical and Political Context   33
      Ethno-genesis of the Kazakhstani Nation and the Rise and
         Fall of the Kazakh Khanate   35
      The Development of Nationalist Movements in Kazakhstan
         under Russian Rule   39
      Soviet Nation-building in Kazakhstan   43
      Post-Soviet Nation-building   50
      Conclusion   59

2. **Between Two Worlds: Kazakh Film and Nation-building in the Soviet Era** — 62
   The Development of the Cinema Industry in the Soviet
       Union and Central Asia — 65
   Antecedents to the Birth of Kazakh Cinema — 67
   The Emergence of Kazakh Cinema and Shaken Aimanov — 71
   1960–1970s: The National Awakening in Kazakh Cinema:
       The Two Worlds of Soviet Kazakh Cinema — 76
   Conclusion: Influence of Kazakh Soviet Cinema — 88

3. **The Disruption of Time: The 'Kazakh New Wave' 1985–95** — 91
   Introduction — 91
   Emergence of the New Wave — 93
   'Kazakh New Wave' as a Disruption of Empty
       Homogenous Time — 97
   The Re-imagination of Kazakh History — 100
   The Negation of Soviet Authority — 108
   Capturing Transition on Screen — 114
   After the 'Kazakh New Wave' — 120
   Conclusion — 122

4. **Naked in the Mirror: The Ethno-centric Narrative of Kazakh Nationhood** — 123
   Introduction — 123
   The Context of the Cinema Industry in post-Soviet
       Kazakhstan — 125
   Defence of the Homeland — 128
   Ethnic Identity — 135
   Power and Regime Legitimation — 142
   Reception — 148
   Conclusion — 151

5. **May the Grass Never Grow at Your Door: The Civic Conception of Nationhood in Kazakh Cinema** — 153
   Inter-ethnic Harmony and Stability — 154
   Kazakh Batyrs as Kind, Open and Hospitable — 162
   Interpretation of History and Soviet Authority — 167
   Reception — 171
   Conclusion — 173

6. **'Hymn to Mother': Tengrism, Motherhood and Nationhood** — 175
   Tengrism — 177
   Literal Representations of Tengrism in Contemporary Kazakh Cinema — 181
   Historical-philosophical Symbolic Representation of Tengrism in Contemporary Kazakh Cinema — 185
   Quasi-primordial Symbolic Representation: Women, Family and the Cycle of Birth, Life and Death — 193
   Controversy and Reception — 195
   Conclusion — 197

7. **The Steppe, Disorientation, Division and Corruption: Social and Economic Visions of Modern Nationhood** — 200
   The Kazakh Steppe — 203
   The Urban-rural Divide — 208
   Struggles with Bureaucracy and Authority — 212
   Home and Family — 221
   Morality and Wealth Accumulation — 226
   The Government's Image of Modernity — 232
   Conclusion — 236

Conclusion — 239
   Heterogeneity of National Identity — 239
   Dissent and Contentious Politics in Cinema — 246
   Film and Nation-building — 251

Notes — 254
Filmography — 308
Selected Bibliography — 315
Index — 328

NOTE ON TRANSLITERATION

Transliterations from the Russian language are based on the BGN/PCGN romanisation of Russian. Kazakh words are also transliterated from their Russian counterparts – except where the word itself derives from Kazakh, such as *Zhauzhurek Myn Bala* (Warriors of the Steppe) and *Akim* (Governor) and where the word, while translatable, does perhaps not provide for a complete cultural translation of its meaning. For example, *kelin* (daughter-in-law), for which the direct translation does not embody the cultural significance of the Kazakh *kelin*.

LIST OF ILLUSTRATIONS

Figures

Figure 2.1 Nurlan Segizbayev as Kozha in *My Name is Kozha* (1963), dir. Abdullah Karsakbayev.   79

Figure 2.2 Elubai Umurzakov and Murat Akhmadiev in *Land of the Fathers* (1966), dir. Shaken Aimanov.   82

Figure 2.3 Still from *Kyz-Zhibek* (1970), dir. Sultan Khodzhikov.   87

Figure 4.1 Asylkhan Tolypov (centre) as Sartai in *Zhauzhurek Myn Bala* (2011), dir. Akan Satayev.   129

Figure 4.2 Jay Hernandez as Ablai Khan in *Nomad* (2005), dir. Sergei Bodrov, Ivan Passer and Talgat Temenov.   133

Figure 4.3 Eljas Alpiev as the young Sultan in *Sky of My Childhood* (2011), dir. Rustem Abdrashev.   145

Figure 5.1 Dalen Shintemirov as Sabyr and Nurzhuman Ikhtymbayev as Kasym in *The Gift to Stalin* (2009), dir. Rustem Abdrashev.   161

Figure 5.2 Bolat Abdilmanov as Oreke in *The Promised Land* (2011), dir. Slambek Tauyekel.   165

Figure 6.1 Turakhan Sadykova as Ene in *Kelin* (2009), dir. Yermek Tursunov.   182

Figure 6.2 Yerbolat Toguzakov as Kasym in *Shal* (2012), dir. Yermek Tursunov.   189

Figure 7.1 Scene from *The Owners* (2014), dir. Adilkhan Yerzhanov. 215

Table

Table I.1 Analytical Framework for Study of Narratives of Nationhood and Identity in Cinematic Works 27

ACKNOWLEDGEMENTS

When I set out on this project in 2012 I thought it would be something of a frivolous piece of work. I would watch a couple of Kazakh films, knock out a quick 8000-word article and be done with it. I saw the project initially as a fleeting moment when my profession would elide with an interest in cinema. Sitting here in 2017, having completed a full book manuscript, comes as something of a surprise when reflecting on my initial ambitions for this work. That I could evolve such an amorphous idea into a full-scale book is in large part due to the significant assistance, support and guidance I have received throughout this project from colleagues and friends.

The fieldwork for the research in Almaty and Astana was undertaken at various points in 2012, 2014 and 2016. I am grateful for grants received from the British Council and the Faculty of Humanities and Social Sciences at Oxford Brookes University, which made those trips possible. Those fieldtrips would not have been fruitful had it not been for the assistance of several research assistants who helped with arranging and conducting interviews, collecting data and interview transcription. I am indebted to Zaure Mederkhanova, Nellie Sarova, Nikolay Shevchenko, Aliya Tskhay, Max Tyan and Yerbolat Yerzhanov for all their help on the project. A very special debt of gratitude is owed to Aidana Abdykulova, who has been an endless source of support throughout the whole research and writing and whose tireless effort in securing interviews, answering my multitude of questions, driving me around Almaty, responding to my requests and being a source of knowledge on Kazakh culture benefited this work considerably. I would like to express a further debt of thanks to Aliya Kadyrova, Yevgeniya Plakhina, Daniyar Sapargaliyev, Saltanat Nauruz and Zhar Zardykhan for all their help in organising the focus groups and interviews with hard-to-reach directors. I was fortunate to meet and speak with many film directors, critics and others working in the film industry in Kazakhstan who generously gave me their time and responded positively to my questions and interest in their work. A special thanks to Gulnara Abikeyeva, Serik Abishev, Kairzhan Orynbekov and Adilkhan Yerzhanov, who were all willing to speak with me on more than one occasion and have continued to take an interest in the book as it developed. I would also like to thank all those who contributed to the focus group discussions. During my stays in Kazakhstan I am grateful to the hospitality of colleagues at the Central Asia Studies Centre at KIMEP, who were always happy to accommodate me with office space and provide a friendly, warm and vigorous environment within which to conduct research. A heartfelt thanks to my surrogate Kazakh-Italian family, Alessandro Frigerio, Nargis Kassenova, Arsen and Anika, who were always at hand with a warm plate of pasta and an open bottle of wine after a hard day's research.

I have presented various aspects of the book at many conferences and invited seminar papers over the last few years. I am grateful to the organisers and audiences of such events and the discussions that prevailed have helped shape my thinking on this work. There have been too many events to mention here, but special note should go to the two papers presented in Kazakhstan at the Central Asian Studies Centre in 2016 and the Almaty Management University in 2014. Getting encouraging feedback from audiences of Kazakhstani citizens was a welcome sign that I was not barking too far up the wrong tree.

At Oxford Brookes, I have been fortunate in the support I have received from colleagues at the Centre for Global Politics, Economy and Society. I am especially grateful for Professor Gary Browning and Dr Abbey Halcli's support and encouragement over the duration of the project. I would like to say a special thank you to Dr Victoria Browne, Sofya Omarova and Dr Sarah Whitmore, who have all read various chapters of this book, while I am eternally grateful to Dr Emilia Pawlusz, Professor Birgit Beumers, Harry Gable and Dr Togzhan Kassenova for agreeing to read the full draft version of the manuscript, as well as two anonymous reviewers. Their constructive and insightful comments have only served to strengthen the book and iron out its weaknesses. Remaining issues with the book are entirely my responsibility.

Among a wider circle of academic colleagues, thanks go to Dr Filippo Menga, who kindly agreed to take on some of my teaching responsibilities in 2016, which allowed me some space to focus on writing. Also, thanks to Dr Abel Polese, my colleague in nation-building studies in Central Asia and the post-Soviet space. I would also like to thank Tomasz Hoskins and Arub Ahmed at I.B.Tauris for helping bring this book to publication.

Finally, thanks go to Peter, Gwen, Bettina, Gino and especially Charlotte for all putting up with me. For too long, working on this book, I spent my days distracted from day-to-day life. Thus, I am grateful for your patience and understanding.

Well, I have decided at length: henceforth, pen and paper shall be my only solace, and I shall set down my thoughts. Should anyone find something useful here, let him copy it down or memorise it. And if no one has any need of my words, they will remain with me anyway. And now I have no other concern than that.

Abai Kunanbayev, *Book of Words*,
Abai International Club (Semey, 2005), p. 78.

INTRODUCTION

FROM CONSTRUCTED TO CONTESTED NATIONS: THEORISING AND ANALYSING NATION AND CINEMA

On a scorching day in July 2011 I was perusing the Meloman store on Gogol Street in Almaty. Amid the racks of *Harry Potter and the Deathly Hallows* and *Rise of the Planet of the Apes* DVDs, I noticed a whole section dedicated to *Kazakhstanskoe Kino* (Kazakh cinema). I had been aware a few years earlier of the regime-sponsored film *Nomad*, a Braveheart-esque big-budget historical epic, but had not realised Kazakhstan had such a vibrant film industry. In all the time spent in Kazakhstan in the preceding five years I had not seen such an assertive campaign for the Kazakh film industry. Where did this come from? I asked myself. Why is Kazakh cinema[1] being promoted now? Most importantly, what were these films about? And what would they tell us about Kazakhstan and its construction of national-self in the post-Soviet period?

This book, therefore, is an effort to address the questions that came to me immediately on that hot summer's day, as well as a more fundamental question — what does cinema tell us about the construction of national identity and a sense of nation-ness? There is an extant literature on cinema and nation.[2] This tends to focus on either a textual analysis of the discourse of cinematic works considered to belong to a nation, and/or the broader domestic and global industrial context of the development of those national cinemas. This body of work belongs to the broader film studies discipline, where the dialectic between nation and history is an entry point to understanding specific cinemas and their particular transnational or post-colonial contexts.[3] The departure point for this book is the opposite. What do cinema and cinematic works tell us about the development of nations and nationalism? How can cinema help shape our understanding of the imagination of nations? Therefore, the aim is to approach cinema not from a film studies perspective, but instead from the direction of nationalism studies and, more broadly, political studies.

The 'nation'[4] as the primary unit of economic, political and social organisation emerged as a function of larger structural changes concomitant to industrialisation, capitalism and the development of communicative technologies.[5] From the eighteenth century onwards, especially in Europe, national political elites sought to match the 'nation' with the state via the consolidation of national cultures, which was achieved, for the most part, through the spread of vernacular languages, often as a consequence of the uneven development of economies and internal colonialism.[6] Print capitalism[7] was initially the central mechanism for the promotion of linguistically defined and imagined national cultures, but radio and film intensified this process throughout the twentieth century.[8] Therefore, the 'nation' and cinema share a close relationship in terms of their emergence and the extent to which they could be observed to constitute one another. Cinematic works in their distillations of time and space contribute to the kinds of imaginings that sustain nation states.[9] As Wimal Dissanayake has argued, 'the discourses of nationhood and history and the representational space opened up by films are all vitally connected with modernity and interpenetrate each other in complex ways'.[10] Understanding this close association between nation and cinema is the broad aim underpinning this book. Through an analysis of cinematic works, this book argues that rather than there being a homogenously accepted interpretation of nationhood among the Kazakh titular majority, what we can instead observe is the multiple and contentious nature of the Kazakh nation.

This introductory chapter sets out to address how we can conceptualise, theorise and analyse the relationship between film and nation-building in the case of Kazakhstan. The first two sections provide an interpretation of nations, nationalism and nation-building as constructed, contentious and multivalent. The third and fourth sections conceptualise the role of cinema in the nation-building process and detail how this specifically applies to the case of Kazakhstan. The fifth and sixth sections then lay out the specific analytical and methodological framework for exploring the relationship between film and nation-building in Kazakhstan, and how it demonstrates the contentious and multiple nature of nationhood.

Nations as Constructed

If cinema is understood to play a role in sustaining the imagination of nations across space and time, then it can be taken as read that the nation is a constructed social phenomenon. In his depiction of the creation of an imagined community made possible by Walter Benjamin's concept of empty homogenous time,[11] Benedict Anderson argued this exact point. In Anderson's view, 'the convergence of capitalism and print technology on the fatal diversity of human language created the possibility of a new form of imagined community, which in its basic morphology set the stage for the modern nation'.[12] Anderson's work followed on from that of Ernest Gellner, who argued that nations materialised as a result of the advent of 'high-culture'.[13] Put simply, Gellner argues nations emerged concomitant to industrialisation with the development of a universally literate, numerically and technically sophisticated, and highly mobilised communicative society.[14] Hobsbawm also concluded, similar to Anderson and Gellner, that nations were a product of modernity, but focused more on their socially engineered nature as invented artefacts.[15] Following this cannon of work, scholars such as Paul Brass pointed to how such construction and imagination of nations was undertaken by political elites for instrumental purposes.[16]

Such accounts of nations as being socially constructed have become a cliché. One is left wondering whether there is anything to add to a constructivist perspective on nations and nationalism. Yet, there is a tendency within these accounts to treat the nation as a homogenous, clearly defined group. Put differently, nations are assumed in their constructed and imagined form as unquestionable social wholes with a reified sense of self-identification. Gellner's work is perhaps most obvious in this respect. In *Thought and Change*, Gellner describes how nations emerge because of the need for standardised education and vernacular languages in the shift from pre-industrial to industrial society.

The result is a uniform social world, an attachment to an impersonalised community and the assimilation of folk cultures into a standardised cultural homogeneity.[17]

Similarly, Anderson understands that, despite internal divisions, the nation 'is always conceived as a deep, horizontal comradeship'.[18] In his analysis of how modern nationalism emerged in the colonial Americas, Anderson conceived of the idea that creole nationalisms were imagined through the 'specific imagined world of vernacular readers of newspapers'.[19] In doing so, he stresses the cultural and linguistic homogeneity of certain imagined communities, not the potential for contention or variation within those imagined communities.[20]

We can see this assumption more closely in Michael Billig's concept of banal nationalism. Building on the modernist and constructivist frames developed by Gellner, Anderson and Hobsbawm, Billig asserts that nations are sustained over the longer term via the reproduction (or what he terms 'flagging'), both conscious and unconscious, of national narratives, symbols, discourses and traditions. According to Billig, 'banal nationalism operates with prosaic, routine words, which take nations for granted, and which in doing, enhabit them. Small words, rather than grand memorable phrases, offer constant, but barely conscious, reminders of the homeland, making 'our' national identity unforgettable'.[21] Yet, Billig's formulation of banal nationalism neglects 'how different constituencies might respond to the particular media texts or political speeches used as examples of the nation being flagged in a routine or taken-for-granted manner'.[22] Not only are there various domestic audiences that exist, but they could also interpret the signs of nationalism and identity differently (such as region, class, gender and so on). Furthermore, there are also international audiences to which the concept of banal nationalism does not translate well (such as Europeanism and Americanism).[23]

That the nation is often assumed as a bounded whole within the constructivist paradigm has not gone unnoticed. As Rogers Brubaker has argued, the concept of the 'group' is taken for granted within the social sciences and 'ethnic' groups should not be reified as homogenous externally bounded groups with a single collective identity and agency.[24] While Brubaker focuses on the category of 'ethnicity', the logic of his critique applies equally to that of 'nation'. Despite constructivist accounts tending towards understanding the contingency and fluidity of nations at the rhetorical level, as Brubaker asserts, constructivism 'has become weary, stale, flat and unprofitable'.[25] Too often, as a result of the reification of the nation as a social category it fails to 'account for the ways in which – and conditions under which – this practice of reification, this powerful crystallisation of group feeling can work'.[26] Equally it fails to account for instances where reification does not work and instead divisions and fragmentations appear within a given social organism. This is not to suggest nations can exist as homogeneous wholes, or that they should exist as such, rather that analytically more is to be gained by focusing on their internal fragility and division. Importantly, the idea of heterogeneity within nation states has been a long-accepted aspect of modern nationalism. Hobsbawm is clear that there were many parts of Europe, and much of the rest of the world, in which nationalities were mixed up on the same territory.[27] The job of the state, therefore, was to spread a particular image and heritage of the nation that sought to bound distinct national groups to a single nation state identity.[28] This, however, as Hobsbawm notes, ran the risk of creating counter-nationalism from nationalities who are not the titular majority.[29] As we saw in the study of post-colonial nation-building the assimilation of different ethnic groups into cohesive 'nation states' was one of the main features of this process.[30] However, the reification discussed here in relation to groupism is about the contested and multivalent possibilities of the nation within a given titular national majority. It is not just about contested accounts or counter-nationalisms amongst different ethnic groups within a nation state. The focus here is the possibility that there exists, internal to specific titular (and non-titular) national groups, contested and contentious interpretations of nationhood and identity.

This book, therefore, provides a constructivist account of the nation by emphasising the contentious nature of the imagination of nationhood and identity within a titular group, an otherwise often neglected aspect of Nationalism Studies. It does so by approaching the subject, and its case of Kazakhstan, with two fundamental assumptions. Firstly, that to understand the construction and imagination of a nation we need to take account of the contentious nature of such imaginaries, especially in relation to the political expediency of certain representations of the nation, either for those involved in the production of national narratives or those who reject, negotiate or produce their own interpretations. By focusing on the contestation of nationhood, and not just along the lines of titular majorities versus ethnic minorities, but within titular majorities themselves, we can observe the fault lines and social divisions that underpin nations, and moreover, point to the fragility of their construction. Secondly, the book uses cinema, because of its concomitant relationship with the emergence of the modern nation, as an analytical lens to explore the construction of representations of the nation over time and to account for how they evolve, adapt and are contested. This second assumption concerning cinema will be addressed in detail in the following section. Before that, I will address the contentious nature of the constructed imaginations of nations and how this leads to their potential multiplicity as a social organism. I will undertake this with particular reference to nation-building[31] in the post-Soviet experience, and our case of interest here, Kazakhstan.

Nations as Contested and Multiple

As we note from Brubaker's critique of groupism above, we cannot assume a nation or its corresponding nationalism, defined here as a movement, organisation or ideology that makes claims regarding solidarity and inter-connectedness of a community of peoples as to their identity, jurisdiction and territory,[32] is singular or reified in any given case. Rather, the construction of nationhood can be observed as an internally contested process akin to the idea of contentious politics. Contentious politics is commonly understood as an interactive process in which 'actors make claims bearing on other actors' interests, leading to coordinated efforts on behalf of shared interests and programs, in which governments are involved as targets, initiators of claims, or third parties'.[33] Within the literature these types of claims have been analysed along three broad lines with contentious politics as either: the result of structurally rooted political process which creates a 'political opportunity structure'; a rational-choice account premised on the resource mobilisation capacity for individuals and organisations to make claims; or finally a constructivist approach, which focuses on the development of identities through the practice of claim-making.[34]

Taking the latter perspective as a point of departure,[35] we can understand the construction of nations and national identity as an inherently ambivalent process, which, as Homi Bhabha has argued, 'emerges from a growing awareness that, despite the certainty with which historians speak of the "origins" of the nation as a sign of "modernity" of society, the cultural temporality of the nation inscribes a much more transitional social reality'.[36] Therefore, an ambivalent reading introduces the idea of competing claims and alternative sites of meaning of the nation.[37] Put differently, examining the construction of nationhood in this way reveals the contested and conflicting process of nation-building; it is as Étienne Balibar has suggested, 'a configuration of antagonistic social classes that is not entirely autonomous, only becoming relatively specific in its opposition to others and via power struggles'.[38] Understanding the nation as a site of contentious politics raises two fundamental issues, one concerned with power and the other with dissent.

Firstly, in political terms some claims will have more power and greater weight than others. For instance, specific constructions of nationhood and identity are engendered by political elites. In the case of Kazakhstan and the role of cinema, I frame these as 'official' regime-led representations of the nation. The regime in the country is utilising the state-funded Kazakhfilm Studios to disseminate its 'imaginations' of the nation. The plural is telling here. The government does not have one, but two representations of the Kazakh nation (ethnic and civic – see Chapters 4 and 5, respectively). As such, it is evidence that even within state-led modulations of nationhood there is a form of contestation. Further, it also points to how the study of nations and nationalism elides with the study of authoritarian politics. In our case of interest in this book, these constructed imaginaries of the nation are the 'official' ideological expressions of nationhood constructed and purported by an authoritarian regime.

This top-down, elite-led understanding of identity formation in post-Soviet Kazakhstan (and the broader post-Soviet space) has underpinned existing empirical work on nation-building in Kazakhstan. This has been because scholars have framed the process through the lens of the concept of the 'nationalising state', which focuses on titular elites' attempts to nationalise the state body politic at the expense of other minority groups.[39] Consequently, scholars have suggested Kazakhstan is emblematic of a 'nationalising state', as the government has sought the Kazakhification of the state, lifting the titular Kazakh nationality to the standing of *primus inter pares* through a practised set of policies related to language, state recruitment, education and the re-writing of history.[40]

Simultaneously, it is argued that the Kazakh government, acutely aware of the ethnic diversity of the population, especially the sizable Russian minority, has sought to establish a civic Kazakhstani identity.[41] This subsequently produced a tension within the broader policy narrative of the Kazakh government, and especially the president, who has tried to appeal to both modes of national identity.[42] Ultimately, however, to see the contentious politics of the construction of a nation as both a top-down, elite-led process and a simple binary choice between an 'ethnic' and 'civic' nation is a largely limiting and simplistic interpretation. This is because it would assume nation-building is solely an elite-driven process and that representations of nationhood and identity correspond only to cultural or political interpretations of group boundaries. As this book will demonstrate, it is possible to observe the role of non-elite actors in nation construction efforts and that there are represenations of nationhood beyond just political and cultural manifestations.

Secondly, understanding the construction of nationhood and identity as a contentious process demonstrates how nation-building can provide a space for dissent, both in political terms (against the regime or political establishment) and in relation to how elite-led, 'official' representations of the nation can be challenged from below. Dissent is understood in this book in a broad way as a spectrum of values and actions that detour from commonly held norms and 'official' expressions of opinions. Therefore, it can include direct and open dissent against an authoritarian regime, but also, and perhaps more commonly in authoritarian systems, subtle indirect dissent, whereby deviance from the norm is understood through the varying interpretations of meaning behind a given expression. In this way, dissent resembles the contentious politics of everyday resistance alluded to in the work of James C. Scott.[43] The type of dissent, observable in cinematic work in authoritarian and bureaucratic regimes, is often subtle and discrete, representing a type of 'hidden transcript'.[44] Indirect dissent in this form can represent any expression that could be interpreted as undermining conventional political, economic and cultural narratives. Cinema and artistic works, therefore, offer a receptive conduit for such dissent in non-democratic settings. This is not to suggest that forms of dissent that appear in cinema represent outright open dissent, but rather are informal and indirect; relying on interpretation of meaning to decode their dissenting content.

Introduction

The above demonstrates how nation-building is not solely an elite-led process. As Eric Hobsbawm has argued, the official ideologies of the state are not reliable guides to what ordinary citizens feel about nationhood and identity.[45] Therefore, we do need to take account of other actors within the process, from those who enact nation-building policies to those who receive them. Adrien Fauve's work on monumentalisation in Kazakhstan is a good example of such an approach. In Fauve's analysis, Nursultan Nazarbayev's regime, through local *akims* (governors), possesses an 'imagined' vision of the nationhood and identity it seeks to represent through monuments dedicated to historical figures (e.g., Zhanybek and Kerey Khan), the interpretation and meaning of those monuments are shaped, however, by local actors (architects and sculptors). It is these actors who possess the agency to 'perform' nationhood and identity and this can compete with the original intentions of the state-led vision.

The logic of the above is that the process of imagining the nation can lead to multiple possibilities of the nation or, put more concretely, multiple nationalisms. Rima Wilkes and Michael Kehl have demonstrated the plurality of nationalisms in their analysis of war and conflict photography.[46] Put simply, there exists the prospect of varying claims of representations/narratives of what constitutes any nation. This should not be limited to interpretations of nationhood played out between a titular majority versus ethnic minorities. It is not just an issue of assimilation. It is, rather, a contestation between competing claims of nationhood as imagined within the titular majority itself. Therefore, we should not treat imaginations of the nation as accepted and understood by all. As scholarly debate on the question of identity in Ukraine has already shown us, the formation of national identity in the post-Soviet space can be ambivalent and consisting of multiple narratives.[47] The literature has demonstrated how the civic-ethnic binary fails to account for nuance within varying constructions of Ukrainian identity,[48] such as where regional identities can be more salient[49] and how nation-building is a heterogeneous process that transcends simple dichotomies.[50] These contributions to understanding national identity in post-Soviet Ukraine have been largely absent from the study of other post-Soviet states, perhaps with the exception of Oxana Shevel's work on Russia.[51] In the case of Kazakhstan, given it too, like Ukraine, is an ethnically heterogeneous state with a complex demographic and historical legacy left behind by both Russian imperial and Soviet rule, makes the continued focus on just the binary between 'ethnic' and 'civic' nationalism analytically unsatisfying.[52] This work, therefore, while identifiying regime-led civic and ethnic narratives in Kazakhstan, also goes beyond the dichotomy revealing alternative narratives of Kazakh nationhood related to religion and the socio-economic. Moreover, even if we returned to Brubaker's original formulation of the concept of the 'nationalising state' we would see he places something akin to the idea of multiple nationalisms front and centre in his definition:

> whether we are talking about perceived nationalising stances or openly avowed nationalising projects, there is a great deal of variation among such stances and projects, not only between states, but within a given state ... we can think of a nationalising state not in terms of a fixed policy orientation or a univocal set of policies or practices but rather in terms of a dynamically changing field of differentiated and competitive positions or stances adopted by different organizations, parties, movements or individual figures within and around the state ... [53]

Therefore, a fixation on only two possible forms of identity related to nation-building (civic and ethnic) overlooks the multiplicity of nationalism(s) and identities in Kazakhstan, especially in relation to religious identity,[54] urban and rural identities,[55] transnationalism[56] and the cross-cutting nature of identity.[57] As this book will demonstrate through its analysis of nation-building and identity using cinematic works, conceptions of national identity in Kazakhstan are heterogeneous, multi-voiced and varied. While there are two representations focused on 'ethnic' and 'civic' representations of nationhood, there are at least two others: the religious and socio-economic interpretations.

To summarise the discussion thus far, it is the contention of this work that while nations are a product of modernity and socially constructed, imagined if you will, we cannot treat such imaginations of the nations as reified and homogeneous even among the titular group. Instead, the construction of nations is a contentious process open to the possibility of multiple nationalisms that are derived at via a multiplicity of actors – not just an elite-led, top-down process. The existing literature on Kazakhstan tends to treat the process of nation-building as elite-led and bifurcated along ethnic and civic lines. This book, through an analysis of the relationship between film and nation-building in Kazakhstan, will reveal the contentious process of nation construction in the country and the multiple nature of nationalism beyond just the ethnic-civic dichotomy. The question to consider now is how we can conceptualise the role of cinema in drawing out these differentiated, competitive (and possibility complementary) positions related to nationhood and identity.

Enter Cinema: Nationalist Myth-making and Myth-breaking

Cinema appears in two specific forms in this book. Firstly, it exists empirically. The book's over-arching aim is to explore the relationship between film and nation-building over time in the case of Kazakhstan. Secondly, cinema is used as an analytical lens to understand the construction of nationalism and identity. This section will deal firstly with the empirical relationship between film and nation-building. Cinema as an analytical lens will be addressed concretely below in the analytical and methodological framework section before the close of the chapter.

Film and Nation-building

There is a tradition within nationalism studies which highlights the important role of social communication in the emergence and maintenance of nations. Philip Schlesinger has articulated the ways in which the nation can be understood as a 'communicative space'. Drawing on Deutsch's idea of how national communities rely upon facilities for social communication to create, consolidate and strengthen a common identity, and Gellner's concept of 'high culture', in which cultural mediums are used to 'invite the audience to consider and understand themselves to be members of a given community', Schlesinger encourages us to see the sociological links between cinema and nationhood.[58] What he acutely expresses is how cinema is part and parcel of a broad range of mediums that communicate ideas about, and conceptions of, national identity and can go some way to shaping nations and identity. This can be further observed in the work of Michael Billig, who has demonstrated how everyday, banal, yet ideological habits allow nations to reproduce a common 'imagined' sense of nationhood amongst their members (e.g., flags, national anthems etc.).[59] While film could be considered tangential to broader structural processes related to nation formation, such as those proposed by Gellner and other modernists, the power of the silver screen can contribute to fostering a common sense of belonging among citizens by creating national heroes and re-imagining collective memory, myths and traditions with the aim of establishing stable cultural meanings. Cinema, therefore, when it comes to narratives and debates related to national identity and nationhood, has 'pride of place on the cultural and technological battlefield'.[60]

As Dissanayake notes, 'the power-wielders in any society strive to enhance their base by making use of all available media of communication at their disposal, and surely film is one of them', if not the most prominent.[61] The power of cinema as an agent of identity formation and political control was evident throughout the twentieth century. The famous (and clichéd) comment attributed to Lenin that 'the most important of all arts is cinema', underscores how cinema was used as an ideological tool for the purposes of propaganda by totalitarian regimes.[62] The Bolsheviks coined the term *kinofikatsiya* (cinefication) to encapsulate their need to transmit the ideas of the October revolution and the society they wanted to build through cinema to reach peasants in the countryside.[63] In both the Soviet Union and Nazi Germany significant resources were ploughed into cinema for the purposes of ideological education.[64] Much of the scholarship which has sought to explore the nexus between culture and politics of Soviet cinema (as opposed to the aesthetic and semiotics of film in the USSR) has tended to focus on the process of ideological education and the state providing films for the masses.[65] Here, of course, it is easy to observe the ways in which political elites can use cinema to create a stable set of ascribed meanings around the nation as a powerful ideological tool for political control. However, as Kenez has argued in the case of the Bolsheviks, such revolutionaries over-estimated the power of film-based propaganda to influence behaviour.[66]

Cinema, therefore, as an ideological tool either for specific political objectives or for nation-building has its limits. These boundaries pertain to how different symbols of nationhood, nationalism and identity, as realised through the medium of cinema, can be interpreted in varying ways. Differently put, the meaning of narratives about nationhood are what Roland Barthes termed polysemic.[67] The concept of national cinema (which will be discussed further below) also reveals the contentious nature of cinema as a site for imaginations of nationhood. As Andrew Higson notes:

> the process of nationalist mythmaking is not simply an insidious (or celebratory work) of ideological production, but it also at the same time a means of setting one body of images and values against another, which will very often threaten to overwhelm the first. Histories of nationalist cinema can only therefore be really understood as histories of crisis and conflict, of resistance and negotiation.[68]

It is here where cinema exists as an important nation-building tool – not just for political and cultural elites seeking to convey their imagined community, but for other actors, individuals and groups to challenge and contest top-down constructions of nationhood. Moreover, cinema can reveal the heterogeneity of nations rather than their homogeneity. As Paul Willemen has noted, cultural formations may also be marked by not just the presence but also an absence of preoccupations with national identity.[69] Narratives of nationalism within cinematic works can point to social divisions that are at odds with the perceived homogenising efforts of nationalist cinematic works. In his work on British national cinema John Hill has articulated how cinematic works within Britain highlight the power of film to 'reimagine the nation, or rather nations within Britain ... in a way which does not presume a homogenous or "pure" national identity'.[70] Similar observations have been made of post-colonial Asian cinema, where films have offered 'contestatory narratives of nationhood and history'.[71]

Cinema, therefore, has played a role not just in the conveyance of nationalist myth-making but also in its ability to be myth-breaking. Film can shape popular understandings of the nation and can be used for political expediency (regime-building) – but cinema can also reveal alternative imaginations of the nation to those put forward by the regime. Representations of nationhood and identity are not fixed within the celluloid form, they shift and evolve over time and often in relation to the contingent political and social context. This is what we see in Kazakhstan. There are specific discrete narratives that can be analytically drawn out, but the fact there are multiple and contentious narratives demonstrates the inessential nature of Kazakh nationhood and identity. Moreover, there is leakage between these narratives. In several instances directors and producers shift across the boundaries of these different narratives, on occasions making a film that represents one specific narrative, before then completing another project that is representative of a different interpretation of the national narrative.

We may wonder why cinema is used by elites for nation-building purposes. Such a question is beyond the scope of this work, but film, like other media texts – newspapers, books, radio – allows people to imagine their connection to people who live within an agreed bounded community to imagine they are part of that shared community.[72] Our response to watching films is often largely psychological and emotional. Despite knowing characters are not real and plots and structures are constructed we still develop an emotional response to signs and signification on screen.[73] Our response to cinema, therefore, is often irrational and located in emotion rather than rational calculation. The appeal to our emotional irrational side perhaps explains its utility to political elites interested in mobilising support for constructions of nationalism. Cinema is not as important as wider social and structural changes which have brought about the emergence of modern nations and nationalism, but as noted previously it is concomitant to them and serves as a useful tool for elites for the dissemination of constructions of nationhood and identity and, as this book argues, also as a site for the contestation of nationalism and political authority more broadly.

Multiple Nationalisms and National Identities in Kazakhstan

This book, therefore, seeks to explore the contentious nature of nationhood and identity through cinema via the case of Kazakhstan. Kazakhstan is an appropriate and compelling case for such an examination of the nature and process of multiple nationalisms. Like the other four Central Asian Republics, the current borders of Kazakhstan were established by Soviet elites in the 1920s; the promotion of what constitutes Kazakh history and identity was also sponsored by the Soviet authorities and often enacted by local elites; therefore understanding post-Soviet nation-building in Kazakhstan cannot be achieved without taking account of the influence of Soviet-era nation-building.[74] Nevertheless, along with the other Central Asian Republics, Kazakhstan stands as an important example of a country seeking to construct a sense of self-identity, and to match the territorial borders of the state with a common sense of national belonging. It does this in the context of not being ethnically homogenous (which state is?); there remains a large Russian minority, and the president speaks of there being over 100 different nationalities in the country.[75] This ethnic diversity makes the process of establishing a common sense of belonging challenging. Besides, Kazakhstan's 'newness' as, depending on your perspective, a Soviet or post-Soviet state, means political and cultural elites as well as ordinary citizens have been engaged since the collapse of the USSR, in an ongoing process of re-discovering or 'inventing' perceived local traditions, myths, folklore and historical events, which are marshalled to constitute a 'national' present. Moreover, political and economic transition in the country, and the legacy left by Soviet rule, lends itself to deep social divisions related to class, language and religion. This complexity only serves to highlight the potential for nation-building as a contentious process capable of producing multiple nationalisms.

The power of cinema to shape national consciousness and to contribute to identity formation has not been lost on Kazakhstan's government. In 2005, the Kazakh authorities turned the old Soviet-era Kazakhfilm Studios into a joint-stock company in which the state maintained the largest share. Simultaneously the government also sought to invest heavily in the Studios updating production facilities.[76] After the furore over Sacha Baron Cohen's 2006 film *Borat*, in which Baron Cohen's fictive Kazakh journalist portrays a wholly negative and absurdist image of Kazakhs and their country, the depiction in the Western media of the government's sponsorship of the film industry was one in which the state authorities were seeking public relations restitution through film to fight back against the 'Borat image' in which the real truth of Kazakhstan, its people and history is revealed.[77] This interpretation of Kazakh cinema belies something much deeper occurring. The government is using film as an ideological tool to present its interpretation of history and its vision of Kazakhstan's nationhood to domestic and international audiences. It is the contention of this book, however, that cinema is a site through which the top-down government-sponsored imaginations of Kazakh nationhood and identity are contested – and where we can see the emergence of multiple nationalisms.

What this book argues, therefore, is the following. Kazakhstan as a national entity has been contested over time – even since its inception as a proto-state as the Kazakh Khanate in the fifteenth century through the Soviet era up until contemporary post-Soviet statehood. There is no suggestion that there is such a 'thing' as an essential Kazakh nation or Kazakh national identity, or that anyone should expect there to be in Kazakhstan or any other nation. Rather, the book seeks to account for the competing representations of Kazakh nation-ness and the social and political context of such a disaggregation of identity formation. While the book highlights discrete analytical narratives for us to understand various representations of the nation, these narratives in and of themselves should not be treated as fixed. Throughout the book the analysis makes clear the fluidity between some of these cinematic narratives either in terms of directors and producers shifting across these narratives, or even instances when the state produces and funds films that challenge regime-sponsored accounts of nationhood and identity. In such instances, as will be addressed throughout, it demonstrates the limitations of the state in terms of its ability to control the cultural production of the nation.

Cinema in Kazakhstan reveals this contested nationhood (at least since the Soviet period and the inception of film as a medium for the representation of national identity) both empirically and as an analytical lens. In the Soviet period, as noted by Kazakh film critic Gulnara Abikeyeva, Kazakh filmmaking revealed two representative worlds on the screen. One pertained to a 'Soviet' world, and the other a 'Kazakh' world where there existed an ethnic representation of Kazakh nationhood and identity based on perceived traditions and the Kazakh *aul* (village). This changed with the advent of *glasnost* and *perestroika* in the 1980s. This period witnessed the birth of the 'Kazakh New Wave'; a coterie of young Kazakh directors who used the space and freedom provided by Gorbachev's reforms to challenge Soviet orthodoxy (both in terms of politics and filmmaking), to re-interpret Kazakhstan's history, to create new heroes, and to depict the disintegration of the USSR and the realities of life for ordinary Kazakhs during the period of transition. Kazakh films of this period reveal the way in which the two worlds of Soviet Kazakh cinema collapse into one another. In other words, the

INTRODUCTION 17

films of the 'Kazakh New Wave' act to disrupt the neat process of Soviet nation-building that had distinguished between a specific political identity (as a Soviet citizen) and a cultural identity (an ethnic Kazakh identity). The films of the late Soviet period also provided a critique of the Soviet system. The 'Kazakh New Wave' represented the figurative shaking of the Kazakh identity snow globe – disrupting representations of identity and understandings of nationhood established during the Soviet period. The consequence of this was the formation of several different representations of Kazakh nationhood and identity that emerged in contemporary Kazakh cinema.

These can be observed through four different narratives that have appeared in Kazakh cinematic works. The first is an ethnic prescription of the Kazakh nation – rooted in an appeal to Kazakhstan's pre-Soviet and pre-Russian past – and the re-interpretation of Kazakhstan's past as a nomadic state. This is a form of national identity that can be understood in terms of Fredrik Barth's notion of cultural identity.[78] This narrative can be seen in state-funded films such as *Sardar* (2003), *Nomad* (2005) and *Zhauzhurek Myn Bala (Warriors of the Steppe)* (2011), which depict nomadic Kazakh tribes' eighteenth-century struggle against invading Mongolian *Oirat* tribes. These films portend to a regime-sponsored, 'official' interpretation of post-Soviet Kazakh nationhood.

The second narrative concerns a 'civic' conceptualisation of the Kazakh nation, premised upon the multi-ethnic and multi-faith nature of the country. According to this narrative contemporary Kazakh nationhood was formed because of the forced Stalinist deportations of different ethnic groups to the Kazakh steppe in the 1930s and 1940s. The narrative implies the modern Kazakh nation was born during this time of mass demographic upheaval, and subsequent inclusion in the nation is not dependent upon cultural identity, but rather the political identity of belonging to the Kazakhstani state. The civic narrative is mostly observable in two films produced by Kazakhfilm Studios: *The Gift to Stalin* (2008) and *The Promised Land* (2011). It can also be understood as a regime-sponsored interpretation of nationhood and identity, and as will be discussed in Chapter 1, reflects a broader policy agenda of the government that aims to provide a civic prescription of citizenship based on rights and obligations to the state. The fact the ethnic and civic narratives can both be understood as regime-sponsored illustrates the inessential nature of representations of Kazakh nationhood and identity even within the regime itself.

The third narrative pertains to a religious identity rooted in the religion of Tengrism. In several films Tengrism is treated as the natural and proper religion of Kazakhs, as it was practised by their nomadic ancestors prior to the adoption of Islam in the Kazakh steppe. Tengrism concerned humankind living in symbiosis with the environment and the spirit world. Thus, Kazakh nation-ness is premised on a psycho-geographical identity. From this perspective, Kazakhs seek to live in harmony and be at one with nature and their environment. This narrative also places woman and mother at its centre – highlighting the important role of woman as the carrier and symbol of the nation. Nations within this narrative are not born through struggle against marauding invaders (as in the ethnic narrative) nor through the forced creation of nations by ethnic displacement and assimilation (as in the civic narrative), but are born in the primordial relations of the family through the cycle of birth, life and death. This conception of nationhood is quasi-primordial because the films within this narrative, especially the work of Yermek Tursunov and his films *Kelin* (Daughter-in-law) (2009) and *The Old Man* (2012), while being underpinned by the religious philosophy of Tengrism, in fact explore several universal themes not specific to Kazakhs or even the broader Turkic population. This Tengrist narrative challenges the state-led imaginations of the nation and it also shows how we can find representations of the Kazakh nation that go beyond just the ethnic and civic dichotomy that has dominated both academic and policy discussion on Kazakh nationalism.

The final narrative concerns nation-ness as realised through the socio-economic reality of the everyday for ordinary citizens. Identity in this representation of Kazakh nationhood is constituted on upon interest. While the other three narratives portray the unity of the Kazakh nation, films within the socio-economic narrative depict the fragility and divisions of belonging to the modern Kazakh nation. We see the tough lives of everyday existence, struggles with bureaucracy and the state, the break-up of the family unit, and all number of social divisions: urban versus rural; Kazakh versus Russian speakers, moral versus immoral and poor versus rich. The Kazakh nation is thus presented as fragmented and precarious. Again, the socio-economic narrative demonstrates the limitations of state-led ethnic and civic prescriptions of the Kazakh nation, while also providing a clear example of how cinema can emerge as a site of dissent against an authoritarian regime.

The way cinematic narratives about nationhood can change and evolve from the Soviet to contemporary period validates the inessential and contentious nature of Kazakh nation-ness. It also emphasises that Kazakh nationhood and identity cannot be reduced to just a simple ethnic-civic dichotomy. The last two narratives are especially revealing of the push-back against top-down representations of nationhood. This is significant given the authoritarian nature of the country.[79] It exemplifies the value of cinema as a cultural space for different modulations and varying intensities of political dissent and critique. While cinema is often viewed as a tool of ideological propaganda[80] for political elites to bind together ruler with ruled and to depict and disseminate a vision of nationhood, politics and identity set against the 'other', it can also be a tool of contention. This is especially the case in authoritarian systems where formal institutions such as political parties and legislatures are unable to perform the function of political resistance. This of course does raise the question of what function cinema, and culture more broadly, performs in authoritarian settings. On the one hand, given the abstract and hidden meanings that can often be ascribed to cultural representations, satire, critique and dissent may be difficult for censors to locate or they may even interpret a different meaning. At the same time, however, regimes may see culture as a safe arena to disperse tension from the system. Thus, culture performs the role of a safety valve, ultimately reinforcing regime stability. In the case of post-Soviet cinema in Kazakhstan, it is arguably the former, although it is possible to observe the latter function in Soviet cinema.

Analytical Framework and Methods

If through an analysis of cinematic work it is possible to understand the multiplicity of narratives pertaining to Kazakh nationhood and identity, then we also need to consider how to analyse the contentious and multiple nature of nationalism in Kazakhstan. This work adopts a two-stage analytical framework. The first utilises the concept of representation and the second national cinema. If nations are socially constructed through narratives, then particular representations and signs are required to give substance to the various narratives of nationhood. Therefore, the purpose of utilising theories of cultural representation (banal nationalism and semiotics) is that it will focus attention on how symbols of tradition, history and identity related to the nation are imagined. The analysis adopts a polysemic understanding of meaning, which is that such nationalist narratives possess multiple meanings depending on who and which audience is interpreting the narrative. As representations and signs of the nation are produced, received, and given value by subjective agents, in this case through the medium of cinematic works, the concept of national cinema will allow for the analysis of such symbols within the wider discursive practice related to the production, distribution, market (domestic and global), technological development and reception of Kazakhstani films. The wider context includes the domestic film industry as well as its broader relationship to the international film business, but also, more importantly, the political background and role of the state in film production. The following sections address the utility of the concepts of representation and national cinema for this analysis on film and nation-building in Kazakhstan.

Representation

If we take the position that nations are socially constructed, and that contrary to typical interpretations, these constructions are inherently contentious and multiple, then for these multiple nationalisms to be realised they need to be channelled through representation. Representation is an important mechanism, which gives meaning to the content of nationalism. Stuart Hall understood representation as 'the process by which members of a culture use language (broadly defined as any system which deploys signs, any signifying system) to produce meaning'.[81]

The concept of representation is rooted in Ferdinand Saussure's work on semiotics and his dyadic model of the signifier (the form a sign takes) and the signified (the concept it represents).[82] Both elements of the sign are required to give meaning, but according to Hall 'it is the relation between them, fixed by our cultural and linguistic codes, which sustain representation'.[83] Therefore, the symbols, myths, narratives and traditions that are conjured up in the discursive construction of nationalism operate as signs in attempts to establish a shared meaning about what the 'nation' is and whose 'nation' it is, and what the shared features are that give meaning to associated feelings of national identity. Signs also do not possess a fixed or essential meaning, they are always defined by the difference to the 'other', and this is especially the case when constructing a representation of the nation and national identity.[84] While there are varying approaches to representation, this work adopts a constructivist approach whereby it is the construction of the system of signs (in this case symbols, narratives and motifs of Kazakh national identity and nationhood) by social actors (in this case those involved in the production of film) that give such signs meaning, not the materiality of the signs themselves.

Cinema through its structured body of signs channelled through image and text provide representations of numerous concepts and ideas that the various social actors involved in the production of film wish to convey. As noted by Shani Orgad, the power of such representations is conditional, 'the representations circulating in the media must be *meaningful* to their viewers'.[85] In effect, this body of signs acts as a 'script' that calls upon viewers to imagine the collective community that constitutes the nation, how that nation was born and the markers of identity that entail inclusion in the nation.[86] The issue of audience reception is key. Audiences will understand national signs in multiple ways. Besides, not only are there multiple nationalisms, there are varied ways of understanding and interpreting such nationalisms. Not only are there potentially various domestic audiences that might interpret the signs of nationalism and identity differently (such as region, class, gender etc.), there are also international audiences.[87] However, not only should perceived acceptance of membership of the nation by individuals and groups not be equated with enthusiasm for nationalist signs, but it also has to be understood that often reception to such nationalist signs can generate 'broad strands of indifference and hostility towards national identity in general'.[88] The relevance of this for the study of film and nation-building in Kazakhstan is that analytically it is necessary to be open to the complexity of the nature of the signs that are produced through film and their assigned meaning by those involved in the production of cinematic works and the varying audiences who receive such nationalist signs.

To achieve this aim it is possible to use two approaches for the analysis of the representation of national signs: semiotic and discursive. In semiotics, representation is concerned with how a system of signs establishes meaning.[89] In the discursive approach the focus is on the effects and consequences of representation.[90] A discourse can include language, images, texts, ideas, forms of knowledge and institutional practices. Here, therefore, the onus is not just on meaning, but on the production of knowledge and the underpinning relations of power. For Foucault, power is central to understanding the production of systems of signification. He noted in 1982 that 'while the human subject is placed in relations of production and of signification, he is equally placed in power relations which are very complex'.[91] This is precisely why media representations such as film matter. As Orgad stresses, 'power relations are encoded in media representations, and in turn media representations in turn produce and reproduce power relations by constructing knowledge, values, conceptions and beliefs'.[92] Therefore, film matters for understanding the development of multiple nationalisms in Kazakhstan, and for our understanding of the power relations relative to nationalism, politics and authoritarianism. However, locating 'power' is not easy. As noted above, the meaning of signs is contested in that meaning is not essential and, therefore, capturing any essentiality to relations of power is challenging.[93]

This book adopts both a semiotic and discursive approach for analysis. Semiotics is necessary to unravel what Barthes termed 'the floating chain' of signifiers, in other words, those elements of a text or image that convey a body of meaning related to a specific interpretation of nationalism and national identity.[94] Through a semiotic approach to cultural representation it is possible to use cinematic works to determine the multiple forms of nationalism. How is this achieved analytically? When writing about the rhetoric of the image, Barthes alludes to at least two processes when analysing images: the literal and the symbolic. The first is to address the literal question of 'what is it?' This involves identifying 'purely and simply the elements of the scene and the scene itself'.[95] This denotes a straightforward description of the image or moving images on the screen. There is also a denominative analytical process, which provides an *anchorage* of all the possible symbolic messages inherent to the image, which relies on the interpretive understanding of the image and text.[96] However, this does not rule out the author's (or a director's) subtle or perhaps even obvious *dispatching* of a meaning chosen in advance.[97] In other words, there is likely to be some ideational element to the image and text which is pre-determined by social actors involved in production. This requires an analysis or deep contextual understanding regarding the production of the film, in both artistic and broader political, social and economic terms. This is discussed in more detail below in relation to the concept of national cinema.

When exploring the role of cinema in imagining nations and nationalism across different historical time periods (in this case Soviet, late-Soviet and post-Soviet eras) it is also important to be sensitive to the issue of temporality. Representations of global and national imagination have undergone substantial transformation in the last 70 years.[98] Shani Orgad has highlighted what Thompson described as 'the new world of mediated visibility'.[99] While Thompson is concerned with how previously invisible actions are now visible through the media because of technological developments and our social interaction with them, something which is not central to film and nation-building in Kazakhstan, it does highlight the need to take account of the changing nature of film. The expansion of social media and internet-based communicative technologies means that films are produced and consumed within this new mediated context. Audiences watch, interact, share and comment on the content of cinematic works in a more intense and extensive way than ever before. And moreover, artistic and political actors involved in the production of films have less control over how the ideational message is received and given meaning by the audience and how the intended meaning could be challenged and distributed in an extensive way through social media. It perhaps explains how cinema can be a forum for dissent and critique because of the expansive opportunities for satire via social media. Control of media representations was something more prevalent during the Soviet period, while the intensive and extensive nature of contemporary global media was not present during the late-Soviet and early post-Soviet periods of Kazakh cinema. In short, any analysis of the representation of multiple nationalisms in film must consider the temporal context of the production and reception of the 'floating chain' of signs that constitute the different narratives of nationalism.

While the above has touched on the semiotic approach to analysing the multiple forms of nationalism in Kazakh cinema, as the previous section highlighted with regards to temporality, these forms of nationalism in cinematic works are also discursive. They are produced within a larger structure of power relations and institutional practices involving different social and political actors. These broader structures include the political context in Kazakhstan, the very nature of the authoritarian system, the role of Kazakhfilm Studios within that system, and how independent studios and directors respond and exist outside of these powerful agencies. In analytical terms, for considering the more discursive element to analysing film and nation-building in Kazakhstan, it is necessary to scrutinise the concept of national cinema.

National Cinema

The concept of national cinema has been ubiquitous within film studies, even if it is commonly solely adopted in a prescriptive sense related to a body of cinematic work within a given territory often situated in contradistinction to 'Hollywood' cinema.[100] Such bodies of cinematic work are then observed to possess some 'putative national spirit'.[101] This original and narrow interpretation of the concept was critiqued for failing to take into account the broader discursive, cultural and international processes related to the production and reception of film.[102] The various ways films are produced and consumed within a given territory, especially in relation to the role of the state, means it is possible to identify multiple forms of national cinema. Stephen Crofts, for example, identified eight varieties of national cinema that take account of different modes of production, the role played by the state and the extent to which the body of work can be considered industrial (applies to Hollywood, Hong Kong and Indian cinemas), cultural (role of state in supporting cinematic production) or political (clandestine and artisanal cinema).[103]

At the same time, the narrow conception of national cinema tended to neglect the international nature of the film industry and how it can be difficult to untangle a particular 'nationality' to a film when it features a multi-national team of directors, producers, actors, writers and financers. Furthermore, films made in a specific territory, whether the directors and producers are seeking to portray a set of nationalist signs or not, continue to be shaped by both the artistic influence of other 'transnational cinema' (such as Hollywood or Bollywood) as well as the demands of the international market. It is as Valentina Vitali and Paul Willemen suggest, that 'like capitalism, cinema is, and always has been, a global industry, but diverse societies and clusters of film are always inevitably positioned differently within the centrifugal expansion of capitalist modes of production, not least because any given culture encountered cinema in different circumstances.'[104] Therefore, a reading of narratives of nationalism and national identity within film has to address the influence of transnational cinematic modalities as well the complexity of the production of cinematic works given the global and capitalist nature of the film industry. This will be evident in the case of Kazakh cinema. Often the financing of a film, while evidently possessing a 'national spirit', is imbued with the complexity of the global film industry. The 2005 film *Nomad*, for example, which will be discussed at length in Chapter 4, was financed to the tune of $37 million by the Kazakh government, was co-directed by a Russian, Sergei Bodrov, and a Czech, Ivan Passer, while also being produced by Czech-born Hollywood director Miloš Forman and featuring two Mexican-American actors in lead roles, playing historical Kazakh figures. Therefore, while the film portrays a specific narrative about Kazakh history, nationhood and identity, it does so in the context of the transnational nature of global cinema.

The notion of 'transnational' cinema has been adopted by many scholars to account for the perceived weakness of the concept of national cinema in 'understanding the production, consumption and representation of cultural identity (both individual and collective) in an increasingly interconnected, multicultural and polycentric world'.[105] However, while the global context needs to be taken into account, at the same time it is important that the concept of the 'national' does not become displaced in the analysis.[106] The 'national' can remain important in literal and symbolic terms and the global context should not make redundant the concept of national cinema. Despite the importance of the international context to both the production and consumption of cinema, a body of cinematic work can still be 'national' if it seeks to represent a coherence, unity and stable set of meanings.[107] However, any attempt to represent a unified social world within any cinematic work can still be challenged by competing representations and ultimately illustrates the inessential nature of national identity.

National cinema, therefore, needs to take account of the production, reception and contestation of such representations of nationalist signs within an international setting as well as domestic context, and at the same time situate the analysis within the broader political, social and economic milieu. Especially important is the extent of state inolvement in determining content as well as the production of cinema, as noted by Crofts in his typology of varieties of national cinema (although often the role of the state can be marginalised in some readings of national cinema due to the eroding of national sovereignty by forces of globalisation).[108]

The concept of national cinema is used in this book to be sensitive to the broader discourse within which narratives about the Kazakh(stani) nation and national identity are represented through cinematic works. It concerns reading the literal and symbolic representation of signs within cinematic works by way of referring to both the production and reception of such films, the global setting and the political and institutional context in which such films are produced and consumed. This is achieved analytically by paying attention in the analysis to the following key categories of national cinema as per Crofts' typology, although these are modified (see Table I.1) for the specificity of this work:

The mode of production, which encompasses all or some of the below:

- *Mode of audience*: targeted audiences through distribution and exhibition and the reception of films which represent a set of nationalist signs by audiences and social actors central to the film industry.
- *Genres:* kinds of genres being produced in relation to multiple nationalist narratives.
- *State subvention*: role of the state in regulating or controlling production.
- *State intervention*: role of the state in regulating or controlling distribution and exhibition of films, typically through a state-funded film studio.
- *Nationalist or anti-nationalist representations*: the specific representations of narratives of nationalism within cinematic works.
- *Local market*: levels of success within local markets.
- *Export market:* levels of success in international export markets.
- *Competing forms of entertainment*: extent to which cinematic works face competition from other forms of entertainment and how that effects production and reception of films; also the role of social media in the promotion, distribution, exhibition and reception of films.[109]

Table I.1 Analytical Framework for Study of Narratives of Nationhood and Identity in Cinematic Works

Narrative(s)	Representation (language of signs)	Temporality	National Cinema
Soviet period cinema	'Soviet' and 'Kazakh' worlds.	Soviet Nationalities Policy and Soviet nation-building.	Production, audience, genres, influence of 'other' cinema, role of the state, local and export markets, competing entertainment
Kazakh New Wave	Re-interpretation of history, negation of Soviet authority and new heroes, and lived experience of transition.	*Perestroika*, *glasnost*, disruption of homogeneous empty time, and the collapse of the USSR.	
Ethnic	Defence of the homeland, ethnic identity and contemporary power.	Post-Soviet nation-building and authoritarian legitimation.	
Civic	Inter-ethnic harmony, national characteristics, and negation of Soviet authority.	Post-Soviet nation-building and authoritarian legitimation.	
Religious	Literal representation of Tengrism, psychogeography of the steppe, primordialism and women.	Globalisation and re-discovering of pre-Russian, pan-Turkic history and traditions.	
Socio-economic	Inhospitality of the steppe, disorientation, urban-rural divide, struggles with bureaucracy, breakdown of the family, morality and wealth accumulation.	Rejection of regime-led narratives, and the lived day-to-day experience of post-Soviet life.	

Each of these analytical categories will be used as guides throughout the book when detailing Soviet Kazakh cinema, the Kazakh New Wave and the four narratives related to national identity and nationhood observed in contemporary Kazakh cinema. However, they should only be understood as heuristic analytical devices and not rigid or fixed analytical categories. The final issue is how the concepts of representation and national cinema are operationalised. The final section on methods, below, addresses this question.

Method

Methodologically, this analysis of the contentious and multiple nature of nationalism and nation-building in Kazakhstan, as realised through cinematic works, is operationalised along two axes: production and reception.

I adopt an interpretive analysis of nearly 60 films from the 1920s to the present day, which, utilising a modernist and social constructivist approach to nations and nationalism, identifies: the contention of nationhood and identity in the Soviet period through the imagining of distinct 'Kazakh' and 'Soviet' worlds, along with the fragmentation of identity in the late Soviet period in the 'Kazakh New Wave' cinema; and four main narratives evident in contemporary Kazakh cinema – ethnic, civic, religious and socio-economic. The films which reveal these contentious and multivalent interpretations of Kazakh nationhood and identity were for the most part an idiosyncratic selection. Having said that, the aim was always to choose films that were the most overt in offering an account of nationhood and identity. In this sense, the most obvious films reveal themselves to the author. It was, however, a subjective process and it is entirely possible that others could write a different account of film and nation-building and perhaps identify other narratives and strands in the representation of nationhood and identity.

The interpretative analysis of films has then been triangulated with data collected in relation to both the production and reception of films. In terms of production, 30 semi-structured interviews were conducted with directors, producers, actors and writers. Interviews were underpinned by an extensive analysis of media coverage, data and statistics related to the film industry in Kazakhstan, documentation from Kazakhfilm Studios and a review of secondary sources on Kazakh cinema both in English and Russian. For Soviet period and 'Kazakh New Wave' cinema a review of issues of *Sovetskii Ekran* and *Isskustvo Kino* from the 1920s to 1991 was undertaken to explore both production and reception (film reviews) of Kazakh cinema during the Soviet period. The issue of reception is much more difficult in methodological terms. Accounting for the reception of these different narratives pertaining to Kazakh nationhood and identity is important as it can determine the extent to which any of these narratives 'stick' in a broader social sense and whether they possess any residue for social and political change vis-à-vis authoritarianism. However, the first challenge is the general lack of exposure of cinema audiences in Kazakhstan to Kazakh films. There are only a few Kazakh-made films released every year (at most, 12 on average) and often many of these films do not get a general release and if they do they are restricted to the main cities of Almaty and Astana. Therefore, engaging a large sample of the population through surveys would be problematic in this context as many of the results could be simply negated by the lack of exposure citizens have had to the films. Naturally, issues of exposure do tell us something about the capacity of these cinematic works to shape citizens' perception of Kazakh nationhood and identity. Nevertheless, a more imaginative approach to analysing audience reception was necessary. In the first instance, three focus groups were held with self-selecting cinema audiences (those who had seen some contemporary Kazakh cinema, or at the very least films that, at the initial stage, had been part of the analysis of this work). Participants for the focus groups were recruited via existing contacts in the film and arts community in Almaty and Astana using snowball sampling. The focus groups attracted those who were pre-disposed to and interested in discussing Kazakh cinematic works. The focus groups elicited discussions amongst participants regarding specific films (*Nomad*, *Zhauzhurek Myn Bala*, *Kelin* etc.) as well as general discussions on Kazakh identity and nationhood, and the general state of the film and cinema industry in the country. The focus group data was then triangulated with data from the website forum kino.kz. The forum features comments and discussion on Kazakh films, and international cinema. Combined with the focus group data the idea was not to achieve definitive generalisable conclusions about how citizens understand and interpret these films. As alluded to earlier, meaning is complex when it comes to the representation of national signs, and the purpose was to get a broad contextual sense of how these films are being understood by those who have watched them, and the extent to which narratives regarding nationhood and identity cut through and how they are given meaning and interpreted by sections of a Kazakhstani audience. The analysis of reception was also underpinned by 'expert' interviews with film critics and specialists in Kazakhstan and by a way of a thorough appraisal of film reviews both nationally and internationally.

Structure of the Book

The case of film and nation-building in Kazakhstan reveals the ways in which nations are not just socially constructed but also contentious and multiple within the titular group. The remainder of the book sets out exactly how these different forms of nation and nationalisms in Kazakhstan can be observed in contemporary cinema and in Soviet cinema too. Chapter 1 explains how narratives pertaining to nationhood and identity in Kazakhstan cannot be separated from the wider contentiousness of Kazakh nationhood, identity and history as well as the political and social context that has shaped government policy towards nation-building in the contemporary period. Chapter 2 analyses the emergence of cinema in Soviet Kazakhstan, providing historical and political context to contemporary cinema, but also outlining the emergence of the 'Soviet' and 'Kazakh' worlds that arose as narratives regarding nationhood and identity in this period. Chapter 3 then explores the emergence of the 'Kazakh New Wave'. Again, it provides the social and political context in the USSR and the Soviet cinema industry in relation to Gorbachev's policies of *perestroika* and *glasnost*, to understand how a group of young Kazakh directors, writers and artists appeared to challenge both cinematic and political Soviet orthodoxies. Through an analysis of several films the chapter also explains how the two distinct worlds evident in Soviet Kazakh cinema collapse into one another. Through a re-interpretation of Kazakh history, a negation of Soviet authority via the creation of new types of heroes and a depiction of the material and psychological realities of transition, the directors of the 'Kazakh New Wave' flattened the cinematic landscape in terms of its portrayal of nation and identity. Instead of two distinct worlds, Kazakhstan was open to new interpretations of national identity.

Four constructions of Kazakh nation-ness and identity can be observed in contemporary Kazakh films and Chapters 4 to 7 provide an account of each of these. Chapter 4 analyses the Nazarbayev regime-sponsored ethnic narrative, which focuses on a re-interpretation of eighteenth-century Kazakh nomadic history and the defence of the homeland against invading forces. The narrative is driven by state-led cinematic projects, which the Ministry of Culture oversees. Films such as *Nomad* and *Zhauzhurek Myn Bala* provide a specific ethnic representation of Kazakh identity. The chapter also provides an analysis of how the ethnic narrative is intertwined with the process of regime legitimation, power and the development of the Nazarbayev personality cult. Chapter 5 details a second regime-sponsored narrative of Kazakh nationhood, but this time instead of focusing on a cultural ethnic identity, it depicts a political civic identity. The chapter provides a reading of films within this narrative that explain Kazakh nationhood by reference to the demographic changes wrought by the Stalinist deportations of the 1930s and 1940s. It also locates Kazakh identity in a series of signs related to the tradition of nomadic hospitality, openness and friendliness, which is counter-framed in relation to a negative portrayal of Soviet authority. The civic narrative is a corollary to the ethnic representation – meaning they both represent regime-led efforts of constructing a specific imaginary of the nation. This is reflective of the broader policy discourse concerning post-Soviet debates between civic and ethnic forms of nationalism. Like the ethnic narrative, the civic imagination of the nation is also linked closely to issues of power and regime legitimation.

Chapters 6 and 7 provide accounts of two narratives within contemporary cinematic works that dissent from these prevailing regime-sponsored narratives. In doing so, these narratives exemplify: the multivalent and contentious nature of post-Soviet nation-building in Kazakhstan; that accounts of nationhood go beyond just the ethnic-civic dichotomy; and how cinema can emerge as a site of dissent from prevailing ideological narratives. Chapter 6 offers an examination of the Tengrist narrative. Through an analysis of the films of Yermek Tursunov, among others, the chapter explains shows how the pre-Islamic religion of Tengrism has defined a precise reading of the nation based on its symbolic practices, the psycho-geographic relationship between Kazakhs and the steppe and a quasi-primordial interpretation of nationhood rooted in the symbolic role of women and the cycle of birth, life and death. The narrative provides for a subtle philosophic dissenting account of the Kazakh nation that challenges the ethnic and civic narratives put forward by the regime. Chapter 7, on the other hand, gives a lengthy analysis of a more critical dissenting narrative rooted in the lived socio-economic experience of Kazakh nationhood and identity. Analysing many films from the contemporary period, it identifies a series of signs which challenge any homogeneous reading of the Kazakh nation. These signs pivot on the internal divisions and fissures within Kazakh society – the steppe as a harsh, inhospitable environment, the disorientation of modern Kazakh society, urban and rural division, breakdown of family unity, struggles with bureaucracy and authority, and the issue of the morality of wealth accumulation. Taken as a whole, Chapters 4 to 7 highlight the contentious nature of imagining the post-Soviet Kazakh nation – something which was only subtly present in the Soviet period and more explicit during the 'Kazakh New Wave' era. The Conclusion provides a brief analysis of how these different narratives of Kazakh nationhood and identity can help shape our thinking on the social construction of nations in cases beyond Kazakhstan and the post-Soviet space.

CHAPTER 1

KAZAKH KHANATE TO KAZAKH ELI: NATION-BUILDING IN KAZAKHSTAN IN HISTORICAL AND POLITICAL CONTEXT

Different conceptualisations of nationhood observable in Kazakh film are interwoven with wider interpretations of nationhood and identity within the country's historical and political discourse. These representations are also reflected through Russian, Soviet and post-Soviet writings of the country's history. This chapter sets out to locate the relationship between film and nation-building in Kazakhstan in historical and political context.

This chapter will reveal that nationhood and identity have always been contested phenomena in Kazakhstan, especially with regards to how history is imagined and interpreted. It traces this contention from the ethno-genesis of the Kazakh nation to modern statehood. However, it should be noted this chapter is not seeking to offer a complete history of Kazakhstan. This is best left to the number of historical accounts which are already available.[1] Rather, the aim is to explore the ways in which the construction and development of Kazakh nationhood and history is a contentious process. The Kazakh nation, as an idea, construct and institutional entity has been subject to contention at historical junctures by politicians, scholars and nationalists as well as being disputed in contemporary historiographical debates. Consequently, it unveils the absence of a fixed or essential meaning to Kazakh identity and nationhood within existing accounts of its imagination, something in which it is not unique. Further, it alerts observers to the ways in which different agents can utilise history, memory and myth, often for very instrumental purposes.

In reviewing important junctures in pre-Russian, Russian, Soviet and post-Soviet periods of nation-building in Kazakhstan, this chapter reveals the contentiousness of nation and identity observed in Kazakh films that form the basis of this book. It is worth being clear that different representations of nationhood evident in the debates focused on the pre-Russian and pre-Soviet periods do not mirror the multivalent imaginations of the Kazakh nation that appear in Soviet and contemporary cinema. Selected elements of these debates, however, such as a historical event or hero, do feature and form part of the re-invention of Kazakh history in the post-Soviet period, both in policy terms and in relation to the four narratives of nationalism within cinema.

This chapter argues that the contentious nature of Kazakh nationhood and identity can be divided into the following four sections. Firstly, pre-Russian disputes centre on the Kazakh Khanate, its inherent divisions, the different intentions of the Kazakh tribes in inviting the protection of the Russian Empire in the region, and the extent to which a continuous line can be drawn between the Kazakh Khanate and contemporary nation and statehood. Secondly, the period of Russian rule features a dispute concerning the extent to which we can observe the emergence of genuine national liberation movements (e.g., Kenesary Kasymov) and debates within the twentieth-century nationalist movement *Alash Orda* regarding nation-building (e.g., sedentarisation and language). Thirdly, in the Soviet period we see an inherent distinction emerge between a Soviet identity and a distinct Kazakh ethnic identity. This is a consequence of the practical changes wrought by Soviet nation-building policies. Esepecially important here are demographic changes brought about by inward and outward migration; the process of sedentarisation and collectivisation; the development of the infrastructure of nationhood (e.g., language, symbols, institutions etc.); the promotion of local Kazakh cadre through *korenizatsiya* (nativisation) and; the eventual diffusion of power to national elites during the Brezhnev era via the mechanism of dual authority (power centred in both Moscow and Almaty). The Soviet period of nation-building is also subject to debate with regards to the extent to which local political and cultural elites played a role in shaping the nation-building process, or whether nation formation efforts were driven top-down by elites in Moscow. Finally, the contention within varied imaginations of the Kazakh nation can be seen in post-Soviet nation-building. Mirroring the representations of nationhood observable in contemporary cinema, debates focus on an antagonism between a civic and ethnic identity, as well as the emergence of a broader Pan-Asian interpretation of Kazakh national identity reflected through Islam, Eurasianism and the Turkic religion of Tengrism. Furthermore, the inherent unity of the social whole is challenged by an understanding of the Kazakh nation that focuses on the fault lines in society between rural and urban communities and Kazakh- and non-Kazakh-speaking populations.

This chapter is divided into the above four sections. In traversing historiographical and contemporary accounts of the Kazakh nation it demonstrates the difficulty in understanding the Kazakh nation as a homogeneous whole, elucidating the multivalent nature of nation and nationalism in Kazakhstan.

Ethno-genesis of the Kazakhstani Nation and the Rise and Fall of the Kazakh Khanate

Conventional accounts of the ethno-genesis of the Kazakh people are rooted in the work of the Russian orientalist Vasili Barthold. Barthold believed Kazakhs emerged in the fifteenth century from disaffected Uzbek Kypchak tribes sometime after the dissolution of the Golden Horde.[2] Led by two tribal leaders, Zhanybek and Kerey Khan, sons of Barak Khan of the White Horde of the Mongol Empire, the disparate Uzbek-Turkic tribes established the Kazakh Khanate in the land between the Chu and Talas rivers in what is known as the Betpak Dala (the Hungry Steppe).[3] This description of the ethno-genesis of the Kazakh people remains the most accepted account found in the English language, principally put forward by Martha Brill Olcott in the late 1980s. Olcott's historical interpretation was based not only on the work of Barthold, but also other Russian and Soviet-educated Kazakh historians' reading of Kazakh history such as S.E. Tolybekov, N.I. Grodekov and G.E. Markov, among others. These sources exemplify the way in which Kazakh history was originally reflected through both

Russian and Soviet interpretations and writings of history, as most of the sources drawn upon were in the Russian language or written by scholars educated in the Russian system. A reliance on such sources has been argued to prove problematic given that intense state censorship led to partial accounts of history, and that the inscribing of history was refracted through a historical-materialist lens.[4] Nonetheless, independence in 1991 brought with it the opportunity for both Western and Kazakh scholars to re-examine existing accounts of Kazakh history.[5] Special focus has been given to the role of 'myth creation' in relation to the evolution of the Kazakh peoples.[6] Given the paucity of primary sources in relation to the establishment of the Kazakh Khanate, the story of Zhanybek and Kerey Khan remains the most privileged, and for the most part undisputed, account of the ethno-genesis of the Kazakh people.[7]

By the end of the seventeenth century the Kazakh Khanate had gradually expanded to most of present-day Kazakhstan.[8] Yet, the Khanate was prone to instability and internal discord.[9] Consolidation was accompanied by the formation of a social composition of groupings based on clan identity.[10] *Zhuz* was the term applied to the broader union under which various tribes became federated. The etymology of the word *Zhuz* is contested. Some suggest it derives from the Arabic word *Juz*, meaning part or branch, while others argue it is from the Turkic *yuz*, meaning 100.[11] Nonetheless, *Zhuz* within Kazakh historiography denotes these tribal unions as being 'conscious of being of one Kazakh nationality and inhabiting a piece of the Kazakh territory fixed in tradition'.[12] The three *Zhuzs* comprise of the *Uly Zhuz* (Elder *Zhuz*); the *Orta Zhuz* (Middle *Zhuz*); and the *Kishi Zhuz* (Younger *Zhuz*). Additionally, within each *Zhuz* exists a confederation of smaller tribal units viewed as geopolitical and ethno-territorial entities.[13]

Barthold believed the formation of the *Zhuz* system emerged concomitant to nomadic pastoralism and the resulting conditions of cattle herding.[14] Local scholars have reaffirmed this, believing the existence of the *Zhuz* was driven by the practice of nomadism and permanent pattern of migration.[15] Others scholars have suggested that they formed for largely military purposes.[16] Under a succession of ruling Khans, the Kazakh Khanate grew in power and strength. By the mid-1500s it was even threatening the sedentary Uzbek populations of Tashkent.[17] Until the eighteenth century, the Kazakhs, along with the Mongolian *Oirats*, were understood to be the most powerful nomadic grouping in Central Asia.[18] As will be discussed below, conflicts with other tribal groupings, the *Oirats* among them, as well as the incursion of the Russian empire into the region, undermined any existing unity underpinning the Kazakh Khanate.

The idea of the Khanate, as represented in Kazakh historiography, is important for post-Soviet political legitimation of the Kazakh state. The Nazarbayev regime has placed great emphasis on post-Soviet independent Kazakhstan being a historical continuation of the Kazakh Khanate. In 2015 the government celebrated what it considered the 550th anniversary of Kazakh statehood, dating its history as a state to the formation of the Kazakh Khanate in 1465. The year of celebration was marked by an educational campaign about the history of the Khanate, as well as the production of a *Game of Thrones*-style epic TV series about the proto-state.[19] Arguably, the 550th anniversary was created in response to remarks made by Russian President Vladimir Putin in 2014 that implied that until 1991 Kazakhstan had never had sovereign statehood.[20] Those comments arrived in the aftermath of the Crimean crisis and thus only served to spur the Kazakh elite into demonstrating the supposed historical longevity of the Kazakh state. The use of the Kazakh Khanate in this manner perhaps validates ethno-symbolist approaches to nations and nationalism that stresses the ancient nature of nations via the use of symbols, heroes and myths.[21] The stories of the heroic Khans of the Kazakh Khanate are used to validate a historical linearity between modern-day Kazakhstan and the Khanate. The Kazakh Khanate is celebrated as a 'golden age' and the basis upon which modern statehood is founded. This has been represented in several films within the 'ethnic' narrative, such as *Nomad*, *Sardar* and *Zhauzhurek Myn Bala* (see Chapter 4). Furthermore, Ilyas Yessenberlin's Soviet-era Kazakh-literary epic *Koshpendiler* (Nomad) is an example of this insidious myth-making. Yessenberlin promotes the founders of the Kazakh Khanate, Zhanybek and Kerey Khan, as national heroes.[22] This is not only the Kazakh government's position, but also that of some Western and many Kazakh scholars.[23]

Some scholars have, however, challenged the idea of direct continuity between the Kazakh Khanate and the modern Kazakh state. Michael Hancock-Parmer, for example, has analysed the etymology of the 'Kazakh' identity and makes a distinction between what we today call Kazakhs, and the term *Qazaqs*, which was a name used originally to mean a young man free of authority from his father, leader or ruler, but came to be associated with a specific language group, or social-political entity like a tribe or society.[24] The term *Qazaq*, which according to Hancock-Parmer does not reflect the usage and pronouncement of modern-day Kazakh, was used at least until the early eighteenth century (around the time of the decline of the Kazakh Khanate), in Russian, Central Asian and other sources.[25] Furthermore, to add to this complexity, other scholars have also claimed that the terms Uzbek and *Uzbek-Qazaq* were used concurrently with Kazakh.[26] This rather small linguistic point demonstrates two larger issues. Firstly, the very nature of the formation of the Kazakh people, perhaps a consequence of their nomadic cattle-herding lifestyle where permanent structures and recorded written history were limited,[27] indicates the ambiguous nature of Kazakh identity and nationhood. Kazakh (or *Qazaq*) identity was traditionally premised on genealogical lineage, not on territorial boundaries.[28] Secondly, it illustrates the problematic nature of trying to establish a continuous and unbroken 'sense of self' for the *Qazaqs* of the 1600s that connects, seamlessly or otherwise, to the 'sense of self' for modern-day Kazakhs.[29] To clumsily paraphrase Wittgenstein, if a *Qazaq* of the 1600s could speak with a Kazakh of the 2000s they would not understand each other. Our *Qazaq* and Kazakh's reference points of culture, identity, ethnicity and territory would be very different, and arguably unrecognisable to each other. Thus, any reference to unbroken continuity is questionable to say the least. From the very beginning of the Kazakh (*Qazaq*) nation as an entity the phenomenon has been replete with complexity and contestation.

The eventual decline of the Kazakh Khanate was driven by two main factors. Firstly, the Khanate was unsuccessful as a unitary state. It was divided and fractious, not least along the diving line of the three *Zhuz*. Unity among the three *Zhuz* was periodic and occurred on occasions when the steppe was threatened by other groups such as the Shaybanids.[30] As Steven Sabol noted, 'rarely in Kazakh history did one leader organize the three hordes into one political and military unit'.[31] It illustrates that it is very difficult to speak of the Kazakh Khanate as a unitary state as understood in the conventional sense of the term. Secondly, Kazakh (*Qazaq*) tribes found themselves pushed out of what are now the southern parts of modern Kazakhstan by invading *Oirat* tribes during the years 1723–5. In what has been termed the 'barefooted flight' in Kazakh historiography, faced with the *Oirat* armies, the Kazakhs retreated leaving behind cattle and livestock, while many were murdered in the invasion.[32] The 'barefooted flight' has been an essential part of Kazakh historiography, however, as Michael Hancock-Parmer has argued, it has not remained static, and in fact it emerges as a contested narrative of history. Russian-centric (and Soviet) characterisations of the 'calamity' are observed as an impetus for Russian colonisation in the region, and eventual hegemony. Indeed, Soviet interpretations of the invasion and exile provided utility in importing to later generations 'a warning against autonomy from Russia, or against a decentralized society open to attack from abroad'.[33] This was most acutely observed in Yessenberlin's *Koshpendiler*. However, in the post-Soviet period, the narrative has been recast with the Kazakhs more victorious and the Russians as by-standers, who in the aftermath of the 'barefooted flight' sought to impose their rule of the Kazakhs.[34] It has become an event of celebrated mythology of national defence, which has been represented cinematically in the film *Nomad* (partly based on the second volume of Yessenberlin's book) and in *Zhauzhurek Myn Bala*. The second factor related to the decline of the Khanate was the eventual Russian hegemony in the region and it is Russian colonisation we turn to next.

The Development of Nationalist Movements in Kazakhstan under Russian Rule

Russian colonisation of the Kazakh Khanate took place gradually. Initially, between 1716 and 1735, the Russian Empire constructed a series of forts along the northern border of the Kazakh steppe in Omsk, Semipalatinsk and Ust'-Kamenogorsk.[35] However, Russian control took more concrete form in 1730 when Abu'l Khayr Khan of the *Kishi Zhuz* sent a letter to Empress Anna asking for citizenship.[36] Abu'l Khayr Khan's letter, and the gradual gravitation of the other *Zhuz* into the Russian imperial orbit, has often been characterised as the Kazakh tribes seeking Russian protection from marauding external forces who threatened the security of the Kazakh steppe.[37] Yet, Steven Sabol has suggested that Abu'l Khayr Khan's intention in sending the letter could be interpreted differently in that the Khan wanted assistance rather than incorporation.[38] The small matter of this letter serves to highlight that there are competing explanations for the emergence of Russian rule in the region. For instance, Russian colonisation of Kazakhstan (and the broader Central Asian region) has been largely explained by Russian, Soviet and other historians as initially being a consequence of Russia's need for new markets and its designs on India.[39] At the same time, a Soviet historical reading of Russian colonial rule in Kazakhstan veered between condemnation for Tsarist imperialism while also plying the idea that Russia did not conquer Central Asia, but rather was invited by the Kazakh *Zhuz* as a form of protection to guarantee stability vis-à-vis Mongolian *Oirats*.[40]

The assimilation of the other two *Zhuz* into the Russian Empire was completed by the early 1820s.[41] Russian administration was to have a profound effect on the development of Kazakh nationhood and ushered in the dawn of modern nation-building in the steppe. The Russians brought Western education, the beginning of sedentarisation, new urban settlements, transport links and changes to legal-administration.[42] It is important, however, not to see the Kazakhs as passive recipients of imperial domination, but rather, as Michael Rouland has noted, 'complicated actors finding their way to adapt to an increasingly repressive colonial system'.[43]

Recent scholarship on Kazakh history has sought to demonstrate how the Kazakhs were complex actors negotiating Russian rule. This research has been notable for two fundamental reasons in relation to nation-building. The first is how particular figures perceived to be central to Kazakh national-liberation movements are interpreted in different ways, and this is especially the case with the resistance movement led by Kenesary Kasymov during the 1830s and 1840s. The second is how the development of a the early twentieth century nationalist movement *Alash Orda* speaks to modernist and constructivist understandings of nations and nationalism. *Alash Orda* illustrates how from the beginning, conceptualisations of the modern Kazakh nation were contested and even ambivalent. The members of *Alash Orda* wrestled over the impact Russian colonisation had on the peoples of the Kazakh steppe and how this shaped the constituent elements of Kazakh identity. I will deal with both points in turn.

Kenesary Kasymov

Kenesary Kasymov was the grandson of Ablai Khan from the *Orta Zhuz*, perceived to be the last Khan who could unite the disparate Kazakh tribes in their fight against the Mongolian *Oirats* (a battle celebrated in the film *Nomad*, which is discussed in Chapter 4). Such a prestigious heritage provided Kenesary with political status as he took up the mantle of leadership in resisting Russian and Kokand (the Kokand Khanate, which was based in modern-day Uzbekistan) designs on the Kazakh steppe. Kenesary's rebellion is believed to have lasted ten years from 1837 to 1847 and consisted of raids on sedentary populations while gradually, at one time or the other, each *Zhuz* sided with his rebellion.[44] The perceived unification of the three *Zhuz* by Kenesary Kasymov in resistance to the Russian Empire has led post-Soviet Kazakh historians to depict his revolt as a symbol of resistance, evidence of national unity and an example of the first Kazakh national-liberation movements comparable to those found in other colonial empires of the nineteenth century.[45] Undoubtedly this has proven an important historical memory with which to construct a national history for the present and legitimise post-Soviet Kazakh nationhood. Sabol has argued, however, that Kenesary Kasymov's revolt did not constitute a national-liberation movement – ultimately the rebellion failed because of the lack of unity from all clans in the Kazakh steppe in support of the campaign. Additionally, the objectives of the revolt rested on the restoration of Kenesary's authority (which had eroded because of colonial rule) rather than national-liberation per se.[46]

The legacy of Kenesary's revolt exemplifies the controversial nature of such use of historical figures in the construction of Kazakh nationhood and identity. Sabol shows us how Kenesary Kasymov's resistance has been characterised in different ways. Initially, after Kasymov's death in 1847, Kazakh poets redefined the nature of the revolt as an expression of national struggle, rather than it being about the interests of a particular *Zhuz*.[47] Then Soviet historians presented the revolt as a reactionary movement of feudal-patriarchal nature, albeit national in character and part of a larger project of the Soviets to use *Batyrs* (heroes) to establish an imaginary national unity for Kazakhstan.[48] Subsequently, as noted, post-Soviet historians have sought to use the rebellion as a demonstration of the emergence of a unified national-liberation movement. What these subtly different accounts elucidate is the way that Kazakh national history, and the process of nation-building itself, was (and remains) an imagined and constructed process open to interpretation with the selection of specific figures used to serve wider ideological objectives.

Alash Orda

A more concrete national movement did appear in the Kazakh Steppe towards the end of the nineteenth century with the emergence of *Alash Orda*.[49] The movement was led by a number of prominent intellectuals who had benefited from the Russian education system.[50] This reflects modernist arguments within nationalism studies, and especially Ernest Gellner, who argued that the promotion of a literate and educated class through the development of 'high culture' is an essential component to the emergence of a national consciousness.[51] The Kazakh national intelligentsia's grounding in Russian education had a profound effect on their understanding of the concept and development of nationhood. As Peter Rottier has argued, the Kazakh intelligentsia adopted Western interpretations of the linear development of nations as a way of explaining the history of the Kazakhs and showing how they should develop in future.[52] This was reflected in a series of debates within the *Alash* movement that sought to promote the settlement of the nomadic Kazakhs because, 'the transition to the sedentary way of life was an important condition of the preservation of the Kazakh people as a nation'.[53] Therefore, influenced by European ideas of nations and nationalism, the Kazakh intelligentsia of the *Alash* movement argued that the development of a distinct national identity was dependent upon making fundamental changes to the social, economic and cultural organisation of the Kazakh peoples.

Kazakh historian Gulnar Kendirbaeva has detailed the lengthy and contested debates regarding these monumental changes. The debates did not focus solely on the nomadism/sedentarism dilemma but also on whether to adopt Islamic or Kazakh customary law, and the role of literature (and print language) in the promotion of the codification of the Kazakh language (and what particular form that standardisation should take).[54] Kendirbaeva argued 'from the outset, the Kazakh intelligentsia was split between those who opposed all Russian, thereby Western, socioeconomic changes, who were characterized as "traditionalists," and those who sought to advance the Kazakh nation via Russian, that is, Western, progress, who were termed "westernizers."'[55] European ideas of nation construction, therefore, were clearly influential in shaping the development of the idea of the Kazakh nation. There was also an attempt to clearly outline the boundaries of Kazakh ethnicity during this period. Saulesh Yessenova has argued that in the period 1890–1925 the Kazakh national intelligentsia developed the *Shezhyre*, a genealogy-based register of historic accounts of all Kazakh tribes and lineages. Yessenova argues that the document was important in crystallising the Kazakh ethnic concept and thus determining which groups constituted and were legitimately part of Kazakh ethnicity.[56]

The *Alash* movement changed over the course of its existence. They began as reformists, altered to become democratic nationalists when faced with the crumbling Tsarist Empire, and eventually became revolutionaries challenging Bolshevik power.[57] When the Tsarist regime fell, the *Alash* movement, which had some deputies in the Duma, supported the new provisional government. When the Bolsheviks took power, however, *Alash* proclaimed autonomy from Soviet authorities and established the *Alash* Autonomy, a state incorporating much of the territory of contemporary Kazakhstan. The state was under the control of the White Army and lasted only from December 1917 until August 1920, when the Red Army gained control of the Kazakh steppe. Nonetheless, the short-lived state has again lived long in historical memory as one of the moments when Kazakhstan had independence. Once the Soviets had control of the Central Asian region they moved quickly to establish a process of nation-building in the Kazakh steppe, but again this was a contentious process.

Soviet Nation-building in Kazakhstan

Understanding contemporary nation-building and identity formation in Kazakhstan, and much of the former Soviet Union for that matter, cannot be achieved without reference to the legacy of Soviet nation-building, and especially the enduring influence of Soviet nationalities policy.

Soviet Nationalities Policy

Soviet nationalities policy was devised by the Bolsheviks as a political strategy to maximise the mobilisation of the industrial working class against the Tsarist autocracy.[58] The policy stemmed from Lenin's doctrine on the 'nationalities question', which according to Seton-Watson, 'upheld in principle the right of every nation to self-determination, including the right of secession'.[59] While classical Marxism treated the nation as peripheral, Lenin and his comrades in the

Bolshevik movement had to countenance and address the issue of the multi-ethnic and multi-national composition of the Russian Empire. Theoretically, such an approach to the 'national question' was underpinned by Stalin's work, which while providing a very simplistic interpretation of 'the nation', as a 'definite community of people', also emphasised how nations are subject to historical laws of change, hence proscribing the harbinger for the uniting of classes and the demise of national differences.[60] According to Ro'i, Soviet nationalities policy can be distilled into four simple principles. The first is the recognition of the connection between national rights and territorial concentration of a particular grouping. The second is that national culture is primarily based on language. Thirdly, national groups that had republic-level recognition had to fulfil specific undertakings as part of the all-Union project, and were materially rewarded for the fulfilment of such tasks. Finally, nationalities should have representation within the administrative cadre.[61]

The consensus amongst scholars is that in practice Soviet nationalities policy saw the promotion of dual identities. On the one hand, Soviet elites were committed to accommodating ethno-national heterogeneity throughout the USSR, while at the same time seeking the assimilation of national groups into a unified *Sovetskii narod* (Soviet People).[62] It was the tensions created by this dual approach, which, it is argued, led to the collapse of the USSR while also being central to many of the ethnic fissures and border disputes that have appeared during the post-Soviet period, especially in relation to the Central Asian Republics.[63]

Such an approach to understanding questions of nationality, ethnicity and conflict in the post-Soviet era assumes that Soviet authorities' ethno-federal policy was successful in institutionalising ethnic (and national) identities across the USSR and that assimilation policies were less prosperous.[64] As far back as the 1950s Russian scholars were arguing that national groups in Russia had 'transformed from "nations in themselves" into "nations for themselves," in other words, from ethnic groups into nations with a more or less highly developed national consciousness'.[65] However, as Gorenburg has argued, this approach tends to overlook the success of some aspects of assimilation policy, especially with regards to the dominance of Russian language across the USSR.[66] Moreover, it is important to note that the success of the institutionalisation of ethnic identity was variable depending on the region.[67] If we take Kazakhstan and the broader region of Central Asia as an example, we can observe the variability of this success in ethnic institutionalisation. On the one hand, some scholars had suggested that attachments to ethnic and national identities had taken as strong a hold in Central Asia as in other parts of the Soviet Union, even if it was not entirely in line with Communist Party diktat.[68] Consequently, scholars noted that the Soviet institutionalisation of ethnic and national identities, combined with arbitrarily drawn borders of the region through the national delimitation process of the 1920s, meant that ethnic or religious conflict was a likely scenario of the post-Soviet period.[69] Nevertheless, at the same time, much has been made of the paucity of home-grown nationalist movements in Central Asia at the time of the collapse of the USSR, and that for the most part the experience of Soviet rule in the region had been one in which the Russians dominated, and traditional and national ways of life were repressed as part of the policy of assimilation.[70] It is this tension between a Soviet identity and a specific Kazakh identity that plays out in Kazakh Soviet cinema. As will be discussed in the following chapter, it is these two seemingly contradictory narratives that emerge in cinematic works from the 1960s onward. A representation of Kazakh national identity through cinema, which contrasted with the ideological transmission of an all-Soviet identity, represents a very subtle form of contentious politics, although not dissent. It also went hand in hand with the emergence of a stronger national Kazakh identity among the political elite during Dinmukhamed Kunayev's long period in office as First Secretary of the Communist Party of the Kazakh Soviet Socialist Republic (Kazakh SSR) (1960–86), closely associated with Moscow's more hands-off approach to the Central Asian Republics.

The Central Asian Republics, and Kazakhstan especially, are compelling examples of the Soviet nationalities policy in practice. Whereas most Soviet Republics had some form of prior nation statehood albeit limited, the five Central Asian Republics of Kazakhstan, Kyrgyzstan, Tajikistan, Turkmenistan and Uzbekistan, had no such previous experience. In the 1920s, in an attempt to secure control of the regions that were previously known as Russian Turkestan, the Emirate of Bukhara and Khanate of Khiva, the Soviet authorities enacted the nationality policy by establishing national units (what would become full Union Republics) for six groups Soviet ethnographers classified as constituting distinct national communities.[71] These six peoples (Kazakhs, Turkmen, Tajiks, Kyrgyz, Uzbeks and Karakalpaks): were assigned their own administrative territorial units; had literary languages standardised for each group, along with compulsory education in these languages; and cultural and folk traditions were protected and promoted through the creation of 'national' cultural institutions.[72] Thus, for some scholars, the Soviet authorities took it upon themselves not just to promote and institutionalise national and ethnic categories, but to actually become 'nation-makers'.[73] It has been argued that this was tantamount to Kazakhstan and the Central Asian Republics being artificial creations in which these new territorial units overrode existing Islamic and traditional structures in the region.[74] Subsequently, in the post-Soviet period a historiographical literature emerged which provided competing explanations for the extent to which local elites in Kazakhstan and Central Asia were involved in the process of 'nation-making'. Some scholars point towards the centrality of Central Asian elites to the formation of their national republics,[75] while others suggest local elites remained on the periphery of what was a Kremlin-directed initiative.[76] Questions regarding the extent of the influence of local Central Asian agency in the process of Soviet nation-building are important as they go to the heart of the extent to which Kazakhstan possesses agency in the writing and interpretation of its own history and nationhood or whether this is something which exists, in part, as a consequence of Russian and/or Soviet re-interpretations of the region's history. Soviet cultural elites are argued to have played a role in selecting the historiography, folklores, myths, traditions, symbols and literature that made up Soviet-approved 'cultural traditions'.[77]

The above discussion on Soviet nationalities policy is important for the context of this study on film and nation-building in Kazakhstan for two fundamental reasons. Firstly, post-Soviet nation-building does not represent a *tabula rasa*. Given the Soviet authorities delimited the existing borders of Kazakhstan and the other Central Asian Republics, the existence of Kazakhstan's current territorial borders is owed, whatever the contribution of domestic elites, to Soviet authorities. Therefore, post-Soviet nation-building begins from the existing process of Soviet nation-building. Secondly, Soviet nationalities policy had a practical influence in relation to the demographic legacy it left for the successor states, and this was especially the case in Kazakhstan because of the settlement of the nomadic population and the deportation of other ethnic groups to the Kazakh steppe.

Sedentarisation, Collectivisation and Deportations

Sedentarisation was an issue that had been central to discussions within the *Alash Orda* in the early part of the twentieth century. During the Soviet period the settlement of the Kazakh nomads was an important element of the social engineering task the Soviet regime had set itself in terms of the collectivisation of the agricultural economy. As Martha Brill Olcott noted, sedentarisation also represented for Stalin 'the final destruction of the nomadic economy and so end the political authority of the old social order'.[78] The settlement of the nomadic population was rapid. In the late 1920s, 23 per cent of Kazakhs were settled; by 1930, this was 56.6 per cent and by 1933 the whole rural population was sedentary.[79] The forced collectivisation of the Kazakh nomads clearly altered the demographic and social fabric of the country. After the Bolshevik Revolution, and during the Civil War, small groups of Kazakh nomads fled to Mongolia. This migration intensified with the institution of sedentarisation.[80] By 1956, 36,700 Kazakhs had migrated to Mongolia.[81] This outward migration had important consequences for the post-Soviet period. Kazakhs seeking to return to Kazakhstan post-1991, known as *Oralman* (returnees), led to a contested discourse regarding Kazakh identity and belonging in the new state. Opinion was divided between those who saw the *Oralman* as possessing the shared ancestry of the Kazakh people and others who viewed the returnees as traitors and a drain on the country's resources.[82]

Collectivisation had a devastating effect on the Kazakh nomads who remained. Poor management of the process, systematic requisition of grain and livestock and climatic changes led to a widespread famine, which tragically claimed the lives of over 1 million Kazakhs, approximately 38 per cent of the population.[83] The Kazakh famine of 1932–3 was largely absent from Soviet history books, as was the equally tragic *Holodomor* famine in Ukraine. With *perestroika*, and then independence, discussion of the famine was finally permissible with a number of historical studies being published.[84] Kazakh historians laid blame on Filipp Isaevich Goloshchekin, the First Secretary of the Communist Party of the Republic of Kazakhstan during the famine, as well as Stalin and the Soviet system.[85] Sarah Cameron has argued, however, that less attention has been paid to the intensity of local-level violence during collectivisation and sedentarisation, and the responsibility of domestic elites in enforcing these policies.[86] The Kazakh famine is notable by its largely absent nature in the commemorative politics of the post-Soviet period. In part, this is down to victims no longer being around to re-tell the story, but also as argued by Isabel Ohayon, it can be explained by the ambivalent relationship contemporary Kazakhstan has towards nomadism.[87] The topics of sedentarisation, collectivisation, famine and outward migration have been largely absent in cinematic works in Kazakhstan. Given that the historical memory has been a central element of reconstituting the boundaries of Kazakh identity and nationhood in the post-Soviet period, only Damir Manabayev's 1991 film *Surzhekey – the Angel of Death* (discussed in Chapter 3) explicitly addresses the history of collectivization, and especially Kazakh resistance to the transformation.

Further demographic changes were wrought by the forced deportations of other ethnic groups to the Kazakh steppe. Russians had been migrating to the Kazakh steppe since the colonisation of the region by the Tsarist Empire, either bringing technical and administrative expertise or seeking out fertile land for pasture. Stalin's leadership of the Soviet Union brought with it the forced movement of populations to Kazakhstan. Firstly, victims of de-kulakization and collectivisation from 1929–31, then Poles and Koreans in 1936–7, Soviet Germans in 1941–5, and then finally Chechens and Ingush in 1944.[88]

Sedentarisation, collectivisation, famine and inward and outward migration not only had a fundamental impact on Soviet nation-building, but also shaped post-Soviet nation-building. The consequences of these events altered not only the social structure of nomadic life, rendering it something that needed to be re-imagined and re-constituted in historical memory, but also the demographic make-up of the country. It is well known that by the last Soviet census in 1989 ethnic Kazakhs only made up 41 per cent of the population of the Republic of Kazakhstan. It represented a significant challenge for President Nursultan Nazarbayev in terms of firstly making Kazakhstan a centre for ethnic Kazakhs, while at the same time ensuring a common sense of belonging for all those other ethnic groups who found themselves living in an independent Kazakhstan once the Soviet Union collapsed. This story of inward migration has been a central theme for one of the dominant narratives within contemporary Kazakh cinematic works (see Chapter 6), as well as reflecting the project of 'civic' nation-building in the post-Soviet period (see below).

The above analysis is only a partial exploration of Soviet nation-building in Kazakhstan. It is important not to downplay the role of the Soviet state in constructing the borders of the current territory of Kazakhstan. Nor must we lose sight of the crucial role of Moscow and local elites in developing important national institutions, education, national literature and symbols as well as culturally repressing aspects of Islamic religious practice. As important was the development of a local cadre through the policy of *korenizatsiya* and during the Brezhnev period the emergence of a form of dual authority whereby power was located not just in Moscow but also in the hands of the First Secretary of the Kazakh Communist Party, Dinmukhamed Kunayev, a Kazakh.[89] Kunayev's power and presence loomed large in Kazakhstan from the 1960s until the 1980s.

Kunayev's rule was significant for two reasons in terms of the process of nation-building. Firstly, a degree of informal autonomy was given to the regions, which ensured Kunayev could distribute resources and positions to key local allies and relatives. This power of patronage is argued to have strengthened a 'Kazakh national consciousness', as it had in other Soviet republics during this period.[90] Secondly, Kunayev's removal from office in 1986 led to one of the first nationalist mobilisations of the *glasnost* period against the Soviet leadership in Moscow. From 16–19 December 1986, thousands of students demonstrated in Alma-Ata, Shymkent, Taldykorgan and Karaganda against the decision to replace Kunayev with the Russian, Gennady Kolbin. The Soviet military moved to quell the protests, with reportedly 200 people being killed. The event has been memorialised as *Zheltoksan* (December) and has become a central symbol of Kazakh national independence with streets being re-named in its memory of the event, while a documentary was also made in commemoration of the event. *Zheltoksan* has emerged as a point of national pride against Soviet repression and a unifying symbol of Kazakh solidarity. The events have been argued to have had an enormous psychological impact, which led to a clear divergence between the interests of Kazakhs and Russians in the country.[91] The emergence of the 'Kazakh New Wave' of cinema, which began to depict on screen the problems and challenges of life in late Soviet Kazakhstan, can partly be understood in the context of the contentious politics that surfaced as part of the *Zheltoksan* events. The above does not represent a linear description of Soviet nation-building in Kazakhstan. Rather the idea was to provide a flavour of some of the key ingredients which point towards the contestation of nationhood and identity during this period – that is, the promotion of two identities (Soviet and Kazakh), debates around who was involved in the process of nation-building (central or local elites) – and critical junctures which have contributed to shaping post-Soviet nation-building and its inherent discourses (migration, deportation and the nature of political rule). Understanding the legacies of Soviet nation-building on post-Soviet nation-building is important for situating the competing and contrasting narratives on identity and nationhood in cinematic works.

Post-Soviet Nation-building

Like any discussion on post-Soviet nation-building in Kazakhstan there is much ground that could be covered, and indeed there are texts on the subject written already.[92] Again, like above, the aim here is to offer a portrait of how questions of national identity, and nation-building more broadly, have emerged as site of contention where we can observe multiple forms of nationalism. The scholarship on post-Soviet nation-building in Kazakhstan has focused predominantly on a perceived antagonism between ethnic and civic nation-building projects. As will be noted below, not only are there more varied interpretations of nationalism and identity in Kazakhstan, but also the ethnic-civic binary is not necessarily one that is automatically in tension. Rather it is quite natural for a state to adopt both positions concurrently.

Ethnic Nation-building

As with the other Central Asian Republics, in the first decade of independence the government of Kazakhstan was understood as a 'nationalising regime'. Premised upon Rogers Brubaker's idea of a 'nationalising state', Central Asian regimes were perceived to be asserting 'the hegemony of their respective titular nations'.[93] As no modern independent state called Kazakhstan had existed before, post-Soviet elites in the country were characterised as 'nation-builders' whom were undertaking the Kazakhization of state and government institutions.[94] This has taken a number of forms including, but not limited to: inscribing the centrality of ethnic Kazakhs within the constitution; language policy; the nationalising of public space; education; and minorities and repatriation. The following section addresses these elements.

The position of Kazakhs within the constitution has changed since independence. As Özgecan Kesici has noted, the original preamble in the 1993 constitution referred to Kazakh statehood in the abstract sense as a state to which all the people of Kazakhstan belonged.[95] In the 1995 constitution, however, the focus shifts to that of ethnic territoriality: 'we, the people of Kazakhstan, united by a common historic fate, creating a state on the indigenous Kazak land ... '.[96] The modification, while semantically subtle, is highly significant. It introduces the idea that those not of Kazakh ethnicity belong to a state that is territorially indigenous to the Kazakh people, rather than a state indigenous to all the people whom live within Kazakhstan. Over the course of the two-and-a-half decades since the collapse of the Soviet Union, the Kazakh government, led by the President, has continued to introduce further Kazakhization of state structures. This has been most notable in state recruitment policy. In the 1990s, preference was given to ethnic Kazakhs in key cadre positions within the government, presidential administration, the police, the army and the National Security Committee.[97] Furthermore, the centrality of Kazakh ethnicity was also enshrined in the 1996 'Concept for the Forming of State Identity of the Republic of Kazakhstan' in which Kazakhstan is claimed to be the 'ethnic centre' and state for all Kazakhs.[98]

Key national emblems also referred exclusively to Kazakh mythology or symbols such as the national flag which utilises the steppe eagle, the *koshkar-muiz* ornamental pattern, and the light blue background, all of which are rooted in either the traditions of the Kazakh Khanate, or older Turkic traditions. Moreover, the replacement of Lenin's statue in the main Republic square in Almaty, with that of Altan Adam, the Golden Scythian warrior, was an attempt to de-Russify the public space, and erect more ethno-centric symbols as monuments of independence.[99] After the collapse of the Soviet Union all old Soviet street names were also quickly replaced with names that honoured the great figures or events of Kazakh history such as Ablai Khan, Zheltoksan, Seyfulin (after the poet and writer Saken Seyfulin) and Kurmangazy (after composer Kurmangazy Sagyrbayuly).[100] There has also been a concerted effort to promote particular historical narratives about Kazakh ethnicity and its history, especially in relation to the idea of the 'nomad'. This has been evident in cinema (as we will see in Chapter 4) but also in other 'soft power' forms such as music videos, literature and television.[101] Some local Kazakh analysts have suggested that wide-scale celebrations of prominent Kazakh Figures (such as poet Abai Kunanbayev, traditional folk singer Zhambyl Zhabayev and Ablai Khan, former political leader of the Kazakh Khanate) are examples of the ethnic discrimination of the public and cultural space against other national groups residing in the country.[102] Ethnic discrimination in favour of Kazakhs was most prominent in a trial balloon released by the president in February 2014 when he suggested dropping the suffix 'stan' and renaming the country *Kazak Eli* (Land of Kazakhs). Nazarbayev suggested 'stan' in the country's title failed to distinguish the country from other states in the region that also used the suffix. Needless to say, the idea never took off given the message it would send to non-Kazakh minorities living in the country.

Since independence the Kazakh government has also pursued a policy of altering the demographic make-up of the county to favour Kazakhs. Kazakhs were in a minority at the time of independence. In 1991 there remained a large Russian minority of nearly 10 million people (37 per cent of the population), which came second only to Ukraine as the largest Russian diaspora outside of the Russian homeland. Consequently, the government of the Republic of Kazakhstan has placed primacy on bolstering the number of ethnic Kazakhs in the country.[103] This was achieved through several policies. There was a rigorous campaign to promote the birth rate amongst Kazakhs, the relocation of the capital from Almaty in the South to Akmola (re-named Astana) in the North where there were large numbers of Russians, and a rigorous campaign for the repatriation of *Oralman* mostly from Mongolia, Russia, Kyrgyzstan, Iran, Afghanistan and Turkey.[104] These policies were a success. The population of ethnic Kazakhs increased to 46 per cent in 1995, to 53 per cent in 1999 and to 63 per cent in 2009. The increase in the Kazakh population has come at the expense of other minority groups, mainly Russians, of whom as many as 4.5 million have migrated back to Russia after the collapse of the Soviet Union.[105]

It is the issue of language, however, whereby there was the greatest effort in policy terms to promote an ethnically exclusive interpretation of Kazakh nationhood. The main language law adopted in 1989 established a commitment to ensuring all official state communication would be in Kazakh by 1995. However, this deadline passed without being met and a further date of 2010 was also missed. The current deadline is 2020. There continues to be a gap between the rhetoric of the government's support for the Kazakh language and the reality on the ground. For instance, while there is pressure to learn Kazakh, the number of hours of Kazakh being taught in schools has been reduced.[106] Furthermore, an on-going campaign to convert the Kazakh language from Cyrillic to Latin script has also yet to be fulfilled, although at the time of writing, in 2017, this does seem to be coming closer to finally happening. In the view of ethno-nationalists, the rationale behind such a move is that Cyrillic is stigmatised by Russian colonialism.[107] Given the large Russian minority, and that there are many Russian-speaking Kazakhs, a language policy that exclusively promotes Kazakh remains problematic. Instead, while Kazakh has been promoted to the official state language, Russian remains the language of inter-ethnic communication and English the language of business.[108] The promotion of the Kazakh language is also reflected in cinema of the late 1980s and early 1990s. Serik Aprymov's films *Akusat* (1988) and *The Last Stop* (1989), with their realist, art-house and ethnographic portrayal of *aul* life, meant the films ultimately used the Kazakh language, preceding later government sponsored efforts of promoting Kazakh language in cinema, especially with *Nomad* and *Zhauzhurek Myn Bala*.

Civic Nation-building

According to Juldyz Smagulova, the legislation on language reflects a compromise between two contradicting ideologies – mono and bilingualism.[109] While this is true, that Kazakhstan requires a language for multi-ethnic communication only illustrates that the promotion of an exclusive identity centred on Kazakh ethnicity is not, and has never been, straightforward. It serves to elucidate the limits of the nationalising state in Kazakhstan. The demographic legacy Soviet rule left behind has meant Kazakhstan was a multi-ethnic state where Russian (rather than Kazakh) was the prominent spoken language. Therefore, the Kazakhification of the state has taken place in an ethnically complex and sensitive environment. The perception of the government is that it has been necessary to satisfy the linguistic claims of Russians, and as importantly, Russophone Kazakhs and other minority groups, in order to maintain inter-ethnic stability.[110]

A tension within policy circles between so-called 'nationalists' and 'cosmopolitans' has been evident in Kazakhstan since the 1990s. For Cengiz Surucu, these two camps 'are struggling to delineate a distinctive posture based on shared attributes of being "urban" inter-ethnic and "Russian-speaking" in opposition to being "rural" and "Kazakh-speaking"'.[111] These two positions reflect the ethnic-civic dichotomy. As Kazakh political scientist Rustem Kadyrzhanov has noted, 'proponents of the idea of Kazakh nationalism advocate a special place for all ethnic Kazakhs in Kazakhstan ... in contrast, advocates of the civil national idea believe that the national idea should reflect the interests of all ethnic groups in Kazakhstan: as the titular and non-titular'.[112] The legacy of Russification meant that most urban-dwelling Kazakhs spoke Russian rather than Kazakh and attended Russian schools. Therefore, the government could not simply impose the Kazakhization on society without the risk of inter-ethnic discord and instability; rather, they have had to balance the demands of the ethnically diverse population as a matter of course for the regime's own legitimation.[113]

This balancing act between ethnic and civic ascriptions of nationhood includes several dimensions. In the first instance, the government utilised institutional mechanisms to embed a commitment to a civic-inspired understanding of post-Soviet nationhood. This included: respect for, and promotion of, different national cultures being enshrined within the constitution; state funding for minority groups; the creation of the Assembly of Peoples of Kazakhstan (APK) in 1995, a presidentially appointed advisory institution made up of members representing different ethnic groups within Kazakhstan (nine members of the Assembly also sit in the parliament); and the outlawing of political parties based on ethnic (and religious) grounds.[114] The last institutional mechanism was especially important for the consolidation of Nazarbayev's power. The early post-Soviet period did see the emergence of several nationalist movements and parties (both Kazakh and non-Kazakh), such as the Russian groups LAD and *Russkaya Obshchina*.[115] Restricting political parties on this basis ensured that at least in electoral terms the political system would not segment along ethnic or national lines, and instead allowed the Nazarbayev regime political space to put forward their narrative regarding a 'civic', inter-ethnic and harmonious Kazakhstan.

The second dimension of the civic narrative is the specific discourse put forward by the regime concerning inter-ethnic and religious harmony in the country. This has been evident in presidential policy statements and speeches since independence – especially in the idea of Kazakhstan as a 'common home' for all citizens within the state. In other words, Kazakhstan is not a nation of Kazakhs, but of Kazakhstanis. For example, at the 2014 *Nur Otan* (Light of Fatherland) congress the president proclaimed, 'we Kazakhs – we are a nation with a united future. That says it all. There should be no dividing line between ethnic groups – we are Kazakhstanis. We have made significant progress in developing our own model of stability and harmony in the country.'[116] This idea of a 'common home' was formalised in the 2010 Doctrine of National Unity. The president had requested the APK draw up a document to develop the idea of inter-ethnic harmony in order to establish a coherent set of values upon which to unify the citizens of the country in spite of their ethnicity.[117] The initial draft version of the document incited disunity rather than accord with a number of Kazakh nationalist movements such as *Ult Tagdyry* (Fate of the Nation) and *Memlekettik Til* (State Language), along with opposition political parties, complaining that Kazakhs should be recognised as the core group in the nation around which the state forms.[118] The debate revealed a number of important cleavages related to the development of a unified nation, not least in relation to the language of the community and the obscured meaning of the Kazakh term *ult* which can mean both nation and ethnicity.[119] Nonetheless, a process of consultation and dialogue followed between the APK and other groups including the Kazakh nationalist movements and those representing minority groups and a form of wording was agreed for the doctrine.

The Doctrine of National Unity was the legal-rational embodiment of the idea of a civic form of nationhood and identity in Kazakhstan.

It advances a conceptualisation of nationhood, which is a consequence of both Soviet nationalities policy and the demographic legacy of deportations to the country in the 1930s and 1940s. This narrative is reflected in a few films in the contemporary period that have been produced by Kazakhfilm Studios, such as *The Gift to Stalin* (2008) and *The Promised Land* (2011).

The two trends of ethnic and civic nationalism within contemporary nation-building in Kazakhstan have been depicted as contradictory in the scholarly literature.[120] They have also been observed as opposites in the way in which they cultivate a sense of victimisation within their constituencies.[121] Yet, it is not necessarily contradictory for the government of Kazakhstan to hold and promote these two interpretations of nationhood. As Taras Kuzio has argued, all civic states possess ethnic cores and therefore all states are in some sense 'nationalising', while at the same time possessing the civic element that appeals to political rights and responsibilities.[122] As this work argues later in Chapters 4 and 5, both the exclusive ethnic narrative and the inclusive civic narrative within contemporary cinema are promoted by the Ministry of Culture through Kazakhfilm Studios. It is not contradictory for the regime to disseminate both narratives. In the first instance, the regime is not monolithic in Kazakhstan (it consists of different interest groups) and secondly, both narratives are important components of the legitimation of the regime in its efforts to appeal to different social constituencies in the country. There is fluidity between the two different conceptions of nationhood and, therefore, despite the emphasis in the scholarly literature, and the policy debate in Kazakhstan too, the complexity of the nation-building process in the country cannot be reduced to an either/or dichotomy.

Pan-Asian (Tengrist) and Social-Economic Interpretations of Nationhood

A core argument of this book is that we can observe multiple forms of nationalism in Kazakhstan. It shows this by providing an account of these multivalent constructions of nation through an examination of cinematic works. Representations of nationhood beyond the ethnic-civic dichotomy are also rooted in broader political discourse. The first of this relates to how religion has underpinned a representation of a national idea. Islam, with its cultural and moral components, has emerged as a potential basis for a unifying national idea in Kazakh intellectual circles.[123] Discredited under the Soviet regime, Islam has resurfaced as a possible representation of national identity as a moral force which constitutes a 'way of life' for Kazakh citizens.[124] However, the Nazarbayev regime has been careful in promoting Islam, wary on the one hand of the sizable Slavic minority in the country, while on the other hand choosing to securitise Islam, responding harshly to the alleged threat from its radical variant.[125] Perhaps because of this, Islam has not emerged as a significant narrative related to nationhood and identity within contemporary film. Nevertheless, what Islam does reveal is a broader interest in pan-Asian identities. This has taken two principle forms. In regime-led policy discourse there is a Eurasian identity. Eurasianism is an elusive concept that has different meanings to various constituencies. Russian Eurasianism, for example, was developed on a geopolitical and European understanding of the concept. Nazarbayev's conceptualisation of Eurasianism (an idea he has been explicit in promoting) links partly to the notion of a multi-ethnic Kazakhstani state, but focuses more on unity within the broader Eurasian region on political, economic and security issues (concretely realised in the Eurasian Economic Union).[126] However, it is a Turkic interpretation of Eurasianism linked to the pre-Islamic religion of Tengrism, which has emerged most prominently with regards to a clear narrative of nationhood and identity in Kazakhstan. This form of Eurasianism relates to an ideology that aims for the cultural and/or physical union of Turkic peoples in the Eurasian region.[127] In Kazakhstan, amongst cultural intellectual circles, this has taken form in the espousal of Tengrism as being a potential basis of a post-Soviet Kazakh national identity.[128]

Tengrism, according to Marléne Laruelle, refers to the Turkic-Mongol cult of the sky god and was traditionally practiced amongst the Turkic-Mongol peoples, until it was gradually superseded by Islam.[129] It is a monotheistic religion grounded in shamanistic, totemistic and animistic beliefs and practices where humans, animals, and nature possess spiritual qualities that form a symbiotic relationship. Importantly, however, it has re-emerged among some post-Soviet Central Asian national intellectual elites 'as a key element in the identity renewal of Turkic–Mongol peoples'.[130] As will be discussed in

Chapter 6, proponents of Tengrism view Islam as a foreign religion to the region and that Tengrism is the rightful spiritual basis of the Kazakh people.[131] This is often couched in psycho-geographical terms in that Tengrism provides Kazakh people with an identity rooted in their relationship with the vast Kazakh steppe. As will be revealed in Chapter 6 when discussing the films of Yermek Tursunov, such a conception of Kazakh national identity and nationhood is problematic. This is predominantly because of the way it adopts religious, social and cultural characteristics that are shared by many Turkic peoples across the Eurasian region, and the tendency for some elements of the discourse to portend toward an exclusive primordialism.

Tengrism as the basis for an alternative construction of the Kazakh nation is not the only variant from the ethnic-civic dichotomy of nation-building. Some Kazakh scholars have argued that any notion that Kazakhstan possesses a common culture and identity is highly questionable. This is driven by the disparity of social, economic and cultural experiences between rural and urban populations.[132] This highlights how a common sense of belonging to a nation can be stymied by divergent socio-economic experiences (both real and imagined) which create alternative social realities of the nation from the ethno-centrist and civic imaginations of nationhood put forward by the ruling regime.

This speaks to is an understanding of nationhood and identity rooted in the 'stress of the post-socialist transitional period'.[133] Under the pressure of the transition to capitalist modes of economic and social organisation, as well as an encroaching globalisation and Westernisation in the country, a unified sense of social belonging is largely absent. Instead, there are developmental discrepancies between the city and the village, an inequality which as argued by Saulesh Yessenova is a legacy of Soviet rule.[134] The post-Soviet period has witnessed significant migration from the rural areas to the cities as people seek economic opportunities. This urban migration has contributed to shaping citizens' identity not toward unity and shared belonging, but instead displacement and adjustment, which causes frustration and dissatisfaction.[135] Citizens who migrate from the *auls* (village) to the urban centres are often viewed as 'social outsiders' who 'have no chance to improve their position by legal means'.[136] Nationhood, therefore, is constituted not by a commitment to an ethnic, civic or religious disposition, but instead is framed by the dislocating and alienating experiences of the post-Soviet transition, especially in relation to the corruption and bureaucracy of the state. What appears, therefore, are a series of social divisions between urban and rural, moral and corrupt, and Kazakh- and Russian-speaking populations.

The linguistic division is particularly potent. There is a tendency within some aspects of Kazakh nationalism to seek purity. Therefore, urban-dwelling Kazakhs who have lived in the Soviet and Russian-constructed cities all their lives and who speak Russian rather than Kazakh are viewed by arch-nationalists as 'Shala Kazakhs'. In other words, they are viewed as half-Kazakhs, not real Kazakhs; Russified Kazakhs.[137] It is these social divisions, underpinned by social and economic tensions of post-Soviet transition, along with the struggles with political authority, which define nationhood and identity. The juxtaposition of these different divisions reveals the contested nature of the construction of the Kazakh nation, undermining any sense of homogeneity.[138]

These additional narratives to the civic and ethnic dichotomy are not obviously present in political discourse. However, when explored through the lens of cinema they become more apparent. The pan-Asian identity that comes through most clearly in cinematic works is that of the Tengrist representation of nationhood and identity. The socio-economic understanding of contemporary nationhood focuses on many of the social divisions mentioned above, but also emerges as a narrative that acts as a site of dissent against the regime in Kazakhstan.

Conclusion

This chapter has sought to provide historical and political context to understanding the relationship between film, identity and nation-building in Kazakhstan. The aim was to show the contentious nature of Kazakhstan's claims of nationhood throughout history. The nature of contention is neither consistent nor stable. Contestation appears at different points and junctures. The historiography of the Kazakh Khanate remains disputed in terms of the extent of its unity and the degree to which it represents a continuum for the modern-day Kazakh state. The period of Russian colonisation also features contention with regards to whether resistance to Russian rule represented a form of national liberation. We also see debates within *Alash Orda*, the late-Tsarist-period nationalist movement, regarding how the Kazakh nation could be built and modernised. The writing of Kazakh history of the pre-Russian and pre-Soviet period is also refracted through a Russian and Soviet lens. Even if local Kazakh historians and elites were involved in the writing of this history, they still benefited from Russian and Soviet education and their modernisation processes. It is challenging, but perhaps not impossible, to completely isolate an independent Kazakh agency in the writing of its history. Also important is the way in which some of these writings of history, especially in relation to the Kazakh Khanate, are being reclaimed by the regime in the post-Soviet period for the purposes of legitimation. Re-imagining historical heroes and myths of the Kazakh Khanate serves an important function in attempting to create a sense of common belonging for the post-Soviet present as well as a continuous link between the historical past and the present Kazakh state.

The Soviet period sees contention along a number of lines: the promotion of dual identities (Soviet and Kazakh); the degree to which local Kazakh elites were responsible for shaping Soviet nation-building; demographic changes (sedentarisation, collectivisation, *korenizatsiya* and dual authority) that ultimately shaped the challenges of post-Soviet nation-building; and the development of dual political authority, which saw a form of political rule emerge dependent upon patronage, clientelism and personalism, a phenomena that continues to shape post-Soviet authoritarianism in Kazakhstan. In the post-Soviet period, it is possible to identify different representations of nationhood and identity both in policy and discursive terms. This includes the ethnic and civic notions of Kazakh nationalism, as well as a religious representation of identity rooted in a pan-Asian form of Turkic Tengrism, and a conceptualisation of modern national identity rooted in socio-economic experiences.

While the nature and points of contention change over time, what is central is that any essential, uncontested understanding of Kazakhstan as a nation is difficult to find. It is this form of contention regarding representation of nationhood and identity that we can observe in cinematic works from the Soviet period into contemporary post-Soviet cinema. The following chapter begins this journey of exploring the multiple interpretations of nationhood and identity in Kazakhstan through cinema. We start by examining how both a Soviet identity and an ethnic ascription of identity are represented in the films of Soviet era Kazakh cinema. As will be shown, it was the development of a national Kazakh identity in the cinematic works of this period that also represents a very subtle form of contention against the Soviet regime.

CHAPTER 2

BETWEEN TWO WORLDS: KAZAKH FILM AND NATION-BUILDING IN THE SOVIET ERA

As the previous chapter emphasised, Kazakhstan's history is replete with contention concerning its construction as an imagined community. The nation is understood in multiple ways at varying points of time by different constituencies. As an imagined entity, therefore, Kazakhstan should not be considered homogenous. It is fractured along different interpretations of nationhood and identity. Examining film-making in the Soviet period in Kazakhstan we can see two distinct identity worlds emerge. This chapter offers an exploration of those two worlds as well as providing a historical context for an analysis of representations of nationhood and identity in Kazakh cinema.

The first film ever to be screened in Kazakhstan was in 1910 in Vernyi (Almaty) at the Mars cinema, on what is modern-day Dostyk Avenue.[1] The introduction of cinematic technology coincided with the development of Vernyi as an urban centre along with the growing influence of *Alash Orda* as a nationalist movement, especially with the publication of their weekly journal *Qazaq*.[2] The emergence of a national awakening in the early twentieth century elided with the introduction of cinema as a form through which to portray representations of the national self. Taken together it illustrates how ideas about what constitutes the Kazakh nation formed because of structural transformations, the gradual settlement of nomadic populations and the emergence of new mass communicative technologies.

The Russian Revolution also coincided with the rise of cinema as mass entertainment. Cinema acted as an important tool for the Bolsheviks as they sought to educate the masses into new patterns of social, economic and political behaviour.[3] Soviet cinema became an essential instrument for establishing an 'alternative' reality through socialist realism and its idealised portrayal of the values of the revolution and heroism of the proletariat.[4] Ultimately, Soviet cinema was not all-encompassing in presenting a singular ideological message. In Kazakhstan, while the promotion of 'New Soviet Man' was present in cinematic works, at the same time elements of a Kazakh national identity also came to the fore. Cinema provided a forum through which representations of Kazakh national identity were constructed and began to emerge. Similar to Soviet nationalities policy in the way it promoted nation-building in the hope that it would ultimately lead to a universal Soviet identity, the promotion of both Soviet and Kazakh identities in film was not necessarily contradictory. Nonetheless, it did establish what Gulnara Abikeyeva has called 'two worlds'. One world was that of the Soviet system, the typical heroes of the revolution and the Soviet project. The other was a 'Kazakh' world in which films from the 1950s and 1960s developed a palette of different national symbols.

While a 'Kazakh' world was represented in films as early as the late 1930s, such as in *Amangeldy* (1939), it was from the 1960s onwards that the distinction between the two worlds became more tangible. The emergence of a group of Kazakh-born directors, actors and producers in this period brought with them a greater confidence and commitment to providing a representation of the 'Kazakh' world. As with cinema in other Soviet republics in this period, socialist realism fell from grace and was gradually replaced by the *bytovoy* (slice-of-life) film. Such films told stories 'about contemporary society, individual lives and relations, current problems and human values'.[5] Films from this period also began to provide a subtle and indirect form of contention. This is not outright political antagonism and opposition to the regime, but these films provided a relief valve in which social concerns and the day-to-day could be expressed along with representations of national cultures and identities that then sat in tension (but not always) with the more universal pan-Soviet identity. Films of this period were able to express a form of deviation from the Soviet norm because of the polysemic nature of cinema with regards to the extent to which we ascribe meanings to images and text – and that such meanings can be hidden. Moreover, it is also possible such forms of subtle deviation from the Soviet 'script' were permissible because of a perceived necessity on the part of the elite to use cinema as a release valve for social and economic frustrations.

The depiction of the 'Kazakh' world within mid-to-late-era Kazakh Soviet cinema does demonstrate a form of contention. The antagonism between the promotion of Soviet fraternal friendship and an ethnic ascription of Kazakh identity, while seemingly presented as complementary, was never resolved. The 'Kazakh' world does in fact form part of the construction of the Kazakh nation, which consequently undermines an all-national Soviet identity. The emergence of a Kazakh national cinema also corresponds to a period of Soviet history under Brezhnev where authority was located not just at the centre in Moscow but also in the regions. Kazakhstan was no exception. The greater confidence in Kazakh representation of identity mirrors the confidence with which Dinmukhamed Kunayev ruled the Kazakh Soviet Socialist Republic. He appointed Kazakhs to leading positions within the economic, cultural and educational institutions of the state. The development of Kazakh cinema in this period was also influential for the development of post-Soviet cinema. The Ministry of Culture in post-Soviet Kazakhstan has been influenced by the 'custom-made' nature of Soviet films in their own efforts to use film to propagate an ideological message and depiction of Kazakh national identity, history and memory.

This chapter is broken down into four sections. The first two sections provide historical context, exploring the development of cinema in the early Soviet period in the USSR and the antecedents for the birth of cinema in the Kazakh SSR. The remaining two sections deal explicitly with the emergence of a distinct Kazakh Soviet cinema, especially in relation to the work of Shaken Aimanov, and the drawing out of the two competing 'Kazakh' and 'Soviet' worlds from the 1960s onward. The conclusion then assesses the influence of Kazakh Soviet cinema on the 'Kazakh New Wave' and contemporary Kazakh film directors.

The Development of the Cinema Industry in the Soviet Union and Central Asia

Once the Bolsheviks had taken control of much of the former Tsarist Empire, cinema provided the new Soviet state with a powerful ideological weapon.[6] It would be misleading, however, to think that it was easy to develop a film industry capable of pumping out movies to educate the masses of the virtues of a communist order. As Richard Taylor has noted, much like the struggles to take control of the former Tsarist state, the Bolsheviks also had to gain control of the production and distribution of the existing cinema network.[7] When they did get a grasp of it they found it in a state of depleted disrepair. As the Civil War raged on, the film industry lost some of its most prominent directors, producers and actors, along with vital raw material such as film, stock and cameras.[8]

The Bolshevik take-over of the cinema industry was thus a gradual process. It began in January 1918 with the creation of a subsection of the Extramural Education Department of the Commissariat of Education (Narkompros) which was set up to oversee matters of film.[9] This evolved into the All-Russian Photographic and Cinematographic Section of Narkompros (VFKO), and over a year later The Council of People's Commissars (Sovnarkom) nationalised all film companies.[10] VFKO was then centralised into *Goskino* in 1922. However, Kristin Thompson has warned scholars from assuming the nationalisation of the industry meant the Bolshevik government fully subsidised the industry in the early years succeeding the 1917 revolution. Given the government was fighting a Civil War, only limited financial support could be given to the exhausted film industry. Valuable raw stock and equipment had to be bought in from capitalist countries and the industry was expected to be self-sufficient.[11] The Civil War had ravaged the industry. According to Peter Kenez, by 1921 'the Studios were idle, the distribution system stopped functioning and film theatres shut down.'[12] A revival only began to take place with the introduction of the New Economic Policy (NEP). NEP saw the reopening of private theatres, some of the old specialists in film production returned and with the signing of the Anglo-Russian Trade Agreement in June 1921 it was now possible for theatres to import more commercially viable foreign films, which made up for the lack of domestic production.[13] When domestic production did restart it was focused on newsreels and so-called *agitika*. These were short five- to thirty-minute films aimed at political education that according to Richard Taylor conveyed a 'simple message on a single subject with directness and economy'.[14] Nonetheless, the quality of such films was perceived to be technically very poor.[15]

The re-birth of the cinema industry is largely agreed by scholars[16] to have taken place from 1924 onwards, when *Goskino* was replaced by *Sovkino*,[17] a joint-stock company that, in the view of Denise Youngblood, possessed a much 'broader mandate and sounder financial footing'.[18] The resurgence is reflected in the increase of film production. From 1918 to 1921 just 16 domestic feature films were produced, by 1924 this rose to 37; and by 1928 to 112.[19] From 1925 onwards the Soviet film industry was perceived to have entered a Golden Age, with directors such as Sergei Eisenstein and Vsevolod Pudovkin among others attracting plaudits for their contribution to the language of cinema-making.[20] From the 1930s onwards the introduction of sound along with urban and rural cinefication was gradual, as were developments to the industry base.[21]

The above illustrates that the imposition of central control over the film industry was a difficult and pained process. If it was challenging establishing cinema and its concomitant industry in Russia as a means of mass political education, it is not hard to imagine how impregnable the task was in the more under-developed region of Central Asia, and especially Kazakhstan. An article in *Sovetskii Ekran* from 1927 affirms how for Lenin the development of the cinema in the 'East was of particular importance'.[22] The rationale was that cinema was important for raising the cultural level of the masses in the East who were perceived to live a culturally backward existence.[23]

As Michael Rouland notes, the first films screened in the region were in Tashkent in 1897, and cinemas were opened in Uralsk and Vernyi in 1904 and 1910 respectively. However, for the most part it was Russian communities setting up travelling cinema exhibitions that was the most common way to screen films in the region.[24] In 1926 Sovkino established a new department, *Vostokkino* (Eastern Cinema), with the intention of representing the eastern peoples of Soviet Russia and to spread propaganda among the 'oriental population'.[25] As Gabrielle Chomentowski notes, 'the creation of *Vostokkino* reflected the nationalities policy and transformations in cultural politics in the

Soviet Union during the mid-1920s'.[26] *Vostokkino* acquired and built cinemas (including a thousand-seat cinema in Alma-Ata) and production sites (also including one in Alma-Ata).[27] *Vostokkino* was charged with training local nationalities to become film-makers, but was also involved in the production of documentary and ethnographic films often termed *kul'turfil'my* (cultural films).[28] These films depicted the lives of the populations of the region as they underwent major industrialisation or collectivisation efforts. It was these types of films and developments of the industry in the Kazakh SSR that provided the antecedents for national cinema in the Republic.

There has been a focus in some scholarship as to what constitutes the 'birth of Kazakh cinema'. This is referred to throughout the following sections. For Baurzhan Nogerbek, Kazakh cinema only begins when the story and production is a solely Kazakh-based.[29] The fixation, however, on pinpointing when Kazakh cinema began overlooks a more important issue. What matters is not so much when Kazakh cinema begins, as this rests on the contested assumption that we can disentangle an essential Kazakh identity from its Russian and Soviet history and legacy, but rather the way in which different forms of Kazakh identity and nationhood have been realised through the cinematic lens. Early films that may have featured non-Kazakh writers and production teams, and been shot in film studios outside of the country, are just as important in revealing the way readings of the Kazakh nation are difficult to separate from the influence of Russian and Soviet interpretations of Kazakh nationhood and identity.

Antecedents to the Birth of Kazakh Cinema

Despite *Sovkino* ploughing significant finances into the creation of movie theatres in Kazakhstan, the organisation was slow to develop unambiguous films related to 'the specific conditions of life in Kazakhstan'.[30] This was despite the perception that there 'were many materials with which to achieve the aim of nation-building' in the country.[31] Nonetheless, *kul'turfil'my* of the early Soviet period represented not only antecedents for the development of national cinema in Kazakhstan, but also more importantly the beginning of the representation of Kazakh national identity on screen. The first documentary shot in Kazakhstan appeared prior to the establishment of *Vostokkino* in 1925. Titled *The Anniversary of the Existence of the KASSR*, the silent documentary depicts the first stages of Soviet power in the steppe and provides a representation of the life of workers in the young Republic.[32] A series of other documentary news reels were also made in the territory.[33] This included, among others, the 1929 documentary news reels *Alma-Ata and its Surroundings*, *The Arrival of the First Train to Alma-Ata*, *An Educational Program of the School*, *Cooperation in the Villages* and *Kyzyl-Asker*.[34] The most widely known of such films was the 1929 documentary *Turksib*, directed by Viktor Turin. *Turksib* was aimed at promoting one of the successes of the five-year plan: the construction of the Turkestan-Siberian railway. As Matthew Payne has noted, the film has been largely neglected by scholars of Soviet cinema who have tended to hold it in low regard both aesthetically and as a piece of socialist realist propaganda.[35] Nevertheless, as Payne argues, *Turksib* 'works at a much deeper level than simply as a justification for a Stalinist industrial project. It is almost a metaphysical call to arms against the forces of disorder and the primitive'.[36] The film, therefore, is a crucial element of Soviet orientalism, and was the first opportunity to represent on screen a depiction of the national characteristics of the Kazakhs and other Central Asian peoples for a mass audience. While *Turksib* portrays the Soviet Union as a civilising force in the region, defeating primitivism and tradition with science and industry, the portrayal of Kazakhs, cotton fields and traditional dress are the earliest cinematic signifiers of Kazakh national identity. Even if created by Soviet orientalists, these representations provide the first 'national scripts' and 'floating chain of signs' that would shape and influence later representations of Kazakh nation-ness in Soviet cinema, and ultimately be situated as in opposite to an all-Union identity.

The release of *Turksib* in 1929 raises questions about what constitutes the birth of Kazakh cinema. Some early Soviet feature films had been based on so-called 'Kazakh material', such as the 1928 *Sovkino*-produced film *Mutiny* (based on the writings of Dmitri Furmanov), and the 1935 Mosfilm-produced *Accursed Trials*, which was based on Ivan Shukov's novel *The Hatred*.[37] For Baurzhan Nogerbek, these films, along with the production of documentaries and news reels in the early 1930s such as *The Freeze* (1931), and *The Secret of Kara-Tau* (1932), do not constitute the genuine beginning of Kazakh cinema.[38] Nogerbek argues that as these films were produced by Russians, and given that at the time of their production there was no technical capacity for producing films in Kazakhstan, they do not constitute the actual birth of Kazakh cinema, rather they represent an important step in its development, but not its real beginning.[39] A technical base did finally arrive in Alma-Ata in 1934, when a newsreel studio was set up in the capital, but production of feature films which touched on Kazakh themes remained the preserve of the Central Studios Lenfilm and Mosfilm. Also, in Moscow during this time the most popular Soviet films were dubbed into the Kazakh language for distribution in the country, all in the effort of popularising cinema in Kazakhstan.[40]

The 1939 film *Amangeldy* is conventionally understood to be the first 'Kazakh' feature film. The film tells the story of Amangeldy Imanov, the organiser of the 1916 rebellion against Tsar Nicholas II's 'June decree', which had sought the conscription to the front line of male populations in Central Asia. *Amangeldy* depicts Imanov's leadership of the peasant rebellion and then his assistance of Soviet consolidation in Kazakhstan and later fight against counter-revolutionaries during the Civil War in which he perished in 1919. *Amangeldy* was produced in response to a request from local party officials in the Kazakh SSR to create a film which celebrated a local popular hero.[41] This was a direct result of the success of the Russian 1934 Civil War drama *Chapaev*, which was based on the life of Vasily Chapaev, a celebrated Red Army Commander during the Civil War. *Chapaev* was a cultural phenomenon and is argued by Birgit Beumers to have 'represented a new stage in Soviet cinema',[42] especially with regards to how it used the pathos of heroism and sacrifice for the sake of homeland as an effective propaganda weapon.[43] *Amangeldy* was situated within the context of the development of cinematic works which provided new Soviet heroes. What is specific to *Amangeldy*, however, is that it also fits within the Soviet efforts of establishing what Harun Yilmaz has called 'red *batyrs*' (heroes) for the Kazakh steppe.[44] In other words, they were national heroes for the Kazakh SSR useful for Soviet nation-building in Kazakhstan.

Amangeldy is significant for two reasons in terms of cinema and nation-building in Kazakhstan. Firstly, if Baurzhan Nogerbek is correct to assert that it was local party officials in the Kazakh SRR who pushed for the celebration of a national hero on the silver screen, then it does point to the central role played by domestic elites in the process of Soviet nation-building in the country. This reflects some of the scholarship within Soviet historiography which has sought to tease out the agency of Central Asian elites during this period.[45] However, at the same time, it is important to consider that any local agency that seeks to construct a form of national representation (in this case, the life of Amangeldy Imanov) does so within the confines of accepted Soviet boundaries, which in this instance is the form of cinematic heroic epics that promote the revolutionary cause. Secondly, during the Soviet period *Amangeldy* was promoted as being the first Kazakh film. For Nogerbek, however, 'the modern film historian's distance allows us to see clearly that Lenfilm's *Amangeldy* was a political film, following traditions of early Soviet agitation films, biopics of Bolshevik revolutionaries, and the work of the Vasil'ev Brothers'. Put differently, it 'stemmed from the ideology and policies of a particular historical time'.[46] While the movie was based on a Kazakh theme (the life and rebellion of Amangeldy Imanov) it was produced by the Russian-based Lenfilm, directed by Russian Moisei Levin and featured a mostly non-Kazakh production team (the major exception was the involvement of Kazakh writers Gabit Musrepov and Beimbet Mailin).

As noted above, focusing on whether *Amangeldy* could be considered the first Kazakh film or not misses a larger issue. Whether we call it the first Kazakh film or not only serves to demonstrate the inessential nature of Kazakh history, nation and identity. An essential Kazakh identity cannot be untangled from its Russian and Soviet history. Later representations of Kazakh nationhood and identity in cinematic works are shaped ultimately by the interpretations observed in the early cinematic works, which in turn were highly influenced by Russian and Soviet orientalist readings of Kazakh identity.

What is important in *Amangeldy* is the visual power of its signification of specific national signs of Kazakh nationhood and identity. The film is an atypical socialist realist film, which mythologises the Bolshevik struggle against the oppressive Tsarist Empire and situates Amangeldy Imanov as a good people's commissar working side-by-side with the Bolshevik forces against counter-revolutionaries. In *Amangeldy*, the interests of the local Kazakh population are shared with those of the Bolshevik revolutionaries in their resistance to the Russian governor and the Tsarist conscription decree and then against the White Army during the Civil War. These common interests evoke a shared sense of identity. Yet, in its portrayal of Kazakh peoples, especially the rural peasant community, local dress, custom and the landscape, the film does carve out a degree of national particularism. For example, we witness Amangeldy in one scene playing the dombra and singing a Kazakh song in a yurt, while a woman performs a traditional dance. Moreover, such signification of Kazakh identity is not necessarily contradictory to the all-Union Soviet identity, given that the film should be understood in the context of Soviet nationalities policy. Yet, these are 'national scripts' and tropes that exist as the 'other' to Soviet fraternity and brotherhood. The Russian characters in the film exist outside of this scene. In other words, Russians are absent from the representation of an ethnic Kazakh national identity. Subsequently, we can observe a distinct cleavage between the two constructs of identity.

Amangeldy's utilisation of Kazakh national signs also provided the template for the representation of Kazakh national identity in cinema. The use of the sublime mountainous landscape in the film, especially in a scene where *Amangeldy* is taken away by Russian soldiers after confronting the new Russian governor over the 'June Decree', is similar to how the Kazakh landscape was used 70 years later in the 2005 historical epic film *Nomad*. *Amangeldy* was criticised for its lack of historical accuracy, its downplaying of the division within the *Alash Orda* at the time on how to respond to the June decree, and its marginalising of other characters central to the rebellion.[47] Despite this, as noted above, the film does represent a significant point of departure for the imagining of the Kazakh nation within cinematic work for the very first time. It also alludes to the contention within the earliest forms of Kazakh cinema regarding the multivalent properties of identity observable in films between a Soviet identity of shared interests and a prescriptive 'Kazakh' identity, represented through landscape, dress and the figure of Amangeldy, who symbolises the Kazakh nation throughout.

The Emergence of Kazakh Cinema and Shaken Aimanov

Amangeldy heralded the real beginning of the development of cinema in Kazakhstan. The onset of war also served to strengthen the technical base and capacity for film-making in the country. While a newsreel studio had been set up in Alma-Ata in 1934, this was then re-organised into the Alma-Ata film studio in 1941. Then in November of the same year, after the Soviet Union's entry into war, the major film studios, Mosfilm and

Lenfilm, along with other studios in the USSR, were evacuated to the Kazakh capital. During this period the studios were merged to create the Central United Studio.[48] Eighty per cent of all Soviet feature films were produced in Alma-Ata between 1941 and 1944 (when the major studios returned to Moscow).[49] Prominent Soviet film directors worked in Alma-Ata during this time, such as Sergei Eisenstein, Vsevolod Pudovkin, Abram Room, Ivan Pyr'ev, Fridrikh Ermler and the Vasil'ev Brothers.[50] Indeed, much of Eisenstein's *Ivan the Terrible* was filmed in Alma-Ata, while the All-Russian State University of Cinematography (VGIK) was also relocated to the city during the war. These developments proved significant in the emergence of a technical base in Kazakhstan capable of producing domestic-made feature films. Young film-makers were trained at VGIK while it was based in Kazakhstan, and major studios retained their links with the Alma-Ata studio even after they re-located back to Moscow.[51] Consequently, film production in Kazakhstan increased after the war. In the first instance the studio focused on the production of news reels and documentaries but by the 1950s focus shifted to the production of feature films.[52] In 1953, eight feature films were produced, in 1954 this rose to 15 and by 1955 to 23.[53] It was also during this period that local-born directors, writers and artists appeared who shaped the development of Kazakh cinema from the 1950s to 1970s. This included Shaken Aimanov, Mazhit Begalin, Sultan Khodzhikov and Abdullah Karsakbayev, among others.[54]

The most influential of all these directors was Shaken Aimanov. Aimanov was born in 1914 into a poor farmer's family in the Bayan *aul* in the Kazakh steppe (what is now the Pavlodar region). His talent for acting was spotted by famous Kazakh writer Gabit Musrepov, and subsequently Aimanov was invited to join the Kazakh Drama Troupe in 1933. Aimanov established himself as one of the leading actors within the theatre scene in Kazakhstan. While also directing theatre work, Aimanov began appearing in films from 1938 onwards too. His first role was a cameo in *Amangeldy*. Aimanov briefly appeared in the 1940 domestic-produced film *Raikahn* (written by Mukhtar Auezov and directed by Moisei Levin), before gradually taking on more prominent roles in a series of domestic-produced films including *The White Rose* (1943), *Songs of Abai* (1946) and *The Golden Horn* (1948). The films all follow a familiar socialist realist pattern. They portray an ideal-type of human destiny story whereby the hero embarks on the path for revolutionary struggle. This was the case even in *Songs of Abai*, a film that celebrated the Kazakh poet Abai Kunanbayev. The main text of the film focuses on the transition from a traditional patriarchal way of life. Typically, however, these films display the central characteristics of the Kazakh village and use traditional Kazakh music, instrumentation and song. In doing so, there is a very similar portrayal of national identity to that which appears in *Amangeldy*.

Fitting neatly into this characterisation is the 1952 biopic *Zhambyl*, depicting the life and times of the famous *akyn* (folk singer) Zhambyl Zhabayev, in which Shaken Aimanov took his first lead role. On the surface, the film fits the typical socialist realist interpretation of Kazakh cinema of this period. Peter Rollberg described *Zhambyl* (along with *Songs of Abai*) as being, 'typically Stalinist biopics with schematic, heavily didactic plots, black and white characterisations, and the obligatory message of the inseparable connection between the people and the artist'.[55] Zhambyl is depicted in the film as a national hero who is persecuted by the Tsarist authorities, and then freed by the Bolsheviks whereby he is able to fulfil his destiny as a poet of the people, penning many songs and poems for the revolutionary struggle. However, the film is notable for two reasons beyond its obvious role as an ideological propaganda tool. Firstly, it placed Shaken Aimanov into the limelight as a national figure within Kazakh cinema and the broader Soviet film industry. His performance as Zhambyl received wide praise. A review of the film noted that 'never does a false note sound in his performance. The viewer believes Aimanov as a young and old man.'[56]

As we will see below, Aimanov's emergence was significant in terms of the development of Kazakh cinema, and in the way in that a more confident national 'voice' appears in Kazakh films of the 1960s. Aimanov saw cinema as crucial to being able to communicate his ideas of the Kazakh land to as wide an audience as possible. He is suggested to have claimed that 'my transition from theatre to film is mainly due to my longing as widely as possible to uncover more deeply the transformation of my native land.'[57] Fittingly, Aimanov's role in *Zhambyl* was the beginning of the transformation of Kazakh cinema, whereby a specific 'national' voice could be made possible.

Secondly, the film provides an interesting representation of Kazakh national identity and its relationship to Soviet power. Like *Amangeldy* and *Songs of Abai*, the film contains a series of national signs: the steppe, mountains, national dress and most obviously Zhambyl himself, his songs, poetry and dombra-playing. These national representations, however, are conditional. They exist within the film in so much as they were given life and freedom to exist by the revolution and establishment of Soviet power. This is captured most clearly in a scene where the Red Army liberates the *aul* where Zhambyl lives. Zhambyl receives one of the commissars, a friend he had previously known in captivity. In greeting as friends the commissar returns Zhambyl's dombra to him that had previously been taken from him by the old regime. In this scene, the dombra is symbolic of Kazakh national identity. It represents the link Zhambyl has with the Kazakh population through his poems and songs. The freedom for Kazakhs to be Kazakhs, therefore, is guaranteed only by the Bolsheviks being able to provide that freedom through revolutionary struggle. It alerts us to how the idea of a distinct Kazakh national identity was taken away under the Tsarist regime and only allowed to flourish through word and song when freed from the shackles by the consolidation of Soviet power in the Kazakh steppe. As part of Soviet nationalities policy, the self-determination of the Kazakh nation (represented in the film via Zhambyl and his artistry) is only achievable via cooperation with Soviet power. Kazakh nationhood and identity is therefore portrayed as inseparable from the revolutionary struggle of the Soviets.

As a cinematic work, *Zhambyl* is revealing of the way in which folk heroes and *batyrs* were selected by the Soviet regime for nation-building. In fact, there has been scepticism with regards to the extent that Zhambyl authored many of his songs and poems, especially after the Soviets came to power. Zhambyl has been referred to as the 'grandest hoax in the history of Kazakhs'.[58] In 2007, an article appeared in the Kazakh newspaper *Svoboda Slova* that featured a series of excerpts from the composer Dmitri Shostakovich's memoirs in which he claims Zhambyl had a 'whole brigade of Russian poets working for him', and that the Kazakh bard essentially just appended his name to poems and songs that were scripted by Russian poets for an expected fee.[59] It was these songs which tended to celebrate Stalin. The claim, therefore, is that Zhambyl was essentially a Stalinist myth used to rally the peoples of the Kazakh steppe around a unifying cultural national figure for the purposes of Soviet ideological propaganda. It is alleged by some that Zhambyl was unaware of what was going on as he did not speak

Russian.[60] Whether these claims are true or not, the Zhambyl portrayed by Aimanov in the 1953 film remains a contested representation of an important cultural icon of the post-Soviet period. Today he is celebrated as a national hero represented in statutes across the country and even with a region named in his honour (Zhambyl Oblast), but as the film demonstrates he was a hero who depended upon the Soviets for his position as a national cultural icon.

Aimanov's stock rose significantly because of his performance in *Zhambyl*. And in 1954 he co-directed alongside Karl Gakkel the film *Poem about Love*. Based on the fourteenth century traditional Kazakh lyrical-epic poem *Kozy Korpesh-Bayan Sulu*, which tells the tragic tale of two star-crossed lovers, *Poem about Love* has been hailed by Baurzhan Nogerbek as the genuine birth of Kazakh cinema because it met his criteria of a film based on a Kazakh theme and produced in Kazakhstan with a Kazah crew.[61] The remainder of the 1950s saw a plethora of 'Kazakh films' released, including *The Girl and the Horseman* (1954), *We Live Here* (1956), *Our Dear Doctor* (1957) and *Botagoz* (1957). All of these films provide some representation of Kazakh national signs, whether it be the steppe or traditional Kazakh music and song. *Botagoz*, for example, explicitly displays the customs of Kazakh village life, and even implicitly provides a social division between Kazakh and Russian language. A 'Kazakh world' begins to emerge in the cinema of the 1950s illustrating 'the uniqueness of the Kazakh national character in home, work and action'.[62] To an extent, however, these films remained within the constraints of socialist realism. It is in the 1960s, however, through films such as Aimanov's *Land of the Fathers* (1966), and *My Name is Kozha* (1963), directed by Abdullah Karsakbayev, that a division between the Kazakh world and the Soviet world becomes expressly concrete. In doing so, it provides a form of contention within Kazakh nationhood and identity, but also a very subtle form of dissent against Soviet ideology. It should be reiterated this does not represent an outright form of political dissent or a rejection of Soviet authority. Indeed, it is far from such forms of dissent. For example, a director such as Shaken Aimanov was a member of the Communist Party and celebrated hero of the Kazakh SSR. Rather, what is important here are the very subtle ways that the polysemic nature of meaning in these films provides us with competing accounts of Kazakh national identity and the social order in the country at the time, which in some instances deviate from Soviet ideology. Whether this was intentional on the part of the directors or the authorities is difficult to discern, but nonetheless it introduces the idea that, in the 1960s, Kazakh cinema, as in other cinemas in the Soviet Republics, provided a forum where very subtle forms of social and political contention emerge — where a distinct 'Kazakh' world, separate from the world of Soviet authority, begins to take shape.

1960–1970s: The National Awakening in Kazakh Cinema: The Two Worlds of Soviet Kazakh Cinema

Kazakh film critic Gulnara Abikeyeva has pointed explicitly to the development of these two discrete worlds within Kazakh Soviet cinema of this period. She references Abdullah Karsakbayev's 1963 film *My Name is Kozha* as the first Kazakh film to benefit from the 'thaw' in Soviet cinema, agruing that it 'showed the national identity of Kazakhs'.[63] *My Name is Kozha* is an important film in terms of nation-building in Kazakhstan, but as noted above, feature films at the height of Stalinist rule such as *Amangeldy* in 1938, and *Zhambyl* in 1953, were also offering an account of Kazakh national identity on the screen. These were crude representations of identity framed through Soviet orientalism — focused on ethnic dress, song and dance — and the representation of Kazakh identity served the larger purpose of depicting the revolutionary struggle — but nonetheless these films featured representative signs of Kazakh national identity and pre-date *My Name is Kozha*.

My Name is Kozha is a re-working of the 1960 children's book of the same name written by Berdikbek Sokpakbayev. The film, like Sokpakbaev's book, focuses on a mischievous and inquisitive child called Kozha who lives in a stereotypical Soviet village. His father died because of shrapnel caught his chest during the Great Patriotic War and throughout the film we follow the misbehaviour of Kozha in school, which leads him to become a pariah among his peers and an example of a bad Pioneer. Nonetheless, we understand that, at heart, Kozha is kind and he wants to do well in school to fulfil his dream of becoming an astronaut. He befriends the local village outcast, Sultan, which gets him into a great deal of trouble, wages war against one of his class mates, and is in love with another, Zhanar. Despite his mischevious nature, Kozha is always shown to repent and display guilt for his actions. He is guided morally by his grandmother, who had one point in the film recounts a famous proverb, 'the wind purifies the air, laughter the soul', the meaning being that the boy should always be clean and open.[64] It is a family-oriented film and over the years has become a well-loved and remembered film from the Soviet era. For example, film director Darezhan Omirbayev spoke warmly of it to this author, and in fact has a scene in his 1995 film *Cardiogram* where the protagonist (also a young boy roughly the same age as Kozha) is shown watching the film.[65]

My Name is Kozha is, however, a significant film in terms of the relationship between cinema and nation-building in Kazakhstan. Abikeyeva points to the way the that film creates two distinct worlds. As she notes:

> The action of the film occurs in two different spaces. Basically, there is the village where Kozha lives. The village has wooden lodges, birches, a Soviet school; Soviet life – all that we have gotten used to seeing in the Soviet films of those years. But once Kozha's older friend takes him away to the mountains; the other world opens-up. This is the world of the Kazakh *aul*; the nomadic world. If the lower world is the artificial world of the village the upper world is natural, it is shot almost like a documentary. This episode shows a feast and we see people sitting in groups, singing songs, cooking food and playing the dombra.[66]

Cinematically, the transition from the Soviet village to the *aul* is well-realised. The scene Abikeyeva is referring to here is qualitatively different from similar representations of Kazakh national identity we have seen in earlier Soviet films because of the ethno-graphic feel. This documentary-style form is echoed in later Kazakh cinema, especially Serik Aprymov's 1989 film *The Last Stop* (see Chapter 3) and Sergei Dvortsevoy 2008 film *Tulpan* (see Chapter 7). Both of those films seek to capture the reality of *aul* life in a much more visceral way than *My Name is Kozha*, and we should be cautious about reading too much into what Karsakbayev was seeking to achieve with this one scene; nonetheless, it illustrates a long thread running from Kazakh Soviet cinema into contemporary Kazakh cinema whereby the perception is that the essence of Kazakh identity is to be found in the *aul*, and it is the *aul* which needs to be captured in order to realise national identity.

My Name is Kozha is significant for nation-building in other more abstract ways. Abikeyeva, in her reading of the film, has been very clear that *My Name is Kozha* can be read as 'My Name is Kazakh'. This, she argues, is because Kozha relates to an old aristocratic Kazakh name.[67] In fact we can read something much deeper going on in the film embodied in the character and actions of young Kozha. Kozha is performed as a disruptive character in the film. He is presented in a humorous manner, such as when he places a frog in his teacher's handbag, much to the amusement of his class mates. This may seem harmless, yet Kozha's behaviour is provocative. The village school is the embodiment of the Soviet system. It is the institution through which children are socialised into becoming good Pioneers for the revolutionary cause. Kozha disrupts and undermines the system and the socialising process through his free-spirited actions. Nonethless, Kozha's constant remonstrations of repentance and guilt ensures the narrative of the film does not drift too far from Soviet ideals of morality and the proper conduct of behaviour befitting of a good Soviet citizen. However, Kozha's behaviour in the context of the 'Kazakh world' created in the film can represent the embodiment of the Kazakh national self kicking against the Soviet establishment. We can read Kozha's transition from childhood to adolescence in the film, represented in his relationship with the older boy Sultan, as well as his 'otherness' to his fellow school pupils, as allegorical of Kazakhstan's transition from complete Soviet control to greater local autonomy under the leadership of Kuanyev in the 1960s.

The film's representation of the Kazakh *aul* combined with the disruptive nature of Kozha's behaviour demonstrates how the film represents not only a very subtle form of contention against the Soviet system, but also a break from socialist realism. This is further realised in the way the film depicts the realities of life in the Soviet Union. This includes a scene demonstrating the long queues for daily provisions in a shop (and the way in which Kozha seeks short cuts to skip the queue) as well as the common practice of child labour (where the children of the school are packed off to the field to collect hay and to shear sheep – again Kozha avoids this labour without significant sanction). A retrospective review of the film marking the 50th anniversary of its release also pointed to the subtle use of religion within the film and how it acted to undermine the official anti-religious Soviet ideology. In one scene

Figure 2.1 Nurlan Segizbayev as Kozha in *My Name is Kozha* (1963), dir. Abdullah Karsakbayev.

Kozha's grandmother encourages him to read the Islamic prayer of Bismillah, while in other scenes she utters the word Allah.[68]

We should be cautious about the intentionality of *My Name is Kozha* either in terms of the representation of national signs or potential for subtle political dissent within the film. *My Name is Kozha* was originally commissioned by the Arts Council of Kazakhfilm Studios because of its desire to make a children's genre film. Some recent archival work has revealed that on completion of the film some members of the Arts Council were critical of the representation of Kozha's misconduct and how this remained unresolved within the film. The implied narrative is that, despite his misbehaviour, Kozha can still be a good Pioneer.[69] Other members of the Council criticised the representation of the school in the film and its failure to sanction Kozha's behaviour. Karsakbayev defended his artistic choices to the Council, noting that, 'this is a feature film, not a didactic manual... it teaches children nobility, if the film portrays a lively, interesting character, then, it has reached its goal.'[70] This exchange reveals the contention at the core of the film's main theme and discloses the degree of intention in how Karsakbayev sought to portray the disruptive behaviour of Kozha, and the extent to which it would cause political consternation. As Peter Rollberg has noted in relation to *My Name is Kozha* and some of Karsakbayev's other works, such as *The Troublesome Morning* (1966), 'at a time of strictly enforced political guidelines and aesthetic norms, Karsakbayev managed to subvert official restrictions in a soft, unobtrusive manner, creating a lasting image of the Kazakhstani people and their plight beyond propaganda and cinematic cliché's'.[71] *My Name is Kozha* was well received by audiences in Kazakhstan, and a review in *Kazakhstanskaya Pravda* praised the film as a success, but interestingly it also picks up on the same criticism of the Arts Council, querying why the script leaves Kozha the same as when he entered the film. That said, the film collected a series of awards at film festivals as well as being nominated for the best children's film at Cannes in 1964.[72]

My Name is Kozha should not be seen in isolation from broader developments in Soviet cinema. The film was part of a much wider trend in which directors in the USSR turned away from socialist realism towards exploring the moral and ethical duties of the artist and making films that featured 'poetic parables, generalised metaphors that deal with the universal concepts of good and evil instead of the categories of "class" and "party mindedness"'.[73] As Soviet flim critic Herbert Marshall noted, such cinematic works were 'difficult films'.[74] Marshall points to a film such as Sergo Paradjanov's 1964 *Shadows of Our Forgotten Ancestors*, a Ukrainian picture which draws out national characteristics, religious rituals, festivals, rites and ceremonies of the Hutsuls.[75] It evokes again the idea of an ethnographic cinema that emerges as part of the 'thaw'.[76]

My Name is Kozha might not have been overtly a 'difficult' film, perhaps because it is hidden under the guise of the children's genre, but it does conform to the idea of a 'thaw' in Soviet cinema. In the context of a broader shift away from socialist realism towards more 'national' themes and characterisations within cinema, *My Name is Kozha* plays an important role in presenting an alternative interpretation of Kazakh nationhood to that presented by Soviet authorities. It illustrates how, even during the Soviet period, in the midst of a specific political configuration (Khrushchev's political thaw from 1956 onward; and the emergence of a more prominent national elite in the shape of Dinmukhamed Kunayev), we can observe contention within conceptualisations of Kazakh identity and nationhood. On the one side we have the Soviet world of institutional order, commitment to the revolutionary struggle, friendship of peoples – a Soviet identity – and on the other side we have an ethnic ascription of identity rooted in the traditions of rural life and religious practices.

This contention, and the cinematic realisation of a 'Kazakh world', takes more concrete form in the 1966 film *Land of the Fathers*. It appears not necessarily in the ethno-graphic documentary style of Karsakbayev's *My Name is Kozha*, but rather in the more confident representation of ideas and themes associated with conceptualisations of Kazakh national identity. The film was directed by Shaken Aimanov and the script written by the young poet Olzhas Suleimenov.[77] The film features an emotive and simple plot in which an elderly *Aksakal* (elder) takes his grandson Bayan on a long journey across Kazakhstan to Leningrad to recover the remains of Bayan's father who perished on the front line during the war. It is ancient Kazakh tradition that sons should be buried with their ancestors. As noted in an article from *Sovietskii Ekran* in 1966, the film captures the guilt associated with burying sons who were soldiers away from home without ceremony.[78]

Stephen Norris has written eloquently about how the film explores the loss experienced by war, especially by those from the periphery of the Soviet Union far from the front.[79] Aimanov expresses a clear Kazakh 'national-self' through the representation of national signs. In the opening scene strains of the dombra play over a shot of the *Aksakal* performing the Salat in the direction of Mecca while the *Aksakal* and Bayan finish building a Mazar to bury the remains once they return. Such depictions of Islamic rituals and sites are brazen on the part of Aimanov, given the anti-religious context of Soviet ideology.

The relationship between space, land and territory is also a central element of the film's national character. The film is a journey – a road trip by train, a familiar motif in Kazakh cinema used in many films such as in Darezhan Omirbayev's *The Road* (2001). As the *Aksakal* and Bayan's journey unfolds we are invited to realise the scope, expanse and geography of the Kazakh steppe. Bayan's emotional journey of dealing with loss is replicated in the actual journey through which he gets to understand the land and its importance to the national self. This is best realised in a scene whereby the *Aksakal* admonishes Vitali, an archaeologist also on the train, who suggests people should travel more to know the land, whereas the *Aksakal* argues forcibly that 'a man must

Figure 2.2 Elubai Umurzakov and Murat Akhmadiev in *Land of the Fathers* (1966), dir. Shaken Aimanov.

know his own land, the hearth, the camping ground, the house where he was born, where the bones of his ancestors are'.[80] This exchange is revealing for the way in which two competing conceptions of nationhood are carved out. On the one hand, a civic interpretation by Vitali that understands that the land is accessible by all, a common entity, and on the other hand the *Aksakal* evokes a more exclusive ethnic interpretation that believes that the land can only be understood by those who come from it. In other words, Vitali cannot know the Kazakh land, despite his scholarly credentials, because he is not from the Kazakh steppe.

Kazakh language also features more prominently in *Land of the Fathers*. This is realised through Vitali's daughter, Sofya, who is a scholar of Turkic languages, and can speak Kazakh, and also in Bayan's relationship with a Yegor, a soldier. Yegor asks Bayan to teach him Kazakh, Bayan does, but mocks his inability to grasp the language and instead teaches him to say *Men Akmak*, which means 'I am a fool'.[81] Language, therefore, operates as a point of contention, even if only as a moment of comedic relief.

Like *My Name is Kozha*, *Land of the Fathers* is also a tale of transition. Whereas Kozha is transitioning from childhood to adolescence, Bayan is transitioning from adolescence to adulthood. *Aksakal* informs Bayan that he cannot become a man unless he completes the journey to return his father's remains to Kazakhstan. Like Kozha, Bayan is an embodiment of the transition to national self-realisation, but in a much more concrete form than presented in *My Name is Kozha*. The confidence in which Aimanov promotes not just the signs of Kazakh national identity through religion and landscape, but also the concept and theme of who can best understand and know the Kazakh lands, speaks to this idea of a transition to another level of national self-identification. Nonetheless, caution should prevail in this interpretation. In the end Bayan decides to leave the remains where they are, buried with his father's comrades. It suggests that despite the 'thaw' in Soviet cinema, which allowed directors and writers to explore more openly issues and themes related to national characteristics, there was a limit to how far this could go. For instance, an article in *Sovetskii Ekran* published at the time stressed the film's appeal to friendship of peoples through shared experiences, rather than its depiction of a distinct Kazakh national identity.[82]

The two films analysed here perhaps best represent the way in which contention of national identity appeared in Kazakh Soviet cinematic work and the way in which cinema could provide a space for subtle dissension from the official Soviet ideological line. Nevertheless, given the extent of party control and state censorship at the time, this does not amount to outright protest or a challenge to the Soviet leadership, and it is not a form of antagonistic dissent. Rather, cinema as an open-ended art form to which multiple meanings can be ascribed means that alternative ascriptions of Kazakh national identity, this discrete 'Kazakh world', emerged as a subtle counterpoint to dominant state readings of an all-Soviet identity.

There were, of course, other films of this period that spoke to Kazakh national identity. Shaken Aimanov's 1964 film *Aldar Kose*, for example, draws on a popular Kazakh mythical folk hero for inspiration. A review of the film outlines the depiction of Aldar Kose:

> He wanders from village to village, town to town. He had no stake in any court, but is always cheerful and in good spirits. He is ready to delve into his pockets at a word and is ready to make fun of

others and of himself. The poor seek his protection and assistance, and the nobles tremble at the mere mention of his name. He punishes injustice and deceives the rich, exhibiting a rare ingenuity.[83]

Aldar Kose is the Turkic equivalent of Robin Hood, and the film was an explicit attempt to create a national Kazakh version of the hero. *Aldar Kose* (in Russian the film was known as *Bezborodyi Obmanshchik* – the Beardless Deceiver) is important, therefore, in its attempt to draw upon universal mythical folk figures for constructing a national hero. Aimanov's playing of Aldar Kose is slightly ambiguous. Typically, Kose is understood as a cheerful and joyful character – but Aimanov's performance was noted for 'his weary gait, haggard face, penetrating eyes, which creases into a smile, but something he ponders painfully'.[84] This performance also lingers on a psychology in which Aldar Kose ruminates on the inability to always protect the powerless.[85] Aldar Kose can be presented on the one hand by Soviet authorities as a national folk hero who challenges social injustice and protects the poor from aristocratic nobles, yet on the other hand can also be understood as a channel between the ruler and ruled. He can act where the authorities are unable, offering social protection and to some extent this could be read as a challenge to Soviet officialdom. Most notability the film creates a very elaborate 'Kazakh world'. This is different to the ethno-graphic portrayal in *My Name is Kozha*. In utilising a mythical folk hero, the film is set outside of the Soviet era; therefore, the viewer is immersed entirely in a Kazakh world of obvious national signs related to Kazakh national identity such as dombra playing, customs, dress and yurts. Unlike *Amangeldy*, *Zhambyl* and *Land of the Fathers*, there are no Soviet institutions or heroes, as viewers we are invited into a Kazakh-only world with no reference to the Soviet world. It is, of course, a very theatrical world, but it is significant that the use of a mythical folk hero gives the director carte blanche to establish a totally imagined Kazakh world without specific reference to Soviet institutions, events and ideology.

The culmination of the 'thaw' in Kazakh cinema was the 1970 film *Kyz-Zhibek*, arguably the ultimate depiction of the Kazakh world within Soviet cinema. The film is said to represent 'the myth, ethnography and legends of Kazakhstan'.[86] Written by Gabit Musrepov and directed by

Sultan Khodzhikov, *Kyz-Zhibek* was based on the sixteenth-century poetic folk-legend of the same name, which details the bloody conflicts between warring Khans and tells the tragic tale of two star-crossed lovers from rival families.[87] Being based on folklore, like *Aldar Kose*, Khodzhikov had free rein to use cinematic language to truly create a distinct Kazakh world. This is achieved in *Kyz-Zhibek* in a more poetic and meaningful way than had been achieved in Kazakh cinema until that point. In his 2016 documentary, *The Story of Kazakh Cinema*, director Adilkhan Yerzhanov compares *Amangeldy* to *Kyz-Zhibek*. He notes that in *Amangeldy* we see formulaic shots and cuts, everything is expressed in content and there is no depth and subtext. With *Kyz-Zhibek*, he argues that we begin to see the emergence of poetic cinema, evident in the use of red poppies in the foreground to represent the blood. Poetic metaphor is central to the film. This is notable from the very first frames, which show the splatter of blood on the steppes inter-spliced with a squawking swan and then cutting back again to a disturbed, unsettled and probably dying horse. For film historian Kabish Siranov from the beginning we are invited as viewers to ruminate on life, death and the eternal problem of good and evil.[88]

While *Kyz-Zhibek* is important in terms of the depth of its cinematic language, it also represented the apex of the relationship between cinema and nation-building during the Soviet period in Kazakhstan. The film represents a critical intervention in the realising of the Kazakh nation, both in terms of its use of folklore and myth, and in the extent to which its imagination of the Kazakh world has had lasting impact. As Baurzhan Nogerbek has noted,

> the film was the most expensive for that time and it broke all attendance records. In modern parlance, it was a blockbuster, it was a film about love, but, most importantly, it also reflected folk traditions, the richness of folk arts and crafts and the oral poetic traditions. It also accurately represented the sentiments and mentality of the nomadic nation. Until this day *Kyz-Zhibek* remains in demand as a world national classic: virtually any Kazakh in any country knows this film.[89]

In the interviews for this book, often, when interview participants were asked to choose a film they felt represented the Kazakh nation, or was the archetypal Kazakh film, they chose *Kyz-Zhibek*. As film producer Sergei Azimov noted, '*Kyz-Zhibek* became a phenomenon, because for the first-time Kazakhs were shown worthily. They were not shown as an unhappy, miserable, poor and suffering nation, it was a nation that lived richly.'[90] Perhaps the reason why the film has lived long in the imaginations of Kazakhs is because of the extent to which Khodzhikov was able to re-create a believable and fully rounded 'Kazakh world'. Khodzhikov undertook a deep and extensive survey of nomadic culture and history for the purpose of making the old nomadic Kazakh way of life come alive on the screen in a vivid way.[91] As Aigul Tuyakbaeva notes, 'we can observe all the signs of nomadism in the film ... the director gives the audience the opportunity to plunge into the extraordinary world of indescribable beauty, where there is a richness of nature in the vast geography of the nomadic Kazakh people.'[92] Wedding rituals and the cult of ancestors were central themes within the film. Consequently, *Kyz-Zhibek* provides a representation of Kazakh nomadism and in doing so gives a cinematic interpretation of the nationally bound Kazakh community. For the first time on screen Kazakhs were introduced to their nomadic past, erased and forgotten through the Stalinist period, the nomad became real and visceral in *Kyz-Zhibek*, the nomad became scared. Along with Ilyas Yessenberlin's epic-prose trilogy *Koshpendiler*, written during 1963–73, and Olzhas Suleimenov's *Az i Ya* (1975), *Kyz-Zhibek* was one of the central pillars of how Kazakhs began to understand, symbolise and represent their nomadic past, not just at the time of their release, but more concretely in the post-Soviet period.[93]

There were struggles and tensions in the production of the film. Khodzhikov is believed to have had to fight off Soviet censors.[94] The film, therefore, signifies the ultimate contention with Soviet identity. No Soviet institutions or identity exist in *Kyz-Zhibek*, the film was the strongest possible statement at the time of a clear-cut construction of Kazakh identity and nationhood. Indeed, one review suggested that despite the film's focus on the warring Khans, the main theme concerns the consolidation of the Kazakh people into a uniform and indestructible nation.[95] This is an idea we see played out again in post-Soviet cinema, in the ethnic narrative put forward by the Nazarbayev regime.

Kyz-Zhibek also represents the end of an era in Kazakh Soviet cinema. Despite producing the most successful Kazakh film up until that point and being lauded with prizes and medals, including the order of the Red

FILM AND NATION-BUILDING IN THE SOVIET ERA 87

Figure 2.3 Still from *Kyz-Zhibek* (1970), dir. Sultan Khodzhikov.

Star, Khodzhikov was not able to produce films for the Kazakh public again until his film *Know Ours* was released in 1985. That film concerned the friendship of two wrestlers: Kazakh Khadzhimukan Munaitpasov and the Russian Ivan Poddubny. Khodzhikov was successful with that film as it fitted the friendship of peoples' message preferred by the Soviet government. He wrote many more scripts but they were rejected by the Arts Council of Kazakhfilm Studios.[96] The political and economic stagnation of the Brezhnev era influenced the type of films that were produced in Kazakhstan. The end of the era was also marked by the passing of Shaken Aimanov in 1970, killed tragically when he was struck by a passing car in Moscow. Many of the Kazakh films produced in the 1970s to the early 1980s moved away from a focus on Kazakh national identity and creating a 'Kazakh world'. Instead they focused on films celebrating war heroes more in the vein of spy and thriller genres, reflecting the tensions inherent in the cold war during this time. A trilogy of films during this period exemplify this trend. *End of Ataman* (1970), Aimanov's last film, *Trans-Siberian Express* (1977) and *The Manchurian Version* (1989) are action adventure films about the revolution.[97] Other films also embody this trend, such as Mazhit Begalin's 1969 *Song of Manshuk*, which depicts a day in the life of Kazakh Soviet war hero Manshuk Mametova; Karsakbayev's 1979 film *Chase in the Desert*, which is set in the 1920s and focuses on a committed and courageous Red Commander; *The Last Transition* (1981) is also set in the 1920s and tells of the Soviet fight against the Basmachi rebels; and finally *Sniper* (1985), which celebrates another Soviet war hero, Aliya Moldagulova.

In the 1970s and 1980s the attempt to create a distinct Kazakh world was no longer central to Kazakh-produced cinematic works. The contention we had seen in the 1960s between a distinct Kazakh and Soviet identity was no longer apparent. It would instead take a shift in the political and economic context of the Soviet Union, alongside the timely emergence of a group of young Kazakh directors in the mid-to-late 1980s for Kazakh cinema to emerge once again as a site of contention both in terms of questions of identity and also in relation to a more explicit rejection of Soviet ideology.

Conclusion: Influence of Kazakh Soviet Cinema

We should be wary not to overstate the case that Soviet Kazakh directors such as Aimanov, Karsakbayev and Khodzhikov were in anyway political dissidents. They were far from it. For the most part they were loyal party members. Nor should we exaggerate the influence of Kazakh Soviet cinema on contemporary directors and cinematic works. Not one contemporary director spoke with any great reverence for the Kazakh cinema of the Soviet period during interviews for this book. These films are sometimes viewed on TV and remembered fondly as a part of childhood (such as *My Name is Kozha* is for Darezhan Omirbayev), but they are not held in high esteem nor do they evidently influence the work of contemporary directors.[98] If anything, as we will see in the following chapter, for young directors emerging in the late 1980s the films of the Soviet period represented a conservative force to react against. For young contemporary directors like Adilkhan

Yerzhanov and Serik Abishev, despite Kazakh Soviet cinema establishing a 'Kazakh world', which offered a series of national 'signs', they do not see any 'truth' in these films and they understand these cinematic works as being 'national in form, and socialist in content', and thus failing to offer a genuine Kazakh cinematic language.[99] Abishev noted that while a director like Mazhit Begalin was a good auteur, 'they all took lessons from Soviet cinema and made films in the language of Soviet films.'[100]

But cinematic works of this period are important for nation-building in Kazakhstan for two fundamental reasons. Firstly, as we have seen in this chapter, cinema played a central role in visually realising the 'Kazakh' nation through a representation of perceived national signs such as the steppe, tradition, rituals, customs, dombra playing, the depiction of rural *auls* and religious practice. This sits in antagonism with Soviet ideas of friendship of peoples beyond national boundaries, revolutionary struggle and anti-religious ideology. An argument can thus be made that Soviet authorities simply pushed nationalities to the margins of folklore and myth and this is what we see in Kazakh cinema of this time. To an extent this is true, but through cinema, such myth and folklore, seemingly non-political representations of national identity were kept alive, if not given breath for the first time. In this way cinema reflects the nature of Soviet nationalities policy in that national ideas, institutions and myths were promoted as long as they were not in conflict with broader ideological goals that could threaten Communist Party rule. However, the way in which the 'Kazakh world' emerges in Soviet cinema from rather simplistic and clichéd beginnings in *Amangeldy*, to the confident and bold vision of *Kyz-Zhibek* demonstrates the gradual imagining of the Kazakh community in the Soviet period before 1985. Cinema, therefore, acted as a mechanism which allowed for the realisation and representation of the Kazakh nation to reach as wide a possible audience in the country for the first time. This is an influence on the development of nation-building in the country that should not only not be overlooked, but also should be viewed as a fundamental building block for the emergence of the Kazakh nation as we know it today.

Secondly, as we will see in Chapter 4, films such as *Amangeldy*, *Zhambyl* and *Kyz-Zhibek* set the template for how the government of Kazakhstan would use big budget historical epics to put forward their interpretation of Kazakh history and their specific representation of the Kazakh nation. Before we touch on contemporary regime-led narratives of nationhood and identity in Kazakhstan we need to traverse the 'Kazakh New Wave'. This was an era in Kazakh cinema, which shook up the staid, old and creaking Soviet system, utilised cinema as a site of dissent against the Soviet authorities and put Kazakhstan on the map internationally for both cinema and its exploration of identity and history.

CHAPTER 3

THE DISRUPTION OF TIME: THE 'KAZAKH NEW WAVE' 1985-95

Introduction

Anna Lawton has noted that from its inception Soviet cinema was 'strictly connected with the national political reality'.[1] Nowhere was this as much the case as in the Kazakh Soviet Socialist Republic (Kazakh SSR) during the waning years of the Soviet Union and the early post-Soviet era. As in other Soviet Republics, the period from 1985 to 1995 was marked by significant political, social and economic transformation in Kazakhstan. Once Gorbachev set the wheels of *perestroika* and *glasnost* in motion the old certainties and rigidity of the Soviet system began to falter. Cracks appeared in the system, new voices began to be heard, new modalities transpired and social protest became more visible. The move towards national self-determination away from the centre across Soviet Republics was reflected in cinema. Structural changes to the Soviet film industry, a freeing-up of the market, reforms to distribution, the complete demise of socialist realism, the advent of new forms and influences, and the emergence of unknown, forgotten and previously censored films all portended to the fundamental changes the Soviet Union was undergoing during the Gorbachev era.[2]

That Kazakhstan should emerge as the vanguard of this new trend within Soviet cinema was something of surprise to scholars, especially given the conservative reputation the country's cinema had always attracted.[3] Whether as a harbinger of the times, or an uncanny coincidence, it was the case that a group of young like-minded Kazakh directors appeared and whose work reflected the new political realities of the age.[4] Collectively known as the 'Wild Kazakh Boys' and the 'Kazakh New Wave', directors such as Rashid Nugmanov, Serik Aprymov, Darezhan Omirbayev, Ardak Amirkulov, Talgat Temenov, Abai Karpykov and Amir Karakulov interpreted the new age as a blank sheet. The directors used their work not just as a site for a renewed representation of Kazakh national identity, but also as an arena for dissent from, and the exposure of, the ailing bureaucratic edifice of the Soviet system. Influenced less by the cinema of the Soviet era (both Kazakh and non-Kazakh), the 'Wild Kazakh Boys' took their cues from the European cinematic tradition, especially the French New Wave.[5] In their work, however, these directors offered new interpretative accounts of Kazakh identity. They were at the forefront of Kazakh independence and their films were the artistic representation of a nation seeking to make sense of the tumultuous changes forced upon the Kazakh SSR.

Cinema of the 'Kazakh New Wave' emerged as a disruptive force to the old Soviet order. Gone were the carefully crafted 'Kazakh' and 'Soviet' worlds of the 1960s thaw period and in their place was a chaotic, disordered cinematic landscape where identity and nationhood were fluid and 'up for grabs'. What we witness in this period is the collapsing of these two previously discrete worlds. This occurs through three specific aspects of the 'Kazakh New Wave'. Firstly, several films seek to offer a re-interpretation of Kazakh history – especially in relation to pivotal points in history as in Ardak Amirkulov's *The Fall of Otrar* (1991) or in the silences of Soviet history as in collectivisation and sedentarisation in Damir Manabayev's *Surzhekey – the Angel of Death* (1991) or the Stalinist terror as in Kalykbek Salykov's *The Balcony* (1988). Secondly, films of this period depict a negation of Soviet authority through the establishment of new types of heroes as we see again in *The Balcony* and most prevalently in Rashid Nugmanov's *The Needle* (1989). This negation of Soviet authority appears via the independent agency of the heroes, their neo-romantic depiction (as opposed to the socialist realist model), the interpretation of time, and the explicit rejection of Soviet taboos such as drug use. Finally, the 'Kazakh New Wave' offered a representation of Kazakh nationhood, identity and belonging rooted in the lived experience of transition from Soviet to post-Soviet rule, both in a material sense – as in Serik Aprymov's *The Last Stop* (1989) and Abai Karpykov's *Little Fish in Love*

(1989)– and in an inner psychological sense as in Darezhan Omirbayev's *Kairat* (1992) and *Cardiogram* (1995). This last aspect of the 'Kazakh New Wave' also begins to point towards the disconnection in both material and ideational terms between the rural and urban areas, something which was to influence contemporary Kazakh cinema in its interpretation of nation-ness and identity (see Chapter 7). Through these three elements (re-interpretation of history, negation of Soviet authority and capturing transition) the 'Kazakh New Wave' culled the cinematic landscape allowing for the emergence of multiple representations of nationhood and identity to be reflected through cinematic works in the post-Soviet period (and which are the subject of Chapters 4 to 7).

This chapter, therefore, addresses these three aspects of the 'Kazakh New Wave' via five main sections. The first provides an account of the emergence of the 'Kazakh New Wave' and the context underpinning the appearance of these young directors. A further three sections then address a trio central themes of cinematic work from this period: the re-interpretation of history; the role and place of the hero and the negation of Soviet authority; and the representation of the realities of the late-Soviet and early post-Soviet period, with special reference to the depiction of the Kazakh *aul* and the distinction between rural and urban life. The final section then addresses the lull of the cinema industry in the mid-1990s, which preceded greater state intervention in the film industry in Kazakhstan from the mid-2000s onward.

Emergence of the New Wave

It is often assumed that the political and economic stagnation of the Brezhnev era was concomitant to conservatism within culture and the arts. Yet, Brezhnev's foreign and domestic policies bought a measure of material comfort that saw the public taste for entertainment become more 'bourgeois'.[6] Consequently, there was a tendency for *Goskino* to produce more commercial films that reflected popular demand.[7] This focus on commerciality brought forward films that provided a space to tell stories about 'contemporary society, individual lives and relations, current problems and human values.'[8] Andrey Shcherbenok has addressed how films of the so-called 'stagnation' period offered a site for a subtle critique of the Soviet system. Shcherbenok points to how the choice of settings within films of this period tend towards a form of realism (not socialist realism), alerting the viewer to the drabness of the everyday, standard apartments, ordinary transportations and dilapidated buildings.[9] Films of this period tend to elucidate contemporary problems and the individual's inability to change their circumstances. As Shcherbenok emphasises, 'a male hero is often stuck in one or several relationships that he can neither develop nor abandon; his work has stopped satisfying him, but he cannot think of anything better do. The same is true for female heroines ...'.[10] In elaborating on this theme Shcherbenok exemplifies his argument by reference to *The Wife Left* (1979), *The Autumn Marathon* (1979), *Dream Flights* (1982) and *A Lonely Women Looking for a Relationship* (1986).

A consequence of this shift towards addressing 'real' day-to-day life was the revival of the so-called *bytovoy* (slice-of-life) film, which tended to reject the socialist realist model. Lawton notes how this new approach concerned problems of the factory such as in Sergei Mikaelian's *The Bonus* (1975), which sees a factory supervisor challenge the falsification of the over-fulfilment of planned targets and reject a financial bonus.[11] While the Party supports the supervisor, the film was a representation of the corruption and inefficiencies systemic to the planned economy. The popular 1976 film *Irony of Fate or Enjoy Your Bath*, directed by Eldar Ryazanov, epitomises this trend in 'stagnation'-era cinema. While the film operates within the romantic comedy genre, it is underpinned by social criticism. This is evident in the opening animated sequence in which an architect is blocked in his creativity by red tape and bureaucracy. The subtext of the film concerns the uniformity of the Brezhnev era in terms of buildings, apartments and commodities. Indeed, the comedy of errors plot hinges upon this social critique as the protagonist, after a drunken New Year's Eve, awakens to find himself in a different city in somebody else's apartment but does not realise because of the uniformity and similarities of every-day commodification. The building looks the same, his key fits the lock, and he has the same furniture laid out in a similar way to this stranger that lives in the apartment. As Lawton notes, 'the lives of dwellers, have become so uniform and depersonalised that this sort of mix-up is conceivable'.[12] *Irony of Fate* was an immensely popular film, but it demonstrates that even during the period of perceived political, economic and cultural stagnation cinema could be a place of subtle critique and indirect political contention within the Soviet system.

That such a critique was possible in Soviet cinema of the 'stagnation' era is perhaps important for understanding how the 'Kazakh New Wave' emerged when it did and how such young directors were confident in their rejection of the ideology of the Soviet system. However, as argued in the previous chapter, the 'thaw' in Kazakh Soviet cinema of the 1960s did give way to a degree of cultural conservatism in Kazakhstan. The forms of very subtle social criticism highlighted above are not as easily observable in Kazakh Soviet cinema of this period.

While there were structural changes to the film industry during *perestroika* and *glasnost*,[13] it was largely the conscious decisions of Kazakh cultural elites that helps us understand why a new generation of young Kazakh film-makers appeared in the 1980s. In 1981, poet, writer and literary figure Olzhas Suleimenov was appointed head of *Goskino* in Kazakhstan. He in turn appointed fellow writer Murat Auezov as head of the Kazakhfilm Studios. Despite having undergone a modernisation process in the 1970s, the studios failed to meet the production capacity of six feature films a year during this period, and according to Ludmila Pruner, they remained in obscurity compared to studios in some of the other Soviet Republics like Kyrgyzstan.[14] In the words of director Sabit Kurmanbekov, 'Kazakhfilm Studios were dormant'.[15] Suleimenov and Auezov set out to change the situation and purposely sought a new generation of creative minds. Auezov felt that 'the talent pool of directors was very thin and decisive measures had to be taken'.[16] To this end, an advert was put out calling for young talent interested in a career in cinema to come forward. Russian film director Sergei Solov'ev had agreed to take on a cohort of young Kazakhs and teach them film-making at the All-Russian State University of Cinematography (VGIK). Suleimenov and Auezov managed to convince the overall head of *Goskino*, Filipp Yermash, to fund the workshop. Their aim, according to Solov'ev, was not just to improve the national quota, but to 'mentally establish a new generation of Kazakhs who could do something that previous generations had not.'[17] As Auezov suggested in an interview in 1987, 'all of sudden, it became a national necessity to realise our cultural identity through cinema. The society itself tries to achieve its cultural goals and the atmosphere becomes very conducive for highlighting talented people, when the public movement starts along with the administration's organising efforts'.[18]

The participants in the workshop came from a range of backgrounds unrelated to cinema. Rashid Nugmanov had trained as an architect, Darezhan Omirbayev had studied Mathematics and Amir Karakulov was a poet. The all-Kazakh class included seven directors, three screenwriters, two art directors and two cinematographers.[19] The chance to participate in Solov'ev's workshop at VGIK in the spring of 1984 was a unique opportunity for the prospective Kazakh directors to break free from the constraints of a typical mundane Soviet work-life and to study the importance and depth of cinema as a cultural tool. The workshop was fundamental to shaping the style and attitude of the new generation of directors. As Nugmanov has noted, 'thanks to Solov'ev and another wonderful professor Anatoli Vasil'ev, we started to make our own style and they taught us a lot.'[20]

In the view of Birgit Beumers the young group learnt from Solov'ev 'how to observe life on the margins of society, where cracks and crisis are more visible than in the centre'.[21] Solov'ev is noted to have told the workshop participants, 'make films that [are] different and [they] will be classy'.[22] The young group followed his advice and rejected the old orthodoxies. While Soviet cinema relied on actor's performances and written dialogue, the 'Kazakh New Wave' 'established new schemes, frames, the internal life of characters, surrealism and symbolism'.[23] The directors sought to detail the reality of late-Soviet and post-Soviet life, but not through the lens of approved Soviet authority, but instead through new influences and their own instincts. As Nugmanov has noted, 'we did not recognise any authority except Solov'ev and our own judgements as classmates'.[24] They were free from the constraints of the old. The directors of the 'Kazakh New Wave' renounced the old ideological patterns, the use of pristine interiors and inspirational dialogue, instead they 'furnished their creations with grey streets and set them in dark and real apartments'.[25] Bound by a sense of adventure imbued within them by Solov'ev they also sought to depict previously taboo topics and subcultures such as drugs and criminal groups. Solov'ev's 1987 film *ASSA* embodied the spirit of the changing times. While *ASSA* included two conventional plot lines, it also featured more experimental elements too, including surreal dream sequences and a focus on the underground rock scene. It also starred Viktor Tsoy from cult rock group *Kino* in a cameo role. Tsoy would go on to have a prominent role in perhaps the defining film of the 'Kazakh New Wave' era, Rashid Nugmanov's *The Needle*

(1988). Tsoy's presence in *The Needle* is notable for how films of the 'Kazakh New Wave' eschewed professional actors, instead the directors used their friends or as in the case of Serik Aprymov's *The Last Stop* (1989) simply the residents in the *aul* he was filming in.

The directors involved in Solov'ev's workshop went on to release feature films that defined the late and early post-Soviet era in Kazakhstan, and the USSR. This includes Rashid Nugmanov's *The Needle* (1988), Talgat Temenov's *A Wolf Cub Among Little People* (1988), Serik Aprymov's *The Last Stop* (1989), Abai Karpykov's *Little Fish in Love* (1989), Amanzhol Aituarov's *The Touch* (1989) Ardak Amirkulov's *The Fall of Otrar* (1990), Amir Karakulov's *Homewrecker* (1991) and Darezhan Omirbayev's *Kairat* (1991). At the same time, some directors not part of Solov'ev's workshop also produced films which also embodied the spirit of the 'Kazakh New Wave' such as Kalykbek Salykov's 1987 film *The Balcony* (1988), Yermek Shinarbayev's *Revenge* (1989) and Damir Manabayev's *Surzhekey – the Angel of Death* (1991).[26]

'Kazakh New Wave' as a Disruption of Empty Homogenous Time

Despite their diverse backgrounds, the directors of the 'Kazakh New Wave' shared some characteristics within their work, shaped ultimately by their participation in Solov'ev's workshop at VGIK. According to Ludmila Pruner, these include: being free of didacticism, with cinematic themes being low-key and subtle; simplicity of plot structure; and a tendency towards light irony.[27] Auezov, however, points to the cultural significance of the emergence of these new young directors and how they shared a profound commitment to 'historical self-identity or historicism and a sense of historical perspective'.[28] Moreover, while the young group of directors abandoned the old Soviet forms of cinematic language, they were highly influenced by other regional traditions, most notably European (nominally French and Italian) cinema.

Most evidently, however, the directors of the 'Kazakh New Wave' used these new influences and freedom of expression to make sense of the changing contours of the Soviet state and implicitly what that meant for Kazakhstan and Kazakh identity. Indeed, what the 'Kazakh New Wave' represented was a step away from the clearly defined 'Kazakh' and 'Soviet' worlds depicted in the cinema of the Soviet era. Instead, there is a collision between the two. Ethnic prescription is not evidently important or central to many of the films of the 'Kazakh New Wave' but neither is Soviet institutional authority. In its place, there is an emptiness of time, a confusion and a search for identity. For Darezhan Omirbayev, this was the peculiarity of the 'Kazakh New Wave', in that they were making 'films when the socialist state and ideological censorship no longer existed, but at the same time there was no commercialisation of cinema yet like in the West.'[29] However, by filling this void with interpretations of history from the vantage point of the present (as in *The Fall of Otrar*); or in negating Soviet authority through the establishment of new heroes (as in *The Balcony* and *The Needle*); or in exploring the process of Soviet transition (as in *The Last Stop* and *Kairat*); these films spoke volumes about the search for identity in late Soviet and early post-Soviet Kazakhstan.

The varied style and influences of films of the 'Kazakh New Wave' can be interpreted as reflecting a shift to post-modernism. *The Needle*, for example, follows closely the multi-layered structure of Solov'ev's *ASSA*, providing a new aesthetic style of post-punk neo-romanticism eschewing both straightforward narrative and socialist realism.[30] Framing the 'Kazakh New Wave' as post-modern perhaps ultimately makes sense. Nevertheless, it also feels an obvious and clichéd observation. Yes, the 'Kazakh New Wave' feels chaotic, un-anchored in tradition and form, playful, and a product of the openness and freedom of the late-Soviet period, but simultaneously these films arrive at a time when Kazakhstan as a sovereign, independent and modern nation is emerging, preceded by the *Zheltoksan* movement of 1986 (see Chapter 1). Despite the lack of explicit reference to national identity, it is possible to see movies of this period as being part of the construction of national identity at a time when identity formation was fluid and filled with open possibilities. Therefore, another way of conceptualising this period of Kazakh film is as a disruption to homogenous empty time.

Walter Benjamin understood homogenous empty time as calendrical – marked by identical units (days, months etc.) – which is manifest by historical monuments (holidays, festivals etc.) and which exists as a corollary to a linear progressive interpretation of history and time.[31] The concept was utilised most famously by Benedict Anderson to explain how individuals who had never met could understand themselves as belonging to the same social organism. Homogeneous empty time for Anderson was analogous to a nation moving steadily through time in which individuals have confidence in their steady, anonymous and simultaneous activity.[32] Yet, Benjamin understood homogeneous empty time as a pathological historical construction that formed because of capitalism, and which was not progressive, linear or determinate.[33] Benjamin alludes to the necessity to disrupt this homogenous empty time 'to explode the continuum of history' and to have 'the concept of a present which is not a transition, in which time originates and has come to a standstill.'[34] While Benjamin alludes to this linear interpretation of time being associated with capitalist development, the inevitability of historical progression is also evident in the conception of the Soviet state, which was underpinned by a historical-materialist conception of history regarding the inevitability of communism. Therefore, the films of the 'Kazakh New Wave' represent the disruption of Soviet homogeneous empty time. Films such as *The Needle*, *The Fall of Otrar* and *The Balcony* are the cinematic equivalent of shaking a snow globe. Time, place, identity and history are free-floating snowflakes, up in the air and yet to settle, and when they do fall to the ground they will align in a very different way. As the director Rustem Abdrashev notes 'they (the directors of the 'Kazakh New Wave') entered a timeless period. The period when time stopped, it did not exist.'[35] Therefore the films of the 'Kazakh New Wave' are central to our understanding of the construction of post-Soviet narratives related to identity and nation-ness in contemporary Kazakhstan.

Therefore, the 'Kazakh New Wave' exists as a transitionary period in terms of exploring identity politics on the silver screen. The old order is crumbling, and the new yet to be constructed. It is this empty space the directors of the 'Kazakh New Wave' sought to fill with interpretations of the present which while reflecting on the past did not see the past as determining the future. Below is an analysis of some of the films of the 'Kazakh New Wave' through three modulations of time and identity:

(1) through a re-imagination and/or re-interpretation of history including previous silences;
(2) the negation of Soviet authority via the creation of new types of heroes;
(3) a capturing of the realities of this period of transition.

In their totality, the films of the 'Kazakh New Wave' demonstrate two fundamental things. Firstly, the journey of different conceptualisations of

Kazakh national identity is inessential, multi-voiced and contested through time and space. Secondly, that cinema emerged as a much more vocal and concrete site of dissension in the late-Soviet period, compared to the subtle contention of 1960s Soviet Kazakh cinema.

The Re-imagination of Kazakh History

One of the most common trends of the 'Kazakh New Wave' was a return to history. Some directors, writers and producers chose to re-visit and re-imagine important turning points, or perhaps more acutely put, the silences and invisibility of Kazakh history long suppressed under Soviet rule. The use of cinema to re-interpret history brought with it a re-evaluation of issues of identity and belonging, as is often the case with consideration of the past. In this regard, while the films are situated within the historical drama genre, they address history with a keen eye on the present. Differently put, they tackle questions of history while also providing a subtext for issues of identity and belonging in the transitional period, offering a comment on Kazakhstan's emergence as an independent modern nation. This section will focus on three films that ostensibly fit this broader characterisation. These films are: Ardak Amirkulov's *The Fall of Otrar* (1991); Damir Manabayev's *Surzhekey – the Angel of Death* (1991); and Kalykbek Salykov's *The Balcony* (1988). Each film will be addressed in turn.

The Fall of Otrar

The Fall of Otrar is a visually stunning epic in the great tradition of historical cinema. The plot concerns the politics and intrigue that led to the obliteration of Otrar, a major silk road oasis. The town was originally located in what is now South Kazakhstan province, just 65 kilometres south of the historic city of Turkestan. Set in the year 1218, *The Fall of Otrar* provides an account of the historical events that led to Chingiz Khan's eventual domination over the Khorezm Empire (which stretched from modern day Iran to Southern Kazakhstan) and the establishment of the Mongolian Empire. The Shah of the Khorezm Empire, Ala ad-Din Muhammad, was too interested in seeking conquest of Baghdad to pay attention to the growing power and threat of Chingiz Khan in the East.[36] Unzhu, a lowly soldier and nomad from the Kipchak Khanate, who had served in Chingiz Khan's army, warns the Shah of the impending threat from the East, but his advice is ignored and Unzhu is tortured. Being able to escape, Unzhu manages to convince Kairkhan, the governor of the border town of Otrar, of the dangers posed by Chingiz Khan, and that a trade mission consisting of 450 Muslim merchants is in fact a caravan of spies staking out the defences of the town. Kairkhan arrests the members of the caravan, seizes their property and executes an ambassador who had been sent by Chingiz Khan to ameliorate the situation and request reparations for the death of the merchants.[37] This affront to Chingiz Khan unleashes his wrath and he sends his army to raze the city to the ground.[38] A siege entails, which ends with the Shah fleeing and Kairkhan defeated. After helping Kairkhan unsuccessfully defend Otrar, Unzhu survives to wander the nomadic lifestyle. What is significant about these historical events is how a seemingly small local dispute led to such global consequences. The film is believed to be a reasonably authentic and faithful portrayal of the historical events that took place.[39]

The Fall of Otrar was a re-interpretation of a part of Kazakh history that pre-dates the Kazakh Khanate, but had been established in mythology as an important element of the Kazakh past and sense of identity. Such mythology had been recognised in Kazakh Soviet literature of the 1960s and 1970s. For example, Dukenbai Doszhanov's 1973 novel *Shelkovyi Put'* (Silk Road) depicted life in Otrar before the fall.[40] Along with Olzhas Suleimenov's *Az i ya*, such literature implanted Otrar as central to Kazakh cultural mentality.[41] It was this mythologising of Otrar that informed Ardak Amirkulov's underlying aim of the film, which was to 'express my pain for us, the Kazakh people. The ancient city of Otrar was the cradle of our civilisation; and we still have not climbed out of its ruins'.[42] Otrar, and a re-interpretation of its fall, is therefore central to Amirkulov's expression of Kazakh identity in the film, even if the film is not formally about national identity. It is a film that seeks to find a symbolic historical moment with which to explain the silence of the Kazakh nation throughout history, not as an abstract mythological idea but as an entity with agency, with sovereignty and power. The film's depiction of Otrar's defence against the Mongolian horde speaks not just to an 'ancestral national archetype of consciousness, but also to questions of national survival both in the past and in the contemporary sense of the late Soviet and post-Soviet period'.[43] One reviewer notes how the film depicts a 'town so much divided by hatred and envy that it could not defend itself against invaders'.[44] The subtext, therefore, centres on the importance of unity, and the message that without unity there is failure and destruction. At the same time, by focusing in the second half of the film on the defence and siege of Otrar, the film sits within a broad tradition of historical epics in Kazakh cinema, stretching from *Amangeldy* to *Nomad*.

A sense of national consciousness is embodied in Unzhu. This character is positioned by the director, Ardak Amirkulov, as a neutral protagonist used to introduce the main characters pivotal to the historical events that are to unfold.[45] Unzhu's position as the objective observer is fundamental to the film's construction of Kazakh identity. While one reviewer likens him to a 'young, bold, beautiful Kipchak',[46] his Kipchak identity in the context of the thirteenth century is significant for Kazakh identity in the present. As we saw in Chapter 1, the Kazakhs are descendants from Kipchak tribes and the character of Unzhu, therefore, embodies the ancestral continuity with the Kazakhs of the twentieth century. More substantively, Unzhu's positionality as a neutral protagonist who mediates between the main powers in the film: Chingiz Khan, the Shah of Khorezm and Kairkhan the governor of Otrar; demonstrates his agency. In an early scene, he declares his autonomy by stating that he 'came back of his own free will' from Chingiz Khan's army. His agency, and willingness to work between major competing powers, mirrors the agency of Kazakhstan as an emerging sovereign country during the late-Soviet period (1990–1).

One notable aspect of *The Fall of Otrar* is the straightforward way the director depicts historical events and characters. The film is a clear shift away from Soviet orthodoxies of cinematic narration and aesthetics, in its rejection of socialist realism the visuals of the movie strive towards historical realism. Amirkulov was most interested in recreating as authentic a portrait of medieval Central Asia as possible. The film captures, in the words of one reviewer, 'the atmosphere of the Middle Ages, it's filth and brutality'.[47] As Amirkulov notes in an interview, he 'was more interested in "how", not in "what"'.[48] This is most evident in a scene near the end of the film where Kairkhan's face is cast in molten silver after his defeat. Reminiscent of Tarkovsky's moulding of the bell in *Andrey Rublev*, Amirkulov has spoken of how he was interested in capturing the technology of the process as a way to demonstrate the specificity of how great warriors were immortalised.[49] The film was compared to *Andrey Rublev*, and the work of Akira Kurosawa.[50] The aesthetic influences of those works are evident, and the director has pointed to that himself.[51] However, as one reviewer notes, 'what distinguishes *The Fall of Otrar* from *Andrey Rublev* is its unpretentiousness, no-nonsense earthiness, its concentration on matters physical and political rather than psychological'.[52] The strength of the film is its ability to convey the reality of the blood, guts and violence of the time. In other words, the film is not an exploration of the inner life of characters. We are not privy to their inner psychological turmoil. The focus instead is on their perceived political interests and the actions they take to achieve them.

The Fall of Otrar is, therefore, as much a political film as it is historical. From this perspective, the film can be read in several ways in relation to the context of *perestroika* and the collapse of the Soviet Union. The fall of Otrar could be understood to mirror the disintegration of the USSR – we are witness to the 'doomed struggle' and 'a people submerged by the tide of events'.[53] At the same time, the film is argued to depict 'the importance of interconnecting backgrounds, with a warning that choosing personal ambitions over global concerns may endanger civilisations and humanity causing an entire way of life to disappear'.[54] Amirkulov's representation of thirteenth-century Otrar is symbolic of the inter-ethnic demographics of Kazakhstan at the time of the collapse of the USSR. Therefore, the subtext of survival, unity and community over personal political ambition, provides a cautionary tale for post-Soviet Kazakh nation-building. Of course, it is important not to over-emphasise this point. The film was four years in production and was released months prior to Kazakhstan's independence. Nonetheless, the search for a historical moment in Kazakh history through film acts as an artistic mechanism to begin exploring aspects of national identity and mentality during *perestroika* and the post-Soviet era. The film disrupts the Soviet narrative surrounding the history of what came before, and provides in the character of Unzhu a symbol of Kazakhstan's opportunity for agency to re-write and re-interpret its history to understand the present.

Surzhekey – the Angel of Death

Another film of this period that acts to disrupt the existing historical narrative regarding Kazakhs and their land was Damir Manabayev's

1991 picture *Surzhekey – the Angel of Death*. Like *The Fall of Otrar*, *Surzhekey – the Angel of Death* re-creates another difficult period of Kazakhstan's history and is also concerned with the destruction of a Kazakh civilisation, or, put more subtly, the nomadic way of life. The film concerns the 1930s collectivisation process and subsequent famine that struck the Kazakhs. It tells the tale of an ordinary Kazakh *aul* in which two brothers differ over their response to the impending Stalinist collectivisation and settlement of nomads. Azbergen believes it is best to leave and travel to China to preserve the traditional way of life, but his elder brother Pakhraddin decides to stay on the land of their ancestors. It is hardly surprising that a film about the terror of collectivisation and the subsequent famine of the 1930s had not been made before in Kazakhstan. However, *perestroika* and *glasnost* provided a window of opportunity for Manabayev to revisit this period. He began production of the film in 1989 but was unable to get backing from Kazakhfilm Studios and so had to seek independent financing.[55] Just its focus on sedentarisation and collectivisation was a challenge to Soviet authority and a Soviet reading of Kazakh history. However, while feeling it was possible to make the movie in the political climate of 1989–91, the director still had to hold back in terms of his representation of Russians. As Manabayev explained:

> I just wanted to tell the story [of collectivization], perestroika had begun, there was freedom and everyone took a breath and I said 'now I will tell this story'. I did not touch on the role of Russians in this process, they are not shown in the film. Collectivization is happening in the *aul* and between Kazakhs themselves. Bolshevik soldiers are somewhat present there, behind the corner. Somehow, they are influencing the process but they are not in the shot. I just wanted to show how collectivization happened among Kazakhs themselves.[56]

In focusing purely on the tensions inherent within the Kazakh community, perhaps best symbolised through the relationship between the two brothers, *Surzhekey – the Angel of Death* makes a significant contribution to the re-construction of national identity. As noted above, like *The Fall of Otrar* the film focuses on the destruction of the Kazakh civilisation. This time, instead of a crumbling medieval city it is a way of life, central to the identity and mentality of Kazakhs, which is shown to slowly disintegrate on the screen. The parting of the brothers is emblematic of the separation of the Kazakh people from their roots and from each other. We are led to understand the process of collectivisation as one that divorced the Kazakh people from each other. This is most astutely observed in the local Kazakh Red Army soldier who enforces the requisition of livestock and grain. It is Kazakhs who are tearing the *aul* apart, not Russians. To some extent this reflects those arguments in Kazakh Soviet historiography that place an emphasis on the role of local agency in the collectivisation and sedentarisation process.[57] Nevertheless, the film does clearly demonstrate the brute force of Soviet power and its impact on the traditional Kazakh way of life, and thus illustrates the ability of cinema to be a mechanism for political dissent. This is shown in one scene where the Soviet officer greets one of the women in the *aul* with 'hello emancipated woman', to which she replies, 'let your emancipation rot'.

Surzhekey – the Angel of Death also provides a mythologisation of Kazakh national identity. This mythology appears in several ways. Firstly, we can observe it in relation to Kazakhs' relationship with the land. A symbiotic relationship to the steppe is a fundamental psychogeographic element of Kazakh nomadic identity. Migration to fresh pastures for livestock to graze is directed by the weather and the environment. Therefore, the land and the Kazakhs' place within in it is fundamental to self-identification. In *Surzhekey – the Angel of Death*, the land is an essential character of the film. The movie was filmed in the barren harsh sands of Mangishlak and the external environment is shot in monochrome. According to Gulnara Abikeyeva, the use of monochrome 'reflects the true psychological state of being in a steppe or desert'.[58] The land is central to Pakhraddin's reasons for staying on in the *aul* even when he knows disaster and devastation await. He proclaims to Azbergen that 'I am rooted into this soil – I'll never move from it'. This all portends to a representation of Kazakh national identity that puts the idea of the land and Kazakhs' relationship with it front and centre. It is a mythological motif that we see play out time and time again in Kazakh cinema. It is most prominent in the Tengrist narrative of Kazakh national identity in the films of Yermek Tursunov, which are discussed in Chapter 6. Secondly, mythology appears in the literal sense via the Turkic legend of Korkut. Korkut is foretold death awaits him and even though he spends his life trying to escape it everywhere he goes there is someone digging his grave. For Abikeyeva, Korkut is used in the film to make clear that collectivisation was the death that followed Korkut.[59]

The film is important, therefore, for amplifying a silent part of Kazakh history. It sought to explain how the Kazakh people became divorced from their own sense of history and place, but the director also saw it as a larger comment on 'the end of an entire historical epoch – a nomadic civilization'.[60] In doing so, the film acts as a harbinger for themes that emerge as important to representations of nation-ness and identity in post-Soviet Kazakh cinema. The underpinnings of the Tengrist narrative have already been alluded to, but the use of the steppe as barren and desolate in which people struggle to eke out an existence evident in the film's depiction of nomadic life in this period is returned to in the socio-economic narrative in Chapter 7. Similarly, the tension between a rural and urban divide and between Kazakh and Russian speakers, which is evident in the contemporary socio-economic narrative in Kazakh cinema, is also present in *Surzhekey – the Angel of Death*. The communist Shege is encouraged to move away from the *aul* to the town, to learn Russian and 'become somebody'. But, for Shege 'becoming somebody' by migrating is equated with betraying people. *Surzhekey – the Angel of Death*, despite its lack of domestic, and even international distribution, is an important film of the 'Kazakh New Wave' period (even if Manabayev was not part of Solov'ev's workshop) because it allows for a reconsideration of Kazakh identity as part of the period of disruption and transition. In doing so, we can see the influence of some of its themes in more contemporary Kazakh cinema.

Balcony

Kalykbek Salykov's 1998 Kazakhfilm Studios production *The Balcony* also offers another reconstruction of Kazakh history. *The Balcony* recreates the late 1950s in Alma-Ata and the street life of young kids during this period. The film lacks a clear and distinct narrative, instead offering fragments of memory, nostalgia and sketches of the postwar 'thaw' period.[61] The film has been praised for its faithful recreation of the time, in 'wonderfully capturing the spirit' of the period after the Stalinist era, 'the poets, artists of the time, love and romance'.[62] The film was partly based on a poem of the same name by Olzhas Suleimenov. Aidar, the protagonist in the movie is tall, handsome, poetic, soulful and clever and was believed to have been written with the image of Suleimenov in mind.[63]

The film hovers between the past, present and future, making a statement regarding Kazakhstan's position at the tail end of the 1980s. Our entry into Alma-Ata street life of this period is from the present of the 1980s. Aidar is performing surgery when he notices a tattoo of the number '20' on his patient's arm. As in Proust's famous scene in *In Search of Lost Time*, where the narrator dips a *petite madeleine* into a warm cup of tea evoking the involuntary memory of a time past in Combray, Aidar's noting of the '20' tattoo conjures the memories of courtyard '20' from his childhood on the Broadway (previously known as Kalinin street and now Kabanbai-Batyr) in Alma-Ata. From then on, the viewer is privy to the atmosphere of the vibrant street-life of the Broadway's inhabitants. Jazz music fills the local restaurants and cafes, there are scuffles in the street, homelessness, drunks, maverick artists, all circumscribed by a continued fear of repression and terror.[64] The film also hints towards the future. This is represented in a scene when Aidar, along with his friends, previously antagonistic gangs, and complete strangers begin running. They run along a railway track and as they pass through a tunnel a portrait of Stalin hangs above. They are running from the past, the terror and the fear, they are running into the darkness of the unknown future. The group disappear, only the fat young Puzo remains, the straggler of the group, he calls out to his friends, 'guys where are you, guys where are you'. There is no response, only silence.[65] The young group's disappearance into the darkness mirrors that generation's (those who were adults in the 1980s) journey into a future without the fear and terror of the Stalinist past. The underlying subtext is that the current generation of Kazakhs in the late 1980s, those whose formative years was the period of Khrushchev's 'thaw', face an uncertain and unknowable future. Soviet time has been disrupted and all that is certain is that perhaps the Stalinist repression is in the past.

The running from the past is also emblematic of the film's propensity to offer a veiled critique of Soviet repression. Like *Surzhekey – the Angel of Death* it touches on a silent part of Kazakh history (as well as broader history of the Soviet space): the Stalinist terror. This re-imagination of the terror reveals itself in a dream sequence. In the dream sequence, we see Aidar's mother (who forbade that Aidar and his sister Joan should speak of their father) look on as his father offers some papers to NKVD officers who are at the door. The officers reject the papers and Aidar and Joan's father is taken away and hustled into a waiting car. In today's context, such a depiction of the terror may seem unremarkable. But in the context of the late 1980s this was a bold statement on the part of Salykov. In 1988, the USSR remained intact with what seemed like no immediate prospect of collapse, and the Party still maintained power. Therefore, it is noteworthy that the director felt able to open this previously taboo subject.[66] To some extent, however, Salykov was following in the footsteps of artistic work which had already begun to deal with the issue of repression. The release of Georgian director Tengiz Abuladze's *Repentance* in 1987 (originally made in 1984 but barred from release for three years) offered an allegorical critique of Stalinist repression.

The Fall of Otrar, *Surzhekey – the Angel of Death* and *Balcony* all offer a re-interpretation of, and try to open, previously closed and silent aspects of the country's history. Their achievement in re-imagining history is that they challenged Soviet authority by dissenting from the prevailing norms of Soviet inflected readings of history, while at the same time offering an account of Kazakh identity. In *The Fall of Otrar* and *Surzhekey – the Angel of Death*, it is a fragmented identity, uncertain, fluid and not fixed – awaiting to settle in the period of flux and transition. In *Balcony*, the notion of identity, and the challenge to Soviet authority, is intertwined with Aidar's position as a new type of hero. Indeed, it is the emergence of this new form of hero within the works of the 'Kazakh New Wave' that is central to the negation of Soviet authority.

The Negation of Soviet Authority

Having re-interpreted and brought alive the gaps within Kazakh history, the films of the 'Kazak New Wave', as we have seen above, also challenge Soviet authority. This is achieved principally via the establishment of a new form of hero. Moving on from a socialist realist representation of the hero, which tended towards the idealisation of the worker willing to sacrifice themselves for the revolutionary cause, the hero in the 'Kazakh New Wave' was more independent, romantic and with their own sense of agency sequestered from broader structures and communities. In other words, the hero is an outsider. We can see this most prominently in *Balcony* and Rashid Nugmanov's 1989 film *The Needle*.

In *Balcony*, Aidar performs this role. He has been described by Gulnara Abikeyeva as 'independent in spirit, free and at the same time a leader of a generation'.[67] He is imbued with honesty, morality and integrity. This is despite his involvement in street fights and the rough and tumble of the Broadway street life. As one reviewer argues, 'he is not an ordinary street yard bully – he knows and understands poetry, is always ready to help someone who needs it and if he sees his friends or entourage are in the wrong he silently gets up and leaves.'[68] Aidar, therefore, is a 'loner and a maverick' standing outside the crowd, which is further emphasised in his interest in the outcast artist who appears in the street periodically.[69] Aidar's outsider status is epitomised most clearly by the central place of the balcony in the film. Aidar is shown standing on the balcony smoking and listening to jazz, but in its elevation from the street it becomes as one reviewer notes a 'space of contemplation and observation ... Aidar loves the balcony because he towers over all life, above the crowd'.[70] This perhaps represents the key subtext of the film in relation to the notion of identity and Soviet authority. At the heart of the film is the relationship between the individual and the crowd. Aidar represents the agency of the individual to stand apart from the crowd, and thus from authority. As a protagonist, Aidar and his confidence as an individual separate from the larger community and wider social structures, which can be understood as symbolic of Kazakhstan (or perhaps any Soviet Republic during the late 1980s). Aidar's separateness represents a search for identity away from the norms of behaviour of the broader Soviet state. It is an identity in transition from the conformity of the crowd under Communist rule, to one anchored in a new existence that provides an internal psychological reflection on the changing external environment.

The Needle

It is Moro, however, the protagonist of Rashid Nugmanov's 1989 film *The Needle*, who has come to embody this new type of hero for the transitionary period. *The Needle* is the most celebrated and famous film of the 'Kazakh New Wave'. Of the generalist monographs written on late-Soviet cinema, *The Needle* is the only Kazakh film usually warranted more than a single sentence. The film has come to symbolise the ethos and politics of the 'Kazakh New Wave'. Gulnara Abikeyeva has even gone as far to suggest that *The Needle* heralded the starting point for *perestroika* cinema.[71] This may be a stretch given *ASSA* preceded *The Needle's* release by two years. Nonetheless, it was Nugmanov who coined the term 'Kazakh New Wave'. He used it as a marketing tool to describe the programme of Kazakh films he and Talgat Temenov organised for the 1989 International Film Festival in Moscow.[72] *The Needle* was a huge hit in the USSR and is reported to have sold 14.5 million tickets.[73]

Nugmanov came to Solov'ev's workshop from a background in architecture and archaeology. His first film was the 40-minute documentary short *Ya-Ha* (1986). The first short film to be produced as part of the workshop, *Ya-Ha* resembles what Nugmanov describes as 'a free-flowing sketch ... and ad-hoc improvisations' of the underground rock scene in Leningrad.[74] Akin to a visual diary, not that dissimilar to D.A. Pennebaker's two Bob Dylan films, *Don't Look Back* (1965) and *Eat the Document* (1966), *Ya-Ha* captures the cramped, claustrophobic atmosphere of the underground music scene in Leningrad.[75] The film never received a commercial release in the USSR, but it set the template for the visual and musical style that Nugmanov would use for *The Needle*. Ludmila Pruner describes this as 'an elliptical, disjointed narrative, written text within the pictorial text, separate soundtracks and juxtapositions between the visual and the audio in the same shot; the visual effects of parallel cinema'.[76] *Ya-Ha* features a performance from Viktor Tsoy and his band *Kino*. Nugmanov and Tsoy became friends in the 1980s during a period when Nugmanov spent summers living in Leningrad where he became acquainted with the underground rock scene.[77]

Nugmanov's opportunity to make *The Needle* arrived at a time when he was still in his third year of study at VGIK. The screenplay had already been written and the original director for the film had come into conflict with the screenwriters. Initially Nugmanov was reticent to get involved fearing it was a typical communist propaganda script. As he explained:

> They said it is about drugs, I thought maybe it is communist propaganda, but when I met with the screenwriter and film makers, I understood it is not this type of movie. I saw it was something new and I said ok, it is a good opportunity for me ... I asked what kind of budget we have ... They said unfortunately

we can't put any more money into the budget so I would have to make this film with what's left of the remainder of the money and I had to start shooting within one month. I put forward my own conditions because the time schedule was tight, I had to recast everything. I decided to invite my friends, they were not professional actors, but I didn't have time to make huge casting calls.[78]

The employing of his friends as the cast because of time and budget constraints was both a serendipitous and inspired decision. Utilising his friends provided the film with a playful spirit, something Nugmanov puts down to his use of rock musicians in some of the main roles (Russian rock icon Pyotr Mamonov also stars in the film) and his background in Soviet sub-culture.[79]

Neo-romanticism

The choice of Tsoy to play the character of Moro was especially inspired for what he brought to this new type of hero on the Soviet screen. Tsoy was already an underground rock icon. He already carried himself with an effortless coolness clad in the Western rock star uniform of black jeans and black leather jacket. Tsoy brought a detachment to the role. As Anna Lawton notes, Tsoy 'is a wonderful interpreter of the neo-romantic spirit. He did not have to act, he just played himself'.[80] Described by one reviewer as a 'post-punk dandy ... and a modernised version of Camus' outsider', Tsoy's character of Moro in *The Needle* provides a new romanticism in Kazakh cinema.[81] Like Aidar in *Balcony*, Moro is imbued with a sense of agency and morality, the simple plot of the film turns on Moro's search for justice and morality, firstly in relation to getting his friend Dina off her morphine addiction, and away from the drug mafia boss (played by Pyotr Mamonov), then in reclaiming money he is owed from the shadowy character of Spartak (played by Aleksandr Bashirov). Moro is a neo-romantic hero, distinct from the romanticism of typical cinematic heroes because he arrives to us without a backstory and an absence of a clear explanation for his actions. We know nothing of Moro's background, we know little of his relationship with Dina beyond the fact he wants to help her, we do not know why Spartak owes him money, or what led to Moro's unfortunate demise by mysterious assailants in the snow inflected streets of Alma-Ata.[82] In other words, Moro is unanchored from the materiality of his existence and he is free-floating between the different realities of other characters in the film. Sergei Sholokhov, however, suggested it was Moro who is grounded in reality and the other characters (the narcotic addicted Dina, the deluded Spartak and the Mafia drug boss) who had 'lost their sense of reality'.[83]

The film, therefore, has been described as a 'neo-romantic paradox'[84] where it is difficult to place characters' actions and motivations and the extent to which they are grounded in a sense of materiality and/or reality. This is reflected in the visual style, with the creation of a disconcerting and disjointed atmosphere. Frames are regularly infused or interrupted with songs, radio broadcasts and TV shows from different time periods.[85] The characters' alienation from reality and each other is also foregrounded by random sounds and words in Russian and foreign languages.[86] The chaotic, playful and disjointed feel is important for our understanding of Kazakh national identity in this period because it demonstrates the transitional social reality of identity. Moro's untethered relationship to the existence of others, and the reality of late-Soviet Alma-Ata, represents a form of liberation. This is a liberation from the past and from the collective totality which had framed social interaction in the socialist state. It is a liberation which reflects the political, social and economic reality of the late 1980s. This was noted in a review of the film in *Sovetskii Ekran* in 1989. As the reviewer contends:

> I do not remember on our movie screen where loneliness could be so worthy and attractive. It does not destroy, and the doomed tragic end is liberating, it leads to a liberation from the bonds of collective thinking, collective life, decisions, choices, words, actions ... this man is not the offender (of the past), not a tramp, not a rocker, none of them ... I do not know what he is doing, but he carries a personal principle.... He is independent, initially free ... He is free in this world, where everything is tied by the bonds of obligation.[87]

Moro is representative of all Soviet citizens beginning to understand the liberation from previously servile bonds. He is emblematic of Kazakhstan, its nationhood and identity, being unanchored from the Soviet past, free, ready to settle and ready to be interpreted and reconstructed without the chains of Soviet authority.

This unanchoring of the character is represented in the film via the concept of time.

Time

While Ludmila Pruner has suggested chronology is an important aspect of 'Kazakh New Wave' films,[88] *The Needle* does not in fact present us with a form of chronological time. Yet, time is central to the film. Periodically a digital display of the time appears in-between scenes and Moro is often caught checking his watch. We have no sense as viewers as to whether different shots are temporally related. Time, therefore, is confused. It is neither the present, past or future. This is realised in a long panning shot of Dina's apartment where old transistor radios, TVs and clocks come into view representing the confusion of time, some show old TV shows, while other sounds portend to a foreign language – the 'other' – the outside world. Then, when Moro takes Dina out into the steppe to the desiccated Aral Sea to dry out from her addiction, time seems to be suspended. The place is calm, still and empty. The Kazakh Steppe is representative of 'empty time' – not the Soviet homogeneous empty time – but a new empty time ready to be filled with new content. The scenes set in the Aral Sea (the embodiment of the Kazakh nation – the steppe) are symbolic of the collapsing in of the previous two worlds we saw in Soviet Kazakh cinema. There is timelessness now in which Kazakh nation-ness and identity can be re-written.[89]

Any notion that *The Needle* speaks to a specific Kazakh national identity should be treated with the utmost caution. Moro is not a hero for the Kazakhs. Moro has been likend to Bruce Lee (without the Kung Fu)[90] or a Western Superman 'descended to the earth to restore order and justice'.[91] While Nugmanov has denied the specific influence of the American Western on his construction of the neo-romantic Moro, instead pointing to influence of Jean-Luc Goddard[92] and the fact that 'Moro is Tsoy',[93] undoubtedly the film operates with a universal language, and as Ludmila Pruner argues of 'Kazakh New Wave' films, it displays 'cosmopolitan interests'.[94] The film, therefore, does not seek to explicitly reference Kazakh nationhood and identity – as much of its cultural reference points are universal. Besides, Nugmanov has suggested the film was made to have fun with his friends.[95] Nevertheless, by virtue of the fact that Nugmanov is Kazakh, the film was shot in Kazakhstan, and indeed the Kazakh Steppe and the Aral Sea are important representations of landscape (geographical and the internal landscape of the characters), the film does provide us with an implicit account of Kazakh nation-ness and identity during the period of transition from Soviet to post-Soviet rule. It is a film in transition about characters in transition set in a place in transition.

It is in the capturing of transition that *The Needle* provides a negation of Soviet authority through the depiction of drug use. Cinematic representation of such a taboo subject would have been unthinkable five or ten years previously. The film also explicitly undermines Soviet authority. The Soviet state is mocked in a rambling speech by Spartak after Moro catches up with him in a disused junk yard. Spartak satirises the communist attitude to the individual by claiming that 'everyman here is a loner, but all men together make us'. But when 'they', the Soviet state, is betrayed within Spartak's reading of Soviet authority by trends of freedom and independence, he takes back such grandiose claims for shared community. He bellows that:

> the conservation of time, that is our motto! But we closed it because you have not been worthy of my good faith, and neither have you. I no longer trust you. I no longer trust myself – to fall and to rise? No! To lay down once fallen. Dear friend! Farewell! I was on your side. Now our companionship will end.

Spartak's rallying cry receives no response either from his henchmen or Moro. It is a satirical slap in the face for the age-old Soviet propaganda regarding brotherly comradeship and the correctness of the leader's vision. In this one scene, *The Needle* pulls the rug from under Soviet ideology.[96] It is also important to notice the reference to Soviet attempts to control and conserve time within Spartak's speech; this is the time which is disrupted in the film.

The 'Kazakh New Wave' presents a new type of hero. It is a hero who is an independent agent seeking morality and justice, who ultimately acts to negate Soviet authority.

Capturing Transition on Screen

With the silences of history brought to the fore, and negation of Soviet authority realised through the establishment of new heroes, the final element of the 'Kazakh New Wave' seeks to capture the material and psychological nature of transition. This capturing of transition also adds weight to the negation of Soviet authority. Elements of the 'Kazakh New Wave' cinema, according to Inna Smailova, revealed 'the exact state of the modern Kazakh' at the point in which the country and its people found themselves at a crossroads.[97] Kazakh cinema of this period, therefore, stood to reflect, in its unique way, the political, economic and social reality of the time. A depiction of reality occurs in two forms. The first is material and we can witness this most prominently in Serik Aprymov's *The Last Stop* (1989), which has been likened to a 'critique of Soviet and Kazakh reality ... a wiping away of the old values and realities', and again to an extent in Abai Karpykov's *Little Fish in Love* (1989).[98] The second is a subtle reading of the realities of transition through the psychological inner journey of protagonists. This is best reflected in the work of Darezhan Omirbayev and his films *Kairat* (1992) and *Cardiogram* (1995). Both strands, however, share two main commonalities: the tension between rural and urban lives; and the lived day-to-day experience of ordinary citizens. These are two aspects that remain fundamental to the contemporary socio-economic narrative of nationhood and identity, which is discussed in Chapter 7.

Material Realism

The Last Stop has a deceptively simple plot. Erken, a young Kazakh man, returns from military service to his native *aul*. For three days, he is in 'a state of post-army syndrome' as he seeks to adapt to civilian life.[99] He seeks to mend relations with his former girlfriend, meet old friends and drink. Yet, the film consists not of an obvious linear narrative, but rather episodic documentary-like scenes that aim to illustrate what one reviewer coined as 'sad but honest realism'.[100] *The Last Stop* is not a celebratory tale of homecoming; rather it reveals the villagers as 'procrastinating in a state of despair and desolation, drowning in the misery of their aimless existence in alcohol and petty crime'.[101] What the film shows are the desperate lives of the inhabitants, trapped in a way of life which seems meaningless and is going nowhere. This is embodied in the suicide of one of Erken's friends. The name of the film itself reflects this – the last stop – the final destination and the end of the line or, as Aprymov noted himself, 'no future'.[102] It is a rebuke of Soviet ideology — there is no future for residents of the *aul* in a Soviet system. It has brought decay and disappointment. Erken understands this and leaves the village at the end of the film. After his time in the army where he had been stationed near to a city, the *aul* holds no allure, it creates boredom and despair.[103]

If the film looks and feels real, it is because Aprymov shot the movie in his native village of Aksuat. He filmed the inhabitants in their real environment going about their daily lives. As Aprymov noted in an interview, 'everything, pedestrians, streets, houses, the interiors are all real; everything that happened — conversations, interactions and relationships'.[104] The search for authenticity is a common theme in the history of Kazakh cinema. We saw this in the documentary ethnographic realisation of *aul* life in *My Name is Kozha*. However, Abdulla Karsakbayev's film presented an idealistic representation of a 'Kazakh world' where village residents were cheerful and fulfilled by the simplicities of traditional village life. In 1963, it was something to behold and for Kazakhs to be proud of. It was a romantic representation of the *aul*. Aprymov provides a similar ethno-graphic style in the way in which he captures day-to-day real life, but this is not an idyllic scene. The 'Kazakh world' of 1960s cinema disappeared — replaced by a contorted, ugly version made decrepit by years of Soviet servitude. Thus, while we can see continuities in terms of the cinematic methods used (in this case some form of ethnographic representation) to construct a version of Kazakh identity between Soviet cinema and the 'Kazakh New Wave', the representations of that identity are very different, contentious even. Yet, the depiction of misery and sadness offended local officials from the village. Consequently, the film was shelved and not released for five years — only obtainable via a pirated copy on VHS.[105] Interestingly, 14 years later in 2003 Aprymov made *The Hunter*, which provides a much more positive take on the Kazakh *aul* and the traditions of the Kazakh steppe.

A central sub text of *The Last Stop* is the theme of the journey. For Erken it is initially the journey home to the *aul*, but is also about a prospective journey to the city. In this way, the film reflects a fundamental dividing line within Kazakh society and identity between urban and rural populations. It is a theme that is rendered heavily in contemporary cinematic works (see Chapter 7). In *The Last Stop* the initial journey back to Aksuat can be read as a search for Kazakh tradition and authenticity considering the homogenising force of being in the Soviet military. Erken's exit from the village, however, can be understood as the search for hope – and that might only be found in the urban centre.

The opposite journey occurs in Abai Karpykov's *Little Fish in Love* (1989) where the protagonist, Zhaken, leaves a suburban village to visit his musician brother in Alma-Ata. Like many of the films of the 'Kazakh New Wave', *Little Fish in Love* features a series of impressionistic scenes with little driving narrative other than Zhaken's attempts to conquer the city. Like *The Last Stop* the film also seeks to provide a form of realism, but it is what Karpykov defines as a 'conditional reality'.[106] While Zhaken has big dreams, the fulfilment of those dreams is circumscribed and he struggles with life in the city and in finding love. However, the important difference with *The Last Stop* is that Zhaken does not give up hope (although he does return to the suburbs) – the city is an optimistic place unlike the pessimistic Aksuat is Serik Aprymov's film. Karpykov uses irony instead of cynicism to deal with the difficulties of life in late-Soviet period Kazakhstan, noting in an interview that 'only irony can speak about the desire that each of us has to conquer the world'.[107]

The film, therefore, delivers a different take on realism. It provides a cinematic account of the ordinary lives of city dwellers and their relationships. Notably, Alma-Ata is realised as a vibrant, exciting and dynamic city. In doing so the film reflects the cosmopolitan nature of the city, as one reviewer commented we can observe 'different lifestyles and religions, different faces of the century, Europe and Asia.'[108] In capturing the multi-ethnic nature of the city (and the country at large), the film speaks to a form of national identity rooted in a civic nationalism.

Zhaken's journey from the periphery to the centre is also symbolic of an internal division within Kazakhstan which reveals the multivalent nature of the nation. This was a division Karpykov was acutely aware of when making the film. As he notes, 'Kazakhs are divided into two nations: the urban and rural. The urban speaks in Russian and the rural in Kazakh. That is a nation divided not only by the way of life, but also with regards to the main language.'[109] *Little Fish in Love* alludes to the challenges facing the transition to a post-Soviet society and especially the necessity of bringing together these two nations. While these 'worlds' were distinct politically and artistically in Soviet cinema, the cinema of the 'Kazakh New Wave' explores the dilemma of them coming together. In both *The Last Stop* and *Little Fish in Love* this division between urban and rural, Russian- and Kazakh-speaking, is not resolved. Furthermore, as we will see in Chapter 7, contemporary cinematic accounts of this social fracture remain as prescient as ever.

Inner Psychological Transition

Much like Zhaken in *Little Fish in Love*, the eponymous protagonist of Darezhan Omirbayev's first full-length feature, *Kairat* (1992), also journeys from the rural periphery to Alma-Ata seeking a new life. This journey is represented consistently throughout the film via the symbolic use of the train. The opening scene is Kairat on a train and a very long shot of the expansive Kazakh steppe as the train passes by. But the notion of the journey is also present in the character of Indira, a girl that Kairat is seeking to court, who works on the train and is often away for days at a time. We are constantly shown close shots within the carriage of the train while Kairat waits for Indira and/or speaks with her co-worker. The train, however, acts an exteriorisation of the inner journey which Kairat is on from adolescence to adulthood. He arrives in Alma-Ata and fails his college test, but can take a job on the buses. He lives in meagre accommodation in a shared dorm and ends up confronting the dormitory bully. Much of the film concerns his pursuit of Indira, his social awkwardness and ultimately his failure in winning her heart. The film, therefore, tends towards the mundanity of the everyday, 'the dull, uneventfulness of daily life'.[110] The only respite we have from mundanity of Kairat's existence are the occasional dream sequences where he lives out his fantasies. Omirbayev's work has been described as possessing a dry 'stubbornly ordinary style, rooted in the particular experience of life in Kazakhstan, either rural or urban.[111] Therefore, the ordinariness of the everyday experience masks the inner psychological transition for Kairat as he navigates his new unfamiliar setting.

Cardiogram (1995) follows a similar pattern to *Kairat*. It follows Zhasulan who is taken from his *aul* on a bus to a sanatorium outside the city. Zhasulan does not speak Russian, only Kazakh, and the film is a meditation on adapting to alien environments. Along with *Kairat* and Omirbayev's 2001 film *The Road*, *Cardiogram* is semi-autobiographical. As Omirbayev explained:

I wanted to show a person that appears in an alien atmosphere. It is a sort of autobiographical story. I was born and raised in a rural Kazakh-speaking area of Southern Kazakhstan. My Russian is poor. I was sent to a sanatorium in Taraz when I had problems with my health after having angina and I was 'in' a Russian-speaking sphere. After that I used this experience in the film *Cardiogram*. I found it interesting that a person gets into a new sphere and he experiences more sharply.[112]

The fact Zhasulan's inner turmoil is driven by a tension along the lines of language and the division between urban and rural sensibilities only serves to reflect the reality of the early post-Soviet transition, and moreover, the inherent tensions undermining claims to a homogenous national identity. Moreover, the film represents an inner psychological transition from childhood to adolescence[113] – as Zhasulan undergoes a sexual awakening – embodied in his fascination with the nurse and his voyeuristic encounters with her by spying on her in the shower.

Omirbayev achieves in his work a demonstration of how identity and nationhood can be encountered in the ordinariness of the everyday, in the small seemingly insignificant moments of existence, in the emotional and psychological reflection of personal journeys of transition to new states of being and new constructions of time. Omirbayev's work is significant, therefore, for our understanding of the nation-building process in Kazakhstan because of its reflection on the internal lived existence in being part of a larger community. However, he does this in a way as not to explain the world, rather in how we feel it.[114]

Like other films in the 'Kazakh New Wave' it is important to not overstate the particularity of these films to Kazakhstan. The focus on this inner turmoil of dealing with the adaptation to new environments and emotional transitions to new stages in life that involve passions, betrayal, discovery and disappointment could be, as Omirbayev argues, 'a story which happened in England'.[115] Moreover, Omirbayev's work has been influenced by European cinema especially the work of Jean-Luc Goddard and Robert Bresson.[116] Besides, some of his later films were adaptations of classic Russian literature. *Shuga* (2007) was inspired by Tolstoy's *Anna Karenina*, while *Student* (2012) was an adaptation of Dostoyevsky's *Crime and Punishment*. Along with his 1998 film *The Killer*, *Shuga* and *Student*, while still utilising Omirbayev's quiet style, offer a more evident critique of how Kazakhstan is losing its purity of soul in the face of the ravages of capitalism and the associated desire for trinkets and expensive commodities, which speaks to the socio-economic narrative in contemporary cinematic works. Omirbayev emerged as perhaps one of the most well-known and internationally lauded directors from the group of the 'Kazakh New Wave'. His films *Kairat* and *Cardiogram*, among others, have been showered with awards from across the globe. Yet, his films often receive limited release and attention among a domestic Kazakh audience.[117]

Nonetheless, whether Omirbayev's films are based on universal precepts or not, what his work shares with other films discussed in this section is that they all sought to capture the reality of life in late Soviet and early post-Soviet period Kazakhstan, albeit in different ways. As directors, they 'adequately described the reality in which they grew up and lived in'.[118] In doing so, they provide a challenge to the conventional representations of Soviet reality which preceded them. This was achieved both through an explicit comment on the social and moral bankruptcy of the Soviet system (*The Last Stop*) and in a subtle more intimate way as in the work of Darezhan Omirbayev.

After the 'Kazakh New Wave'

The tide of the 'Kazakh New Wave' began to pull back soon after the collapse of the USSR. The Kazakh film industry struggled in the early post-Soviet period. The 'Kazakh New Wave' gave the country's cinema a great deal of international cachet. The new-found freedom of expression which the directors of this period offered saw a burgeoning of private and independent studios spring up in the country. However, these studios did not last long and could not withstand the competition from the black market and the costs of film production in an economy that was in deep recession.[119] Moreover, during the 1990s the absence of a legislative framework for financing the film industry meant private investors were subject to high taxes, which put off potential investors. Kazakhfilm Studios went through some significant changes – in 1997 *Kazakhkino* (the equivalent of *Goskino*) was abolished and replaced with a National Production Centre, which was responsible for administration of the industry and working with independent studios,[120] while studio production was separated out to the Kazakhfilm studio. Then in 2000 the National Production Centre and Kazkinoprokat was merged into the state enterprise national company Kazakhfilm Studios in the name of Shaken Aimanov.[121] Despite the re-organisation of the industry, film production slumped in the 1990s. In 1991, at the pinnacle of the 'Kazakh New Wave', 13 Kazakh-produced feature films were released, by 1997 this had fallen to just four and in the two years of 1999 and 2000 it was just one.[122]

Consequently, for the directors of the 'Kazakh New Wave', post-Soviet Kazakhstan proved a difficult environment to raise finances to produce their work. Many of the directors continued producing films via co-productions and funding from abroad. Omirbayev, for example, worked closely with French production companies on *The Killer*, *The Road* and *Shuga*. Rashid Nugmanov directed another film in 1993, *The Wild East*, influenced by Kurosawa's *Seven Samurai*, which was a political allegory for the banditism and wildness of early capitalism in the former USSR. After its release Nugmanov moved to France permanently and has not produced a new feature film since (a remix of *The Needle* was released in 2010). Nugmanov instead got involved in politics – supporting the Peoples Republican Party of Kazakhstan, led by former Prime Minister Akezhan Kazhegeldin. He returned to Kazakhstan in 2014 and, at the time of writing, was working with the Ministry of Culture and the Presidential Administration on a series of historical films about Kazakhstan. Ardak Amirkulov and Serik Aprymov continued to make films in Kazakhstan throughout the 1990s. Amirkulov worked with Kazakhfilm Studios on a historical bio-pic of the famed Kazakh poet Abai, which was released in 1996. His most recent film was an adaptation of Chingiz Aitmatov's story *Farewell Gulsary* released in 2008. Serik Aprymov made a series of films throughout the 1990s and early 2000s, some of them were international co-productions, such as *The Hunter* (2003). While these directors' films remained popular outside of Kazakhstan, lauded by critics at international film festivals, their domestic appeal remained limited. As Abikeyeva notes, 'these and other films have travelled to many international film festivals, suggesting a fairly high status and the artistic level of Kazakh cinema. But then came the new millennium, and it became clear that it was time to break out of this prestigious, yet hermetically sealed circle of art-house cinema.'[123] A problem then, as it remains now, was the issue of distribution and low audience numbers.[124]

Therefore, while the 'Kazakh New Wave' spoke to issues of memory, belonging and identity in the transition to the post-Soviet period, these were not films that broadly engaged or reached domestic audiences in the country. The art-house style was too remote for popular and commercial appeal. However, this is not to suggest the that 'Kazakh New Wave' was not influential on directors of contemporary cinematic works. As we will see in Chapter 7, the influence of the 'Kazakh New Wave' movement loomed large on how younger contemporary directors approach filmmaking and their specific construction of representations of Kazakh identity and nation-ness.

Conclusion

It would be fair to say that a single chapter in a book could not in itself do justice to all the films of the 'Kazakh New Wave', and this is not attempted here. Rather, this chapter has sought to concentrate on how the films of the 'Kazakh New Wave' arguably laid the foundation for the multiple nationalisms that can be observed in contemporary Kazakh cinema.[125] Films such as *The Fall of Otrar*, *Surzhekey – the Angel of Death* and *Balcony* focused on revisiting the silences of the Kazakh past – making open what had previously been closed. Other films such as the *The Needle* concerned the negation of Soviet rule – while *The Last Stop*, *Little Fish in Love*, *Kairat* and *Cardiogram* sought to depict the realities of everyday existence. They projected what it meant to be a citizen of Kazakhstan during this time. To be a member of nation of Kazakhstan was to be concerned with transition, one's place in the world, and to journey from the periphery to the centre. What they represent was the collapsing of previously discrete 'Soviet' and 'Kazakh' worlds. The certainty of empty Soviet homogenous time was disrupted. What was to follow was a filling in of 'time' by way of exploring what Kazakh national identity and nation-ness meant. This was a process that began to be reflected in cinematic works in the new millennium and it concerns the next four chapters of this book. They outline the multivalent narratives that are represented in films that speak to different conceptualisations of Kazakh nationhood and identity. The first of these is an ethnic-centric narrative employed by the regime of Nursultan Nazarbayev, to offer an 'official' version of Kazakh history and nation formation.

CHAPTER 4

NAKED IN THE MIRROR: THE ETHNO-CENTRIC NARRATIVE OF KAZAKH NATIONHOOD

Introduction

The representation of Kazakh nationhood within Soviet cinema can be understood as containing two distinct worlds: 'Soviet' and 'Kazakh'.[1] In the previous chapter, the way in which the 'Kazakh New Wave' flattened the cinematic landscape in its portrayal of nation and identity was discussed in detail. The levelling revisited silences of Kazakhstan's past; negated Soviet rule via its depiction of the neo-romantic hero; and provided a representation of belonging situated in the lived material and psychological experience of transition from Soviet to post-Soviet rule. The 'Kazakh New Wave' cleared the way for new and multiple representations of nationhood. This book identifies four constructions of the imagined Kazakh nation in contemporary cinematic works that emerged after the period of the 'Kazakh New Wave'. These are the ethnic, civic, religious and socio-economic narratives.

The first of these, the ethnic narrative, is the topic of this chapter. It is arguably one of two narratives which pertain to an official, regime-sponsored construction of Kazakh nationhood. The ethnic narrative also mirrors Rogers Brubaker's concept of 'nationalising state'.[2] The films considered within this analysis offer an emotional appeal to the perceived bounded ethnic group of Kazakhs, to their history, people and homeland. It is a representation of national identity couched in cultural terms, in expressions of blood, language and motherland.

If the 'Kazakh New Wave' razed the old order to the ground, allowing for the emergence of the new, then it is important to recognise the influence of state-led film production on this narrative. Much like the Soviet regime, the government in Kazakhstan has used cinema as an ideological tool. Film director Adilkhan Yerzhanov has termed them 'custom-made' films, in that Kazakhfilm Studios are seen to make them on the order of the Ministry of Culture.[3] The Kazakh government has placed great store in the films produced within this narrative in offering an official account of nation formation and historical memory.

There are three central motifs that run through this narrative. The first is the idea of defending the homeland from foreign invading forces. This narrative depicts nation formation as a process achieved through the defence of the motherland in the eighteenth-century struggle against the Mongolian *Oirats*,[4] and the unification of the disparate Kazakh *zhuz*. Secondly, the narrative constructs an explicit representation of Kazakh ethnic identity. This is realised through three signs: traditional *aul* life, landscape and language. However, this attempt to construct a culturally specific identity finds itself compromised to some extent by the global nature of the cinema industry. Films within this narrative are often seeking to appeal to international as well as domestic audiences. Thirdly, the narrative also speaks to the nature of contemporary power in Kazakhstan. These films are associated with the political leadership of Nazarbayev and are part of a broader legitimation strategy. This is most effectively realised in a series of films dedicated to portraying the president's life.

This chapter provides a discussion of the three central elements to the ethnic narrative through an analysis of *Sardar* (2003), *Nomad* (2005), *Zhauzhurek Myn Bala* (2011), *Sky of My Childhood* (2012), *River of Fire* (2013) *Iron Mountain* (2013), *Breaking the Vicious Circle* (2015) and *So There Were Stars* (2016). The chapter is divided into five sections. The first provides a brief account of the cinema industry in post-Soviet Kazakhstan. The second explores the theme of 'defence of homeland', the third the symbolic representation of ethnicity and the fourth the theme of power and personality cult. The final section examines audience reception.

The Context of the Cinema Industry in post-Soviet Kazakhstan

As we saw towards the end of the previous chapter, Kazakhstan's cinema industry went into a period of decline from the mid-to-late 1990s. By the turn of the millennium film production had reached a nadir with only one film being produced by Kazakhfilm Studios in the years 1999 and 2000.[5] This lack of investment in the industry was a consequence of poor marcoeconomic performance and recession in the country during the 1990s.[6] While the 'Kazakh New Wave' had been successful with international film critics, the films' auteur sensibilities proved to have limited commercial viability or popular domestic appeal. Inevitably, the 'Kazakh New Wave' could not be sustained by a film industry in which private financing collapsed and there was little finance because of poor tax incentives for investors.[7] The situation did shift once the Kazakh government sought a more direct role in the film industry. The improved economic situation in the second decade of independence, driven largely by high oil rents, eventually led to more government investment into Kazakhfilm Studios. Financing went into specific film projects such as *Nomad* (2005) and into production facilities and new technology at the Studios. This was principally achieved by governmental decree in 2005 which reformed Kazakhfilm into a joint-stock company.[8] The exact amount of expenditure the government put into Kazakhfilm is unclear, but conservative estimates put it at annual $37 million.[9]

Increased government expenditure had a significant impact on the direction of the industry. The most notable effect was the that government, through the Ministry of Culture, has had greater control over the films being produced. Consequently, Kazakhfilm Studios is characterised as working to 'government order, with writers and directors working on themes in accordance with plans written by the Ministry of Culture'.[10] This puts power in the hands of the Minister of Culture and illustrates how cinema is used for ideological purposes.[11] Moreover, with the dearth of private financing, Kazakhfilm remains the central agent in the film industry. Those working at Kazakhfilm argue that, while it is true the Ministry of Culture dictates the topics of films to be produced, Kazakhfilm has control of the creative, developmental and production process.[12] The studios decide which projects are green lighted and which directors are sponsored for work.[13] Moreover, the increased role of the government is not viewed by all as a negative phenomenon. For Darezhan Omirbayev, 'the big advantage of Kazakh cinema is that it still receives government funding ... as there is no expectation or question to return the money.'[14] Given Kazakhstan has such a small market for domestic-produced films (a population of 17 million), government finance can be critical to energising the industry. Moreover, Kazakhfilm works closely in co-productions with private studios based in Shymkent, Astana, Kokshetau, and Almaty as well as working in international co-productions such as *Nomad* (2005) and *Mongol* (2007).[15]

A further impact of greater government investment is the attempt by Kazakhfilm Studios to produce more commercial cinema. In contemporary cinema, directors and their works can be understood under two rubrics: art-house (the successors to the Kazakh New Wave) and commercial. These two rubrics do not neatly correspond to Kazakhfilm only producing commercial cinema and independent studios only producing art-house. The relationship is very fluid. Often indepdent studios seek to produce commercial films, such as Akan Satayev's production company Sataifilm, while Kazakhfilm continue to sponsor the production of art-house cinema such as Emir Baigazin's *Harmony Lessons* (2013), which was also a co-production with German and French companies. A film such as *Nomad*, while a regime-led re-imagining of Kazakh history (more below), was also an attempt to break into the international market. By all accounts it failed. Despite costing $37 million dollars, the film returned $2.4 million from the Russian market and only $19,000 in the United States.[16] Outside of historical blockbusters there has been a commitment to producing more commercial Hollywood-style films such as Akan Satayev's *Liquidator* (2010) and Farkhat Sharipov's *Tale of the Pink Bunny* (2010). Such efforts at commercialisation were not warmly welcomed in all circles, with some critics bemoaning the move towards 'movies about morons for morons, about cops and gangsters'.[17] The shift from the art-house European sensibilities of the 'Kazakh New Wave' towards schematic Hollywood production techniques and thematic motifs were viewed by Sergei Azimov, producer and former Kazakhfilm Studios president, as 'not very positive nor promising'.[18] This characterisation of commercial cinema is perhaps unfair. As discussed in Chapter 7, many commercial films provide alternative imaginaries of Kazakh nationhood and identity to than those put forward by the Ministry of Culture, and because of their commercial nature possess the potential to reach a wider audience, something not always possible with art-house films. Despite Kazakhfilm's efforts of co-producing with private studios, and international co-productions as well as a move towards commercialisation, the regime's involvement with the studios only cemented the perception the government was seeking to use cinema for reasons of political expediency. Cinema became an important political tool for the regime to create a narrative regarding the past and the formation of the nation. Most significantly, however, some films within this narrative are believed to have been initiated directly on the order of Nazarbayev himself. The idea for *Nomad*, for example, was said to have belonged to the president[19] and that the project was under the control of the presidential administration.[20] It exemplifies the importance cinema holds for the president and the broader regime in terms of inculcating a narrative about Kazakhstan's history and nationhood, as well as how we can construe this narrative as being 'official' and regime-sponsored. While *Nomad* is one example, *Sardar* (2003) and *Zhauzhurek Myn Bala* (2011) are also similar efforts to create big blockbuster historical movies with which to instil a regime-approved representation of Kazakh history and national identity.

These films were not the first efforts at developing such ideological historical epics in the post-Soviet period. In the mid-1990s Kazakhfilm Studios produced two historical biopics. *Abai*, released in 1995, told the story of the life and work of the much-celebrated nineteenth-century Kazakh poet Abai Kunanbayev. The film depicts Abai's learning of the customs and traditions of the nomadic population and draws on key elements of Kazakh identity such as the nomads' relationship with the steppe and the veneration of ancestors. The film was directed by Ardak Amirkulov and featured other members of the 'Kazakh New Wave' including Serik Aprymov (as a writer), Yermek Shinarbayev (as producer) and Alexander Baranov (who wrote the screenplay for *The Needle*, as a writer). 1996 saw the release of *The Young Zhambyl*, directed by Kanybek Kasymbekov. The film is a straightforward biopic of the early life of Zhambyl and was released to coincide with 150th anniversary of his birth. *Abai* and *The Young Zhambyl* were estimated to have cost $2 million each, but both were viewed as commercial failures and neither reached a wide audience, partly because of the absence of a comprehensive distribution system.[21] Baurzhan Nogerbek, however, has also suggested their failure was a consequence of 'directors trying to reconcile the irreconcilable: art-house film, folk genres and commercial cinema'.[22] Given that *Abai* was directed by Amirkulov it is perhaps no surprise that it tended towards auteur cinema. Nonetheless, Gulnara Abikeyeva has argued that 'the production of these expensive films crippled the cinema industry.'[23]

Both films are notable for their continuity with Soviet cinema. While they do not possess the revolutionary zeal of Soviet biopics like *Amangeldy* (1938) and *Zhambyl* (1953), these mid-1990s films are reminiscent of state-led projects of the Soviet period in their appeal to national heroes as 'custom created movies about prominent personalities and anniversaries.'[24] This is the view of Adilkhan Yerzhanov who has argued that 'we (Kazakh cinema) are repeating the path of Soviet cinema when directors were just making films on the orders of the government rather than making their own'.[25] Therefore, we can trace a lineage in Kazakh cinema from *Amangeldy*, released in 1939, to *Nomad* and *Zhauzhurek Myn Bala* in the way they represent a regime-led effort to re-interpret and mythologise the Kazakh land, nation and people. Taken together they form a narrative rendering visible an ethno-centric interpretation of the Kazakh nation. It is a nation of ethnic Kazakhs seeking to defend itself from invading foreign forces. It is a narrative that is culturally specific and rooted in processes of political legitimation. The following sections unpack the three elements of this narrative: defence of the homeland, ethnic identity, and personality cult and power.

Defence of the Homeland

Sardar, *Nomad* and *Zhauzhurek Myn Bala* are all set in an approximate time (the eighteenth century) and each feature a plot that focuses on the Kazakh struggle against the Mongolian *Oirat* tribes' invasion of the Kazakh steppe. *Sardar*, released in 2003, concerns two protagonists, Kulzha and Akberdy, who vow to find and release Kulzha's father, imprisoned by *Oirats*. *Nomad*, released in 2005, tells of the coming of age of Ablimansur, his fight against the *Oirats* and his eventual transformation into Ablai Khan, the great Kazakh statesman and warrior of the steppe. In 2011, Kazakhfilm Studios released *Zhauzhurek Myn Bala*, another big-budget historical epic focused on the Kazakhs' struggle against the *Oirats*. The film depicts the struggle of a band of teenagers (The Thousand Warriors) led by the hero of the film, Sartai, who throw off the yoke of the *Oirats* by defeating them at the Battle of Anyrakay in 1729.

Each film represents an effort by the directors, production team and Kazakhfilm Studios to re-interpret a central part of Kazakh history. In doing so they sought the arousal of patriotic feelings, a sense of belonging to the modern Kazakh nation and the education of the masses to Kazakhstan's past, a history obscured by the lens of Soviet rule and censorship. As director Slambek Tauyekel noted:

> we need to find how we are different from other nations. And this process now has a trendy name – self-identification. This is the dilemma now, if to say metaphorically we are sitting in front of a huge mirror naked and studying ourselves. And our goal is to see in this reflection our real image as a nation. We make historical movies not for entertainment of people like they do in Hollywood, our goal is to introduce history to the younger generation and to learn more about ourselves.[26]

Figure 4.1 Asylkhan Tolypov (centre) as Sartai in *Zhauzhurek Myn Bala* (2011), dir. Akan Satayev.

The image of modern Kazakhstan that is imagined in these three films is a nation born through defence of the homeland to ensure it is protected from invading forces. Each film portends to this theme. In the first scene of *Sardar*, younger versions of Kulzha and Akberdy are recounting the Kazakh legend of Sargul, which speaks to the idea of national defence:

> Sargul raised his weapon and cried out 'better to perish in freedom than die in slavery'. Not to protect one's homeland means to lose it and to be condemned to disgrace. Your mother will bless the son expecting victory. The holy Khan Tengri is pinning his hopes on you. I swear by Ushekun, Sargul's voice resonated like a lion roaring and he challenged the hostile batyr, beheaded him and threw his head to the envoy's feet.

The struggle for the homeland was also the opening gambit of *Nomad* – where the ancient link between Kazakhs and the Kazakh steppe is evoked: 'from ancient times the space between the Altai Mountains to the Caspian Sea has been home to my people the Kazakhs. For centuries hordes of enemies have attacked this land leaving only ashes and bones behind. The worst disaster was the invasion of the Dzhungars (*Oirats*)'. And again, in *Zhauzhurek Myn Bala* a similar theme is conjured up at the beginning of the film; however, this time the narrative implies that the Kazakhs' fight against the *Oirats* was akin to the nationalist struggles that appeared in other parts of Europe and the Middle East. As the opening dialogue of the film states:

> the great powers of Europe were torn apart by irreconcilable contradictions: the war for Spanish independence, the Great Northern War and the Middle East that was under the yoke of the Ottoman Empire for 200 years began waking up from two-centuries of hibernation. The time of devastating war also covered Central Asia. Taking advantage of domestic warfare in the once mighty Kazakh Orda, Dzhungar tribes occupied the Kazakh lands. Enemy squads razed all the villages they met in their path.

These opening statements all demonstrate an imagined 'historical' retreat to a specific period of Kazakh history seen as nation-defining.

As we saw in Chapter 1, Kazakhstan in the eighteenth century was under threat from invading armies. It led to the so-called bare-footed flight, which to some extent is depicted in all three films, and the eventual protection of the Russian Empire – leading to the disintegration of the Kazakh Khanate. Modern nationhood, therefore, is defined through these films in relation to the struggle for the motherland and the defence of the nation.

Ingrained from the very beginning of all three films is an innate sense that the Kazakh nation is an ancient primordial one. In *Sardar*, the focus is on the legends of previous Khans and *Batyrs*, in *Nomad* it is shown that for centuries Kazakhs have always lived on the land between the Altai mountains and the Caspian Sea, and in *Zhauzhurek Myn Bala* it is couched in term of venerating the 'mighty Kazakh Orda'. This primordial appeal was not just to 'make people proud to live in Kazakhstan',[27] but also an attempt to draw a line of heritage from the ancient Kazakh Khanate (and even before) through to the battles of the eighteenth century, all the way to the modern post-1991 Kazakh nation. As noted by one reviewer, 'this segment of the country's history is extremely important for the creation of the national state and the historical consciousness of every self-respecting Kazakh'.[28] The imagining of the nation for the present is achieved via several representative signs fundamental to the defence of the homeland narrative.

Firstly, the films seek to instil patriotism in the audience. According to Baurzhan Shukenov, 'by using historic films and praising the best pages of the country's history one can give an audience not just patriotism but also touch the strings of peoples' souls.'[29] *Nomad* was 'intended to awaken in us the patriotic emotions, feelings of admiration for the great feats of ancestors bequeathed to posterity the vast expanses of the native land.'[30] *Zhauzhurek Myn Bala* director Akan Satayev has stated the ideological nature of his film was deliberate:

> initially, when we were discussing the project with Kazakhfilm, we stressed that it was not a commercial project, but an ideological project. We said straightaway that the budget was huge and it would not be possible to make it profitable in Kazakhstan, the question was not about the profitability of the movie, but rather about the ideology, about the fact that we should know our history of the 18th century.[31]

The patriotic appeal comes in two forms in these three films. Firstly, the films promote the Kazakh *batyr* (hero). As we saw in Chapters 1 and 2, the Soviet authorities were deliberate in their use of so-called red *batyrs* in the promotion of ethnic Kazakh national identity.[32] This was translated onto the screen in films such as *Amangeldy* and *Zhambyl*. These were national-patriotic figures that citizens could rally around because of their selfless guile and love for the Kazakh people and motherland. In this respect, *Sardar*, *Nomad* and *Zhauzhurek Myn Bala* are very alike to Soviet-era films. At the beginning of *Sardar*, Akberdy asks Kulzha, 'where are the *batyrs* now?' Their lament for the lack of heroes to defend the homeland against the *Oirats* spurs them on to become proud warriors defending the Kazakh steppe. In *Nomad*, Ablai Khan is a constructed as the national *batyr*: a figure to unite all Kazakhs, a strong warrior who will protect the Kazakh people and their land. Ablai Khan has become central to the nation-building process in Kazakhstan. Nearly every major city and town in the country has a street named after him.

Secondly, the positioning of Ablai Khan in *Nomad* demonstrates how the patriotic appeal of the narrative is also concerned with unity. As discussed in Chapter 1, the Kazakh *zhuz* which constituted the Kazakh Khanate, possessed a tendency towards discord. In the post-Soviet period, the potential for disunity exists in relation to the multi-ethnic demographic of the country and its geographic position vis-à-vis Russia and China. In *Nomad*, we see unity take shape when an army of Kazakhs from across the steppe stand to Ablai Khan's attention; their swords held high, pledging allegiance to the new national *batyr*. But the historical setting is loaded with contemporary relevance, especially in relation to the country's tenuous position in the world. Like Ablai Khan, Nazarbayev has put much stall in his leadership offering unity and stability by using a 'multi-vector' foreign policy which navigates the threats and interests of China and Russia.[33] One scene in *Nomad* encapsulates this perfectly. Ablai Khan's teacher, Oraz, takes his army of young Kazakh children to a sacred tree where he asks them to pray to their nomadic ancestors to protect them from the 'fire spinning dragon' in the East (China) and the grizzly country in the figure of a bear in the West (Russia). Oraz explains there is only one answer to meet this dual threat and that is via unity because 'where there is no unity, there is no security'. In modern parlance, the implication is that unity needs to be built around Nazarbayev. One deputy from the president's party suggested, the country's future success was dependent upon everyone uniting around the president, arguing that, 'if everything is united, people, party and president then we will be able to build a really good future for Kazakhstan'.[34] Therefore, the film, while providing a depiction of the past regarding Kazakhstan's position between Russia and China, and the need for unity to ensure the country's security between these powers, also reflects Kazakhstan's regional position in the post-Soviet period.

Thirdly, these three films turn on a specific re-interpretation of history. Whereas the historical films of the 'Kazakh New Wave' sought to tackle the silences of Kazakh history, or negate Soviet authority, the films in the contemporary ethnic narrative provide a mythologisation of the past to legitimate the authority of the present. In the case of *Nomad*, Gulnara Abikeyeva has argued the film's retelling 'is not a historical drama where the characters are authentic and the time, place and action are accurate. Rather here we are dealing with pure mythology'.[35] Interestingly, this criticism concerning mythologisation is focused less on the fact of mythology itself, and more that the mythology was not Kazakh enough. Abikeyeva and other critics have pointed to the structure of *Nomad* being based upon an American template (the hero prepares, suffers, is tested and eventually wins) – meaning the 'era and geography are only important as a setting',[36] creating a 'sterile westernised action-film'[37] that does 'not depict the familiar folklore and historical image of Ablai Khan and was rather a love story with a pure Hollywood stamping'.[38]

Figure 4.2 Jay Hernandez as Ablai Khan in *Nomad* (2005), dir. Sergei Bodrov, Ivan Passer and Talgat Temenov.

That *Nomad* should be observed as being historically off-piste reflects the different production contexts of each film. While each purports the same narrative regarding nationhood and identity, and each was sponsored by Kazakhfilm Studios, there are differences with production, the broader purpose and intended audiences. *Sardar* was financed with just $1 million and initially was intended to be a co-production with the Chinese Tien Shan studio, but the contract was never followed through.[39] The film followed the earlier efforts in the 1990s of Kazakhfilm Studios (with films such as *Abai* and *The Youth of Zhambyl*) to push for a wider domestic audience and to move away from a reliance on the art-house movies of the 'Kazakh New Wave'. As Bolat Kalymbetov noted in an interview, 'from the beginning, it was conceived as a film for the people ... the idea to make a "movie for the viewers" came after criticism of modern Kazakh filmmakers, including me ... Then I asked myself, "why do we have so few films for a mass audience?" Thus, was born *Sardar*.'[40] However, *Sardar*'s budget was too small to make it an effective historical epic that could capture the public's imagination.[41]

Consequently, a different strategy was utilised for *Nomad*, which received a larger budget of $37 million.[42] Without a mass audience with which to claw back the movie's financing, attention shifted to attracting an international audience for promoting Kazakh cinematography as a potential co-producer in future global cinematic projects. The production team, therefore, was international. The screenplay was written by Azerbaijani Rustam Ibragimbekov, it was co-directed by Czech-born Ivan Passer, Russian Sergei Bodrov and Talgat Temenov, and the Executive Producer was Miloš Forman. The film was also distributed overseas through Miramax. Many of the lead roles in the film were also non-Kazakh. Ablai Khan was played by Mexican actor Kuno Becker, Erali by American Jay Hernandez, Oraz by Jason Scott Lee, while American actors Mark Dacascos and Archie Kao played key *Oirat* characters.

Zhauzhurek Myn Bala was an attempt to return to the educational aims of historical movies and to introduce Kazakh history to a younger audience. The budget at an estimated $10 million was significantly less than *Nomad*. The film was directed by Akan Satayev, who had made a name for himself with his 2007 independently produced film *Racketeer*, which was a gritty picture depicting the economic difficulties and moral

Ethno-Centric Narrative of Kazakh Nationhood   135

dilemmas of post-Soviet Almaty life (see Chapter 7). His drafting in by the Ministry of Culture and Kazakhfilm Studios as director for *Zhauzhurek Myn Bala* led some critics to suggest Satayev was constrained as a real artist by taking on a film on the orders of the government.[43] Nonetheless, Satayev's role in directing such a big regime-sponsored picture, while also producing other work such as *Racketeer* and *Strayed* (2009), which offer a very different imagining of the Kazakh nation, illustrates the fluid nature of cinematic production in the country and the way in which directors, writers and producers can cut across different narratives. *Zhauzhurek Myn Bala* was a Kazakh domestic production between Kazakhfilm Studios and Satayev's company Sataifilm. Using unknown young Kazakh actors, the film was perceived to have the desired effect in terms of its ideological objective. It was noted for being 'really patriotic and emotional. It is intended to awaken in the hearts of young Kazakhs, regardless of nationality and other characteristics, the feeling of love and devotion to the country, as well as awareness of how difficult it was to give us our independence.'[44]

Despite their differing production contexts, all three films demonstrate how the authorities have attempted to establish a foundation myth, in their depiction of the eighteenth-century struggle against the *Oirats*, as a starting point for the beginning of the modern Kazakh nation. They aim to portray the destiny of the Kazakh nation and how it was born through the struggles and suffering endured by ancestors. This is a foundation story which is also underpinned by an exclusive ethnic representation of identity, to which attention now turns.

Ethnic Identity

Sardar, *Nomad* and *Zhauzhurek Myn Bala* all feature similar symbols constituting a series of signs amounting to an ascription of ethnic Kazakh identity. The representation of these culturally inflected signs is nothing new to Kazakh cinema. Indeed, across all three films we can observe cinematic echoes of the past. Aside from technological advancement, these three films share similar tropes with the representation of Kazakh ethnic identity presented in Soviet era cinema. The representation of ethnic identity can be observed in relation to three themes: *aul* life, landscape and language.

Aul Life

Each film provides a representation of traditional *aul* life. In a very early scene in *Sardar* we see yurts, traditional Kazakh dress, elders taking council and one young woman, Kunash, signing a Kazakh folk song to the strains of the dombra. This is familiar to a scene from *Amangeldy* (see Chapter 1) where Amangeldy is sitting in a yurt playing the dombra, singing while a woman dances. It also like the key ethnographic scene in *My Name is Kozha* where we move from the 'Soviet' to the 'Kazakh' world. We see the bustle of *aul* life and the small pleasures in the traditional lived way of the nomadic population. The depiction of *auls* is central to both *Nomad* and *Zhauzhurek Myn Bala*. In a very early scene in *Nomad* we are witness to the peaceful life of the Kazakhs on the steppe. Yurts sit, chimneys quietly smoking, while livestock mills near-by. All of this is set against the backdrop of the effervescent steppe. This cuts to a scene where *aul* life has been disturbed. Flames tear down the yurts and smoke fills the screen as *Oirats* on horseback slaughter the pastoral Kazakhs. This one scene sets up the premise of the film. The peaceful nomadic way of life for Kazakhs is at threat from foreign invaders. By burning the *aul* and attacking the serene existence of the nomadic population, the *Oirats* are destroying the essence of Kazakh cultural identity. Only through defence and unity can Kazakhs restore their way of life. *Zhauzhurek Myn Bala* features an almost identical scene at the beginning of the film. Peaceful *aul* life is attacked by *Oirats*, who burn down the village and slaughter Kazakhs. It is witnessing this attack that inflames Sartai and his friends who resolve to revolt against the *Oirats* and defend the Kazakh homeland.

A great deal of attention went into the recreation of *aul* life, its traditions, customs and especially clothing, as they are viewed as central to Kazakh identity. In *Nomad* and *Zhauzhurek Myn Bala* male characters are donned in the finest and most colourful *Shapans* (a long dressing gown) and *Kalpaks* (hats), while female characters adorn headdresses dependent upon their social position. For Akan Satayev, the *aul* life, with its traditions and customs is the epitome of Kazakh life – the vivid portrayal of which 'carries the mentality of the nation'.[45] *Nomad* utilised over 250 experts in its attempt to carefully recreate the tents, dress, battles scenes, traditions and customs of life in the steppe in the eighteenth century.[46] Rustam Ibragimbekov, screen writer for *Nomad*, has noted that the uniqueness of Kazakhstan is in the 'protection of national customs and traditions and this applies to features such as the kitchen, family life and architecture' – all of which are depicted via *aul* life in these films.[47] In *Nomad*, we see the traditional game of Kokpar being played at Oraz's training camp.[48] In *Zhauzhurek Myn Bala* we are treated to the local pastime of young boys coming from different *auls* to wrestle each other (Sartai emerges victorious). It is a scene almost lifted directly from *My Name is Kozha*. When Kozha entered the 'Kazakh' world of the *aul* he participates in a wrestling match, and like Sartai, eventually overcomes his opponent. The films rely on the same ethnic motifs and symbols used by directors during the Soviet period. It is no wonder a review of *Nomad* noted that 'Kazakhstani cinema is in a hard rut of ethnographism and exoticism.'[49]

This appeal to these traditions and customs has been likened to a form of 'nomadic nationhood'.[50] Yet, in these films, and in many cinematic representations of the nomadic way of life in Kazakhstan we rarely see the process of migration. One of the most important aspects of nomadism – the journey – the seasonal search for new pasture – is often absent. In *Sardar*, following the destruction of the *aul* at the beginning of the film we witness the migration of Kazakhs from their land, providing a cinematic account of the 'barefooted flight'.[51] Horses and camels are loaded up, a migratory caravan trundles across the screen, while a pregnant woman is carried in a large basket. The scene enforces the depiction of the struggle of the fleeing Kazakhs. Yet, it does not portray the ordinary form of nomadic migration; it is the exceptional situation of forced displacement. We do see the erecting of yurts in the final scene of *Zhauzhurek Myn Bala* after the Kazakhs are victorious in the battle of Anyrakay. This portrayal represents the re-building of the Kazakh nation after the war. The construction of the yurt is a metaphor for nation-building in Kazakhstan. Text appears on the screen over a distant shot of the half-finished yurts stating that victory at Anyrakay marked a new era for Kazakhs' 'struggle for independence and freedom', yet 'only after three centuries did Kazakhstan gain its true independence' and then it places Nazarbayev's role for nation-building front and centre as 'the Kazakh nation was led to the historic victory which our ancestors dreamed of by the leader of the nation, N.A. Nazarbayev.' As we will see below, it is evidence of the way in which representations of the past are used for legitimising the politics of the present.

Landscape

Landscape is another cultural trope inherent in these films. The vast Kazakh steppe and its sumptuous beauty is an easy motif with which to express a distinct Kazakh national identity. Indeed, it is the land, the endless steppe, that is being physically defended. Therefore, the steppe is central to the inner psychological relationship between nomadism and the land. Each film utilises the steppe as the character of the Kazakh nation. *Sardar* is perhaps less successful in this respect. With a much smaller budget than *Nomad* or *Zhauzhurek Myn Bala*, much of *Sardar* is shot in the impressive but more closed-in Charyn Canyon, an 80-kilometre canyon close to the Chinese border. With larger budgets, *Nomad* and *Zhauzhurek Myn Bala* offer sweeping panoramic shots of the steppe. Yet, they remain familiar and clichéd.[52] The utilisation of the steppe in both *Nomad* and *Zhauzhurek Myn Bala* recalls its appearance in *Amangeldy*, while recurrent shots of riders bounding over the landscape were clearly inspired by *Kyz Zhibek*.

The steppe is used in these films to represent the space of Kazakhstan; and its openness and almost borderless nature. It epitomises the country's position as the crossroads of the Eurasian continent. In *Nomad* and *Zhauzhurek Myn Bala*, the beauty of the steppe in its vastness is also presented as its weakness. Kazakhs do not have natural defences with which to repel the invading *Oirats*. Nonetheless, the steppe is represented as life affirming; the motherland all Kazakhs must defend. International film critics praised the epic depiction and the breathtaking vistas of the landscape, especially Satayev's *Zhauzhurek Myn Bala*.[53] For director Akhat Ibrayev, the steppe is used in this way to 'make it mystical and to wow European audiences', rather than to demonstrate the essence of Kazakh-ness.[54] Indeed, Satayev is acutely aware that the landscape is not necessarily imbued with properties that make it distinctly Kazakh. Rather, the steppe must be placed in the context of other national signs that, when added together, create a specific Kazakh national representation.[55] One complementary sign which contextualises the steppe is the Kazakh language.

Language

For primordialists any construction of a specific national identity based on a bounded ethnic group has to rely on a shared language.[56] Differently put, human populations are only able to become emotionally attached to ethnic ascriptions if they are able to absorb information via shared communicative equipment.[57] The use of language within *Sardar*, *Nomad* and *Zhauzhurek Myn Bala* reveals the complexity behind attempting to cinematically present an ethnically exclusive account of Kazakh nationhood and identity, especially in relation to the Russian and Soviet legacy and the constraints of the global cinema industry.

Sardar and *Zhauzhurek Myn Bala* are more straightforward than *Nomad* when it comes to language. Both were filmed in the Kazakh language using Kazakh actors. Therefore, the signs of Kazakh ethnicity highlighted above, and the background of the steppe, are made distinctly Kazakh by using the Kazakh language. However, in terms of the audience, the consensus amongst figures within the cinema industry is that there remains a divide between Kazakh- and Russian-speaking audiences.[58] This is not a simple binary division between Kazakhs and Russians, rather there is also a significant element of the population, typically urbanite and whose formative years were during the Soviet period, who are Kazakh but non-Kazakh-speaking. For a Kazakh-language film to be commercially successful it often includes a dubbed Russian version. The issue of language also affects the depth and quality of the Kazakh film industry. For Baurzhan Shukenov, 'it is very problematic since there are very few people who professionally know the language'.[59] This in turn, according to Shukenov, creates a problem with audience numbers as 'popular actors, whom people would like to see, cannot act in the Kazakh language'.[60] For others in the industry, however, language is straightforward – according to Zhanna Isabayeva, 'it all depends, if you make a film about history in the city, then you would make the film in Russian ... if you make a film about an *aul*, you don't have the choice to make it in Russian since even in *auls* even Russians speak Kazakh'.[61] Therefore, the use of a particular language is often driven by efforts to capture authenticity. This is the case with many contemporary cinematic works (several of which are discussed in Chapter 7), but also films which re-imagine history such as *Sardar* and *Zhauzhurek Myn Bala*. The use of Kazakh language for these films is central to their ability to offer a representation of Kazakh nationhood and identity which is clearly Kazakh and not clouded by the experience of 250 years of Russian and Soviet rule. However, the fact that there may not be a large enough audience of Kazakh speakers for this to be effective – so much so the films needed to be presented dubbed in

Russian – serves to demonstrate the difficulty in cinematically representing a widely intelligible construction of an ethnic and cultural Kazakh identity.

Nomad is more problematic with regards to language. As noted above, while pertaining towards ethnic exclusivity, the film featured non-Kazakh, English-speaking actors in lead roles. During filming those actors spoke in English while Kazakh-speaking actors responded in Kazakh. Russian and Kazakh were then dubbed over the English-speaking actors. Therefore, a mostly dubbed Kazakh and Russian version was released domestically in Kazakhstan, while the international release had English layered over the dubbed Kazakh language – rather than the original English audio spoken by the actors. Clearly, having both non-Kazakh actors in lead roles alongside having to dub the titular language over the original dialogue does not present the viewer with an overly confident representation of an exclusive ethnic identity. But the film was only partially for domestic consumption. *Nomad*, therefore, needs to be understood in relation to its position within the global cinematic context. While the film was an attempt by Nazarbayev, the Ministry of Culture and Kazakhfilm Studios to 'to make a genuinely patriotic film and strengthen national consciousness within Kazakhstan',[62] it was also intended for an international audience, an 'image-making', nation-branding exercise aimed at introducing the world to Kazakhstan[63] and to bolster the international image of Nazarbayev.[64] The use of non-Kazakh, English-speaking 'star' actors, as well as the international production team (and being a co-production with the French company Wild Bunch) was driven by the desire for the film to connect internationally. However, in doing so, especially in relation to the muddled and complex use of language between actors and different presentations of the film depending on the market, the film only served to undermine the appeal to patriotism.

Problems with an Ethno-centric Account in *Sardar*, *Nomad* and *Zhauzhurek Myn Bala*

Despite offering distinct representations of Kazakh ethnic identity, *Sardar*, *Nomad* and *Zhauzhurek Myn Bala* encountered significant problems in doing so – albeit in different ways. *Nomad* was perhaps the most problematic in this respect. *Nomad*'s characterisation of Kazakh ethnicity and mentality was considered by domestic reviewers to be undermined by using non-Kazakh actors. According to one reviewer, 'perhaps in the eyes of Talgat Temenov and Sergei Azimov, Kuno Becker looked like Ablai Khan, but for the spectators, including for us ... we have not seen the generosity of steppe peoples, and the authoritativeness, dignity and wisdom inherent in the genuine Ablai Khan. This role was quite beyond the power of Kuno Becker, who despite his talent, is not suited for it'.[65] For Baurzhan Nogerbek, Ibragimbekov's script failed to demonstrate the customs of the Kazakh people and the Kazakh mentality.[66] Additionally, it was felt by another reviewer that the film's use of familiar and traditional Soviet-era tropes of patriotism failed, revealing that 'there is an urgent need to re-interpret our domestic patriotism'.[67] The international reception of *Nomad* was also complicated by its international release coinciding with the release of Sacha Baron Cohen's *Borat: Cultural Learnings of America for Make Benefit Glorious Nation of Kazakhstan* (2006).[68] The British comic's absurdist character, Kazakh journalist Borat Sagdiyev, became the immediate lens through which international audiences unfamiliar with Kazakhstan saw the country, not the historical, sweeping-epic of Ablai Khan. Therefore, despite Nazarbayev wanting to see on the big screen a blockbuster that would advertise Kazakhstan, its people and history,[69] *Nomad* failed to present a clear sense of Kazakh identity to the world.[70]

The ethnic ascription of *Sardar* and *Zhauzhurek Myn Bala* were also observed to be undermined by their universalism. It has already been noted that *Sardar* struggled to offer a sweeping historical epic story because of budget limitations, and this led the director to fall back on a script that focused on the universal themes of 'love, jealousy and betrayal',[71] rather than historical accuracy.[72] The plot of *Zhauzhurek Myn Bala* was argued to revolve on a very simple and ubiquitous threat, as one reviewer notes, 'a child sees his parents killed, he firmly decides to take revenge, there is a love story, there is a conflict between the protagonist and his friend who goes over to the dark side, the rehabilitation of the hero, another penance and the final battle.'[73] The plot was perceived as interchangeable by one reviewer who suggested, 'switch the costumes and their stirring portrait of a raggle-taggle bandit army rising up against brutal imperial oppressors and it could equally apply to Robin Hood, the French Resistance, even Star Wars. There certainly are echoes of Luke Skywalker in Sartai's childhood backstory.'[74] The universality of the plot saw the film compared to big

Hollywood blockbusters *300*[75] and *Braveheart*[76], while local critic Oleg Boretskiy considered the film to be little more than 'light entertainment'.[77] Nonetheless, despite these criticisms, the film received positive press in Kazakhstan[78] and was a hit taking $2.5 million at the Kazakh box office in its first two months of release – breaking all existing domestic box office records.[79] *Zhauzhurek Myn Bala* was then understood by international journalists to be the counter-punch to Borat, the film that would show the world the 'real' Kazakhstan, succeeding hopefully where *Nomad* had failed.[80] Nonetheless, the film's lacklustre performance in international markets, as well as its failure to be selected for the best foreign film at the 2012 Oscars, indicates that if the film was specifically intend to show the world the 'real' Kazakhstan, then it seems the effort went largely unnoticed.

In *Sardar*, *Nomad* and *Zhauzhurek Myn Bala*, landscape and language provide a semi-coherent narrative in relation to an exclusive Kazakh national identity through their depiction of *aul* life. It is only semi-coherent because it is undermined by the complexity of language in Kazakhstan, and the global context in which some of the films were produced, especially *Nomad*, and the extent to which they rely on universal Hollywood tropes, as well as draw on the long lineage of the Soviet custom-made historical movies. This ethnic narrative, however, also serves a larger purpose, which concerns the legitimation of the Nazarbayev regime.

Power and Regime Legitimation

In her excellent historical analysis of *Nomad*, Saulesh Yessenova explains in detail the mismatch between the historically recorded account of Ablai Khan and his mythologisation in the film. Yessenova argues that *Nomad* provides a sanitised account of Ablai Khan, which overlooks the transgressive nature of his leadership. Drawing on Yessenberlin's novel, Yessenova portrays Ablai Khan as a 'gifted politician and a committed leader' who was also 'a cruel and insecure man who used his power and sword against his enemy as much as against his own people.'[81] The question Yessenova poses is why was Ablai Khan chosen for the film given the ambiguous nature of his leadership? The picture was ultimately an attempt to show modern-day Kazakhstan in a positive light – but Nazarbayev's close involvement in the film led to suggestions he wanted to draw an analogy between himself and Ablai Khan – albeit with the historical reality of Ablai Khan's true character removed.[82] Ablai Khan's achievement within the film of defending the homeland and ensuring unity of all Kazakhs could be construed as the same message Nazarbayev wished to convey for contemporary Kazakh politics. Kazakhstan is a demographically multi-ethnic country, which, through much of the 1990s (and to an extent in the present post-Russian annexation of Crimea period), lived in danger of Russian revanchism. The subtext of *Nomad*, as we have already seen, suggests that if the country unites behind a strong leader then there will be security. Therefore, it can be read that Ablai Khan was that leader in the past and Nazarbayev that leader for the present. *Nomad*, and much of the ethnocentrist narrative, therefore, is directed towards legitimising Nazarbayev's leadership as much as it is to offering a specific account of Kazakh nation-building and identity. This much we know because of the president's close involvement in *Nomad* and *Zhauzhurek Myn Bala* and his government's support of Kazakhfilm Studios.

Nowhere was this cinematic process of regime legitimation more evident than in the films dedicated to the story of Nazarbayev's life. *The Way of the Leader* is a series of five films released over a five-year period depicting Nazarbayev's childhood, youth and gradual rise to power. *Sky of My Childhood* (2011), *River of Fire* (2013), *Iron Mountain* (2013) and *Breaking the Vicious Circle* (2015) were all directed by Rustam Abdrashev, who had won acclaim for his early films *Renaissance Island* (2004), *Kurak Korpe* (2007) and *The Gift to Stalin* (2008). After the release of *Breaking the Vicious Circle*, Abdrashev took on directing duties for a ten-part TV series on the Kazakh Khanate led by the Ministry of Culture (which was supposed to be released to coincide with the 550th anniversary of Kazakhstan's statehood in 2015 – but was delayed until the autumn of 2016). In place of Rustam Abdrashev, Russian director Sergei Snezhkin took the helm for the fifth film, *So There Were Stars* (2016).

The initial reaction upon the release of *Sky of My Childhood*, especially from international film reviewers, was to treat it as another piece of the Nazarbayev personality cult jigsaw puzzle.[83] However, the film series is not just the story of the president's life but also the story of the birth of the modern Kazakh nation. This is achieved by the director in two ways. The first is to associate Nazarbayev with an old Kazakh figure from the time of the formation of the Kazakh Khanate, Asan Kaigy, who was thought to be an advisor to Zhanybek and Kerey Khan and who was charged with finding land for the Kazakh tribes to settle. This is confirmed by the director, who has said of *Sky of My Childhood* that:

> it is a story of young boy, but there is a fictitious character of a hunter on a white camel who is teaching him how to hunt with an eagle. His name is Asan, in Kazakh mythology there is such a character Asan Kaigy. In the period of the formation of Kazakh Khanate he was riding on a white camel on the steppes and was searching for the promised land for his people. So, this is a dream of the nation for our free territory and own statehood.[84]

In connecting Nazarbayev with Asan, the film seeks to establish an imagined link between the time of the Kazakh Khanate, the progenitor of the Kazakh state, and the formation of the modern Kazakh state. The 'old man is the link with the past and history, so this archetype of the hunter is the character of a hero that finds a chosen one who should accomplish his mission.'[85] In the film, Asan teaches young Sultan how to hunt with an eagle.[86] Independence was just a dream for Asan, only made realisable by the hard work of Nazarbayev. In the series of films, therefore, Nazarbayev is positioned as the man of destiny for Kazakhstan, the chosen one, the man with all the right qualities to lead the nation to the promised land of independence. Even the depiction of his birth in the film portends as a quasi-mythical divine conception. This is realised in a scene where his parents, after initially struggling to conceive, attend an ancient ritual at the Mazar of the eighteenth-century Kazakh leader Raiymbek Batyr. After this Sultan arrives and his birth is greeted by his parents and village elders in religious overtones ('heavenly blessings') and by spiritual omens (a shooting star).[87]

Nazarbayev is less than subtly imbued with the characteristics of greatness in *Sky of My Childhood*. He is an accomplished dombra player, wins horse races against adults, recites poetry, makes all the right decisions and respects his elders.[88] He is portrayed as an almost picture-perfect man – the man who would eventually lead Kazakhstan into the brightest future.

The second link between Nazarbayev and the Kazakh nation is expressed by dovetailing Nazarbayev's progression from childhood to adulthood with that of Kazakhstan's history from Soviet offspring to

Ethno-Centric Narrative of Kazakh Nationhood 145

Figure 4.3 Eljas Alpiev as the young Sultan in *Sky of My Childhood* (2011), dir. Rustem Abdrashev.

fully fledged post-Soviet nation. *Sky of My Childhood* portrays the multi-ethnic demographic changes that Soviet rule brought to the Kazakh steppe and *aul* life. *River of Fire* and *Iron Mountain* emphasise the modernising force of education (Nazarbayev trains in metallurgy at the steel plant in Temirtau, Karaganda, as well as being sent to Kamianske in Ukraine for training too), but also, with its persistent and beautifully crafted shots of the raw power of the steel-making process, the films evoke how modern Kazakhstan, like Nazarbayev, was made in the searing heat of the blast furnace of steel plants like Temirtau. Over shots of his motorcade driving past modern-day Temirtau, the real Nazarbayev explains at the beginning of *Fire River* that:

> my generation can rightly be called a steel generation and not only because we have built a factory and melted metal. This generation of people have a character of steel, with an unbending will and determination. These qualities allow us, despite all difficulties, to solve the challenges, conquer all peaks and pass the river of fire.

The message is clear. As much as modern-day Kazakhstan was fashioned in the steel works of the Soviet period, so was the character of the president. The formative experience of both Nazarbayev and the nation ensured he had been tested by fire and was ready for the difficult problems of post-Soviet nationhood. If not to make the connection between Nazarbayev and the nation any more obvious, the final shots of *Iron Mountain* give us an eagle-eyed view of modern-day Astana – a new, pristine city of steel; steel burnt in the furnaces of Temirtau, but made reality through the vision of the president. If we were unsure of the extent to which Astana was the vision of the president, a scene in *Sky of My Childhood* reassures the audience. Young Sultan is shown playing with rocks on a mountain-side and subsequently constructs a model city out of stones which looks remarkably like Astana.[89]

In providing a portrayal of the president's life so closely entwined with the story of the nation, the films are an attempt to legitimise Nazarbayev's power. The scripts were written under the guidance of the president himself[90] and based on several of his autobiographical works, including *Without Right and Left*, *The Epicentre of Peace* and *In the Centre of Eurasia*.[91] Thus, his close association to the production of the films (they were produced and released by Kazakhfilm Studios) indicates they were made with one eye on his legacy. Differently put, this cinematic representation is the official version of his rise to leadership and how he would like to be remembered and revered. The films are about elevating Nazarbayev to the status of a new Kazakh *batyr*. As Abdrashev emphasises:

> this is the story of the roots of our independence ... through obstacles he faced and the system he was living in he chose the way through and he became the hero and leader. He became a worker first, and then a party member, then a big public figure in the Soviet system, but the system itself gave birth to him. But the seed of the desire to be free was growing inside this boy and around him. This is a new myth about our independence, but based on factual truth and with a real character. The hero is not invented and the biography is real.[92]

As we will see in the following chapter, these films straddle both the ethno-centric and the civic narratives. While this is the case,

Sky of My Childhood still provides a clear depiction of Kazakh identity. Symbolically, this is realised via key objects which represent Kazakhness, including: horses, yurts, the steppe, Islam, the fable of Bayterek and Samruk,[93] veneration of ancestors, nomadism, the dombra and Kokpar.[94] Moreover, like *Sardar, Nomad* and *Zhauzhurek Myn Bala*, *Sky of My Childhood* also provides an account of Kazakh identity through its depiction of *aul* life, language and landscape. The first hour of the film shows young Sultan growing up in the mountains in the wilderness – living in a yurt and being socialised into the practices of pastoralism. There are stunning picture-postcard shots of the beautiful Kazakh landscape and lingering shots of teams of horses running across the steppe. The film also returns to some elements of Kazakh Soviet poetic cinema with its 'slow pacing and quiet tone, and its ethnographic focus on folklore, everyday life, kinship, and the landscape'.[95] However, the *Way of the Leader* series also marks a return to the cinematic representation of distinct 'Kazakh' and 'Soviet' worlds. This time, however, the transition from one world to the other is reversed from how it appeared in *My Name is Kozha*. In *Sky of My Childhood*, the Kazakh world is in the mountains in the early years of Nazarbayev's life – the peaceful and pastoral life of Kazakh nomads living in yurts speaking the Kazakh language and venerating and remembering seven generations of ancestors. The 'Soviet' world only comes into view once Sultan and his family move back down from the mountain to the village of Chemolgan (now called Ushkonyr). Sultan is exposed to other nationalities and learns Russian in school. *River of Fire, Iron Mountain* and *Breaking the Vicious Circle* are all set in the 'Soviet' world as they depict Nazarbayev's steady rise from steel plant worker to communist apparatchik. The 'Soviet' world is characterised by modernisation, industry and interethnic relations. The 'Kazakh' world creeps through, however, by way of old photographs and visits to the family. Or by the often-present dombra – and occasional bouts of folk singing, which boosts morale of the Kazakh workers at Temirtau. In this sense, there is more interaction between the two worlds than in the cinema of the 1960s.

The role of Nazarbayev is crucial in these films for what it says about modern Kazakh national identity. The films demonstrate that Nazarbayev has lived through and in both worlds. He is shaped by both. Therefore, he is best positioned to negotiate the coming together of these two worlds in the post-Soviet period. Nonetheless, that there is a return to the Soviet tropes of cinematic representation of identity in the *Way of the Leader* series illustrates how the post-Soviet leadership in Kazakhstan is reliant on Soviet methods to engender broader social attachment to its official representations of identities. Just as the Soviets utilised custom-made government ordered films to promote the virtues of heroes who epitomised the spirit of the Kazakh proletariat, *The Way of the Leader* series applies the same method to the case of Nazarbayev.

Reception

The final question to address in this chapter is how has the appeal to patriotism been received by the Kazakh audience? Do the ethno-nationalist themes of defence of the motherland, the appeal to a culturally exclusive Kazakh identity and the position of Nazarbayev resonate with audiences? Or is it viewed as propaganda perpetuated by the government?

Broadly speaking, *Nomad* and *Zhauzhurek Myn Bala* are two of the most watched films in Kazakhstan. This should not be surprising given they were sponsored and heavily promoted by the Ministry of Culture. Across the three focus groups and the kino.kz forum there were extensive comments on these films.[96] As these films also dominate the ethno-centric narrative, it should be possible to get more of a definitive sense of audience reception to these films (albeit not complete) especially compared to other contemporary films which have had a much smaller domestic audience. As to be expected with any cinematic work, the reaction to these films amongst the domestic audience was mixed with an equal balance between positive and negative responses. Nonetheless, to get a qualitative sense of audience reception it is best to draw out a few themes that emerged as part of this mixed response.

Firstly, *Nomad* and *Zhauzhurek Myn Bala* were largely observed as entertainment films that were an attempt to replicate the Hollywood model of cinematography. For example, one member of a focus group commented on *Zhauzhurek Myn Bala* that they 'watched it as entertainment and not for national ideas',[97] while others appreciated the production values noting that they 'really loved the costumes and sets and everything. I don't know who was the designer but for the first time I loved costumes from this kind of historical movie.'[98] One commentator on kino.kz confirms this, noting that 'the film is very good and to international standards'.[99] This led some viewers to 'feel proud of the domestic film industry'[100] for being capable of producing a film of such quality. Likewise, with *Nomad* there was a sense from audience members that it was a good example of Kazakhs being able to create good movies albeit 'with the involvement of Hollywood actors'.[101] And, moreover, there was praise for Nazarbayev for supporting *Nomad*, as one commentator states, 'in the end, we must thank the ideological mastermind of the film, the President of Kazakhstan, Nursultan Nazarbayev, and his support of our cinematography because it is the first steps towards Kazakhstan in Hollywood.'[102]

Secondly, *Nomad* attracted the most criticism and this rested predominantly on the use of non-Kazakh actors in Kazakh roles which, in turn undermined the ability of the film to represent a perceived Kazakh mentality. One focus group participant alluded to this noting that, 'the screenwriter Ibragimbekov could not metaphysically show in the first scenes of the movie the context we are talking about. This context was shown in the scene where this American actor is riding a horse and thinking about who the Kazakhs are, but this is a foreigner's representation'.[103] The use of non-Kazakh actors was widely received to be problematic amongst the reviewers on kino.kz. A selection of comments revealed this: 'oh, horror, the horror! The film is weak; I am sorry for the time spent on it. A Latino appearing in the title role is generally a nightmare;'[104] 'I do not like the two actors, one feels that they are so far removed from the concept of Eurasianism ... put Suimenkul Chokmorov in the role of Don Corleone in *The Godfather* and then we can understand the absurdity of Kuno Becker as the choice for the role of Ablai Khan!';[105] 'it's a bad film, not in the spirit of the Kazakh people, why was it necessary to invite Mark Dacascos, if they wanted to attract the attention of Western audiences, they forgot about the Russian audience. I was not happy to see our American film even Ablai himself was played by an American'.[106] Indeed, the use of foreign actors saw one reviewer note that '*Nomad* joins the piggy bank of failures of custom made movies'.[107] Arguably, therefore, *Nomad* failed to generate widespread patriotism. The ethno-centric appeal was undermined by the film's efforts to break into the international market.

Thirdly, *Zhauzhurek Myn Bala* was more successful in this respect and evidence suggests that some portion of the audience bought into the patriotic narrative pivoted on defence of the homeland, ethnic identity and especially the appeal to history. One focus group participant indicated this noting, 'the audience is used to coming to watch Kazakh films and being disappointed, but this time there were a lot of young people and they were reacting quite positively. They were applauding.'[108] Comments on kino.kz support this claim, with one reviewer noting, 'young people gave their lives for the Motherland! We must live worthy lives so the feat of our ancestors was not in vain',[109] while another stated, 'I enjoyed the native landscapes, native music, native speech, the Kazakh embroidered carpets and clothes, it opened my national self-identity.[110] Another proclaims, 'the film is very patriotic! From the beginning of the film I had tears streaming down my face.'[111] A scrawl through the 54 pages of comments for *Zhauzhurek Myn Bala* on kino.kz will find many more such comments. Therefore, the appeal to Kazakh-ness is acutely understood by the audience.

Fourthly, focus group members were less endowed with the patriotic sentiment of *Zhauzhurek Myn Bala* and viewed it as a form of propaganda aimed solely at a young audience.[112] For instance, one participant noted: 'these films give the younger generation heroes. We do not have heroes, except for the leader. Now they inspire them to be heroes too, because *Zhauzhurek Myn Bala* is about young people who fight for their motherland'.[113] For others, however, the lack of historical knowledge in Kazakhstan means, 'it is the best safe option to make this kind of propaganda. This is history that no one knows. So, you can do whatever you want.'[114] From this perspective, therefore, the creation of new heroes is easy when there is a lack of knowledge regarding the country's history. Overall, focus group participants were less critical of *Zhauzhurek Myn Bala* than they were of *Nomad* or the *Way of the Leader* series.

Finally, focus group respondents generally interpreted the *Way of the Leader* films as a form of propaganda. There was a focus on the idealised nature of *Sky of My Childhood*, 'it's a picture-perfect world they are living in and these are perfect characters, perfect boy with perfect family and with his perfect granny'.[115] Another participant argued, 'it's actually a propaganda film'.[116] *River of Fire* and *Iron Mountain* get similar short shrift on kino.kz, although comments are roughly equal between positive and negative feedback. Nonetheless, there is sense the films are 'boring, overdone with patriotism', 'full of lies',[117] 'no feeling of truthfulness' and 'primarily a patriotic film'.[118] Simultaneously, audience members recognised the power of Nazarbayev's story and his

Ethno-Centric Narrative of Kazakh Nationhood 151

position as a modern hero. One focus group member noted, 'it is just a story about good guy, about a guy among us, a normal guy. He was working in this metal plant ... he was from a normal family, lower than middle class. He just had strength and will.'[119] To some extent, this narrative of an ordinary man, who achieves great things by being hard working and honest, resonates with the audience. As one reviewer notes, 'the main purpose of the film is not about the president and how to become one, but through the prism of the main character of Sultan and how to be an ideal type of citizen'.[120] Such a perspective was evident in the case of *Sky of My Childhood*, where there were very few negative comments on kino.kz. Instead, reviewers left comments stating they were 'more and more proud of our first president', and saw it 'as a film about an ordinary Kazakh family and Kazakh way of life.'[121] The later point indicates the underlying ethno-centrism of the film had traction with the audience. This is illustrated by one reviewer who proclaimed: 'the most valuable thing in the film is the traditions and values of the Kazakh *aul*'.[122]

Conclusion

The above discussion on reception reveals the indeterminate nature of the ethno-centric narrative. Audiences interpret the meaning of the narrative in multiple ways, some observe it in a positive light, embracing the patriotic appeal to the homeland, and others see it as a form of historical revisionism. The extent of its reach, therefore, must be qualified. Clearly, the government, under the leadership of Nazarbayev, has seen the promotion of an ethno-centric narrative which carves out a distinct Kazakh identity rooted in notions of the motherland, history, landscape and ancestral traditions as important. Otherwise, Kazakhfilm Studios would have not been put to the task to produce films such as *Nomad*, *Zhauzhurek Myn Bala* and the *Way of the Leader* series. In doing so, as highlighted at various points in this chapter, the films produced within this narrative have displayed a tendency to repeat the model of state sponsored movie-making during the Soviet period. We can see echoes of Soviet Kazakh cinema past in the utilisation of landscape, the creation of *batyrs* and through the depiction of Kazakh traditions and *aul* life. In the *Way of the Leader* series we even see the return of the distinct 'Soviet' and 'Kazakh' worlds of 1960s Kazakh cinema although they reappear in the film series in a different way.

To be clear, the different ethnic signs that constitute this cinematic narrative are not entirely invented or imagined. They have grounding in history, albeit a selected history, and the traditions and customs of *aul* life, ever-present in these films, are conceivably distinctly Kazakh. Nevertheless, it should be noted that Turkic peoples all over the Eurasian steppe had similar customs and traditions. For instance, the mythology of Bayterek and Samruk, the game of kokpar and the dombra, which all appear in *Sky of My Childhood*, and at varying points throughout other films within this narrative, are symbols and objects rooted in a Turkic history rather than being specifically Kazakh. It illuminates the challenge of regime-sponsored attempts to present an ethnically exclusive version of Kazakh nationhood. This can be further observed, as we have seen in this chapter, with regards to the role of language too. Relying only on the Kazakh language risks marginalising large sections of the population who are not Kazakh-speaking.

Above all, the ethno-centric narrative reflects political efforts to instil patriotism and a sense of belonging among the titular majority. The problem is such efforts run up against the diverse and multi-ethnic composition of the country. The ethnic-centric narrative only tells us part of the story of regime-influenced cinema in Kazakhstan. With the flattened cinematic landscape after the 'Kazakh New Wave', the space was available for competing narratives to emerge regarding nationhood and belonging. As there has been an 'ethnic' narrative promoted via films like *Sardar*, *Zhauzhurek Myn Bala* and *Sky of My Childhood*, so there has also been present a 'civic' narrative in cinema that speaks to the multi-ethnic and multi-faith demographic composition of the country, as the subsequent chapter explores.

CHAPTER 5

MAY THE GRASS NEVER GROW AT YOUR DOOR: THE CIVIC CONCEPTION OF NATIONHOOD IN KAZAKH CINEMA

Nursultan Nazarbayev often quips that Kazakhstan is home to over 100 different nationalities.[1] This has become a maxim widely repeated throughout public discourse. It is held up as a badge of honour, which suggests that, despite the complex demographic composition of the country, the president has steered a course that has created inter-ethnic stability. The significance of this multi-ethnic demographic composition should not be lost on the multivalent nature of conceptualisations of nationhood and identity. As discussed in Chapter 1, as much as the government has sought to promote an ethnically exclusive Kazakh identity, they have also purported a civic identity that appeals to the notion of a 'common home' for all ethnic groups. These two policies related to identity are often viewed as existing in tension with one another.[2]

As we have seen in previous chapters, the 'Kazakh New Wave' led to a flattening of the cinematic landscape, which created space for the re-imagination of Kazakh nationhood and identity. The regime-sponsored ethnic narrative discussed in the previous chapter is one narrative to appear in the post-Soviet period. Its appearance in cinema mirrors its emergence at the policy level too. Nonetheless, a civic narrative which promotes Kazakh identity as a Kazakhstani identity – a nation that is the 'common home' to all nationalities – is also present in cinematic and public discourse. Cinematically, this narrative has been realised through two films produced by Kazakhfilm Studios, Rustam Abdrashev's *The Gift to Stalin* (2009) and Slambek Tauyekel's film *The Promised Land* (2011).

The narrative has three components. The first is an underlying message of inter-ethnic harmony and stability. The second concerns a particular ascription of Kazakh identity typically represented in these films via the protagonist. This is a Kazakh character that is friendly, hospitable and caring. This is a different type of Kazakh *batyr* than that realised in the ethnic narrative. Here the hero is not a warrior defending the land from the invading 'other', but is instead an open-hearted, kind and nurturing hero who welcomes outsiders and treats them as equals. The final element is a historical re-interpretation that roots the Kazakh nation not in the eighteenth-century conflicts with *Oirat* tribes, but instead in the forced Stalinist deportations of the 1930s and 1940s of different ethnic groups (Koreans, Germans, Chechens, Poles etc.).[3] This historical re-interpretation provides a depiction of this troubled period in Kazakh history and a negative representation of Soviet authority at the time. The narrative alludes to the demographic changes wrought by the movement of such large groups of people to the Kazakh steppe, which led to the establishment of the modern Kazakhstani nation. It is a nation based on inclusiveness, tolerance and harmony between peoples. This chapter addresses each of these elements of the narrative and considers the films' relationship to the regime as well as audience reception.

Inter-ethnic Harmony and Stability

As noted in the previous chapter, *Sky of My Childhood*, while offering a representation of an exclusive Kazakh identity, also portrays an inclusive identity linked to a multi-ethnic conception of nationhood. This is depicted when young Sultan moves from the 'Kazakh' world in the mountains down to the 'Soviet' world in the village of Chemolgan. It is in the village, amid the joyous celebrations of Victory Day, following the conclusion of the Great Patriotic War, that Sultan is exposed to the diversity of peoples in the Kazakh lands for the first time. He witnesses, as one reviewer notes, 'Russians playing the accordion, Chechens dancing, Kazakh wrestlers and a marching band playing victory songs under a Soviet banner'.[4] Sultan notes in his commentary that 'these people came from faraway places and were deported to the once quiet and serene village', thus alluding to the significant impact the demographic changes wrought by the forced deportations had on the life of the Kazakh village. Nonetheless, the scene portrays the idea of stability and harmony between different ethnic groups in Kazakhstan. The overhead shots of returning soldiers running into the crowd of open-armed villagers from all different ethnicities is signification of interethnic harmony in Kazakhstan and the 'common home'.

As also noted in Chapter 1, the idea of Kazakhstan being a 'common home' for all the different peoples who found themselves citizens within the territory of an independent Kazakhstan after the collapse of the Soviet Union has been a fundamental discourse perpetuated by the Nazarbayev regime in relation to nationhood and identity. Within this interpretation of Kazakhstan's nationhood, membership of the nation belongs to all based not on ethnicity but instead on citizenship, rights and responsibilities. And this is a model of the nation premised on interethnic and interreligious harmony.[5] This civic conception of nationhood was also realised legally in the so-called Doctrine of National Unity adopted in 2010. The Doctrine sought to find a common set of ideals around which a multi-ethnic and multi-faith Kazakhstan could coalesce. However as also noted in Chapter 1, this caused significant tension amongst different groups, not least Kazakh nationalists who felt the central and leading role of Kazakhs in the nation was being watered down.[6] Nevertheless, the notion of a 'common home' has always been driven by political concerns regarding stability and national unity, ultimately two factors that could undermine the political authority of the president. This is something Nazarbayev has always been acutely aware of, especially when drawing up the 1995 Constitution. As he noted in one memoir, 'the constitution we were devising had to unite the people, not divide them on the basis of their nationality'.[7] The policy of a 'common home' was also constitutionally embodied in the Assembly of People of Kazakhstan (APK), a presidentially appointed 384-member body which represents different ethnicities in the country. It was set up in 1995 after the president had dissolved the *Mazhilis* (parliament) while drawing up the new constitution. The president pushed the Doctrine of National Unity through the APK.

Most importantly, however, this discourse around a civic conception of Kazakhstani nationhood seeks to provide a narrative to underpin Nazarbayev's political authority. This is the idea that Nazarbayev has brought peace, stability and harmony to Kazakhstan, despite its inter-ethnic and inter-faith composition. As he himself noted in a speech he gave on Independence Day in 2013:

> we were able to turn our country into a cradle of peace. Calm reigned in our country; it was stability through agreement and cohesion. Unity, harmony – this is our greatest wealth, a priceless treasure. If our foundation is calm, supported by an agreed desire for stability, our country will take its rightful place in history. Independence united the people under a single Shanyrak – the guardian of peace and harmony. Our spiritual unity – the main foundations of the secular state and society.[8]

Much like the ethnic narrative, which is connected to questions of Nazarbayev's power, the civic narrative is also part of a broader strategy of regime maintenance. Nazarbayev is explicitly linked to being the key person who has ensured the country has maintained political stability given the complex inter-ethnic make-up of its demography. For members of the president's *Nur Otan* (Light of Fatherland) party, the correlation between the president's efforts at establishing a 'common home' and stability is almost self-evident, with one noting that Nazarbayev 'has been working to maintain ethnic stability in the country and consequently there have been no inter-ethnic conflicts',[9] while another more directly notes that the 'president has been working on keeping ethnic and national stability in the country and Kazakhstan has not suffered any inter-ethnic conflicts'.[10] Therefore, the films which form the civic narrative within contemporary Kazakh cinema need to be understood in this broader policy context regarding the notion of the 'common home', the Doctrine of National Unity and its utility in terms of the political authority of the president. This is not to suggest that the films are created expressly by the directors with the representation of the 'common home' specifically in mind, rather they reflect the post-Soviet narrative concerning inter-ethnic stability and harmony.

The two films considered here, *The Gift to Stalin* and *The Promised Land*, are ultimately historical films but, like *The Fall of Otrar*, they speak to contemporary political and nation-building issues. Both films, however, can be viewed as regime-sponsored. As far back as 2002 the president expressed how 'stories about positive developments, the story of good people, and these heroes of our time are of great political importance to the state. After all, they strengthen the public health of our citizens; promote our expertise which is unique and important for others. Above all it creates the image of the state'.[11] Both *The Gift to Stalin* and *The Promised Land* fulfil these objectives, even though they are films set in the 1930s and 1940s. They have contemporary relevance for providing an account of how the modern multi-ethnic and multi-faith independent Kazakhstani state appeared – and how that emergence was driven by a commitment to tolerance and harmony. Therefore, the films had backing from the Ministry of Culture and the Ministry of Finance, especially *The Promised Land*.[12] Notably, these were not the first films to focus on the notion of a multi-ethnic Kazakh identity. Abai Karpykov's *Little Fish in Love* (1989), while a very impressionistic film, as noted in Chapter 3, also provides a representation of Alma-Ata as a multicultural city where Kazakhs, Europeans, Russians and even Africans are seen side-by-side, comfortable with one another and at ease with their life in the city.[13] Alexandr Baranov's 1996 film *Shanghai* also touches on the issue of the multi-ethnic basis of the post-Soviet Kazakh nation and explores 'the complex generalisations about relationships among various ethnic groups living in the same territory'.[14] Both *Little Fish in Love* and *Shanghai* are art-house films that implicitly and tangentially address the issue of multi-ethnicity – they are more philosophical pieces of work. *The Gift to Stalin* and *The Promised Land* are more commercial and explicit attempts to address the idea of a multi-ethnic, inclusive and civic rendering of the post-Soviet Kazakhstani nation.

Consequently, the most notable way in which we see the cinematic representation of the 'common home' in these two films is through a depiction of village life, whereby people from different ethnic backgrounds ultimately find a way of working together in harmony. *The Gift to Stalin* is the most obvious example. The film, set in 1949, and unfolding at a poetic pace, tells the story of how a young Jewish boy, Sashka, is deported from Moscow to Kazakhstan with his grandfather. Sashka's grandfather dies during the journey and at an isolated railway stop in the Kazakh steppe, Sashka is found among the bodies of dead deportees who perished on the journey by the elderly Kazakh local rail worker, Kasym, and his friend Faty. Kasym takes on paternal responsibility for Sashka (or Sabyr, as Kasym renames him – meaning 'humble of heart') and endeavours to bring the boy up in the local village with other Kazakhs and deportees including Vera (a Russian), Jerzy a doctor (who is Polish), Faty (a Dungan) and Gleb (a Korean). The relationship between the different villagers, and their commitment to caring and bringing up Sabyr, goes to the heart of the film's universality, but also speaks to the idea of multi-ethnicity and the 'sources of tolerance and unity of Kazakhstan'.[15] In the portrayal of village life we see the relationships between people as being based on respect, tolerance and shared commonalities. We see them getting a along, falling in love (Vera and Jerzy), celebrating (Vera and Jerzy's wedding) and guiding the young Sabyr. The relationship between the different ethnicities within the film was recognised as embodying the idea of 'the friendship of peoples, but not the one portrayed in Soviet propaganda'.[16] The film does not provide the idealised 'friendship of peoples' but instead a representation of community in which people maintain friendship from different backgrounds despite the tough and arbitrary power of Soviet rule (as will be discussed below, the film is also a comment on the moral bankruptcy of Soviet power). It is fate, therefore, that has thrown these diverse peoples together, via the decisions of Soviet policy makers, but it the indomitable spirit of the Kazakhs, in this instance represented by Kasym, which ensures they make the most of their situation by practising tolerance and kindness to one another. As one reviewer noted, it illustrates how the community of modern Kazakhstan 'lay in the most brutal era of the Soviet Union, but despite the terrible conditions of life, full of hopelessness, the arbitrariness of those in power, here each one is a friend, a comrade and a brother'.[17]

The director of *The Gift to Stalin*, Rustem Abdrashev, began his career in the film industry as a production designer in some of the major works of the 'Kazakh New Wave', including Ardak Amirkulov's *The Fall of Otrar* and Rashid Nugmanov's *The Wild East*. Abdrashev is the son of famed Kazakh poet Zharaskan Abdrashev. Rustem Abdrashev's 2004 directorial debut *Renaissance Island* is based on the biographical poems of his father and tells the story of the first flush of love between Zharas and the daughter of a newly arrived Communist Party official, chronicling the disapproval of the local school and party officials of their relationship. The film is set in 1960 in a small village in the Aral Sea region of Kazakhstan, in which Zharaskan Abdrashev grew up. The film's quiet, poetic and tranquil pace framed much of Abdrashev's later work, especially *The Gift to Stalin* and *Sky of My Childhood*. The film also introduced two themes that were explored in much greater depth in his later work. The first was a critique of Soviet authority and the impact of its policy towards the environment in Kazakhstan. This is most evident in *Renaissance Island* with the background of the gradual desiccation of the Aral Sea and its impact on the local environment. An analysis of the issue of Soviet authority in relation to this civic narrative and Abdrashev's work will be discussed in the following section. The second notable theme in *Renaissance Island* relates to the idea of a multi-ethnic Kazakhstan. While it does not feature heavily in the film, rather the film is ultimately a story of love and desire, the depiction of school and village life provides a representation of Soviet Kazakhstan that gives an indication of how the republic's demographics had shifted in the postwar period. This is epitomised in a scene within Zharas' classroom where an elder Zharas narrates, telling us how the deportations brought different ethnicities to the Aral Sea region. The shot then cuts to the classroom where we are shown the faces of Zharas' classmates; they represent the different ethnicities deported to Kazakhstan during the 1930s and 1940s. Zhibek, a girl in the class, then stands up and reads a Soviet poem about the people of the country. She reads aloud 'the Soviet peoples like one family united, our country stronger than granite, the Soviet soldier is on guard of peace and happiness.' On the one hand, this is naturally a reference to the Soviet policy of the friendship of peoples, but on other hand it also represents the idea of multi-ethnic harmony in Kazakhstan and how the roots of a civic nation of Kazakhstanis is ingrained in the experience of the forced deportations of the Soviet period.

Abdrashev's *The Gift to Stalin* evokes not just the spirit of multi-ethnicity and the flourishing relations of peoples from different ethnic groups, but also the harmony between diverse religious faiths. The president often holds Kazakhstan up as a model for religious tolerance and inter-faith harmony.[18] The notion of inter-faith relations can be observed in the film in two ways. Firstly, it is implicit in the relations between the different characters who make up the surrogate family which care for Sabyr. Kasym is Muslim, Verka Christian and Jerzy Jewish (as of course is Sabyr).[19] The depiction of the characters getting along with one another, caring for Sabyr, supporting each other in the face of the brutal and inhuman nature of Soviet authority despite their varied spiritual backgrounds, is emblematic of the religious tolerance and of peaceful relations between faiths that defined Nazarbayev's discourse regarding a civic and multi-ethnic Kazakhstan. The message regarding religious tolerance emerges in a quiet scene between Kasym and Sabyr at a grave where they break bread and pray:

- Who is your God, grandpa Kasym
- God is for everyone. For me and for you.
- For Jerzy, Mamma Vera and for Faty and Gleb also?
- For all son
- What language does he speak?
- He knows all languages. The main thing is that the word would come from the heart.

The conversation reveals the way in which the diverse communities that compose the population of Kazakhstan (both in the Soviet past and in the present) may not share the same faith, but they do share the same God. It emphasises that Kazakhstan is a county which contains multiple faiths, but they are faiths that respect and tolerate one another. This is further demonstrated in a scene at the very end of the film where an older Sabyr returns to the exact spot in the steppe where he held this conversation with Kasym. There at the grave of Kasym he recites a Jewish prayer in honour of the man who looked after him. It promotes the idea that all faiths are applicable in Kazakhstan so long as people are respectful, kind, tolerant and look out for one another.

The Gift to Stalin is not the only film to have been produced in contemporary Kazakh cinema that provides a representation of national identity based on inter-ethnic and inter-faith respect. Slambek Tauyekel's 2011 Ministry of Culture and Information-commissioned film, *The Promised Land*, tackles the same subject as *The Gift to Stalin*. *The Promised Land* is a re-imagined account of the Stalinist deportations of different ethnic groups to Kazakhstan in the period from 1937 to 1945, with the story beginning with the deportation of Koreans in 1937. The protagonist is Orynbay-ata (or Oreke for short), a village elder, and head of a collective farm, who discovers a group of Koreans abandoned in the freezing, snowing and isolated steppe. Oreke,

Figure 5.1 Dalen Shintemirov as Sabyr and Nurzhuman Ikhtymbayev as Kasym in *The Gift to Stalin* (2009), dir. Rustem Abdrashev.

representing the consciousness of humanity, takes them back to the village and encourages the local Kazakh villagers to look after the new arrivals to their land. As the film progresses, other deported nationalities are introduced to the collective farm, including Germans and Chechens. The different ethnicities are observed living harmoniously and in unity in face of the ongoing threat of Soviet repression. This unity is noted by Oreke in a short speech he orates when the collective farm work together to build a makeshift place of worship: 'brother and sisters, everyone has their own faith, his own religion, but those who are in the same boat, share the same fate'. This one scene encapsulates the theme of both inter-ethnic and inter-faith harmony and the way in which Kazakhstan became a second home for the exiled during the years of Soviet repression.[20]

The inter-ethnic nature of Kazakhstan is also reflected in the use of language in both films. As Rustem Abdrashev noted, 'the music of language of each ethnicity is in itself very cinematic'.[21] This musicality plays throughout both films as dialogue shifts frequently between Russian and Kazakh. Russian is used as the language of inter-ethnic communication in the films, while Kazakh is spoken between Kazakh characters when they have scenes together. The interplay of language in this manner reflects government policy, which states that Kazakh is the language of the state and Russian the language of inter-ethnic communication. The deployment of language in this way, while common in many contemporary Kazakh films (as will be discussed in Chapter 7), especially those which seek to provide authenticity in their representation of everyday life, emphasises the inclusive nature of the civic narrative.

Importantly, *The Promised Land*, and to an extent *The Gift to Stalin*, also provide an alternative foundation story for modern Kazakhstan to that which exists in the ethnic narrative. According to one figure in the film industry, *The Promised Land* shows how contemporary Kazakhstan was created. 'Other nationalities were deported here and they had no food or shelter. Kazakhs accepted them as relatives and helped them survive and until today their friendship with Kazakhs is preserved and rooted in those times'.[22] This connection between the Soviet period and the constitution of modern Kazakh nationhood is seen most vividly in the very final scene, when an elderly Korean who had been just a baby when he arrived to Kazakhstan in 1937, is stirred by a speech given by Nursultan Nazarbayev on television at the APK discussing the Soviet deportations and how they defined modern Kazakh nationhood and were central to Kazakhstan being a nation of tolerance, unity and diversity. On hearing the president's speech, the elderly Korean gets up from his chair, opens his window and looks out on to the new gleaming futuristically designed capital of Kazakhstan, Astana, where below a parade of different nationalities dance and walk by. The scene is a less than subtle encapsulation of the key signifying chain of the film. Modern Kazakhstan was born because of the forced deportations of different ethnic groups to the territory in the 1930s and 1940s. However, in this narrative, national unity is only achieved because of the central characteristics of Kazakhs.

Kazakh Batyrs as Kind, Open and Hospitable

In the ethnic narrative, the archetypal Kazakh hero is represented in the form of courageous warriors who were willing to sacrifice their lives to preserve the Kazakh homeland against marauding invading forces. They are men (usually men – although in *Zhauzhurek Myn Bala*,

Korlan, played by Kuralay Anarbekova, is as fearless as a warrior as her male counterparts, but she is the exception), who like Ablai Khan in *Nomad* are able through strength of personality to unite Kazakhs across the steppe to fend off foreign attackers. These types of heroes, as we saw in the previous chapter, have been used for legitimising purposes by the Nazarbayev regime to suggest that the president, like Ablai Khan, is the only person capable of uniting the peoples of the Kazakh steppe during a turbulent period of its history and that he is in a long line of Kazakh *batyrs* who have fought for an independent sovereign Kazakhstan, which has only been fully realised under his leadership.

The civic narrative provides a different interpretation of the Kazakh hero. In *The Gift to Stalin* and *The Promised Land*, the Kazakh *batyr* is not a fearless warrior out to remove foreign elements from the Kazakh steppe, but a gentle, wise, open and hospitable character who welcomes outsiders. This characterisation of the Kazakh *batyr* is to some extent an attempt to provide a specific representation of the national character. Like the depiction of the hero in the ethnic narrative, the idealisation of the hero in *The Gift to Stalin* and *The Promised Land* is rooted in an interpretation of a mythologisation of Kazakhstan's nomadic roots and the relationship between the Kazakh people and the vast steppe, as well as Kazakhstan's geographical position as a place between East and West. As suggested by director Slambek Tauyekel, historically the lone yurts in the vast steppe represented a stopping place for travelers taking the Silk Road.[23] The Kazakh steppe, with its openness and lack of topographical and material defence, has defined Kazakhs' idea of themselves in that the lack of geographical boundaries makes them open, tolerant and hospitable. This sense of identity was encapsulated by director Satybaldy Narymbetov, who has noted that:

> there was a tradition that a traveller who stopped at a Kazakh home was not asked his name for three days. The host waited until his guest had enough food, water, rest, and had got used to the place, and only then would he listen to the traveller's story ... We had a lot of heroes in our history, they were called heroes not because they were attacking someone or conquering territories, Kazakhs were always defending and that is how they became heroes.[24]

In this conception of national identity, the natural disposition of Kazakhs is to be open, cordial and religiously and racially tolerant.[25] In *The Promised Land* this interpretation of national identity is symbolised in Oreke. The protagonist's kindness and open-heartedness is realised in a series of important relationships he has with other characters. Very early in the film we are made aware of Oreke's concern for a Polish member of the community, Barbara, who has gone missing, believed to have been taken away by the NKVD. He spends time going in and out of local Communist Party officials' offices asking after her and pleading to know of her whereabouts. Through his concern for Barbara, and for Peter Pak, a Korean deportee, Oreke demonstrates his humanity and thus by default the humanity of the Kazakh people. This is further epitomised in a scene when Oreke and other local villagers are told by the local Party official that cannibals will soon be arriving to the steppe and that they should have no communication with them otherwise they will be shot. Oreke, of course, defies such orders. On discovering the abandoned Koreans, he rallies local villagers to care for the deportees. This is perhaps typified in a scene where local Kazakh women bathe and take care of a new baby born to one of the deportees on the journey. We are left in no doubt as to the message of these scenes and who Oreke represents. As noted in one review, 'in our history the embodiment of the friendly village elder is Oreke. Thanks to his open and friendly nature, he is trying to unite all nationalities'.[26]

In *The Gift to Stalin*, these national characteristics are embodied in Kasym. As Jamie Miller has noted in his review, Sabyr observes closely 'Kasym's simple, honest, rural way of life, his kindness and respect for others'.[27] Kasym is perceived to have a 'heart-of-gold'[28] and to display dignity and an innate human goodness which ties the diverse members of the community together, keeping them united in the face of the brutal and arbitrary power of Soviet authority.[29] It is, as one reviewer noted, the 'exact embodiment of the national character'.[30] Further, the performance of Nurzhuman Ikhtimbayev, who plays Kasym, 'almost without words creates an incredibly powerful image of a man who is not embittered despite incredible trials and losses – who is the only one who thought of the terrible fate in store for those lost in the Kazakh steppe – and who sought to save the few he was able to save'.[31] Differently put, Kasym is the beating heart of the film. It is his kindness and thoughtfulness that saves Sabyr, not just at the beginning of the film when he intervenes

Figure 5.2 Bolat Abdilmanov as Oreke in *The Promised Land* (2011), dir. Slambek Tauyekel.

when the local police officer Balgabai is stabbing each corpse (among which Sabyr lay – alive) and stops Balgabai from inserting the knife into Sabyr. It is also evident at the end of the film, when he arranges for Sabyr to return to his family members in the aftermath of Balgabai's death (by an unknown assailant – but the implication is that it was Kasym who acted in revenge for Balgabai, killing Jerzy on his wedding day to Verka). However, Kasym's embodiment of the national character is not just in terms of tolerance, respect and kindness. Rustem Abdrashev sought to tell a deeper story of the nation through the character of Kasym. There is a scene in the film where Kasym is riding with Sabyr on horseback and he is being wistful about the past, explaining to Sabyr where there used to be yurts and *auls*, elements of the traditional nomadic way of life lost because of sedentarisation and collectivization. For Abdrashev, in this scene, Kasym is speaking of the fate of the Kazakh nation. As the director notes:

> when Kasym is telling the story of his family and himself to Sabyr, he is telling the story of the fate of the Kazakh nation. When he talks about the years when he was young and there were lots of kettles, horse riders and everyone was rich and happy. This is not

imagined I have talked to people who said that before the war nearly 700 young people used to gather round an *altybakan* (a swing) in the local *aul* for entertainment. After the war, there were only 70 young people around the *altybakan*. Can you imagine the demographic impact?[32]

As will be discussed below, *The Gift to Stalin* is also a film that is concerned with the destructive nature of Soviet power in Kazakhstan and this is what Abdrashev is alluding to here when he is noting how Kasym embodies the Kazakh nation. Kasym is a survivor in the film. He survived the settlement of the nomads, he survived the war, and now with his quiet patience and dignity in the face of the Soviet authorities, he is ensuring that the local community, which is made up of all different ethnicities, survives too, and that it survives together in unity. Nonetheless, Kasym ultimately fails. Jerzy is killed by Balgabai and Sabyr leaves for fear of being caught by the authorities. The underpinning logic is that Kazakhstan as a family of different nations brought together by fate, under the cruel leadership of the Soviets, could only be brought back together again with independence, once the Soviet authorities had gone. Moreover, that it is only possible under the leadership of the president and his policy of a 'common home'.

There are limitations to this civic narrative, and indeed to the broader policy of a civic national project in Kazakhstan. As Taras Kuzio has noted in his critique of the civic-ethnic dichotomy, all civic states have ethnic cores.[33] In other words, nation states which claim to be civic, in which membership of the nation is inclusive and based upon rights and responsibilities of citizenship, as opposed to ethnic ancestry, still feature an ethnic core at their heart in which assimilation to the culture of the titular majority is the general expectation of membership of the nation.[34] In the civic narrative in contemporary Kazakh cinema, the ethnic element remains important, if not primary. The underlying message in both films is that the unity of peoples in Kazakhstan, and the idea of inter-ethnic and inter-faith stability and harmony, is dependent upon the national characteristics of the Kazakh psyche of being a tolerant, open and hospitable people. Differently put, the ability of the deported groups to settle peacefully in the Kazakh steppe, and the prospect of a 'common home' in the post-Soviet period, was largely due to the very nature of the Kazakh national character.

Interpretation of History and Soviet Authority

Naturally, a significant aspect of *The Gift to Stalin* and *The Promised Land* is their representation of a difficult and dark part of Kazakh history.[35] Both films follow the tradition of historical films within the 'Kazakh New Wave', such as *The Fall of Otrar*, *Surzhekey – the Angel of Death* and *Balcony*, which all sought to re-interpret moments of history that had been either taboo or silent during the Soviet period. As Slambek Tauyekel has noted, *The Promised Land* concerned opening concealed elements of the country's history:

> Our young generation needs to know what was hidden in a box by Stalin. When we opened this box, we felt happy, but the same time we were horrified. It was a horrendous happiness. Why was our real past hidden from us? That is the question that bothers us.[36]

But both films also followed earlier post-soviet cinematic works that sought to critique Soviet authority and its impact on Kazakh society. Most notable was Satybaldy Narymbetov's 2002 film *Lelia's Prayer*, which provides an account of the effect of the Soviet's nuclear testing site in Semipalatinsk, known as The Polygon, on near-by residents of an *aul*, and the disastrous impact on their health. *The Gift to Stalin* and *The Promised Land* instead focus on depicting and critiquing Soviet authority during the period of the 1930s and 1940s, the process of deportation, and how the arbitrary power of Soviet authorities on multi-ethnic communities had a significant impact on the shape and development of Kazakhstan in the post-Soviet period. Both films, therefore, seek to capture the difficult and challenging conditions of deportation. There are two almost identical scenes, which feature the cramped and squalid conditions of the deportees' journey by railway. In *The Promised Land*, we see the fetid, dank, cold and cramped conditions within the train carriages of the Koreans arrival to the steppe – including a woman having to give birth in such circumstances (the same baby who is an old man at the end of the film – who looks out in wonder at the multi-cultural utopia that is Astana). A similar scene portrays Sabyr's arrival to the steppe, and again we are made conscious of the inhuman and squalid situation. Sabyr's grandfather dies on the journey and he is thrown off onto a cart with other dead bodies, amongst whom Sabyr hides until being discovered by Kasym. *The Gift to Stalin* was singled out in one review for the accuracy of its detail in relation to deportations and the treatment of exiles and women by the Soviet authorities.[37]

Both *The Gift to Stalin* and *The Promised Land* realise Soviet authority as arbitrary, brutal and inhumane. The films provide a two-layered account of Soviet power. The first is that each gives a characterisation of 'local' Soviet authority. In *The Gift to Stalin*, Balgabai is a local Kazakh policeman who wilfully complies and does the bidding of senior Soviet military and Party officials.[38] He is portrayed as both a bully to those he believes beneath and less powerful than him and also as a fearful coward to those in senior positions. The only person in the village willing to stand up to Balgabai, and who Balgabai is fearful of, is Kasym. Nonetheless, as the embodiment of local Kazakh Soviet authority, Balgabai is a menacing and bullying presence in the film and this is most acutely realised in the scenes where he rapes both Verka (although she seemingly acquiesces to the sex to distract Balgabai from inquiring about Sabyr) and a local Kazakh girl. Balgabai's full brutality is tragically revealed when he drunkenly disrupts Verka's and Jerzy's wedding and in a jealous rage fights with Jerzy and accidently shoots him in the violent tussle. The fact Balgabai is Kazakh raises a rather interesting paradox in relation to the civic narrative. If the characteristics of the Kazakh national identity are openness, kindness and hospitality then why does Balgabai behave in this way? The answer perhaps lies in the corrupting and corrosive nature of Soviet power that morally underpins the film. In *The Promised Land* the local Kazakh NKVD officer Zhylkybay is a much more moderate figure than Balgabai. He is more likely to provide information to Oreke and the local villagers and does not possess Balgabai's violent streak. Nonetheless, he uses his position of authority to spread misinformation (it is Zhylkybay who states to Oreke and other villagers that the Koreans are cannibals) and to warn against criticism of the Soviet authorities in relation to famine in the steppe (as he does with Oreke's grandson Temirzhan). In other words, Zhylkybay plays the role of mouthpiece and communication tool for the Soviet authorities as he passes down dictats from his senior officers. Nevertheless, he is also acutely aware of his position in the community as watchdog for the authorities, noting early in the film that he 'hears and sees everything'. His character, like that of Balgabai, reflects the role some Kazakhs played of being the local enforcers for Soviet authority.

In this way, cinema has captured a trend within historiography of the Soviet period in Kazakhstan that seeks to pay more attention to the role and agency of local elites in the enforcement of Soviet power in the region.[39]

The second level is an interpretation of Soviet authority as non-local. It is encapsulated in the military power of Soviet authority, most fully realised in Aleksandr Bashirov's (who also played Spartak in *The Needle*) performance as an Army Major in *The Gift to Stalin* who according to one review 'epitomised the Soviet totalitarian system'.[40] He also rapes Vera and intimidates Kasym, Sabyr and others in the local community. But the Major is realised as an external force who is doing the bidding of higher-up officials in the Party, such as collecting livestock as presents for Stalin's birthday. This is something Sabyr contributes towards too – giving the Major a new born lamb as a gift for Stalin in the hope that he will release his parents who are in a labour camp. In *The Gift to Stalin* the external authority of Soviet power is depicted in the impending testing of the first nuclear bomb in Kazakhstan, foreshadowed throughout the whole film. It speaks to a narrative regarding the Soviet's abandonment of the environment of the Kazakh steppe. In *The Promised Land* non-local Soviet authority is represented in the senior communist officials Oreke visits in the local administration, among them is Kovalev whom Oreke plays off against Zhylkybay in his effort to extract information about the whereabouts of Barbara. Senior officials are characterised as more rational figures – seeking to fulfil Party orders that they channel through Oreke and his management of the collective farm. One such order is to use the Koreans as economic migrants for the fulfilment of the plan for growing rice, which Oreke must implement despite his reservations. It provides an evocative interpretation of the abstraction by which Soviet authority understood people as tools for the fulfilment of strategies and targets. In this context, Soviet authority is seen in contrast to Oreke and his humanity and compassion for the exiles and deportees. He sees them as humans and not simply as economic labour. *The Promised Land* also revisits the issue of the purge and the arbitrary arrest of individuals, previously explored in Kalykbek Salykov's 1987 film *The Balcony* (1987). Twice Peter Pak, one of the deported Koreans, is taken away by the NKVD. One scene where he is arrested and put into a truck is similar to the scene in *The Balcony* when in a dream sequence we see Aidar's father taken away by NKVD officers and hustled into a car.

This critique of Soviet authority, and the negative consequences of Soviet rule on Kazakh society, has emerged as a much more overt and prominent strain of post-Soviet cinematic works in recent years, best realised in Akan Satayev's 2016 film *The Road to Mother*. The film concerns Ilyas and his efforts to be reunited with his family during the 1930s and 1940s. The beginning of the film includes a collage of pictures from this period of Kazakhs who suffered at the hands of Soviet policy, which led to the deaths of millions through collectivisation, sedentarisation, famine, persecution and the Great Patriotic War. The film is perhaps the most explicit critique of Soviet authority in Kazakh film to date.

The civic narrative provides, therefore, for an interpretation of Soviet authority that positions Soviet power in contradistinction to both the ability of different ethnic groups to cope in these trying conditions and the role played by Kazakhs in ensuring harmony in such an intolerable context. It reveals something important about the nature of this post-Soviet narrative of nationhood and identity. Examining the early films of Rustem Abdrashev, especially those that are historically set in the Soviet period *Renaissance Island* and *The Gift to Stalin*, the viewer is treated to a negative portrayal of Soviet authority. This depiction in relation to *The Gift to Stalin* is highlighted above, but in the case of *Renaissance Island*, it is the local Soviet authority figures, the local Party chief and the school, who admonishes the two young lovers and keeps them apart.[41] It suggests that there is an anti-authoritarian streak in the work of Abdrashev through his negative depiction of the power and destruction of Soviet authority in his movies. It exists even in the *Way of the Leader* films too. In those films, especially *Breaking the Vicious Circle*, the Soviet authorities are shown as meandering, ineffective and inefficient bureaucrats.

This anti-authoritarian element illustrates the fluidity between these different narratives of nationhood and identity in post-Soviet Kazakh cinema. Despite offering a critique of Soviet authority within the civic narrative, decrying the inhumane ways in which the Soviet authorities behaved towards the exiled deportees to Kazakhstan, Abdrashev films in the *Way of the Leader* series are also an important component of the more exclusive 'ethnic' narrative as we saw in the previous chapter. Moreover, within that narrative, the *Way of the Leader* films provide an important function in the legitimisation of Nazarbayev's authoritarian personal rule.

The existence of fluidity between the ethnic and civic narratives exists is no surprise given both have been supported and sponsored by the government through the Ministry of Culture and both reflect broader policy trends towards either greater Kazakhisation of the state or a discourse regarding harmony and stability among the different peoples of the country. While the regime-led nature of the ethnic narrative is rather obvious in films such as *Nomad*, *Zhauzhurek Myn Bala* or the Kazakh Khanate TV series (also directed by Abdrashev), the government of Kazakhstan continues to support cinematic works that also focus on the civic narrative. While *The Gift to Stalin* and *The Promised Land* have only been two examples of contemporary feature films, the Ministry of Culture also sponsored an animated series in 2015 called *Kazakhstan the Common Home*. The series was commissioned on the initiative of Nazarbayev to celebrate the 20th anniversary of the APK and consisted of nine short animations, each based on folk tales from different ethnic groups, which included Kazakhs, Russians, Turkish, Tatars, Uzbeks, Germans, Ukrainians, Koreans and Uighurs.[42] The animation cycle was produced to 'promote patriotism and tolerance',[43] with the educational aim to 'help children to learn more about the people among whom they live'.[44]

Reception

The final question to address in this chapter is the issue of reception. How have these films been perceived by audiences in Kazakhstan, and to what extent does the civic narrative resonate with cinema audiences? Like the other narratives, the civic narrative suffers from a lack of domestic exposure. Therefore, any reading of audience reception is partial at best. Across the three focus groups only a handful of participants had seen *The Gift to Stalin*, and none had seen *The Promised Land*. Nevertheless, the kino.kz forum website features eight pages of comments for *The Gift to Stalin* and two for *The Promised Land*. It illustrates there was a least a small audience for the films, while *The Gift to Stalin* is often praised in the media and typically included in top-ten lists of the must-watch contemporary Kazakh films.[45]

From the focus groups and the kino.kz website, audiences clearly picked up on and appreciated that this period of Kazakhstan's history was being cinematically represented on the screen. As one focus group participant noted in reference to *The Gift to Stalin*, 'it touches on an important part of Kazakhstan's history as a multinational country',[46] while a respondent on kino.kz noted the film 'subtly touched on some very important historical facts regarding the modern history of Kazakhstan'.[47] In reference to *The Promised Land*, one commentator noted that it was a 'great movie which portrayed the tragedy of the many nationalities who suffered in those terrible times',[48] while another opined that 'the film shows a story that everyone should know'.[49] All in all, there was an appreciation for films which covered this period of Kazakhstan's history. That said, not all were happy with the acting, especially in *The Gift to Stalin*,[50] and some criticised the crude interpretation of history.[51]

Importantly, however, some of the key elements of the civic narrative were picked up on by audiences. There was recognition that the films were offering an account of inter-ethnic stability, the friendship of the peoples and the idea of a 'common home'. As one focus group participant noted with regards to *The Gift to Stalin*, 'the director demonstrated the friendship of different nations, of Polish people, Russians, Kazakhs and others'.[52] Furthermore, there were a plethora of comments on kino.kz for the film which supported this view. For instance, one respondent commented it was 'a very strong film perfectly illustrating the friendship of the peoples in those times: Kazakh, Russian, Polish, Dungan, and Jews – all living together as one family'.[53] A similar comment also alluded to the film indicating that the different ethnicities living together represented a united family suggesting that 'in spite of all the difficulties in the postwar period in Kazakhstan, people of different nationalities and religions lived as a happy family.'[54] In perceiving of the film in this way, some commentators understood the film as representing the Kazakh nation, seeing it as an appeal to patriotism, describing it as just that, a 'patriotic movie'[55] and recommending that 'those who value their homeland should go and see this movie'.[56]

Audiences also seemed to respond to the depiction in the films of the perceived Kazakh characteristics of tolerance, openness and kindness. In referring to *The Promised Land*, one respondent on kino.kz noted that 'this film reflects the soul of our nation: our kindness and hospitality. Kazakhstan has become home to many immigrants. There is no other country where so many people lived in peace'.[57] Those audience members commenting on *The Gift to Stalin* noted how the film 'showed the kindness and humanity of ordinary people, true human values',[58] noting how 'if it were not for the Kazakh people many would have died',[59] while a Korean who had seen the film declared, 'I myself am Korean and I love to listen to stories about the past, about the evacuation and deportation, inhumane difficulties which our ancestors overcame and the heartfelt kindness and generosity of Kazakhs'.[60] Thus, there is a sense, or at least a strain, of audience reception which recognises the representation of those characteristics of Kazakh identity that both films portray, essential to the civic rendering of the nation in the film. Indeed, one audience member who left a comment for *The Promised Land* noted the importance of this period in history, the friendship of peoples and the hospitality of Kazakhs as 'the first step to Kazakhstan becoming a multinational country'.[61] Broadly speaking, therefore, both films did seem to provide an account of the Kazakh nation, rooted in their interpretation of history, which emotionally resonated with audiences who watched them.

Conclusion

Even though there is fluidity between the ethnic and civic narratives, and even though they are both sponsored by the regime, the two narratives still offer distinct visions regarding Kazakh nationhood and identity. The ethnic narrative is based on a specific reading of Kazakh identity that is exclusionary, while the civic narrative is premised on the inclusive appeal to tolerance, harmony and friendship of peoples, and portrays Kazakhstan as the 'common home'. Both have a different reading of the traditional Kazakh *batyr*. The ethnic narrative focuses on the hero as a warrior seeking to defend the homeland from foreign forces, and the civic narrative has a *batyr* who is kind, open-hearted and tolerant of outsiders. The two narratives also have a different interpretation of when the modern Kazakh nation was formed. In the ethnic narrative, the nation was born in the bloody struggles against the *Oirat* tribes when the Kazakhs could unite the disparate *zhuz* against their enemy. In the civic narrative, the modern Kazakhstani nation was formed because of the inhumane deportation policy of the Soviet authorities that saw numerous ethnic groups forcibly migrate to the steppes.

Both the ethnic and civic narratives in contemporary Kazakh cinema, therefore, conceivably offer regime-approved accounts of Kazakh nationhood and identity. Films within these narratives, despite their differing accounts of nation formation and national identity, are often initiated by the Office of the President, supported by the Ministry of Culture and channelled through Kazakhfilm Studios. Yet, they represent only two trends in recent cinematic works when it comes to representations of the nation. The flattening of the cinematic landscape by the 'Kazakh New Wave' also created space for alternative imaginations of the nation that do not correspond to the ethnic and civic narratives. The following two chapters will explore two other narratives pertaining to nationhood and identity that are present in contemporary Kazakh cinema. These are the religious-Tengrist and socio-economic narratives. These are readings of the Kazakh nation that, in their own distinct ways subtly challenge, or at the very least provide an alternative prescription, of prevailing government sponsored representations. What the Tengrist and socio-economic narratives demonstrate is how film can provide a space for critique and pluralism in an authoritarian regime. The next two chapters provide a detailed analysis of these two non-regime sponsored narratives, beginning with an interpretation of the Kazakh nation as founded upon the religion of Tengrism.

CHAPTER 6

'HYMN TO MOTHER': TENGRISM, MOTHERHOOD AND NATIONHOOD

This is the first of two chapters that explore narratives within modern Kazakh cinema that are distinct from the 'civic' and 'ethnic' accounts put forward by the regime. The first of these narratives pivots upon a reading of nationhood and identity rooted in the pre-Islamic religion of Tengrism. We can see in this construction a selection of cinematic works revolving around the literal practice of shamanism associated with Tengrism through rites, rituals and the appearance of animals. At the symbolic level, Tengrism exists as a philosophical, moral and spiritual device used to carve out an identity for Kazakhstan in relation to its history as a nomadic population and the Kazakhs' relationship with the steppe. This is situated in contradistinction to the encroachment of global (Western) capitalism and other universal values. Moreover, within the Tengrist narrative women are symbolically placed and celebrated as mothers of the nation. The narrative situates the family and the cycle of birth, life and death as central to conceptions of Kazakh nationhood and identity. In this sense, this representation of Kazakh nationhood and identity is a quasi-primordial one, based on a respect for ancestors, kinship ties and the symbolic role of women as guardians and guarantors for the survival of the nation.

The Tengrist narrative exists mostly in the work of Yermek Tursunov, Akhat Ibrayev, Sergei Bodrov and Guka Omarova. Tursunov's films *Kelin* (Daughter-in-law) and *Shal* (The Old Man) are especially indicative of this narrative and much space is given over to a discussion of them. Analysis of the production and reception of these films, however, illuminates the tension between aspects of universalism evident in these Tengrist-inflected films and the effort to represent a Kazakh national particularity.

Ultimately, the Tengrist narrative provides a subtle dissenting voice on issues of nationhood and identity in post-Soviet Kazakhstan. It represents an alternative ideological perspective to those postulated in regime-led narratives. Consequently, this elucidates the contentious nature of the nation-building process in Kazakhstan. Moreover, it also exemplifies the fluidity of cinematic works as a site for representations of nationhood and identity and the limitations of the state as an agent for only pursing regime representations of nationhood and identity. Tursunov's films were produced by the state-run Kazakhflim Studios, yet offer a representation of Kazakh nationhood off-script from the ethnic and civic narratives. It illustrates that, even if the state is funding the industry to display the regime's preferred imaginations of the nation, there are limits to the extent to which it can dicate the use of these funds. Moreover, the state is unable to control the multiple meanings attached to cinematic works because of the polysemic nature of images.

The chapter proceeds by providing a general discussion on Tengrism before addressing the literal representation of Tengrism in contemporary Kazakh cinema. This is followed by an analytical discussion on the symbolic representation of Tengrism and how it is channelled through a psycho-geographical interpretation of the relationship between Kazakhs and their environment. It also explores the way in which the discourse around Tengrism seeks to establish a distinct sense of Kazakh identity vis-à-vis the encroachment of Westernisation and global consumerism on post-Soviet Kazakhstan. Finally, the chapter unpacks the quasi-primordial symbolic representation of the nation through its positioning of women, family and the cycle of birth, life and death, and shows that this evokes a mixed audience reaction. On the one hand, some members of the audience appreciate the central place of women within the Tengrist narrative and how it celebrates the centrality of the family to Kazakh identity. On the other hand, some political officials took offense at the way in which Kazakh women were portrayed, especially in relation to their overt sexuality.

Tengrism

Tengrism has a long history in the Eurasian steppe. Written archaeological sources date the practice of Tengrism by the Turkic-Mongol population of the Central Asian steppe as going back to the sixth to eighth centuries.[1] Nevertheless, the Turkic Khaganate practised Tengrism prior to their conversion to other religions such as Buddhism, Manichaeism and Islam. Furthermore, Tengrism's influence is thought to have even stretched as far afield as modern-day Hungary[2] and is argued by some to date back as far as the Sumerians.[3] The religion is monotheistic and centres on the relationship between humankind and nature, sanctifying humans' relationship with the sky.[4] *Tengri* refers to the Sky God, the supreme deity and first of the celestial beings believed to rule the fate of all peoples including powerful Khans. This is clearly expressed in the eighth-century Göktürk-erected inscriptions, located in the Orkhon Valley in Central Mongolia, where it is noted that 'all human sons are born to die in time as determined by *Tengri*'.[5] The number of gods believed to exist within Tengrism varied from population to population.[6] The cosmological worldview of the ancient Turks was based on the unity of the three levels key deities represented. *Tengri* represented the sky and the upper level, *Yer Sub* the earth and the middle level and *Erlik* the underground and the lower level. The Turkic interpretation of Tengrism identified 14 other gods – all related to aspects of the natural world. This included *Umai* (mother earth – goddess of fertility and virginity), Earth, Water, Fire, Sun, Moon, Star, Air, Clouds, Wind, Storm, Thunder and Lightning, and Rain and Rainbow.[7]

The religion and practice of Tengrism was closely tied to peoples' relationship with nature and animals. Animals were totemistic symbols for specific gods. Sheep were associated with fire, camels with the earth, horses with wind and cows with water.[8] Animals, therefore, were central to Turkic folktales and mythology, especially in often repeated fairytales where an animal helps and guides the hero.[9] This is most evident in respect of the 'heavenly wolf' that was descended from heaven and infused with the spirit of ancestors. The 'wolf' was revered as an intelligent, selfless and loyal friend that was the leader among the beasts'.[10]

What is most striking about Tengrism in relation to questions of post-Soviet Kazakh national identity is how as a broader philosophical and spiritual outlook it has become tied to a specific conceptualisation of a 'Kazakh' mentality. Specifically, the relationship between humankind, environment and animals, essential to the cosmological outlook of Tengrism, is seen to influence Kazakhs' *tusinik* (understanding) of themselves as possessing a distinct identity. It has been argued that 'the understanding of mutual relations with nature served as a bridge in understanding reality. Kazakhs always understood nature and did not contrast themselves to it and always aspired to be in harmony with it'.[11] This accord with nature was central to patterns of migration practised by the nomadic population of the steppe. Turkic-Mongol nomads did not 'lag behind the sun's circulation. They were there, where the sun was ... they surround time with the circle and drove it with their sheep. This circle, the circulation of the sun, distinguished nomads from settled people.'[12] In sum, Tengrism provided a belief system that gave meaning to life through a psycho-geographical relationship with nature and the vast open Central Asian steppe.

A critical aspect of the practice of Tengrism, both in its original pre-Islamic incarnation, and its revival in post-Soviet Kazakhstan (Kyrgyzstan and Mongolia too) is the role of the shaman. *Baksy* (shaman in Kazakh) are in possession of extremely rare and valuable gifts because of their perceived special connection to the spirit world. They have been noted for their ability to act 'as the bridge between heaven and earth'[13] and as 'a channelling voice of the spirit world'.[14] This bridge took physical form in the shamanic rituals, in which the *Baksy* would fall into a whirling dervish-like trance state to establish a connection with the other world. However, Devin DeWeese has suggested that the Central Asian people's inner religious life 'is much richer than the label shamanism suggests'.[15] Shamanistic figures performed a central function in the normative reproduction of communal rites, which served, in the words of James Thrower, to 'maintain material and social life — that is, with success in the hunt or agriculture, with fertility, and with the preservation of social identity and social cohesion'.[16]

Shamanistic figures also served an important role in maintaining contact with ancestors. The cult of ancestors was fundamental to Tengrist beliefs. For the nomadic population of the Kazakh steppe identity was not based on geographic boundaries, but rather on genealogical lineage and the ability to retain knowledge of ancestry as far back as seven generations. Children were inspired to venerate and respect their ancestors and, of course, their elders.[17] As Kazakh scholars note, this is reflected in a famous Kazakh proverb that 'ignorance of ancestry to the seventh generation is a sign of abandonment'.[18]

Essential to the reverence of ancestors within accounts of Tengrism is the role of women. Deities in Turkic culture were often represented in the image of a woman, and this is most obvious with respect to Umai, who represented mother earth and fertility, but who was also symbolised by the sun as the giver of life.[19] Woman was also imagined via animism in the protective figure of a wolf or snake.[20] This alludes to the recognition of women within Tengrism both symbolically and in practice as guardians, teachers, creators and guarantors of the Turkic populations.[21] This was further emphasised in Lev Gumilyev's classic text on the ancient Turks where he highlighted the respect afforded to women within Turkic culture and their perceived importance in terms of matrilineal descent for holding high office and for the continuation of the Turkic race through biological reproduction.[22] The situating of women in such a way echoes the gendered analysis of nationalism put forward by Floya Anthias and Nira Yual-Davis, who reveal the ways in which women are central to nationalist projects symbolically, as border guards, participants and as biological producers of the nation.[23]

While Tengrism was arguably the dominant religion of the Turkic-Mongol population of the Central Asian steppe, this is not to suggest there was no influence from other religions prior to the incursion of Islam from the seventh century onwards. Not least Zoroastrianism, Buddhism and Manichaeism. These were all state-sponsored religions at one time or another in the broader Persian and Asian region, which Central Asian nomads encountered, were converted to and/or integrated aspects into the practice of Tengrism.[24] It was Islam, however, which was to have the most profound effect on the Turkic religion.

The conversion of the Central Asian region to Islam was slow and both violent and peaceful. The initial invasion began under Usman in 649 AD and lasted until 715 AD.[25] Demographically, Central Asia has been traditionally depicted by historians as divided along sedentary and nomadic lines.[26] While some suggest that there is no such thing as pure nomadism, in that nomadic populations traded with settled communities in the region, and according to some accounts emerged from settled agricultural populations rather than the other way round,[27] this demographic fault line was extremely important for how Islam developed in Central Asia. While Islam initially took hold in the sedentary population through the early Arab invasions into the Oxus valley,[28] a long-lasting impression was not made on the settled populations until the more peaceful process of conversion through missionaries and merchants between the ninth and twelfth centuries.[29] The nomadic population, on the other hand, was converted to Islam much later, even as recently as the twentieth century. The reasons for such delayed conversion are numerous. Initially, Islamic missionaries and merchants had to compete with the Mongolian Empire of the thirteenth and fourteenth centuries, which promoted a form of state-sponsored Tengrism. Chingiz Khan and four generations of his successors were committed to the religion until Öz Beg Khan pursued the conversion of the Horde to Islam in the early fourteenth entury. At the same time, conversion of the nomadic population of the steppe was gradual because of the sheer distance for missionaries to travel and because of the migration of nomads. It meant the types of Islam to develop in the region were the more moderate, liberal Hanafi school and a somewhat mystical version of Sufism.[30] Rituals of Tengrism, and the shamanistic practices associated with it, continued to co-exist alongside, if not become synthesised with, Islam once it became the dominant religion in the region.[31]

In contemporary post-Soviet Kazakhstan, the idea that Islam remains a foreign religion non-native to the steppe and an external force gradually imposed on the population, means that Tengrism can take on both political and nationalist significance. The emergence of a Tengrist 'national' revival can be traced back at least to the late Soviet period in the short section on the subject that featured in Olzhas Suleimenov's 1975 book, *Az i Ya*.[32] In the post-Soviet period, however, Kazakh historians, journalists and cultural philosophers such as Kurmangazi Karamanuhli and Akseleu Seidimbek have venerated Tengrism as the 'native tradition' and pushed forward the argument that Islam was a foreign religion aggressively forced upon the Kazakh people and their ancestors.[33] Similar evocations of Tengrism as the 'national religion' have also found voice in movements in Kyrgyzstan and Tatarstan. Marléne Laruelle argues that these movements see Tengrism as constituting a possible version of a Kazakh (or Kyrgyz or Tatar) nationalism and that, as can often occur with conceptualisations of nationalism, it appeals to an exclusionary interpretation of national identity that espouses a form of biological primordialism and a commitment to ethnic purity.[34] This is highlighted by Raphael Bezertinov's statement, cited by Laruelle, that 'the spirit of a nation is oriented along three main lines: the unity of blood, language and religion'.[35] Tengrism, therefore, becomes the religious underpinning of a potentially distinctive Kazakh national identity. While these exclusionary and more extreme interpretations of Tengrism in Kazakhstan are limited to a small intellectual circle, the political power of Tengrism is obvious, and has already been taken up by some mainstream politicians. The former leader of the Party of Patriots, and ex-presidential candidate, Gani Kasymov, declared in 2010 that he supported Tengrism, which for him has a 5000-year history, while Islam had only been in Kazakhstan for 800 years.[36]

This above discussion on Tengrism highlights the way in which this ancient religion of the Turkic peoples has, in some circles, provided a spiritual basis for a form of Kazakh national identity that is distinct from the ethnic and civic forms sponsored through government policy. It provides for a grounding of post-Soviet Kazakh national identity that conjures up a continuation of the past. It offers a quasi-primordial account of national identity – venerating the cult of ancestors and ties to nomadic traditions. It advocates the importance of blood ties, kinship, families (and the central role of women in the continuation of the nation) and the cycle of birth, life and death. It uses myth, folklore, the supernaturalism of deities and shamanism to demonstrate the 'natural' and inseparable relationship between nomads and nature.[37] It is these key elements of Tengrism, as understood as the basis of Kazakh nationhood and identity, that we can see represented in contemporary cinematic works.

Literal Representations of Tengrism in Contemporary Kazakh Cinema

Tengrism appears in contemporary Kazakh cinema in a literal sense through the actions of characters or via the depiction of animals and symbols. This is most evident in Yermek Tursunov's film, *Kelin*. Set in the pre-Islamic second-century snow-capped Altay mountains, *Kelin* is on one level a simple tale about a girl who is married off to the wealthiest suitor in the locale who is not her preferred choice, and her struggle to acclimatise to her newfound matrimonial relations. The protagonist adapts to her circumstances, becomes a central part of her new family, and is guided by her mother-in-law, Ene, an elderly shaman. Part of her inner journey is represented by the development of her own sexual agency and her involvement initially in a love triangle, which later becomes a quadrilateral involving her lover, husband and her brother-in-law.[38]

Tengrism in *Kelin* is most obviously embodied in the elderly shaman character Ene and the rituals and practices she undertakes, such as drawing a map on the body of her deceased son of the underworld where Erlik resides and where spirits of the dead pass on to.[39] Similarly, we see Ene draw a circle of fire around the protagonist to purify her soul as part of a fertility ritual.[40]

In *Baksy* (2008) we also observe shamanistic practices and rituals. The film centres on the elderly Aidai, a shamanistic folk healer, who lives out in the wilderness of the steppe. People visit her to seek happiness and health, to find missing relatives or to be cured of ailments and problems (e.g., infertility, alcoholism, nymphomania).[41] The plot concerns a local businessman's efforts to buy Aidai's land to build a gas station, and the subsequent tension this produces vis-à-vis the immorality of the pursuit of wealth set against the moralistic and life-affirming practices of Aidai.

Figure 6.1 Turakhan Sadykova as Ene in *Kelin* (2009), dir. Yermek Tursunov.

Aidai practices traditional Turkic folk healing. For instance, in the opening scene a woman who initially has to walk on crutches is told to smother herself in the blood of a lamb while Aidai chants incantations. On completion of this healing practice the woman can walk, albeit unsteadily, without the aid of props. While Tengrism is not explicit in the film, there are a few specific references to Turkic mythology; for example, the opening credits allude to the ancient Turkic religion with a series of cave paintings. Moreover, there are two central scenes where Aidai falls into a whirling dervish-type trance, seemingly summoning the power of nature and the mystic spirits. The first occurs when she is confronted with the enforced sale of the land and because of her spinning trance falls to what appears to be her death (although she later rises from the mortuary slab). The second is at the end of the film where she dances upon a hill top, again summoning natural sprits, in what one review likened to a 'demented Kazakh version of Julie Andrews in the *Sound of Music*', to heal a young boy emotionally paralysed by the death of his father.[42]

In Russian director Sergei Bodrov's 2007 film *Mongol*, Tengrism is explicitly practised by Temüjin in a scene where in need of guidance he prays directly to Tengri. Throughout the film there are literal representations of the symbols and practices of the religion, which show how Tengrism became the state religion for the Golden Horde. *Mongol*, however, is difficult to qualify specifically as a Kazakh film. The subject of the film, Temüjin, is a Mongolian national hero, and the film was a co-production between Russian, German and Kazakh production companies with the Kazakh government reportedly ploughing $37 million dollars into the picture.[43] The film was partially shot in Kazakhstan, but mostly in China and Inner Mongolia, and the film's language was also in Mongolian and Mandurian. Despite the film also being Kazakhstan's entry into the Best Foreign Language Film for the 2007 Oscars, the complex and multi-national nature of the production makes it challenging to see it as a distinctly Kazakh film. That said, the underpinning literal representations of Tengrism, combined with the depiction of Chingiz Khan as a central part of the history of the Kazakh steppe (as we saw in Ardak Amirkulov's 1991 film *The Fall of Otrar*), makes it possible to understand why it could be perceived as a Kazakh film. However, aside from its strong reference to Tengrism (as part of a broader trend and narrative in Kazakh cinema), *Mongol* only serves to highlight the way representations of Kazakh nationhood and identity can rely on interpretations of historical events, figures and myths shared with other Turkic nations. In other words, it is not easy to tease out a distinct Kazakh identity when its history and religion are situated in a broader universal Turkic culture.

A further example of Tengrism's literal appearance in cinematic works is through the depiction of Tengrist gods and myth in the plot. Akhat Ibrayev's 2012 film *The Book of Legends: The Mysterious Forest* is perhaps the only film in contemporary Kazakh cinema that explicitly used Tengrist gods and myths. The film sits within the children's fantasy genre and was noted for being the first Kazakh domestic-produced CGI film. It concerns the adventures of two mischievous young brothers, Tahka and Bahka, who come across the mythical tale of the Queen of the Turkic Amazons who is fighting a battle against evil. They agree to help the Queen of the Amazons in exchange for the chance to bring their mother back to life. Tahka and Bahka are sons of a prominent businessman but cause much trouble with their step-mother who arranges to have them kidnapped. The boys are left in a forest that possesses a portal to the magical world of the Turkic Amazons. Throughout their journey in the magical forest they meet different creatures and gods who aid them on their quest.[44] They come across the key gods in the Tengrist pantheon, Erlik, Tengri and Umai. However, the film is shaped by more universal influences. The plot is based partly on the O. Henry short story *The Ransom of Red Chief*, while the kidnappers evoke the 1990 American family film *Home Alone*.[45] Moreover, the director has spoken of the influence of Joseph Campbell's comparative mythological work *Hero of a Thousand Faces* on his movie.[46] Nevertheless, as Ibrayev has argued, the use of Tengrist gods in the film was a deliberate attempt to add a Kazakh twist to the universalist models of mythology developed by Campbell.[47] The tension between the specificity of a Kazakh-infused Tengrism versus the universalism that often informs cinematic works in Kazakhstan will be discussed below.

Stylistic tensions aside, Tengrist mythology is literal to *The Book of Legends* not least in the way in which animals are present in the film, most notably the grey wolf who initially guides the boys in the search for their mother. The literal depiction of animals is central to *Kelin* too. Fourteen species of animals appear in the film, including wolves, vultures, owls and mice.[48] The appearance of animals often acts as a representation of a human spirit or an omen of unfortunate events.

For example, Ene is made aware that her son has been killed by the presence and movement of an owl. Similarly, in a scene when Kelin is in rapture after being given a necklace by Mergen, her lover and the man who killed her husband Baktashy, she is only made aware of her disloyalty to her deceased husband by the appearance of a bird, suggestively representing the spirit of Baktashy. This totemism was not lost in the reception of the film. One review noted that 'almost each character corresponds to a key animal – marking the identification with nature'.[49]

The music scores in both *Kelin* and *The Book of Legends* also provide a literal representation of Tengrism. For *Kelin*, the music score was composed by Edil Khusanov, a classically trained musician who specialises in ancient Asian (and Turkic) instruments. It is these instruments and the double-throated singing that comprise the music for the film. Combined with the lack of dialogue, the use of ancient Turkic instruments and natural noises of animals and nature add to the sense of a connection with the ancient Turkic world.[50] For *Book of Legends*, the composer Nikita Karev also wrote 120 minutes of original music based on Turkic and shamanic chants.[51]

While the literal representation of shamanistic practices, the use of Turkic myths and gods, the depiction of animals and the use of music demonstrate that Tengrism has emerged as a small, but nonetheless important aspect of contemporary cinematic work, it is the symbolic significance of Tengrism that is most imperative in relation to conceptualisations of Kazakh nationhood and identity. It is the deeper philosophic and moralistic undertones of Tengrism's representation in film that provide something concrete in terms of offering a distinctive form of Kazakh nationalism.[52]

Historical-philosophical Symbolic Representation of Tengrism in Contemporary Kazakh Cinema

The psycho-geographical idea of man living in harmony with nature, a notion central to the philosophy of Tengrism, appears as a fundamental aspect of *Kelin* (2009) and *Shal* (2012). These films are part of a trilogy of movies written, produced and directed by Tursunov. The third film, *Kenzhe* (young brother), was released in 2015. The trilogy is framed by Tursunov as 'the evolution of the nation from ancient times to modernity

... *Kelin* is set in the mountains, *Shal* is in the steppe and *Kenzhe* is in the city. As an ethnic group, we came from the Altay mountain, then we went down to the steppe and now we live in cities'.[53] 'It is the evolution of the ethnic group. Where we have been and where we are going'.[54] Therefore, all three films are seeking to represent a narrative regarding Kazakhstan's nationhood and identity. It is *Kelin* and *Shal*, however, which most overtly connect nationhood and identity with Tengrism.

Tengrism in these movies emerges re-imagined. It acts as a philosophical system of belief that reconnects the nation with a distant 'lost' nomadic past. Tursunov has been explicit regarding using the idea of Tengrism and ancient Turkic rituals, rites and myths in his work, stating it is 'an attempt to return to ourselves. We have forgotten who we are'.[55] The director further argues that remembrance of the past to create a sense of distinct identity for the present requires:

> a study of the history and development of ancient Turkic tribal unions. It is necessary to build a study of the general history of Turkic blood brotherhood and kinship. History of the Great Turan state and the Great Steppe should really become that foothold ... and we must remember that in the world there is nothing worse for a nation than spiritual assimilation.[56]

From this perspective, national distinctiveness for post-Soviet Kazakhstan stems from the traditional nomadic way of life and how Tengrism provides a belief system rooted in the psychogeographical relationship between nomads, nature and the steppe. Again, Tursunov alludes to the importance of this:

> nomads had their own system of values which was completely different from those of a settled population. Nomads didn't have an idea of a state, because they were constantly moving. A settled way of life implies having some territory: some limited spaces where he grows his crop. The nomad was tied to his cattle: he followed his cattle wherever it went. This is why for the nomad the land is infinite, he doesn't know where it ends, and he is not even asking himself this question, he just follows his cattle. This is a source of the nomad's worldview and religiousness. We didn't have

Islam here, we were pagans, Tengrians. It was cult of fire, cult of mountain and cult of ancestors.[57]

These themes are recurrent through *Kelin* and *Shal*. *Kelin*, for example, portrays the return to this traditional and 'national' way of life. This is expressed through the symbolism of animals and the ways in which Ene appeals to higher spiritual forces throughout the film. *Kelin*, however, was not intended as an expression of a specific 'Kazakh' identity. Some criticism of the film centred on whether the characters were meant to represent Kazakhs or Kyrgyz, and whether or not the film was supposed to be a depiction of their lives at that time.[58] It was not. As film critic Oleg Boretskiy argued, 'Tursunov did not make this movie about Kazakhs. It states in the opening titles the setting is Altay in the second century AD: there was no Kazakhstan back then. Some Kazakh things can be recognised, but the film concerns a general Asian mentality'.[59] *Kelin* is thus concerned with reminding the audience about the connection to this Turkic past, it was not a definitive statement on Kazakh national identity.

Shal, on the other hand, develops the philosophical ideas of Tengrism begun in *Kelin* and applies them, in a much more specific but less literal way, to the idea of a Kazakh identity or at the very least, as one cinema viewer framed it, to the notion of 'the Kazakh spirit'.[60] This is expressed in the underlying theme of *Shal*, which concerns humanity's need to live in harmony with nature, not to be the master of it but rather act as an organic part of the environment. The film concerns the story of an elderly shepherd, Kasym, who gets lost in the freezing and foggy step after agreeing to move his neighbour's flock to new pasture. While lost in the steppe he also protects the flock of sheep from a pack of wolves. Kasym survives in the steppe through the strength and resilience of his character, but also because of his empathy and appreciation for the necessity of equilibrium between humankind and nature.[61] Nature in the film is represented by the wolves and especially the mother of the pack (another example of the way in which the film is influenced by Tengrist ideas of totemism). Kasym's position and relationship with nature and the wolves is juxtaposed with those of a Russian hunting crew who, despite Kasym's warnings that it is closed season because the wolves have just given birth to their pups, go ahead on their hunt and treat the environment with abandonment. Their demise in the steppe is sealed by their failure to respect the necessary balance between humankind and nature. As the director noted, 'the steppe can either be a caring mother, or act as a wicked stepmother ... it all depends on how you treat it – as a big dumpster or as your own god'.[62]

The character of Kasym embodies this national 'Kazakh' spirit. He is patient, resilient, has a sense of humour and cares about future generations. He represents the fathers and grandfathers who had difficult lives, but understands the steppe and the need to preserve nature and the important traditions of the past in the face of modernity.[63] He symbolises the tradition of the Kazakh elder – who, as Tursunov explained is not 'a person of advanced age. An elder is someone with a moral and ethical code.'[64] Inter-generationalism is embodied in the relationship between Kasym and his grandson Erali. There is a disconnection between the two characters' frames of reference. Kasym wants Erali to be interested in his archaic wisdom and the old-fashioned practices 'which have helped him and his people survive for centuries'.[65] Erali is more interested in his handheld computer game and the expensive SUV driven by the Russian hunters than his grandfather's old ways. Kasym nicknames Erali *Shaitan-bek* (mischievous one) because of his cheekiness towards him. Despite this, their relationship in the film is close, as evident in Erali's concern for his missing grandfather and the lengths and effort he goes to in searching for him. Their relationship is symbolic of a central theme of Tengrism – the cult of ancestors. Kasym is seeking to pass on the traditions of the steppe to Erali in an increasing complex and disinterested modern world of false values. He is seeking to teach him the wisdom of ancestors and to respect the traditional ways of life of the Kazakhs out in the steppe and their eternal values: to be a good person, to raise offspring and to live in harmony with nature.[66] The film implies it is these values, the norms of the ancient Kazakh nomadic Turks, which form the national character and which need to be preserved for future generations.[67]

Shal is also a purposefully biblical film. The sight of Kasym wandering lost in the brittle and unforgiving steppe, alone at the mercy of mother nature and her pack of wolves, certainly evokes the 'wilderness' story found in Christianity. Kasym was even compared to Moses 'wandering over the steppe' by one film critic.[68] Yet, the film's religiosity centres on a tension between Islam and Tengrism within the Kazakh national psyche. This tension is played out in a

Figure 6.2 Yerbolat Toguzakov as Kasym in *Shal* (2012), dir. Yermek Tursunov.

conversation between Kasym and one of the hunters (who is Kazakh) when both are lost and find shelter in what looks like the outer casing of an abandoned rocket.[69] The hunter and Kasym discuss religion, with Kasym noting that he had not visited Mecca, but made the steppe his god.[70] The hunter and Kasym are construed in the film to represent the polarisation between Islam and Tengrism (the hunter tells Kasym how he had built a mosque) and the argument regarding two religious identities in Kazakhstan. As film critic Oleg Boretskiy has argued, 'Tursunov believes Tengrism is the spiritual base of Kazakhstan, its nomadic spirituality, and he believes Islam is not really the religion of Kazakhs ... if we look at the social aspect of Islam today in Kazakhstan it becomes a kind of fashion, for many it is part of their identity, if you ask a young man he will tell you that he is a Muslim, but there is not a deep belief behind this'.[71] As noted earlier in the chapter, the type of Islam that developed in Kazakhstan was fundamentally shaped by the nomadic way of life. Consequently, Tursunov argues that 'Islam is sedentarism, you must go to mosque, you can't travel far from the mosque, you have to pray five times per day. The nomad just packed his yurt and moved away. He cannot carry a mosque with him.'[72]

All the films within the Tengrist narrative use the Kazakh language. Russian is only spoken if a Russian character is on the screen. This reflects the natural interplay of languages in contemporary Kazakhstan. Kazakh would be widely spoken in *auls*, but Russian is used to communicate with other nationalities. Therefore, what we see in this narrative is not just an underlying religious and philosophical basis for a Kazakh identity that returns the Kazakh people to a 'lost' past rooted in the psychogeography of the steppe, but also a confidence in the group's specific communicative tool. This makes the films unashamedly Kazakh with a clear sense of group boundary. Of course, the films all have a version where Russian is dubbed over the top. Commercially, the market is not there for Kazakh-language only releases. The fact, however, that Kazakh is the primary language of these films, combined with the focus on Tengrism and specific Kazakh/Turkic myths and a relationship with nature, demonstrates the extent to which the Tengrist narrative is seeking to carve out a conceptualisation of identity and nationhood that is distinct and in opposition to the encroaching forces of globalisation.

The Tengrist cinematic narrative, therefore, is often situated in contradistinction to the conforming forces of modernity. This is especially the case with Tursunov's underlying approach to *Shal*. One reviewer noted how the fog that hangs over the steppe in the film is an allegory for the 'Kazakhs long wandering in the fog and when the fog dissipated an evil world of globalisation has materialised in the form of a pack of hungry wolves'.[73] While this may be a rather sharp characterisation, the director evidently did seek to say something regarding the place of traditional values in a globalised world. In his own words, he has argued that:

> when a nation is losing its traditional values, its religion and its important moral values that were intrinsic to nomadic life, like respect for elders and personal responsibility, it is losing its position and getting washed away. It is becoming more and more difficult to distinguish this nation from other nations ... we sit here now and see the cars driving outside, none of them were made in Kazakhstan ... we are driving things created by others and we consume everything foreign ... this is the Western steamroller which is flattening everything. Our youth is losing important

national values, and it is bad not only for us, but bad for the rest of the world.[74]

It would be unfair to paint Tursunov as anti-modern and a primordial ethnic exclusionist based on his desire to represent a commitment to 'important moral values intrinsic to nomadic life'. The picture is much more complicated. Firstly, *Kelin* and *Shal* are both films based on universalist precepts. *Kelin* is a film without words. It relies instead on the guttural sounds of human communication and the sound of nature. This is a film that can be watched by anyone. Moreover, its themes of family, kinship, preservation and the struggle for existence are relatable in any social community around the globe. Secondly, *Shal* is based on Ernest Hemingway's *The Old Man and the Sea*. Rather than Santiago being stuck at sea battling against sharks, Kasym is lost in the wilderness of the Kazakh steppe, pitting his wits against wolves. While Santiago's young apprentice Manolin speaks of his love of baseball and Joe DiMaggio, Kasym has a love of football and names his flock after the 1970 Football World Cup-winning Brazilian team. *Shal* is not a unique or distinctive Kazakh story. Like *The Old Man and the Sea*, it is an allegorical tale about the natural cycle of life and the importance of passing on important values to the next generation to maintain this natural order. Kasym, like Santiago, is an archetypal character upon which we can impose our own set of culturally specific values and moral codes. For some of the audience, the universality of *Shal* left them feeling that 'it did not in any way bring out the Kazakh spirit', seeing it simply as an international adaptation of Hemmingway's story.[75] It demonstrates Tursunov has no intention of espousing an exclusive 'national' identity and set of values. As he has said himself, he is 'not against modernity rather that while becoming modern we should preserve our values'.[76] *The Old Man and the Sea* was used simply to present a 'Kazakh' version of an age-old story – the biblical wandering into the wilderness. It is the same for Akhat Ibrayev and his desire to use the mythological templates developed by Joseph Campbell but instead give them a Kazakh/Turkic spin using Tengrist gods and myths.

Shal was met with significant domestic acclaim. Reviews were complementary of the film's key theme regarding overcoming constant struggles using moral and physical strength.[77] Simultaneously, critics noted how the film spoke to questions of 'national identity about what we should do now, and what principles we should use to build relationships with each other.'[78] However, despite recognition that the film portrayed Kazakhstan with a unique face, Tursunov was criticised for using the Hemmingway plot as a template – with one reviewer asking 'why use someone else's story? Why copy samples of Western literature?'[79] The claim here is that by using a plot derived from *The Old Man and the Sea*, Tursunov is contradicting his assessment of how the encroachment of Westernisation or globalisation is eroding national values.

The film's tension of universalism versus a distinct Kazakh identity was mirrored in focus group discussions with cinema audiences. Some argued the film lacked national specificity because of the similarities with Hemmingway's plot, while others felt that he did represent the 'Kazakh spirit' because as one participant noted, 'what Tursunov did was take a classic story and just give it national characteristics'.[80] This was negatively received by other participants, who argued Tursunov's cinematic technique created ambiguity because 'he gives room for many interpretations depending on our values and views.'[81]

Outside of film critics like Oleg Boretskiy, audience reception of *Shal* did not touch upon the influence of Tengrist philosophy on the film. Nonetheless, it was clear that many cinema-goers recognised that *Shal* evoked a sense of national spirit. Numerous comments on the kino.kz website allude to the film resonating with audiences in terms of its national message. A series of comments portend to this, such as, 'excellent film that transmits the "spirit" of the Kazakh steppe and our Kazakhstan', 'the film makes you think about life and the values in it', 'Kazakhs, patriots of our country, go see the film, you will definitely enjoy it', 'the film has soul, our proud ancestors' and 'it is a masterpiece, our, small Kazakh masterpiece. This is more than a movie – this is life, this is poetry . . . '.[82] This sample give a sense of the extent to which the film was received positively and with a degree of national pride. There were criticisms, most notably in terms of some of the unrealistic elements of the plot and some issues with actors' performances, but by-and-large the film was met domestically with praise.[83] Likewise, internationally[84] the film was well-received. Reviews focused on the deep-layered meaning of the film and its semi-religious quality.[85]

There is a further element to the Tengrist narrative fundamental to representations of nationhood and identity to be discussed, and that is the role and centrality of women to the Kazakh nation.

Quasi-primordial Symbolic Representation: Women, Family and the Cycle of Birth, Life and Death

The multifaceted role of 'mother' as the personification of the nation, the protector, carrier of traditions and giver of life is central to this narrative of nationhood. This is represented by the vivid portrayal of the primordial role of 'mother' within Kazakh families. The shamanistic character in *Baksy*, Aidai, is symbolic of the importance of women for protecting and passing on the traditions of the people and thus acting as a metaphor and symbol for the nation.[86] Similarly, Ene is a powerful figure of authority in *Kelin*. She guides her daughter-in-law, passing on traditions and ensuring the family continues. The final scene has Kelin alone feeding her newly born infant as Ene walks away. The imagery tells us that responsibility for carrying the progenetic line lies now with Kelin. The symbolism is stark: without the mother – without the role of women as biological reproducers – the nation cannot survive.

Biological reproduction is represented in both *Kelin* and *Shal* through the symbolism of the circle, used to illustrate the cycle of birth, life and death. In *Kelin* Ene draws a circle of fire around her daughter-in-law as part of a fertility ritual, while in *Shal* Kasym builds a circle of fire around his flock of sheep to protect them from wolves. Amid the chaos as wolves break through the circle of fire to maul and kill Kasym's sheep, a new black baby lamb is born. The lamb ends up being the only survivor of the flock by the end of the film. The message is clear. From death comes life. As Oleg Boretskiy noted – 'the symbolism of the circle is a key element of the film. Human life is a circle. Man in born naked and will die naked. Man, is born out of the ground and goes back into the ground'.[87] The death ritual depicted in *Kelin*, where Ene draws a map of the underworld on Baktashy's body and the scenes of infant feeding, also demonstrate the centrality of the cycle of birth, life and death.[88]

Baksy and *The Book of Legends* also highlight the importance of 'mother' to narratives of nationhood, but through absence. In *Baksy*, one of the central characters, Asan, is a young boy without a mother, who is left in the care of Aidai by his father because she previously cured the boy's mother of infertility (even though the mother then died in childbirth). In *Book of Legends*, the central aim of Tahka and Bahka's quest is to bring their deceased mother back to life. The absence of the mother in these two films, therefore, is startling. Without the mothers the characters are incomplete and without mothers, nations are incomplete. Nevertheless, Aidai takes on a surrogate mother role for Asan, while the mythic characters that Tahka and Bahka meet on their quest play a similar surrogate role for the two brothers, especially the wolf, a totemic figure for motherhood within the Turkic tradition. The wolves in *Shal* are also representative of mothers. In one key scene Kasym stares down the mother of the pack. In this one moment, the wolf and Kasym connect on a deeper spiritual level, as Tursunov explained, 'the wolf in this final scene looks at the old man's human eyes – as a mother'.[89] The symbolic focus on the wolf in both *Kelin* and *Shal* is significant for the imaginary of Kazakh nationhood too, as according to legend the ancestors of the Kazakhs were nurtured by a wolf.[90] This Turkic myth informed the philosophical approach Tursunov took to *Kelin*. As he commented in an interview, 'our wolf gave birth to a boy, who had 10 sons, whom in turn produced another five hundred families. Their blood flows in the veins of Kazakhs today.'[91]

The above pertains to a depiction of nationhood that is rooted in a quasi-primordial understanding of nations. In *Kelin*, especially, we see that the Kazakh nation is not born from the violent struggles against invading Mongolian *Oirats*, nor is it created through the forced deportations of the Soviet period, rather the Kazakh nation is formed as all nations are created, in the cycle of birth, life and death, in families, endogamy and the process of reproduction. The symbolic importance of mother in *Kelin*, *Shal*, *Baksy* and *Book of Legends* evokes the idea that nations are tied together by their ancient practices and the primordial ties of kinship, blood and loyalty that cement group unity. Blood ties are particularly evident in the films. Early on in *Kelin* the protagonist takes a blood oath with Mergen (her preferred lover), while blood features heavily in the healing practices of Aidai in *Baksy*. Here nations are interpreted as the embodiment of extended families[92] – and it is the continuation of those families and the traditions and rituals inherent to them that are most important to the survival and reproduction of the nation, especially in the face of the globalisation. In reference to *Kelin*, Tursunov has argued, 'we will survive as long as we have such women. I believe that the biggest achievement of nature – is the creation of the fairer sex, which keeps our world going. Underlying all of this is the female. Women are resilient, even though they suffer more than men. This film is a hymn of Turkic women, our mothers, our foremothers'.[93]

The representation of women in this way is problematic for many reasons. The role of woman is reduced to that of a totemic symbol of biological reproduction. It undermines the agency of women in these films. Even the sexual agency of the protagonist in *Kelin* is performed in such a way that her actions are driven by the perceived necessity of biological reproduction. The lack of voice in *Kelin* is instructive too. Kelin has no voice and no authority in the film. Authority for women only appears once they have fulfilled their role as reproducers of the nation, as in the case of Ene in *Kelin* and Aidai in *Baksy*. In addition, the absence of mothers (we never see Kelin's mother, the mother in *Book of Legends*, nor the mother in *Baksy*) in these films underlines the reductive position given to women within this narrative. Even when the mother is shown on screen, as in *Shal*, she is both a silent and peripheral figure. In this sense, the depiction and positioning of women and mothers within this narrative reflects, to some extent, the patriarchal nature of Kazakh society. This is especially relevant in the post-Soviet period where the government has been criticised for failing to protect the rights of women, particularly with regards to domestic violence and sex trafficking.[94]

Controversy and Reception

The representation of women within this narrative, and their centrality to the depiction of nationhood, was met with some criticism and controversy. *Kelin* received an especially stormy reception because of the numerous sex scenes and the perceived promiscuous nature of the protagonist. Deputies from the *Mazhilis* (parliament) were highly critical of the film's portrayal of Kazakh women, believing it to be an affront to their dignity, immoral and crossing the line from eroticism to vulgarity.[95] It is alleged that many ordinary citizens wrote to the Administration of the President and Minister of Culture complaining about Tursunov's depiction of Kazakhs.[96] Nevertheless, the director defended himself by noting that the film is a universal tale about the strength of human spirit and an anthem to Turkic women in general, not just Kazakhs.[97] In reality the sex scenes are minimal and not explicit, at least not by the standards of Western cinema.[98] Evidence from cinema audiences suggest that the controversial sex scenes did not detract from their perception that *Kelin* was a significant Kazakh film, not least for its deeper Tengrist meaning. One audience member who participated in a focus group commented that, 'this film impressed me. Why? Because for me it was the first time a Kazakh film shows a saga. It's just a family saga in a very historical context in the pre-Muslim and pre-Islamic periods . . . for me this film was good because it showed a very primordial order of family relations . . . Tursunov wanted to demonstrate the best of the best of Kazakh Tengrism and authentic culture'.[99] Such a reaction is notable on two accounts. The first being that the Tengrist theme and its implications in terms of the primordial basis of nationhood is clearly recognisable to some audience members. Secondly, despite the universal qualities of the film, the inherent symbolism of the picture was still interpreted, at least in this instance, as recognisably Kazakh. This perhaps explains why the film garnered such voracious criticism from so-called 'national patriots' who felt the movie disrespected Kazakh women and showed Kazakhs as a primitive people.[100]

Tursunov commented in an interview that people who liked the film, such as the focus group participant cited above, were a minority.[101] The evidence perhaps suggests otherwise.[102] Other participants in the focus groups were acutely aware of the symbolism and the message Tursunov was trying to push, despite the universal themes. For instance, one audience member noted that the film is:

> trying to fill in this empty niche of ideology we don't have. If we don't believe in the leader, the great leader, what do we believe in? Do we believe in Allah? Do we believe in Tengri? I think we can see in these films this identity crisis that has been going on for the last 20 to 25 years. Some people like the idea we are pagan tribes roaming in the steppes, but on the other hand you cannot take out 500 years of Islamic history.[103]

Notable in this comment is that films (and this includes *Kelin*) are perceived to act as a social canvas upon which these complex debates and ideas about post-Soviet Kazakh (and Kazakhstani) identity can play out. *Kelin* is understood by this audience member as an effort to speak to questions of post-Soviet identity and in this case the movie provides an interpretation of identity rooted in pre-Islamic Tengrist philosophy.

The evidence from the kino.kz forum suggests the broader cinema audience were positive about the film. *Shal* received significantly more comments than *Kelin*,[104] which perhaps says something about the differentiated social reach of each film, with *Shal* seemingly more popular. Nonetheless, while there were two notable negative comments stating that *Kelin* was a 'disgusting, horrible movie', and 'trash, mockery of the audience' with a 'script perfect for a porn movie', most feedback was broadly positive, or at the very least not openly hostile. Some commentators alluded to the importance of symbols within the film, with one describing the movie as 'ethnographic', and others picking out the centrality of gender and biological reproduction to the continuation of nations, noting the film to be about 'the struggle of a woman, of life, and the continuation of humanity'.[105]

Tursunov found himself under pressure from Kazakhfilm Studios, who financed the film, to cut the sex scenes from *Kelin*. The director, however, did not relent, and while the picture belonged to Kazakhfilm Studios, Tursunov owned the copyright for the film and his lawyers explained to him the studio could not re-edit the picture without his consent.[106] Amid the controversy, Tursunov compared the film to a baby child. 'For me this film is my child. Imagine if you had a baby who was born with a crooked ear, do you give them to the doctor to heal or give up the offspring? My child may have a slanting eye and a crooked ear, but I will not cut it. That is my position and I will not change it'.[107] Despite threats of public prosecution, and a physical attack on the director,[108] Tursunov reached out successfully to the then director of Kazakhfilm Studios, Yermek Amanshayev, and the film was released to much international acclaim, including being the country's entry into the foreign film category for the Oscars in 2010, where it made the semi-final.[109] The director's conflict with Kazakhfilm studios, and his position as the perceived 'black sheep' within Kazakh cinema, is indicative of a broader complex issue when it comes to determining the relationship between the state, Kazakhfilm Studios, and these narratives around nationhood and identity, which is discussed below.

Conclusion

Tursunov's use of Tengrism in his films and his depiction of Kazakh women provide us with a narrative regarding nationhood and identity in post-Soviet Kazakhstan that is distinct from the two regime-led narratives which focus on ethnic primacy and civic inclusivity.

The Tengrist narrative is, therefore, dissenting in some respects. Indeed, the director has described himself as not a rebel but a 'dissident spirit'.[110] His willingness to go to the wall against Kazakhfilm Studios, even though they funded the film, and to not falter from his conception of how his films should be realised, is representative of a contentious strain. Tursunov's films exemplify that he is not bound by a national ideology framed and constructed in the corridors of the Ministry of Culture or *Akorda* (Presidential Administration). The controversy his films received at the official level demonstrates that Tursunov's conception of Kazakh identity is not regime-approved and thus represents a challenge to the ethnic and civic narratives. Through films like *Kelin* and *Shal*, Tursunov has illustrated that cinema can be a site for dissenting voices. While he is not challenging the power of Nazarbayev, nor the political system itself, his films and the deeper symbolic meaning inherent within them, have confronted the narratives on nationhood and identity that have monopolised the public space in cultural terms through films such as *Nomad*, *Zhauzhurek Myn Bala* and *Sky of My Childhood*. It is important not to overstate the case, however. The political influence of this narrative is limited and the reach of these films to a broader audience is partial. Nevertheless, it illustrates that despite the way Kazakhstan is viewed both internally and externally as an authoritarian system with space for public dissent becoming increasingly narrower and narrower with each passing year of the Nazarbayev tenancy of the presidential office, there are in fact marginal spaces for opposition and alternative prescriptions on at least one core social and political issue – that of nationhood and identity.

The above leaves us with two issues to reflect upon. Firstly, it illustrates that there is fluidity and complexity to these narratives on nationhood and identity. Kazakhfilm Studios is the state-funded and Ministry of Culture-sponsored cinematic arm of the state. As noted in previous chapters, the studio often acts in accordance with prescriptions put forward by the Ministry of Culture for the types of films to go into production. Yet, despite this, a director with an independent artistic voice can produce and finance films through the studios, which to some degree act in dissonance with the preferred cultural prescriptions of the regime. It demonstrates, therefore, the second issue of note, which is that there are limitations to the extent of the regime's monopoly on culture in this authoritarian environment. It suggests narratives with a dissident strain can creep through the cracks of the system. While Tursunov is a dissident voice, his work is more thoughtful, spiritual and philosophical than radical. It is a meditative voice, which ruminates on the psychogeography of the Kazakhs' relationship with the steppe and the primordial importance of women to nationhood and survival. The latter aspect is a universal concern in some respect, and perhaps Tursunov's use of universal values and parables (e.g., *The Old Man and the Sea*) are part of the reason he can succeed in making films with Kazakhfilm Studios that are not in line with the regime's preferred narratives on nationhood and identity. There are, however, cinematic voices that go beyond the philosophical and spiritual narrative of Tengrism that provide a representation of nationhood in Kazakhstan, which are considered more realistic and more concrete in terms of the lived day-to-day socio-economic experiences of ordinary citizens. It is this narrative, which is perhaps more robust in its political dissidence, that this book turns to next.

CHAPTER 7

THE STEPPE, DISORIENTATION, DIVISION AND CORRUPTION: SOCIAL AND ECONOMIC VISIONS OF MODERN NATIONHOOD

The previous chapter demonstrated how aspects of contemporary Kazakh cinema reflect the heterogeneity of nationhood and identity. The Tengrist narrative in the work of Yermek Tursunov provides a quasi-primordial conceptualisation of Kazakh nationhood rooted in a reading of national identity founded upon the pre-Islamic religion of Tengrism, a psycho-geographic interpretation of Kazakhs' relationship with the steppe and the centrality of woman to the nation and the cycle of birth, life and death. The narrative illustrates that it is possible to observe multiple and contentious readings of the nation within cinema, particularly after the flattening of the cinematic landscape caused by the 'Kazakh New Wave'. The Tengrist narrative provides a moderate and philosophic voice which challenges, or at the very least is at odds with, the regime-led ethnic and civic narratives concerning post-Soviet nationhood and identity. This chapter details another, and final, narrative that also challenges these 'official' conceptualisations of the Kazakh nation, but does so in a more direct and critical way than the Tengrist narrative.

The socio-economic narrative offers an account of contemporary nationhood rooted in the internal divisions of the Kazakh nation and the struggles of citizens in their day-to-day lives. In this narrative, it is the experience of post-Soviet hardship that captures the essence and meaning of post-Soviet nationhood. The emergence of the socio-economic narrative coincided with an expansion in the capacity of the cinema industry in Kazakhstan. The government's bolstering of finances to Kazakhfilm Studios, combined with the emergence of some privately financed films, led to a rise in the number of domestic-produced films. From 2004 to 2008 Kazakhfilm Studios was producing four films a year. From 2008 to 2014 this increased to ten.[1] When accounting for independent films, as well those produced by the state-funded studios, 2012 saw 14 Kazakh-produced films released, 2013 16 films and 2014 20.[2] Underpinning this increase in domestic production was an expansion in the network of cinemas across the country. In 2001 there were only 37 cinemas in Kazakhstan, all of them single-screen. By 2011 this had increased to 94 with many of the newly created cinemas being modern multiplexes featuring digital technology.[3] By 2017 it is estimated that there are 270 screens in total across the whole country with an average of 10 million visits to the cinema.[4] The period has also witnessed greater cooperation between distributors and exhibitors, and increased collaboration between local and Russian distributors.[5]

It is within this context we see the emergence of two broad sets of directors in this period: those interested in commercial cinema, seeking to make the most of the new conditions within the cinema market; and those who continued to pursue auteur cinema and carried the torch of the 'Kazakh New Wave', less concerned with the domestic market and more interested in exhibiting their work on the international film festival circuit.

Inspired by the form, modes and aesthetics of Hollywood cinema, yet with an artistic sensibility for social realism, Akan Satayev was at the vanguard of a group of directors committed to making popular cinema along with other directors such as Akhat Ibrayev, Farkhat Sharipov, Nurtas Adambayev, Kairzhan Orynbekov and Bayan Yesentaeva.

As noted in a previous chapter, this division between commercial and art-house directors does not neccesarily correspond to commercial cinema only being produced by the state or art-house being solely produced by independent studios. Kazakhfilm Studios continue to support directors from the art-house camp, while independent studios often seek to produce commercial blockbusters.

There is also fluidity within this narrative. Despite being perceived as the cinematic arm of the state, Kazakhfilm Studios is responsible for financing and producing some films that undermine and challenge the regime's preferred narrative on nationhood and identity, including the work of Adilkhan Yerzhanov, whose films offer the most critical reading of contemporary nationhood. This is indicative of the complexity and messiness of production models in Kazakhstan. Not all commercial blockbuster films are funded by the state (Kairzhan Orynbekov's *The Kazakh Robbery* is but one example) and some art-house films are produced by Kazakhfilm Studios. Moreover, international co-productions also play a significant role in the financing of films within this narrative. Nevertheless, the films produced by this new generation of directors (both art-house and commercial) inscribe in their celluloid form a writing of post-Soviet existence that is troubled, focusing on the trials facing the lived day-to-day experiences of citizens in the country. Inherent to this narrative is the implicit idea that to be a member of the Kazakh nation is to face the challenges and traumas of everyday life.

The two forms of cinema also raise issues in relation to audience reception, which will be discussed throughout the chapter. While more commercially minded films might not offer original aesthetics and form, relying instead on the tropes and conventions of Western cinema, they did find a domestic audience in Kazakhstan and were successful at the box office, suggesting perhaps greater potential in shaping audience identity formation. Art-house films, while being more original in content and form, and offering a far greater critique of contemporary post-Soviet life, demonstrate less purchase with domestic audiences. Many of the art-house films achieved international acclaim and awards, but their domestic distribution has been restricted and the films have received significant criticism from government officials unhappy at their representation of the realities of post-Soviet life in Kazakhstan. This alludes to the more challenging task art-house films have in shaping audience attitudes.

This chapter unpacks this socio-economic narrative of nationhood and identity in Kazakhstan by analysing a series of fundamental signs constituting this representation of national identity. This includes: the difficult, dislocating and disorienting conditions of living in the steppe; the division between rural and urban life; struggles with bureaucracy, authorities and officialdom; challenges to the family unit; and questions of morality and the desire for wealth accumulation. Taken together, these signs represent a cohesive narrative regarding the lived day-to-day experience of post-Soviet nationhood. This narrative also challenges the government's conception of modernity, which understands the country as affluent and prosperous. The government's rendering of contemporary life is also discussed at the end of the chapter.

The Kazakh Steppe

In Adilkhan Yerzhanov's 2016 documentary *The Story of Kazakh Cinema*, Yerzhanov asks director Satybaldy Narymbetov if there is a difference between Kazakh cinema and the cinema of other countries. Narymbetov's answer includes three distinguishing factors – the first, and most important of which, is landscape.[6] We have seen earlier in this book that landscape has been fundamental to representations of national identity, even from the earliest film of the Soviet period, *Amangeldy*, while in contemporary works such as *Nomad* and *Zhauzhurek Myn Bala* the landscape is the symbolic topographical representation of Kazakhstan. It is observed as expansive, opulent, beautiful and fertile. It is realised on screen as life-giving and, as we saw in *Shal*, central to the psychological make-up of the Kazakh mentality. This, however, is only one depiction. In *Tulpan* (2008), *Strayed* (2009) and *Constructors* (2013), the Steppe is not the sumptuous, bountiful and vast land of beauty; rather it is, as one director noted, 'a beautiful, but very harsh, inhospitable land'.[7]

Tulpan, a film by Kazakh-born Russian director Sergei Dvortsevoy, evokes this representation of the steppe as infertile and hostile. The film tells the story of Asa, who returns from serving in the Navy to live in the wilderness of Betpak Dala. He joins his sister Samal and brother-in-law Ondas, who make their living herding sheep. Asa is seeking to fulfil his dream of owning a flock of sheep and a yurt. But before he can take ownership of livestock Asa is required by tradition to marry. Asa cannot be a responsible man unless he has a wife. Tulpan is the only potential bride in the vicinity and much of the film centres on Asa's ultimately failed attempts to convince Tulpan (although we never see Tulpan in the film) and her parents that she should marry him.

The representation of the steppe in *Tulpan* is of a place that presents difficult living and working conditions. The ample dust and meagre grass has been compared to 'a half-forgotten outpost on a distant planet'.[8] The vast steppe is portrayed as a place of suffering for both humans and animals. This is reflected in one story arc where several lambs are found to be stillborn. The vet's diagnosis is not that the animals are ill, but rather the pasture and land is inadequate and demonstrates that the family needs to move on.[9] A violent dust storm that has Asa and Ondas struggling to pen their flock visually embodied the steppe as a remorseless place. The storm was a serendipitous part of the shoot and its inclusion reflects Dvortsevoy's background as a documentary maker.

The director had made a series of documentaries from the 1990s onward that captured 'simple people living difficult, marginalised lives'.[10] For example, his 1998 short *Bread Day* shows life in a part-abandoned Russian village whose only residents were alcoholics, old people and goats. They are only able to survive by way of a weekly delivery of bread, which is left at a railway station 5 km from the village.[11] This documentary style and philosophy behind Dvortsevoy's work, which he describes as 'observations of life', are evident in *Tulpan*.[12] For instance, Oleg Boretskiy described *Tulpan* as 'a vivid example of visionary work at the crossroads of fiction and documentary films' and in this synthesis of two forms produces a style of 'ethnographic cinema'.[13] *Tulpan's* documentary feel is somewhat reminiscent of Abdullah Karsakbayev's ethnographic depiction of the *aul* in *My Name is Kozha* (1963), while we can also see the influence of Serik Aprymov's *The Last Stop* (1989) on the film in its depiction of the struggles of rural life.

While we are made aware throughout *Tulpan* that the topography of the steppe makes for harsh and often infertile conditions, Asa understands the steppe as essential to his identity. For the protagonist the steppe represents a potential fairy tale. He is aware of the difficult conditions the land presents but reconstructs this as a Martin Luther-type 'I have a dream' of owning a white yurt and large flock 'under the starry sky of the Kazakh steppe'. In seeking to impress Tulpan, he insists they would make a success of it, not like others who have failed and migrated to the city. Asa is deliberate in choosing this existence because of its romantic qualities and significance to his identity as a Kazakh. He ultimately resists the lure of the city, even though he faces rejection from Tulpan. His destiny is for a pastoral life, despite the challenging conditions, because it is this way of life that is fundamental to Kazakh identity.[14]

This romantic appeal to nationhood was not lost on critics or the audience. Oleg Boretskiy declared 'Tulpan is more than a movie. It is Kazakh in the full and profound sense, in the context of culture, nomadic culture, visual representation of this culture in its entirety, authenticity and originality'.[15] Audience responses noted that the film reflected 'current reality, the problems of man and the environment and that Kazakhstan is not only the cities of Astana and Almaty. There are villages and people living there, who are also dreaming'.[16] A focus group participant stated that the film was 'realistic, because not everyone lives in the cities — the majority live in the periphery, they live in the *auls* that are lost in the steppe'.[17] The film, therefore, speaks to the reality of ordinary Kazakh lives and what it means to be a member of the nation of Kazakhstan. That *Tulpan* should have such a realistic feel for audiences in its depiction of landscape was no accident. Filming in the Betpak Dala presented the director and production team with significant technical problems. For example, when the tractor broke down it took three days for parts to arrive from the nearest city of Shymkent, 500 kilometres away, and when one of the camels ran away it took them three days to locate it.[18]

While the film foreshadows a conception of national identity rooted in carving out an existence in the steppe, it was an international co-production with companies from Russia, Germany, Poland, Switzerland and Italy. The film was independent from Kazakhfilm Studios and its strong European backing ensured it had distribution on the international film circuit and it was duly rewarded with a tranche of awards.[19] The attraction of international audiences to the film has been attributed to the way in which Western audiences seek out the exotic and alien.[20]

Comparable to *Kelin*, *Tulpan* found itself subject to a great deal of criticism. The depiction of Kazakhs living in the tough terrain of Betpak Dala was scorned by the *Akim* of Astana as portraying the country as backward and patriarchal and in effect doing more harm to Kazakhstan than Borat.[21] *Tulpan* was considered as 'not consistent with the concept of the young independent state'. In its focus on the desolation and hopelessness of life on the steppe, the film challenges the narrative of a flourishing, modernising vibrant country.[22] Director Adilkhan Yerzhanov praised *Tulpan* for being a more honest film and 'showing the steppe as it is in reality', but at the same time he lamented the film's conservatism in relation to its melodramatic imagination. As Yerzhanov argued, 'it is a very good movie, very honest, but what we need now is radical protest movies'.²³ Therefore, despite offering a degree of social realism, which is embodied in its depiction of the steppe, it remains a film which is focused on simple storytelling, rather than a substantive critique of post-Soviet life.

Analogous depictions of the steppe can also be observed in Emir Baigazin's 2013 film *Harmony Lessons*. Set in a rural *aul*, the film concerns Aslan, a young adolescent, and his trials against the vicious and dehumanising bullying system within school. The bleakness of the landscape mirrors the literal violence we see in the school. The desolation of the steppe is symbolic of the inner psychological struggle of Aslan. We are led to understand that in this environment (both the inhospitable steppe and the inhumane school system) only the strongest survive. Extrapolated to contemporary Kazakhstan – the steppe, as depicted in *Harmony Lessons*, can represent the struggle faced by those left behind in a post-Soviet transition that rewards violence, bullying, corruption and bureaucratic incompetence. This is a far cry from the sumptuousness of the steppe as represented in the ethnic narrative. A similar austerity of landscape is realised in Adilkhan Yerzhanov's 2013 work *Constructors*. The film depicts two brothers' attempts at constructing a home on the outskirts of Almaty. In *Constructors*, the steppe is a wearisome place as the brothers steal materials from a nearby construction site under the cover of darkness. The land offers no protection or shelter as they sleep and live without a home. The film is allegorical for the idea that modern Kazakhstan does not offer a home, safety or protection for the dispossessed, poverty-stricken and losers of post-Soviet economic transition.

Landscape and Disorientation

The steppe in its vastness of space is also often used as an aesthetic trope to symbolise the potential for personal disorientation. As a consequence of the endless wilderness, key characters find themselves lost or astray in the enormous montane and shrub grasslands. It demonstrates an alternative psychological relationship with the geography of the steppe. Rather than being in symbiosis with it, as suggested in the Tengrist narrative, the steppe overwhelms individuals in its enormity. This can be observed most notably in Akan Satayev's 2010 film *Strayed*, where the protagonist finds himself lost in the steppe while driving with his wife and son after attempting to find a short cut. Realising he is lost and has been driving around in circles his wife and son disappear and he becomes drawn to an isolated house that appears in the distance inhabited by a mysterious man and his daughter. The film's narrative hovers between the supernatural and reality and we eventually discover that these events are a part of an elaborate hallucination that the protagonist is experiencing to escape the reality of his existence. Principally this concerns his involvement with a criminal gang in which he was charged with transporting a consignment of drugs which he failed to deliver.[24] The protagonist is entrapped by his own actions in relation to the criminal world of modern Kazakhstan and the extent to which he has morally strayed from a righteous path. His disorientation speaks to larger issues of social disorientation in modern Kazakhstan – the influence of criminal gangs, corruption and the tough moral choices of post-Soviet economic conditions.

A comparable phenonmenon occurs in Yerzhanov's *Realtors* (2011) where the lead character, Darik, is temporally disoriented by finding himself in the past, but this temporal confusion is symptomatic of his disorientation within modern society. As described by Yerzhanov himself, Darik is a loser and socially disaffected. He has no job and has no hope.[25] He is a gambler and an alcoholic who is in debt. He is depicted as a figure that will go as far as selling his parents' land to pay off the money he owes. In a montage of early scenes Darik loses his clothes, faces imminent death, is locked in the trunk of a car and handcuffed to the debt collector Kurban, and eventually transported a thousand years into the past. Through these quick-paced events the viewer has a lens into the disorientation of post-Soviet contemporary life in Kazakhstan. When Darik and Kurban find themselves in the past faced with nomadic warriors in an unforgiving, violent and bloody steppe, Darik questions what is going on. Kurban simply replies 'this happens to everybody'. This disorientation, therefore, is not isolated to Darik. It is universal. Darik's search for self throughout space and time is also the nation's search. The move from modernity, which is shot in black and white, to the past, which is in bright brilliant colour, suggests that the Kazakh self can be found with a reassessment and consideration of the past.[26] In this view of things, the present is found to be monochrome, devoid of hope and only through a reconnection with the past can personal and national salvation be discovered. It evokes a different form of membership of the nation. The nation of Kazakhstan consists not of warriors or kind and generous heroes, but of ordinary citizens who are lost, isolated, and disoriented. Indeed, as one nomadic character notes to Darik, 'no one needs you here, you are an alien with no family and tribe'.

The Urban-rural Divide

As discussed in Chapters 4, 5 and 6 one of the central themes in Kazakh cinematic narratives is national unity. Establishing a common-sense of belonging is fundamental to nation-building as a process. Therefore, these cinematic narratives all strive to establish communal unity albeit in different ways. For films like *Nomad* and *Zhauzhurek Myn Bala* it concerns the unity of Kazakh tribes in defence of the nation against an invading 'other'. In *The Gift to Stalin* and *The Promised Land* it focuses on the unity of different ethnicities under a civic Kazakhstani national banner. And in *Kelin* and *Shal* national unity is achieved when man is in symbiosis with nature. In the socio-economic narrative, however, we are witness not to the unity of the nation, but to some of its fault lines. This finds form in depictions of the cultural divide between rural and urban populations.[27]

In *Tulpan*, urban life is positioned as the 'other' to Asa's dream of an idyllic life on the steppe. Its allure only exists in that it may offer economic opportunities not available in the Betpak Dala. The tension between rural and urban life is symbolic not literal. In *Constructors*, this friction is evident in the very opening scene of the film. City life is represented through the three protagonists' eviction from their apartment for failure to pay the mortgage. Rauf, Yerbolat and Aliya's migration in *Constructors* is to the steppe in their effort to build a home. A similar migration from the urban to the rural occurs in the hit 2014 comedy *Kelinka Sabina* (The Bride Sabina), directed by Nurtas Adambayev. The film concerns the kidnap of the spoilt, city-living Sabina Karsybaeva by a rural Kazakh. In an early scene with her parents, Sabina is dismissive of Kazakh traditions, culture and language, expressed most clearly in her rejection of the 'national' dish *beshbarmak*.[28] She is more smitten with the luxuries of urban life, her smart phone and night-clubbing. With her kidnap, Sabina is forced to come to terms with the traditions and customs of *aul* life.[29] She learns how to pour tea, cook *beshbarmak*, milk a cow and speak Kazakh.[30] The tension and comedy lie in the fish-out-of-water scenario, but also draw on stereotypical differences between a fast-paced, modern and glamorous city life compared to the traditional way of life in Kazakh villages. Despite its obvious clichéd humour, the film expresses the fracture between rural and urban life, and the disconnection between the gilded life of young, affluent urbanites compared to citizens whom live in the *auls*. Nonetheless, *Kelinka Sabina* does feature pathos. While Sabina is initially resistant to and mocking of village life and customs, she eventually realises the importance of holding national values and the traditional way of life, even if she does eventually return to the city. At the same time, the exchange is two-way, as Sabina ingratiates the villagers to aspects of urban life.

The film was hugely successful for a domestic-produced Kazakh film, reportedly making 112 million Tenge in the first five days after its release.[31] The movie created controversy though. Committed Kazakh nationalists complained *Kelinka Sabina* showed village residents in a derogatory manner. The journalist Toktar Zhakash launched an online campaign against the film, declaring that it was only popular with 'Shala Kazakhs'[32] and that 'real' Kazakhs were indignant over the film. Others called for a DVD-burning ceremony of the film at the Bayterek monument in Astana and some even went as far as calling for Adambayev to be put on trial for inciting social tension.[33] Echoing the disapproval of Yermek Tursunov's *Kelin*, criticisms focused on the portrayal of the traditional 'Kazakh' Kelin. By creating such an emotional response with self-perceived Kazakh traditionalists, the film only highlights the inherent social tension in finding a unified idea of Kazakh nationhood and identity. While this is played out on the screen as a divide between the urban and rural life, in real life the division is between those who proclaim a purity of 'Kazakhness', disavowing any mocking or satire of perceived traditional ways of life, and the 'other' they establish in opposition to this purity. For nationalists, the 'other' is people they consider 'Shala Kazakhs', in other words those who do not speak the language properly and who are willing to laugh at Adambayev's invented Kelin.

A comparable focus on the challenges of migration is evident in Farkhat Sharipov's 2010 movie *Tale of the Pink Bunny*. The film was popular with a young audience, and like *Kelinka Sabina* it was a deliberate commercial movie, utilising Hollywood teen-movie tropes to tell the tale of Erlan who moves to the city from the countryside, his initial struggle to make ends meet through a job as a big promotional pink rabbit and his attempts to ingratiate himself into the wealthy, young urban elite.³⁴ Sharipov's film echoes the earlier 2003 film *Little People*, by Nariman Turebayev, where the two protagonists are trying to carve out a life in Almaty as street salesmen. While we never see any depiction of rural life in *Tale of the Pink Bunny*, as Tatiana Bakina has noted, we are made aware of the 'bitter reality' of city life for someone coming from the regions juxtaposed to the glamorous life of the city's elite.³⁵ While some compared Sharipov's film to Akira Kurosawa's 1940s and 1950s work, which explored the rapid prosperity and social changes of postwar Japan, and the conflict this created with those who get left behind,³⁶ other critics have suggested that the film portrays an exaggerated version of a clash between poverty and wealth in contemporary Kazakhstan.³⁷ The director himself commented that 'the film is more glamorous than reality, which is harder and tougher ... the film is a caricature of reality'.³⁸

Zhanna Isabayeva's film *My Dear Children* also alludes to this rural-urban divide. The film's narrative concerns a mother who arrives from the village to visit four of her children in the city, asking each one of them to contribute financially to the wedding of her youngest and laziest son. The division of classes is most clearly played out in the opening scene of the film. The mother and the youngest son, Eldos, first visit the eldest son Kanat, who is hosting a dinner party with his boss whom he is seeking to impress so he can obtain a loan that will enable him and his wife to buy their own home. Here we are witness to the economic concerns of modern city dwellers seeking to rise-up to the middle classes. The dinner party is interrupted by the mother and Eldos and their perceived lack of social refinement, evident in their grabbing and eating *Beshbarmak* with their hands,³⁹ Eldos singing the traditional, seemingly never-ending, Kazakh song *Dudarai* on the dombra, and the mother taking a bath during the dinner party, which has the effect of making the boss storm out of the flat because of his desperation to relieve himself.⁴⁰ Central to this scene is the tension between urban sensibilities and the uncouth social norms of those from outside the city. While this antagonism is positioned as a comedic device, perhaps easing what is essentially a social drama of modern urban life (see below); the depiction of these traditions, customs and attitudes towards rural behaviour is delivered as a stereotype.

Nonetheless, *Tale of the Pink Bunny*, *Kelinka Sabina* and *My Dear Children* all evoke the fault line within a unified nationality, despite their teen, commercial and comic modes of genre. They point to a division of classes that, for the most part, can be observed between an urban and rural divide and Russian and Kazakh-speaking populations. The division of language is especially pertinent for post-Soviet Kazakhstan. It is not a division between ethnic Russian speakers and ethnic Kazakh speakers. Rather it is the distinction between Kazakh-speaking Kazakhs and Russian-speaking Kazakhs. During the Soviet period the division of language existed between the perceived cosmopolitanism of the cities (especially Alma-Ata) where Russian was spoken, and the Kazakh-speaking rural *auls*. This has changed significantly since the collapse of the Soviet Union. As noted by director Darezhan Omirbayev, this division of language is reflected in cinema:

> now in Kazakh cinema you can see two extremes, not only in cinema but in society. The first extreme is 100 per cent ethnically Kazakh-speaking and the other is urban life is Russian-speaking. Before the position of Kazakh language was supported by rural areas where almost 60 per cent of the population lived. After the government stopped financing agriculture young people have moved to the cities. Thus, there is now a weakening of Kazakh language since the rural areas are now shrinking.[41]

Films such as *Kelinka Sabina* demonstrate this division of language. Sabina is an urban Russian-speaking Kazakh who does not have a grasp of the Kazakh language and who only begins to appreciate the language, tradition and customs of Kazakhs after being forced to spend time in an *aul*.

The division between Kazakh and Russian languages and between urban and rural populations is reflected in audience reception of these films. As noted earlier, *Tale of the Pink Bunny*, *Kelinka Sabina* and *My Dear Children* were successful films in the domestic market. All, except for *My Dear Children*,[42] could be considered commercial films. While there was some negative response to *Kelinka Sabina* on kino.kz, which in particular echoed the frustrations and complaints of Kazakh nationalists, suggesting it 'made a mockery of Kazakh traditions', overall there was a positive response, especially with regards to the theme of 'bringing Russified Kazakhs back to the village'.[43] Other commentators reflected that the film could only be understood by those who have a 'Kazakh mentality' and the moral message of the film is that young people are 'moving away from their traditions towards glamour' and to 'learn the language and respect traditions'. The division of language was also noted by participants in the focus groups. One member suggested that:

> there are at least two Kazakhstan's – Russian-speaking and Kazakh-speaking ... it is difficult to be a Kazakh who speaks Russian and not Kazakh fluently – the main problem in the future is that this will be the true divide in Kazakhstan with Russian-speaking TV, Russian-speaking movies and newspapers and then the Kazakh language. The gap is growing. It is like parallel worlds.[44]

This illustrates the way in which national identity, in this context, is fractured and non-cohesive. It shows how the ideas presented in some government sponsored films that seek to detail contemporary modern life in Kazakhstan as prosperous and affluent (see below), are evidently challenged, not just in how the films are represented by the directors, but also interpreted and understood by the audience too.

Struggles with Bureaucracy and Authority

The director whose work best encapsulates the division of classes is Adilkhan Yerzhanov. Born in Zhezkazgan, a city in the Karaganda region in 1982, Yerzhanov graduated in filmmaking from the National Academy of Arts in Almaty in 2009. As part of his studies he attended Damir Manabayev's directing workshop alongside other young directors Serik Abishev and Emir Baigazin. As early as 1999 Yerzhanov won state TV channel Khabar's competition for best screenplay for an animated version of Kozy-Korpesh – Bayn Sulu, a Kazakh lyrical poem from the thirteenth and fourteenth centuries.[45] He won awards for his early short *Bakhytzhamal* at the 2007 Eurasian film festival and international recognition for his graduation short *Karatas* in 2009. But it has been his four feature films, *Realtors* (2011), *Constructors* (2013), *The Owners* (2014) and *The Plague in the Village of Karatas* (2016) and his documentary *The Story of Kazakh Cinema* (2016) that have seen him emerge as one of the leading artists of Kazakh cinema. His work possesses thematic characteristics constructed to elucidate a reading of contemporary Kazakh society that constitutes a very different form of nationhood and identity from those depicted in the regime-sponsored narratives. Eschewing what he terms 'bourgeois cinema', in other words safe, conservative, non-confrontational and clichéd forms, genres and aesthetics of cinematic language, Yerzhanov has sought to avoid, and even challenge, the trend of both commercial and custom-made cinemas in Kazakhstan.[46] As the director noted in an interview specifically about the film *The Owners*:

> Kazakh cinema has long been bourgeois. A bourgeois philosophy involves reconciliation with reality, so-called escapism – when eyes are shut to the shortcomings of contemporary society. By saying only those things that are allowed and do not affect anyone, so in Kazakhstan people are trying to produce melodrama or a historical film ... I believe that to turn a blind eye to this problem and not to take on this movie is a crime.[47]

Yerzhanov explicitly sets out to confront the status quo in cinematic terms. He challenges the tendency towards commercial and government-sponsored films such as *Nomad* and *Zhauzhurek Myn Bala*, instead offering up his interpretation of the reality of everyday lives of Kazakh citizens. This is a social realism focusing on the struggles people have with bureaucracy and institutions of authority and the dispossession of property.

These struggles and tensions first appear in *Realtors* where Darik is struggling to pay off his debts. His asocial behaviour and willingness to 'sell his own mother' is driven by a dislocation with contemporary society – a sense of being lost and out of time.[48] However, it is in *Constructors* where Yerzhanov's ideas become fully formed. The two brothers struggle not just with the dispossession of their flat and the construction of their own home, but also with state officials and bureaucrats who persistently place obstacles in their way. They are visited three times by forms of authority (local administrators, the police etc.), who on each occasion put barriers in place to halt the brothers' attempts to build a home. The austere monochrome aesthetics of the film were suggested by one reviewer as transmitting the emotion of fear that the brothers felt when faced with the pervasive power of the authorities.[49]

The theme of struggle with authority continued in Yerzhanov's follow-up film to *Constructors*, *The Owners*. The film acts as a companion piece to the previous film using a very similar plot. The film depicts a tragic situation in an *aul* whereby two brothers and their sister return to a family home left to them by their deceased mother. Their ownership of the property is contested by Zhuba, an alcoholic and brutal village elder whose brother is the local police chief. The story details the young brothers' struggle 'to build a rural home in defiance of corrupt obstructive bureaucracy'.[50] This is best encapsulated in a scene where the younger brother, Yerbol, is seeking to file a complaint with the local administration about the arrest of his brother John and the attempt by Zhuba to evict them from their property. When he files his complaint, it is to a faceless and indifferent bureaucrat. Yerbol is told that the complaint will be processed in two months and then is abruptly dismissed. In this scene Yerzhanov encapsulates the carelessness, rule-bound and impersonal nature of bureaucracy in modern Kazakhstan.

The tussles with authority are a comment by the director on the nature of Kazakhstan's political system, especially in relation to corruption. It is as one reviewer noted, 'a familiar Kazakh story: the criminal struggle for property, blackmail, beatings, corrupt police, a criminal case, lawlessness and an almost absurd inability to seek justice and protection'.[51] Indeed, the director himself noted how *The Owners* 'is in some way a sad verdict on what is happening in our society now, it is a protest against what is happening, it is the cry of a soul and if nothing changes then everything will collapse'.[52] The film constitutes a conception of modern national identity rooted in citizens' struggles and frustrations with local authorities and security officials, often with deeply tragic consequences, and by doing so it is markedly political.

The challenges of facing bureaucracy and authority in Kazakhstan again appeared in Yerzhanov's 2016 documentary *The Story of Kazakh Cinema*. The documentary features Yerzhanov and actor Arslan Akubayev wandering around Kazakhflim Studios late at night having found themselves locked in after working late. The documentary features many of the key characteristics of Yerzhanov's films: quiet, austere and at times unusual and imaginative shots which often pre-empt an impending doom. In one scene Yerzhanov and Akubayev are sitting against the wall when a security guard appears and asks them what they

SOCIAL AND ECONOMIC VISIONS OF MODERN NATIONHOOD 215

are doing there. Despite being locked in the guard refuses to let them out because he is the internal guard and it is the outside guard who is responsible for opening the door. Later, when they ask another security official where they can find the chief of security they are directed to the third floor and to a door drawn on the wall. When told to come back in 15–20 minutes to the imaginary door Yerzhanov responds that 'it's drawn on the wall', to which the response is 'yes everyone knows that it is drawn, but no one says it out loud'. Yerzhanov captures in this one scene a common absurdity of Soviet and post-Soviet existence, in that even when people know the falsities and imagined nature of the discourse of authority no one can speak of it. As Yerzhanov noted in an interview, 'things like corruption and theft are obvious at all levels, but officially it's decided to keep silent about it'.[53] Just as everyone knows the gleaming façade of Astana is not representative of life in Kazakhstan; the government continues to peddle the myth of a modern, affluent nation while neglecting the representation of those it leaves behind.

As evidenced above, the director utilises comedy and the absurdity of real life as devices to provide an honest portrayal of the Kazakh social world. This is realised to greatest effect in *The Owners*. It is a film of bright brilliant colour, a striking contrast to the austere monochrome of *Constructors*. The film comes alive on screen as a living breathing Van Gogh painting, a deliberate attempt by Yerzhanov to capture

Figure 7.1 Scene from *The Owners* (2014), dir. Adilkhan Yerzhanov.

expressionism and establish his own form of cinematic language.[54] The viewer is often disoriented by surreal scenes that break from conventional cinematic narratives, much in the same way achieved by David Lynch in his famous *Twin Peaks* TV series. A good example in *The Owners* is a scene where Yerbol is standing at the grave of John who has died in police custody. In the background, the rumbustious henchmen associated with Zhuba loudly play rock 'n' roll music from a car stereo. Facing Yerbol, Zhuba declares 'we will all die, all of us deserve death, we have nothing left but dance'. In that moment, slowly, but awkwardly, Zhuba begins to dance by John's graveside while gradually an inane grin appears on his face. Yerzhanov has referred to the mixture of surrealism and realism as 'a caricature of realism style'.[55] This is a distinct move away from the quasi-documentary realism of Serik Aprymov's *The Last Stop*, which as we saw in Chapter 3 sought to depict the realities of *aul* life for the first time. Instead, Yerzhanov's film defines contemporary life by its absurdity, by the obvious forms of corruption in everyday life of which everyone is aware, but no one speaks. To an extent, therefore, his use of surrealism to represent social problems shares some similarities with Rashid Nugmanov's *The Needle*.

The director positions his work, therefore, in opposition to commercial and custom-made films in Kazakhstan. As he notes, 'there is either an attempt to return to the heroic past, or to imitate Hollywood romantic comedies ... the problem is the real world is so distorted today that expressionism with all its exaggeration is the most honest thing that you can offer'.[56] Therefore, Yerzhanov seeks to achieve a dissenting, and what he views, honest account of contemporary nationhood. We are witness to a satire of the absurdities in the everyday struggles of ordinary citizens. It is the cinematic equivalent of political resistance to the prevailing discourse and the norms that the Nazarbayev regime has perpetuated for at least the last decade-and-a-half.

Struggle and resistance can also be seen in two short films directed by Yerzhanov's collaborator, Serik Abishev. One short film, *Bureaucrats*, satirises officialdom and the bureaucracy of the state by simply showing a series of 'bureaucrats' shuffling papers and moving them from one side of the desk to the other.[57] In another short film called *Butter*, a worker is paid only with a box of butter. Despite his absolute consternation at the turn of events, he then seeks to find the village of Akchibuk in the steppes to sell the butter before it melts in the searing heat.[58] Desperate for money due to debts, he ultimately fails in his task. Despite the absurd situation, the major motif of the film is 'money or lack thereof in the economic inequality of the new market economy'.[59] *Butter* demonstrates that films within this socio-economic narrative of nationhood and identity are not always explicitly setting out to dissent, but rather subtly offer a representation which focuses on the difficulties and challenges that are commonly experienced by citizens. As Abishev explained:

> the main idea was not social protest. It was to make something interesting in the conditions of our difficult life. At that moment when I was making that film in 2008, the situation where the salaries were being paid in butter was not there. It was 10 years before when I was younger. However, this is a situation familiar to all in Kazakhstan and those who live in the CIS.[60]

The hero in *Butter* has limited agency and is at the mercy of an unjust and unfair economic system and the natural environment. He is 'searching for something ideal or beautiful in life', such as a picture of Audrey Hepburn, which is a means to escape the absurdity of life.[61] Therefore, Yerzhanov and Abishev's work is indicative of an understanding of national heroes not as warriors or hospitable Kazakhs, but as ordinary people struggling against the state and coping with social and economic disparity.

The dissenting and satirical nature of Yerzhanov and Abishev's work is evident by the reaction to it.[62] Kazakhfilm Studios financed and produced *Realtors*, but the President of the Studios was not happy with the results. After the initial script was approved Yerzhanov changed the hero of the movie from an typical hero to the asocial and morally ambiguous Darik that we see in the final version of the film. The film was devised as a protest and as Yerzhanov notes:

> I made it slovenly and maybe dirty on purpose as a protest to films in Kazakhstan like *Nomad*, *Zhauzhurek Myn Bala*, etc. I wanted to rip apart the historical genre. I wanted to explore with that character *{Darik}* what is the motherland to any person. And with

the film I concluded that motherland is a group of people, a group of likeminded people that come together in a group and try to survive in this world.[63]

A consequence of Yerzhanov's effort to challenge conventional cinema and conformist interpretations of Kazakh nationhood, the film never received domestic distribution even two years after its release.[64] This was despite the work collecting a plethora of awards at international film festivals.[65] His experience with Kazakhfilm Studios led his next project to be financed privately through the Soros Foundation and the Network for the Promotion of Asian Cinema. Nonetheless, without the backing and financing of Kazakhfilm Studios, the film again failed to receive any domestic distribution in Kazakhstan. With *The Owners*, Yerzhanov returned to Kazakhfilm Studios for funding, but on completion of the film the president of Kazakhfilm Studios, Yermek Amanshayev, refused to release it. According to the director, Amanshayev 'did not like the way the lives of Kazakhs was shown and nor the combination of comedy and tragedy'.[66] However, when Cannes offered the opportunity for Yerzhanov to show the film at the 2014 Festival, Amanshayev agreed to allow the film to be shown there but on the condition the Kazakhfilm logo and any reference to the film having been financed with public money was removed from the picture.[67] This caused a great deal of controversy and ensured the film received a great deal of attention at the Festival, and consequently it received great acclaim on the international film festival circuit, winning awards[68] and plaudits from reviewers such as Geoff Andrews, who described the film as 'bleak, sometimes angry and even entertaining'.[69] The director was confused about Kazakhfilm Studios' attitude towards the film. As Yerzhanov explained in an interview, 'in the film, there is no policy, no calls to overthrow the constitutional order, it does not discuss any forbidden names and themes, not even hints or allusions – it's just a film about conflict over a private house which is shot in a black comedy genre'. The decision of Kazakhfilm, in the view of the director was 'the logical continuation of the policy of the state film studio in recent years'.[70] 'Kazakhflim' owns the screening rights to the film and this means that it is very difficult for Yerzhanov to get screenings of the movie in Kazakhstan, despite its success internationally. To be able to show the film domestically the director needs to get a special distribution licence from the Ministry of Culture. Yerzhanov's understanding is that he would not be given the licence, and frustrated by Kazakhfilm's position and attitude towards the movie, he decided to instead establish a new independent collective cinematic movement called *'Partizanskoe Kino'* (Guerrilla Cinema). This movement was set up to be in opposition to the perceived 'current stagnation' within the film industry in Kazakhstan which 'currently ignores reality'.[71] The movement is built on three central pillars. The first is to produce films on no budget (which is a misnomer – really it means limited budget). The second is to focus on social realism and the third is to establish new forms. The first film to be released by the movement was *Toll Bar*, directed by Zhasulan Poshanov and co-written by Adilkhan Yerzhanov. It is characterised by the familiar themes within this narrative, such as social division and the loneliness of contemporary life.[72] Yerzhanov's 2016 film *A Plague in the Village of Karats* was also produced as part of the Guerrilla Cinema movement on a budget of just $6000 from a grant given by the Soros Foundation.[73] The film is even more overtly politically than Yerzhanov's previous work. It is a dark and foreboding picture, which has a hint of *The Wickerman* about it. A young man arrives to take up a position of *Akim* in the small *aul* of Karatas, where to him it is clear a plague has broken out infecting the village residents. The mayor wishes to report the outbreak to senior regional officials, but local authorities declare it is only an influenza and seek to force the new mayor to sign the budget for the village in which 90 per cent goes on the medication for influenza – a corruption scam where authorities in the village and senior regional officials are taking kickbacks. The new mayor's efforts of reform are thwarted at every turn and he is told that this corrupt scheme is a 'national tradition', as is the fact that people are dying.[74] The film is clear statement on the corrupt nature of the bureaucratic system in Kazakhstan and the culture, which means that even though everyone is aware of the malfeasance, and its absurd nature, no one speaks of it.

Yerzhanov's work has proved controversial with the authorities in Kazakhstan. In October 2015 the Minister of Culture, Arystanbek Muhamediuly, declared *The Owners*, along with Emir Baigazin's *Harmony Lessons*, 'a disgrace to Kazakhstan' that show 'Kazakhstan from an unsavoury perspective'.[75] At a private screening of the film in Astana, with Yerzhanov and Abishev present, viewers were highly critical of the film with some comparing it to *Borat* while others in the audience suggested the film was 'far from reality'.[76] However, prominent film critics Oleg Boretskiy and Gulnara Abikeyeva did come out in defence of the film with Abikeyeva arguing that the young directors (Yerzhanov and Abishev) were making 'socially meaningful cinema'.[77] The director himself was nonchalant about the Minster's criticism, pointing to the fact that Minister is not an expert in film and that 'what he says is superficial and it explains the general amateurism of our entire system. When a person without a speciality begins to judge something, it's bad. I think people should talk only about what they understand, especially when he speaks on behalf of the government'.[78]

General audience reception of Yerzhanov's films is very hard to gauge given the lack of domestic distribution of his work. Only *Realtors* and *The Owners* appear on kino.kz, and it is only *The Owners* that features any comments from viewers, of which there are only two. Both of those comments are positive with one noting that the film is a 'deep reflection of life in which we live, dancing and grovelling before the masters of life'.[79] Of those who participated in the focus groups only a handful of participants had seen any of the films. The strong dissenting voice in *The Owners* resonated with some of the audience who understood the film as 'the hard truth about how the country works'.[80] Others recognised that the film 'was a tragic situation about corruption and nepotism and all that "nice" stuff in our country which can be extrapolated to the bigger situation'.[81] But, for others the political message was too strong, they found the film 'too socialist'[82] and they 'did not like that the director was so upfront in accusing the government and all the forces like the police, rather than thinking about the mistakes made by main characters themselves'.[83] Another participant who had seen *Constructors* commented that they 'did not want to see *The Owners*' as watching *Constructors* 'gave them bad thoughts'.[84] Another participant suggested that the people whose lives the film sought to represent would not be interested in seeing these types of films and would perhaps prefer the escapist films that Yerzhanov and Abishev have rallied against. The participant commented, 'people who live like this in *The Owners* or in *Harmony Lessons* they don't want to go and watch themselves on screen. Would you? Would you rather not be taken to another world?'[85]

That these films should produce such mixed reactions does not surprise the filmmakers. Abishev noted that if *The Owners* was ever to receive a wide distribution inside of Kazakhstan 'we would just see audiences walking out'.[86] Yerzhanov has spoken of the country not possessing 'the culture of the viewer',[87] but he has also gone further in suggesting that he has 'no concept of the audience'.[88] What he is interested in, therefore, is making films that correspond to his own vision and interpretation of society. Yerzhanov has no ambition in making popular films.[89] He is interested in constructing his own original cinematic language. It is a language which within its text offers a critique of the social reality of ordinary lives, but does so by expressing the absurdity of the current political and economic system. However, that there is such a limited distribution of the films brings to light the partial reach of their scope in shaping domestic attitudes towards identity and nationhood. The reaction of Kazakhfilm and the Ministry of Culture to the work of Yerzhanov also demonstrates that even if film does provide a space for dissent, critique and satire, and the state is unable to control the production of such narratives, it can and does control and limit official domestic distribution, although not informal online distribution.[90]

Home and Family

Realtors, *Constructors* and *The Owners* are united by two other themes central to this conceptualisation of nationhood and identity: the necessity for a home and the breakdown of the traditional family unit.

According to Yerzhanov, all three films are devoted to the 'problem of man and his territory and how he is trying to defend it'.[91] *Realtors* concerns Darik's willingness to sell off his mother's home because of economic strife. In the end, after Darik's sojourn to the past he understands the value of the ancestral home and is willing to protect it from Chinese investors. *Constructors* in its literal form is about the construction of a home for the dispossessed family. Yerzhanov has argued that the construction of the house in the film is representative of the ongoing construction of Kazakhstan.[92] Moreover, the opening shots of the film provide a pocketed guide to Kazakhstan's history. We move at pace through a description of the different tribes, nomadic empires and states that existed on the Kazak steppe from the Mongols, the Kazakh Khanate, the Soviet republic all the way to independent Kazakhstan. Then the voiceover simply states, 'and now we are being evicted from our apartment for the non-payment of rent'. In this way, the film makes a direct connection between Kazakhstan's supposed glorious pre-Soviet history (as nomads and the Kazakh Khanate) and the economic reality of ordinary Kazakhs in post-Soviet Kazakhstan. While *Constructors* is about the building of a home (and a nation), *The Owners* is about the contestation of ownership — the opaque nature of property rights — and the contentious nature of land, property and belonging. The absence of a home within the film, and the disconnection of modern citizens from a sense of place which contributes to the disorientation of post-Soviet life, was something identified by one participant in a focus group who noted that they were 'struck when Zhuba says your ancestors used to move to another place when there was no grass, but now there is no place to move'.[93] The film, therefore, evokes a loss of place, history and space, which is in stark contrast to the idea of reclaimed history and place that emerge from the 'custom-made' films, like *Nomad* and *Zhauzhurek Myn Bala*.

Related to the contestation of land and loss of place is the theme of the breakdown of the family unit. The family, which is represented as the primordial basis of the unity of the nation in the religious Tengrist narrative, is observed in a different light in this narrative. For example, *The Owners*, according to the director, 'is a film about how the unit of society — the family — is destroyed'.[94] From the beginning of the film the incompleteness of the family unit is evident. The mother has recently died and there is no mention of a father. Moreover, throughout the film we see the slow and eventual disintegration of the family. In *Constructors*, we are made aware of the strained relationship between the two brothers with the younger brother blaming the elder for their predicament. This is only seemingly resolved when prior to the elder brother being taken away by the authorities he orders his brother to finish the house and then when the authorities pull it down the state would be obligated to provide him with a flat.

The disintegration of the family unit is central to the work of Zhanna Isabayeva. Isabayeva is one of the few female directors in Kazakhstan, and the only woman who makes 'art-house' cinema.[95] Like Yerzhanov,

Isabayeva possess an independent creative vision in terms of cinematic language, and has also railed against commercial cinema, comparing it to slavery because it will 'do anything to please the audience'.[96] With this artistic mindset, Isabayeva has used her films to establish a reading of the post-Soviet world in Kazakhstan. Often the focus is on lonely figures disconnected from the world around them and their families. This is most evident in her 2007 film *Karoy*. The protagonist, Azat, is a morally ambiguous character who gambles, rapes, steals and cheats people and distant family members out of money and is a character who 'transcends all laws of human morality'.[97] However, while Azat behaves in a heinous way, in particular by raping his friend's wife and stealing their money, Isabayeva uses Azat as a way to explore the contentious nature of absolute good or evil.[98] In the first half of the film Azat is the embodiment of immorality, willing to do anything for self-interest and personal gain. However, in the second half of the film, he returns to the family home and we see a loving Uncle to his nephews and a man who dotes on his mother. This tension between good and evil culminates in the act of him reluctantly agreeing to kill his ailing mother by euthanasia. The film ends with him on the road again, alone. With the death of his mother, he is dispossessed of family. Set in rural Kazakhstan, depicting the tough social and economic conditions and poverty many citizens face, we are left as viewers to ponder the disintegration of the family through the eyes and actions of Azat, in spite of the adoration his mother praises upon him.

In her 2014 film *Nagima*, Isabayeva explored the 'confused and desperate' lives of two orphan girls scraping a living in the dilapidated Almaty microdistrict of Shanyrak.[99] The narrative explores the protagonist's (Nagima) search for her biological mother while also being left with her friend's baby after she dies in childbirth. Nagima feels incapable of caring for the newborn because of her young age and because she never had a role model for a mother to aspire to. The absence of 'mother', and the missing familial unit, was a central element the director sought to portray. In an interview Isabayeva noted that, 'refusing to bring up your child – it's a shame, it is the scourge of our time, it is a kind of social disaster. I was very upset by many things in our country; this fact is one of them'.[100] Inspired to an extent by the realism of the 'Kazakh New Wave',[101] Isabayeva cast Dina Tukubayeva as Nagima, still a student at The Kazakh National University at the time, and herself an orphan. The essence of the film concerns the failure of the family unit in post-Soviet Kazakhstan. It provides an account of post-orphanage existence and the failure of the state to act as a substitute for the absence of the family. Unlike the Tengrist narrative, which depicts the strength of national unity as starting from the basis of the family, Isabayeva's films within this socio-economic narrative underscore the fragility of national unity, starting from the dearth of the family and how it establishes a nation of lost and dispossessed souls without the anchor and security of family life.

My Dear Children, released in 2009, is also evidently a representation of family life. The story arc of a mother visiting her children in Almaty to solicit money from them to pay for the wedding of her youngest and laziest son, is one in which stresses the importance and solidity of familial relations. For Isabayeva:

> in our Kazakh society family comes first. The interests of the family are more important than individual interests. You are firstly a member of the family and then all the rest. You can be a famous person, a millionaire or something else, but you come to the family and play a function or a place that you have in your family, despite your status. It is a good thing on one the hand, and bad on the other hand, because the stronger family members are carrying the weaker ones.[102]

This interpretation of family life, and the importance of ensuring there is large expensive wedding, irrespective of whether it was affordable or not, was easily recognised by audience members for whom it 'demonstrated the Kazakh mentality'.[103] While a participant in the focus group noted that even though people could not afford to pay for such huge weddings 'it was tradition'.[104] The film and its use of comedy were felt by audience members to 'show the real life of the modern Kazakh people, with all the problems of everyday life and national humour'.[105] This combination of focusing on tradition and key aspects of national identity (Kazakh songs, *beshbarmak* etc.) through comedy made the film popular with domestic audiences. However, the film is a social drama that highlights familial tensions and the socio-economic difficulties of everyday post-Soviet existence.[106] There is no father in the film – suggesting the incompleteness of the traditional family. In fact, in all Isabayeva's films there is an absence of the father. Moreover, and more importantly, the economic despondency of post-Soviet life is antagonised by relations within the family. The mother asking for money interferes with her son and daughter-in-law's attempts to buy a house; her other daughter's efforts of keeping financially afloat by working two jobs as a single mum; and her other son's ability to scrape a living working at the bazaar. The mother's demand to her children to pay for the wedding puts their economic security in jeopardy. The only offspring who is not in financial difficulty is in an unhappy and controlling marriage. While Isabayeva has argued that the film is about 'the strength of family, about the spirit of family', in Kazakh national form,[107] it also depicts the tense and fractious nature of family relationships, and importantly how the overbearing nature of the family engenders an obligation that undermines economic security.

Like Yerzhanov, Isabayeva's films provide a very different picture of Kazakh nationhood to those portrayed in the government-sponsored narratives. They are films which dissent from the conventional narrative put forward by the government. Isabayeva 'never accommodates to her audience ... and always tries to uncover the less than best aspects of our nation'.[108] Like Yerzhanov, Isabayeva struggles with the financing and distribution of her work. Her films have never received funding from Kazakhfilm Studios and she also feels that her position as one of the few female directors in Kazakhstan counts against her when trying to obtain funding. According to Isabayeva, she is 'not given money because we have very strong mistrust for women in general [in Kazakh society]. I was rejected many times when people said this openly. I'm grateful for their honesty, but we have much prejudice here.'[109] Isabayeva's two most recent films, *Nagima* and *Losing Virginity in Almaty*, were independently financed.[110] Distribution of her work at international film festivals is common and her films have proved popular on the festival circuit.[111]

Reception to Isabayeva's films are difficult to gauge. While there was a good reception for *My Dear Children*, as noted above, much of this was to do with the relatable representation of Kazakh mentality central to the film and the use of a comedy genre. For *Karoy* and *Nagima* it is much more difficult. Both films had limited distribution in the country, although *Karoy* as a debut offer had wider distribution and does seem to have found an audience in the DVD market.[112] On kino.kz there are several reviews for *Karoy*, all of them positive about the film, noting its deep philosophical meaning and that it is a film intended for Kazakhs – being 'about our Kazakh life in the villages and towns'.[113] Isabayeva's work finds a self-selecting audience in this sense, from those who relate to the rather austere and unsettling portrayal of post-Soviet life that paints the broken nature of family life. Only two comments feature on kino.kz for *Nagima*, and the film did not come up in discussion in any of the focus groups. Both comments on the forum are negative and indeed, in contrast to those for *Karoy*, suggest *Nagima* features 'a lot of clichés for a foreign audience', in that the film is not for or about Kazakhs and Kazakh life.[114] While it validates the difficulty in assessing the extent to which some of the films within this narrative, even with their dissenting nature, can shape identities and understanding of post-Soviet nationhood and identity, at the same time it reveals how representations of post-Soviet livelihoods can be unsettling for audiences. Isabayeva's work has sought to offer a vision of post-Soviet Kazakhstan that portrays the harsh realities of post-Soviet existence, the fractured tensions that undermine family unity and the moral ambiguity that difficult social and economic conditions create.

Morality and Wealth Accumulation

The immoral behaviour of Azat in *Karoy*, and the other moral ambiguities in Isabayeva's work, lead us to exploring the final sign within this socio-economic narrative of nationhood and identity: questions of morality and the pursuit of wealth.

The issue of morality that appears in contemporary Kazakh cinema is part of a post-Soviet psychology. This has been described by film director Kairzhan Orynbekov as a form of 'post-traumatic stress'.[115] A part of Soviet rule consisted of a denial of Kazakh history, a sense of place and tradition that was lost. As we saw in Chapter 3, when discussing the 'Kazakh New Wave', Kazakhstan emerges from Soviet rule as a country caught in a process of transition. In the post-Soviet period this is a transition from Soviet rule and a centrally planned economy to capitalism, the slow rise of a middle-class society and the impact of globalisation. As Darezhan Omirbayev has argued, to be Kazakh is 'to be a transitional person. I'm standing with one leg in that society, since I was born there, and with another one I'm standing in the bourgeois urban society.'[116] It is this confusion and process of identity transition and how it leads to the crossing of, or failure to see, moral boundaries that emerge as part of a representation of post-Soviet nationhood and identity. In a country awash with oil rents, that mostly reach a gilded elite, the aspiration of wealth, at the cost of both financial and moral corruption, has become a core aspect of post-Soviet identity.

This theme appears most prominently in films produced with a commercial market in mind.[117] These films, such as Akan Satayev's *Racketeer* and *Strayed*, Kairzhan Orynbekov's *The Kazakh Robbery* and Farkhat Sharipov's *Tale of the Pink Bunny*, all take inspiration from the Hollywood gangster/crime thriller genre. Each seeks to draw as broad an audience as possible. They are professionally shot films which make use of special effects and a tendency to use Russian as the main language of dialogue. What does this tell us about post-Soviet national identity? It is an identity which is uncertain of itself – not confident in its Kazakhness as in *Zhauzhurek Myn Bala* or 'Kazakhstaniness', as represented in *The Gift to Stalin*. Instead, the legacies of Russian and Soviet rule loom large with regards to the issue of language. The ability to carve out a national distinctiveness is compromised by the need to draw on the cinematic models, genres and language of 'others' to compete in the global or even Russian cinema market. These films are often privately financed too. *The Kazakh Robbery*, for example, was funded to the tune of $2 million by Alidar Utemuratov, son of a prominent Kazakh businessman and politician Bolat Utemuratov.[118] Akan Satayev has also been able to privately finance some of his films, *Racketeer* and *Strayed* among them, although he has also received funding through Kazakhfilm Studios.

Orynbekov's *The Kazakh Robbery* is a film where this form of post-traumatic post-Soviet stress plays out in one of the main characters, a Kazakh mercenary, Oraz. Having studied film-making in Los Angeles, Orynbekov utilised professional methods of cinema with an aim to develop a Kazakh version of British director Guy Ritchie's *Lock, Stock and Two Smoking Barrels* and *Snatch*. The film centres on the story of four friends who have inadvertently stolen €10 million from Chinese triads but end up being sought after not just by the Chinese but also corrupt police officials. Oraz is a paid mercenary on behalf of the Chinese with a traumatic back story (having in the past killed his friend for money). The character, in the view of the director:

is basically some kind of a prototype of a Kazakh person. He'll go over there and work for the Chinese; he'll work for anybody, because he doesn't believe in his own. He goes out there and later he gets fucked over by those guys. You know [he will] come back begging for forgiveness, but he never gets forgiveness. For me this is what the country is going through right now.[119]

Kazakhstan as a character in the film is represented through *Oraz* – a character who has 'post-traumatic stress ... Wolverine in the X-men saga, a guy who has been experimented on for a long-time and is tormented'.[120] From this interpretation Kazakhstan was experimented on by the Soviet Union, it lost its past, its sense of history, its sense of place and identity. Oraz, therefore, is the embodiment of this identity crisis, in that he is willing to kill his own friend and compatriot and willing to sell himself out to the Chinese, but in doing so is regretful about the moral ambiguity of his actions.

While the film is for the most part an action-comedy film and a mediation on friendship, it also touches on the pervasive issue of corruption. The degradation and moral corruption of Kazakh society in the post-Soviet period is a common theme among local film directors. *Racketeer*, for example, provides an account of early post-Soviet Almaty's criminal gangs warring over territory to lucrative bazaars and protection rackets. Yet, it also offers a morality tale of the modern Kazakh nation. Sayan, the protagonist, descends into criminality because of the lack of economic opportunities and a general despondency with the conditions of the post-Soviet economy. However, Satayev's commentary on the immorality of the informal black economy through protection rackets and extortion is most evident in a scene where one of Sayan's former associates is released from prison, and after having found Islam warns Sayan of how the immorality of his actions will affect him negatively later:[121]

> you know Sayan, I met many people in prison. There was an old man. He told me many things. He taught me to endure and to treat life as it was with contentment. You know every man has a bowl over his head. That bowl fills with all the injustices that person does. Someday that bowl might overflow. And all that evil will pour out on that person.

While some critics saw no thematic connection between *Racketeer* and *Strayed*,[122] both films deal with the issue of morality and the extent to which individuals, because of post-Soviet trauma and economic and social dislocation, can stray from a moral path. While *Strayed* is situated within the psychological drama genre, Satayev did attempt to realistically recreate the economic and social dislocation of post-Soviet Almaty in *Racketeer*, and tell the tale of this period. As he noted in an interview, 'we wanted the viewer to believe us and we attempted to re-create real life as much as possible'.[123] Satayev's stress on a form of realism also explains the use of both Russian and Kazakh language. He notes that:

> in *Racketeer*, we used two languages. This is typical; people from the city are speaking Russian, while those in villages are speaking Kazakh. We take such details into consideration to be as sincere as possible. Of course, as a Kazakh, I would like Kazakhs to speak their language, however if it does not reflect the reality, then it is useless. Everything should be real and honest. We need the audience to believe us that is why we must do everything as it is in reality.[124]

By portraying a form of realism, through language and the careful reconstruction of life, and by way of costumes, social mores and street language, despite the commercial ambitions and foreign modes, genres and aesthetics of the film, *Racketeer* implicitly offers up a form of dissent from the prevailing regime-driven narrative of nationhood and identity realised through custom-made films such as *Nomad* and *Zhauzhurek Myn Bala*.

Strayed and *Racketeer* were both successful at the box office. The audience, therefore, is much larger for Satayev's work than Yerzhanov's or Isabayeva's, as an examination of comments left on kino.kz elucidates. *Racketeer* attracted 36 pages of comments and *Strayed* 16. The overall reception to the films is mixed. The audience appreciated the success of a Kazakh film, and the attempt to make Kazakh cinematic work accessible to a wider audience, rather than art-house cinema, which was seen to be aimed at intellectual elites or foreign audiences.[125] However, some comments criticise the acting. What is most important, however, is the extent to which audience reception recognises the theme of morality and the attempt at social realism. Most comments do not focus on these themes, rather in drawing in a wider audience the appreciation is levelled at the professionalism of the film and its focus on familiar tropes within commercial cinema, such as guns and exciting car chases. However, some reviewers did pick up on these key themes.

For *Strayed*, reviewers noted how the film concerns 'man's search for himself, the moral compass of life' and 'our fears and weaknesses, destructive beginnings, for which we can catch and throw into the abyss of passions and emotions, you need only evil. But evil is a product of us'.[126] Some also noted that as the film was about morality, and good and evil the 'film is banal beyond recognition – nothing has been learned. Yes, morality, yes evil ... but how is this different from a religious pamphlet. Our cinema is still in the ideological darkness as perhaps is the whole of our country'.[127]

For *Racketeer*, comments which recognised the key theme were less critical, noting the film represented 'our lost generation', while others thought that the film 'really showed the processes which took place throughout the former USSR', 'emphasised realism', 'showed the history of the formation of criminal groups', 'how the creators wanted to show morality and how we are all mortal and equally responsible for our actions before God', 'how people have experienced all difficulties, frustrations and perhaps many brothers went down this path' and 'how young people come to the metropolis with healthy ambitions ... but in reality to a harsh life'.[128] This recognition of the film's portrayal of early post-Soviet life was also reflected in focus groups discussions too. One participant noted how 'I remember I was watching it and it was mostly like what was happening back in the day and it was so close to you. I remember this and I remember that. Everything is like yes, yes, yes. He gives us this spirit of Kazakhstan in the 90s.'[129]

Coming to the city to seek wealth was also a facet of *Tale of the Pink Bunny*. The film shows not just the disparity between the wealthy Almaty elite and Erlan, but also the immorality of desiring wealth accumulation above anything else. Sharipov himself has suggested the film is attempting to illustrate the temptations and trappings of the new capitalism, arguing that the young characters in the film 'try to set up their lives in a magic manner only believing in the power of money and nothing more than that'.[130] *Cocktail for a Star* (2010), a film produced by TV producer, actor and singer Bayan Yesentaeva, also depicts the pursuit of fame and wealth aspired to by younger people. *A Cocktail for a Star* tells the story of an orphan girl who aspires for a career in music. Partly the film details the intrigue and rough and tumble of the entertainment industry, but it also offers an aspirational, Americanised Cinderella rags-to-riches story. Aimed primarily at a young audience, the film was a financial success, recouping the $500,000 cost of the film by taking in $1.5 million.[131] Like aspirational teen-Hollywood films, *Cocktail for a Star* offers its audience false and unrealistic hope. The most notable aspect of the film is its attempts to replicate the realism of language identity in Kazakhstan by utilising both Russian and Kazakh language throughout the film.[132] This was something picked up on amongst focus group participants too who noted that by using language in this way in the film 'they were applying how language is used in daily life'.[133] A similar aspirational story was used in Yesentaeva's 2014 film *Beware of the Cow*. Again, it concerns how one girl can change her life, overcome obstacles and achieve her dreams. In the film the protagonist was an overweight and unloved teen who goes on to lose weight, become a successful businesswomen and member of parliament. Unlike other directors however, Yesentaeva's films lack any deeper interpretation of the morality of wealth aspiration and how it might lead citizens to act in corrupt ways.

Questions of morality and corruption are present in Baigazin's *Harmony Lessons* in the way the hierarchy of bullies in the school extort money from the weaker and more vulnerable pupils. What all these films portend to, despite their commercial nature (except for *Harmony Lessons*), is how a state of moral decay, corruption, criminality and the desirability of wealth at all costs, is a part of everyday post-Soviet life. While these films provide a caricature of life for melodramatic imagination to draw in a general audience and make profit for the film, they all signify important social issues in contrast to the picture of affluence and modernity depicted in government-sponsored films. Even when not explicitly seeking to do so the comercially oriented cinematic works are a moderate form of dissent. As Satayev had noted 'we are not only making films and earning money, but we also would like to be useful to the society. We would like to be useful to people, to make society a bit better.'[134] There is an effort to show the reality of post-Soviet Kazakh life to as wide an audience as possible, because there is a greater chance such representations will resonate. To an extent that is reflected in the reception of these films by cinema audiences, even if only what is presented here is only a self-selecting sample. Nonetheless, it does tell us that those who watch these films recognise the representation of their lives on the screen and that reflects an aspect of their identity formation.

The Government's Image of Modernity

This moral decay, the persistence of corruption and the desirability of wealth accumulation represents a very different picture to that presented by government-sponsored films and their depiction of modern Kazakhstan. While there has been a preference for state-ordered films which focus on the past to establish a sense of history for the present, there are also works that provide a regime-approved account of contemporary Kazakh life. Instead of providing a representation of nationhood and identity that shows the nation as fractious and economically precarious, these films project a selective image of Kazakhstan as successful, affluent and prosperous.

Two motion pictures that illustrate this trend are *Dolphin's Jump* (2009) and *The Conspiracy of Oberon* (2014). Both films were produced by Kazakhfilm Studios on the commission of the Ministry of Culture. To further illustrate that these films are closely related to the government's preferred representation of contemporary Kazakhstan, the screenplays were written by current Head of the Presidential Administration, former *Akim* of Astana and former Minister of Defence, Adilbek Dzhaksybekov. Dzhaksybekov had studied cinematography in Moscow in the early 1980s, so his sojourn into the world of film-making is not arbitrary. Dzhaksybekov is also a close confidant of the president and one of the most senior members of the political elite. He is also often included in lists of potential successors to Nazarbayev.[135]

Dolphin's Jump is a political-detective story promoted as 'being based on true events', which centres on a planned assassination attempt of the president prior to the 2005 parliamentary elections. A criminal group seeks to use a bomb attached to a bottlenose dolphin to kill the president when he is overseeing a yacht race on the Caspian Sea. The film does demonstrate aspects of corruption and criminality in Kazakhstan but it is rendered in what one critic described as a 'naïve way'.[136] The bad guys in the film are Russians, not Kazakhs, and the good guys are the Kazakh intelligence services who all have the interests of the country at heart.

A similarly ludicrous James Bond style-plot unfolds in *The Conspiracy of Oberon*, in which Kazakh scientists discover some powerful previously unknown highly explosive earth metal called Oberon, of which only a small amount can cause devastation, wiping out entire cities. The narrative arc revolves around different criminal groups seeking to get their hands on the rare material and the Kazakh intelligence agency's efforts to thwart them. The political message of these films is abundantly clear. The Kazakh authorities, rather than being obstinate and bureaucratic, as we have seen in *The Owners* and *Constructors*, are instead there to protect and provide security to the citizens of the country. This is best exemplified in the very final scene of *The Conspiracy of Oberon* where the main intelligence protagonist, Chingiz, is sitting on a park bench with one of the country's leading scientists, Kairat. Under the gleaming modern façade of Astana, Kairat notes that none of the media reports on Chingiz's secret efforts of ensuring foreign criminal elements did not get access to Oberon – suggesting Chingiz should be an example for all. Chingiz replies that his anonymity is worth the price for 'peaceful skies'. Chingiz walks away and the camera pans across the pristine, picture-perfect Astana skyline. It takes in the magnificent looking Ministry of Defence building, before panning across to *Akorda* (the President's White House) and then lifts upwards to the top of the Bayterek monument for a view of a serene blue sky. This scene was suggested by one reviewer to represent the 'apotheosis of patriotism'.[137] In this reading of contemporary Kazakhstan we are left in no doubt that the authorities, led by the Ministry of Defence and the President, are there to provide security and safety for ordinary Kazakh citizens. They are the guarantors of peace and stability. This is further emphasised in *Dolphin's Jump*, where it is implied that it is was the political opposition group Democratic Choice of Kazakhstan who disrupted the elections through strategic violence, making citizens believe that the elections were falsified, and who conspired to assassinate the president. Again, it is the intelligence services that save the day, and in doing so protect the president and secure the nation from internal and external threats.

The final scene of *Conspiracy of Oberon* is notable for its presentation of Astana as the focus of a modern and prosperous Kazakhstan. This is also a prominent element of *Dolphin's Jump*. For Dzhaksybekov, the presentation of Astana was a fundamental aim of the film. As he noted in an interview, 'the idea was to tell the world that Kazakhstan has a history of nomadic tribes, but is a modern country which is no worse than others. Astana is very good, I hope you like it, and my aim first and foremost was to show the new city and the new country'.[138] Indeed, the extended opening credits of the film operate almost as a tourist advert for the city, as the camera glides around the new capital in all is glory. Shots of modern, beautiful and shiny Astana are juxtaposed with scenes set in Moscow that are rain-sodden and dreary. The film is an explicit attempt to demonstrate the modernity and affluence of the pristine capital, and consequently the nation. As one reviewer noted, 'the film smells of money ... the picture is replete with expensive cars, Mitsubishi and Toyota and the most sought after whisky'.[139]

The mini-TV series *Astana – My Love* (2010) also personified on screen the use of Astana as a symbol for an affluent and prosperous Kazakhstan. Jointly produced by Kazakhfilm Studios and the Turkish Radio and Television Corporation, the 12-part series is a romantic tale which concerns two lovers who were promised to each other by their parents on a flight over the old city Tselinograd, one the wife of a Turkish construction worker who was pregnant and gave birth on the flight, the other a Kazakh doctor who deliverers the baby. The deal, however, was forgotten for 25 years until fate transpired that their offspring should meet again in the new capital of Kazakhstan. The TV series depicts Kazakhstan as young, vibrant and successful, providing citizens with a lifestyle comparable to that available in the West.[140] The project was the idea of the then Minister of Culture, and leading Kazakh producer Gulnara Sarsenova was brought in to work for the state and 'make a good film about our wonderful capital Astana, for all to see this young and promising city, a city of hopes and dreams'.[141] Despite coming from an independent background, Sarsenova was 'not ashamed. I wanted to serve the Fatherland. And it's not just words – it's true. I am a patriot'[142] 'Kazakh New Wave' director Yermek Shinarbayev was also brought on board. Shinarbayev had been involved in the popular soap opera series of the 1990s called *Crossroad*.[143] For Shinarbayev his involvement with *Astana – My Love* was an opportunity to return to the format of a TV series and to take advantage of the large finances given over by the state to the project.[144] However, for Adilkhan Yerzhanov, Shinarbayev's involvement is testament to his conviction that directors from the 'Kazakh New Wave' have become conservative, 'right wing and make films that follow the politics of the state'.[145] In other words they have become co-opted by the government. The TV series was given a gala premiere at the Central Concert Hall in Astana with Nazarbayev in attendance.[146] The money and attention given over to the series demonstrates the ideological importance of the TV show to the regime.

Peter Rollberg has provided an analysis of how *Astana – My Love* represents a 'dramatization and visualization of ideological and cultural officialdom'.[147] Rollberg points to several factors that demonstrate this regime-sponsored interpretation of nationhood. Firstly, a quotation from Nazarbayev appears before every episode, which states that 'cities create a country, the capital creates a nation'. Secondly, the characters in the show are all in high-earning occupations (e.g., entrepreneurs, media, doctors and architects) creating the impression of an affluent, rich and beautiful society.[148] Therefore, rather than depicting the struggles of ordinary citizens, the show makes visible the ultra-capitalist class of Kazakh society – in other words the 'winners' of post-Soviet transition. Finally, Rollberg notes the complete absence of history and religion within the series. There is neither an effort to reconnect with Kazakhs' proud history as nomads nor any mention of the Soviet period. According to Rollberg, history is replaced with the concept of destiny, showing how Kazakhstan and the Nazarbayev national project have a pre-determined shiny future, as does the relationship between Turkey and Kazakhstan, represented through the two central characters and their destiny for a romantic relationship.[149]

Astana – My Love was not the only cinematic effort to use the Capital as visual device to depict a representation of nationhood as modern and affluent. The 2012 film *My Heart Astana* featured ten mini-film novellas by various directors in Kazakhstan, including Rustem Abdrashev and Farkhat Sharipov, which all 'show a modern country, with a beautiful capital, stunningly beautiful – both externally and spiritually' based around the lives and dreams of young people.[150] However, the film, along with a series of documentaries which were made about the capital such as *Astana – a Dream Come True* and *Astana Arisen*, amount to an advertising drive for the city.[151] Their ideological potential is not lost on those who work in the film industry, and some have argued that these films are 'blockbusters which praise Kazakhstan as a second Rome'.[152]

Like all other films that are analysed in this volume, it is difficult to ascertain audience reception and the ability of these works to shape identity formation because of the lack of viewing figures and opinion polls. The audience reception on kino.kz to *The Dolphin's Jump* was mixed, some liked the professionalism of the film, but others complained of poor acting and a weak script. Comments were limited to only three pages.[153] There was a similar mixed reaction for *Conspiracy of Oberon*, with only one comment in the two pages of feedback noting how the scene at the end of the movie was 'directly impregnated with fanatical patriotism'.[154] The four pages of comments on kino.kz for *My Heart Astana* feature much criticism of the film as 'continuous PR for Astana', 'most of the film features Astana airport advertising' and as being 'solid public relations'. However, just as many were moved by the film's portrayal of the city, noting that it 'presented the advantages and successes and that it is necessary to make films for an international audience', 'showed how dreams can really come true in a beautiful city, which is located at the junction of Europe and Asia', that it presented Astana as 'beautiful, modern and dynamic city' and that it was a 'wonderful, warm, sincere film about Astana', which anyone 'with at least a modicum of patriotism would enjoy'.[155] It demonstrates that such ideologically charged regime-driven films do have some purchase with a wider audience and can contribute to shaping their identity and how they perceive Kazakhstan as a modern and successful nation.

Conclusion

The regime-ordered representation of modern life in Kazakhstan as realised through cinematic works, TV series and documentaries clearly jars with the series of signs in contemporary films analysed in this chapter. The depiction of the steppe as hostile and barren, the disorientation of post-Soviet existence, the struggles with officialdom, corruption, the urban-rural divide, the longing for a home and the breaking down of the family unit and the immoral temptations of contemporary life in Kazakhstan all add up to a representation of nationhood and identity that contests regime-sponsored nation-building narratives. Understanding nationalism and nation-building as an ambivalent, socially constructed and contested processes has opened up the marginalised narratives and voices within cinematic work. In doing so it demonstrates that cinema has become a site of dissent. This dissent can be observed in both the art-house and commercial forms of cinema in Kazakhstan, with the former being more explicit than the latter. The implicitness of commercial cinema is rendered because of the willingness to reveal the realities of everyday life, even if that only amounts to replicating the varied use of Russian and Kazakh language in daily interactions. It is dissenting because rather than attributing a picture of society that is united and bound by a common sense of belonging, instead we see the divisions within contemporary society. This is most notable even in successful commercial films such as *Kelinka Sabina*, which depicts the social divisions of urban and rural life. In films such as *Racketeer*, *Kelinka Sabina*, *Strayed* and *My Dear Children* the dissention is unspoken, but its meaning as a subtle critique can be observed, as it has been throughout this chapter, through the production and reception of the films, however limited or large the audience.

We have also witnessed much stronger critique and satire in this chapter, especially in the work of Adilkhan Yerzhanov and his collaborator Serik Abishev. Yerzhanov's work has been attempting to construct a Kazakh-specific cinematic language which aspires to an honest reflection of social reality. Consequently, he reveals a portrait of modern nationhood as one where citizens struggle against bureaucracy, power and authority. In this reading of post-Soviet nation-building, the nation is not made up of warrior *batyrs* or kind and gentle heroes or even the affluent 'winners' of the post-Soviet transition to capitalism, it instead consists of the lost, the dispossessed, the disoriented and those without a family to offer emotional and economic security. We can detect this representation of post-Soviet nationhood because in using a social-constructivist framework that recognises the multiple possibilities of nationalism in any given context we are alerted to contentious narratives of nationhood and identity not detectable in regime-driven accounts of ethnic and civic nationalism. Yerzhanov, Abishev and Isabayeva's films are marginal because of their art-house form, their use of austere aesthetics and morally ambiguous heroes. While marginal, politically their message is clear. They offer a distinct site of dissent against the prevailing political system in Kazakhstan and its modes of ideological production through film and the bureaucracy that sustains power. The extent to which these contentious narratives have social reach to a general audience is questionable. Domestic distribution is muted despite international acclaim. The work produced by Yerzhanov has been unsurprisingly viewed as too challenging for domestic audiences by the state film studios and distribution companies across the country.

Nevertheless, that directors such as Yerzhanov, Abishev and Isabayeva are able to produce films that challenge status-quo narratives about nationhood, identity and politics in Kazakhstan vindicates the two fundamental arguments of this work: nation-building in Kazakhstan is a contested and multi-voiced process among the titular majority with no essential meaning given over to what constitutes nationhood and identity; and that cinema, and art more broadly, has emerged as a site for dissent and critique in a way that formal political institutions have been unable to do thus far in the post-Soviet period.

CONCLUSION

At first glance, a study on the multiple forms of nationalisms that can be observed in Kazakh cinema across time may seem a niche endeavour. Yet, such a survey as presented in this book does speak to broader themes regarding the nature of nations and nationalism and the interplay between politics and cinema in contemporary authoritarian states. This concluding chapter seeks to place the findings of this study of film, identity and nation-building in Kazakhstan within the context of these broader themes. It consists of three parts: a discussion on the heterogeneity of nationalism and national identity; an examination of cinema as a site of dissent within authoritarian politics; and a consideration of the relationship between film and nation-building.

Heterogeneity of National Identity

The previous chapter alerted us to the way in which conceptions of Kazakh nationhood and identity in the post-Soviet period, seen through the lens of cinema, can be located, and in fact realised, in the everyday relationships and interactions ordinary people have with each other, the land, their families and the state. For example, the Kazakh nation is composed of all kinds of people from diverse backgrounds. It is the middle-aged accountant working for an international university in Almaty and it's the taxi driver working two jobs. It is the ethnic Russian born in Zhezkazgan, but who owns an apartment in Almaty and likes to spend the winters skiing in Shymbulak and it is the German who likes to go fishing at the Kolsai lakes at the weekend. It is the young woman from Shymkent who moved to Almaty to study and makes ends meet in a coffee shop in an *podzemkas* (underpass) and it is the young women who perform in national dress at the Alasha restaurant. It is the university professor who studies ethno-politics and it is the Kazakh emigres who study abroad in New York, London, Oxford and Berlin. The Kazakh nation is the young people who return from studying abroad to work at Nazarbayev University in Astana or in the civil service. It is the ethnic Tajik who sells dried fruit at the local bazaar and the young actress who returns from America to make a career in Kazakh cinema. It is the street sweeper and the sharp-suited banker. It is the young boy who gets on the bus from Taraz to Almaty and who prays for a safe journey for the passengers. The Kazakh nation is those who live by the desiccated Aral Sea, it is the ethnic Russians and Ukrainians who work for local and international NGOS. It is also the ethnic nationalist who sees portrayals of village life in cinema as an insult and a national betrayal. At the same time, it is also the young Kazakh director who rallies against corruption in the system as well as the Minister of Culture who considers the director's work a denigration of Kazakh culture.

This list of people is neither definitive nor exclusive, but it does represent an approximation of what constitutes Kazakh national identity and the boundaries of the nation. They are representative of the difference that exists within conceptions of the national. This is not to argue that Kazakhstan is unique in this sense, but given the internal antagonisms that can exist between: rural and urban life; the state and citizens; the family unit; and the moral and immoral; to what extent can the Kazakh nation or any given nation hold?

Scholarship within Nationalism Studies tells us that nations are bound by agreed shared conceptions of the national community. Ernest Renan's famous 1882 lecture at the Sorbonne, *Qu'est-ce qu'une nation*, evokes that:

> a nation is a soul, a spiritual principle. Two things, which in truth are but one, constitute this soul or spiritual principle. One lies in the past, one in the present. One is the possession in common of a rich legacy of memories; the other is present-day consent, the desire to live together.[1]

CONCLUSION

Being in possession of shared commonalities is indeed important for the establishment of nationally bounded groups. But Renan also points to how nations exist because they are a form of daily plebiscite where the 'desire of nations to be together is the only real criterion that must always be taken into account'.[2] In other words, nations exist because we will them into existence through our desire to relate, share and interact with others and through our creative imagination to define our relationships by way of a shared sense of solidarity based in interpretations of the past as well as visions of the future. Renan's account of nations undoubtedly shaped the later social constructivist explanations especially those of Anderson and Hobsbawm.[3] Craig Calhoun has gone even further to suggest that nationalism 'is a discursive formation that gives shape to the modern world. It is a way of talking, writing, and thinking about the basic units of culture, politics and belonging that helps to constitute nations as real and powerful dimensions of social life'.[4] But understanding the nation, and the nationalism that underpins it, as a socially constructed and discursive phenomena, rather than a fixed, given, organic and essential fixture of social life, entails being open to the extent to which there can be multiple constructions and discursive formations of the nation. At the same time, as Anthony Smith has argued, this cannot be some sweetshop 'pick and mix' in which symbols, myths and histories are simply cobbled together by political and cultural elites; multiple nationalisms must exist as convincing accounts.[5] Therefore, the daily plebiscite must be persuaded of one or more specific conceptualisations of the nation. But they do not have to agree on all the different elements that might constitute a discursive formation of the nation. This is how it is possible to have a bounded national group that features social and political antagonisms and in which there are multiple accounts of what constitutes the nation in terms of its interpretation of the past and fundamental symbols, myths, heroes and motifs. The daily plebiscite can agree that such a bounded national group like the Kazakh nation exists with perhaps territory and the political state being the more universally accepted boundaries, but the constituent elements in that willed construction of the Kazakh nation is partly contested and this is where its multiple forms appear.

As we have seen in the book with regards to the realisation of multiple forms of the Kazakh nation through cinematic works, and its congruent industry, these narratives can be both complementary and competing. The ethnic and civic narratives discussed in Chapters 4 and 5 complement one another, not just because they are both regime-led and produced by the largely state-funded Kazakhfilm Studios, but also because they serve a larger political goal of regime legitimation (and to some extent regime stability) vis-à-vis the complex demographic make-up of the country. The narratives speak to different audiences in the country. However, at the same time, they both possess distinct ways of conceptualising the nation. The same could be said for the 'Soviet' and 'Kazakh' worlds of Soviet Kazakh cinema. Both constructions served the larger goal of Soviet power, underpinned by Soviet nationalities policy, while at the same time possessing distinct and competing conceptualisations of the Kazakh nation.

The idea of multiple nationalisms that has emerged throughout this book's analysis of cinematic works in Kazakhstan is not entirely original. As noted in the introduction, Rima Wilkes and Michael Kehl used the term as a way of noting the changing meaning images can have across space and time with regards to the nation.[6] This book has revealed how multiple nationalisms can be realised across larger constructed narratives, rather than a single image, and in a broader social and political context of a given state. In doing so it complicates three areas in relation to the study of nations and nationalism: elite-centred approaches; the notion of national homogeneity; and the 'civic' and 'ethnic' dichotomy.

Firstly, many accounts within the modernist and social constructivist traditions in nationalism studies tend to focus on the pre-eminence of elites in the formulations of nationalist ideologies and their promotion.[7] John Breuilly, for example, understands nationalism as a form of politics tied to the objective of obtaining and using state power.[8] However, by focusing on the multivalent conceptions of nationhood and identity that can be observed in film, this work demonstrates that the 'political archaeology' of nation-building is not necessarily an elite-centred exercise.[9] Differently put, the invention or re-invention of myths, symbols, national histories and traditions, expounded most acutely in Hobsbawm and Ranger's edited volume, is not just the work of elites.[10] Like in Homi Bhabha's work on how the cultural narratives of colonised subjects are translated through an interstitial passage between fixed identities (the coloniser and the colonised) establishing a form of hybridity,[11] this study on film and nation-building in Kazakhstan has demonstrated that in Kazakh cinema, we can see the emergence of alternative and dissident types of nationalist narratives, thus creating the multivalent nature of nationalism. As we saw in Chapter 2, in Soviet-era Kazakh cinema, originally Kazakh ethnicity and culture is realised only through the lens of Soviet orientalism in documentaries such as *Turksib*, and then via more concrete policy form in Soviet nationalities policy, represented by the passing of the dombra from the Russian solider to Zhambyl in the 1952 film of the same name. In this context, Kazakh identity only exists because it is delivered by Soviet authorities. But as the political and cinematic thaw reaches the 1960s, there is an emerging subtle contention and a more fully realised Kazakh national identity that appears on the screen. It features elements that are antagonistic to the 'Soviet world', such as religion and the Kazakh language, as we saw in *My Name is Kozha* and The *Land of the Fathers*. These films in some very small way, like the cinema of this period in other Soviet republics such as the poetic cinema of Ukraine,[12] subvert the narratives of the Soviet authorities, thus establishing a form of hybridity. In the contemporary period of Kazakh cinema, we can see a similar but perhaps more concrete and noticeable process taking place. Both the Tengrist and socio-economic narratives provide a subversion of the ethnic and civic narratives put forward in Ministry of Culture-sponsored films. Both of those narratives, perhaps the socio-economic more than the Tengrist, pertain to the way in which we can observe nationhood and identity in the every-day. These are not the top-down regime-led ascriptions of identity which we find in the ethnic and civic narratives. In the work of directors such as Adilkhan Yerzhanov, Sergei Dvortsevoy, Serik Abishev, Zhanna Isabayeva and Emir Baigazin nationhood, is realised in everyday interactions and the way that individuals and families struggle and cope with the challenges of contemporary life. This is what constitutes being a member of the nation. We are bound in Renan's daily plebiscite by way of recognised shared struggles. Our belonging together is the belonging of common challenges faced in the lived day-to-day. Thus, like we have seen in recent scholarship on nation-building in the post-Soviet space, the construction of nationhood and identity is a dialogical and negotiated process between elite-oriented policy narratives and how they are received, understood, interpreted and fed back from below.[13] This is precisely what the films within the socio-economic narrative illustrate – that the direction of travel is not one which is always top-down and elite-oriented – instead there is engagement, interruption and the creation of nationalist narratives from below.

Secondly, non-elite, or at the very least non-regime, nationalist narratives demonstrate the heterogeneous nature of nationalist ideologies. In other words, that it has been possible to carve out the distinct philosophic Tengrist narrative, with is quasi-primordial understanding of Kazakh nationhood and identity being rooted in a psychogeographic relationship with the land, the cycle of birth, life and death, and the symbolic role of the mother, alongside the contemporary socio-economic narrative, illustrates that there is not just one nationalism within a given nation. The analysis of film and nation in Kazakhstan has exemplified the ways in which conceptualisations of a nation can be multivalent and fluid across time. The argument of this book is that it was possible to observe two distinct depictions of the Kazakh nation in Soviet cinema: The Soviet and Kazakh versions (although as noted above the Kazakh world was one which was initially formed through a form of Soviet orientalism). The 'Kazakh New Wave', however, flattened these conceptions through a re-interpretation of history, negation of Soviet authority and by its depiction of the realities of the political, social and personal transition from Soviet rule. As the 'Kazakh New Wave' receded back to the shore, disrupting Soviet empty homogenous time, representing the failure of the conservation of time as Spartak notes in the *The Needle* (1989), what constituted nationhood and identity for Kazakhstan was up for debate. In cinema, reflective of broader policy debates across the post-Soviet period, this has been realised in both complementary and competing ethnic, civic, Tengrist and socio-economic narratives. Despite some overlap, each narrative has a distinct understanding of the content of national identity and nation formation. Each represents a different form of identity with the ethnic narrative focused on culture, the civic on the political, the Tengrist on the religious and the socio-economic on interest. But above all, these different nationalist narratives from the Soviet period to the post-Soviet era demonstrate how the group boundary is not fixed, it is fluid across time and space, and to some extent contingent upon context. The heterogeneity of nationalism is not about competing ethnic claims for domination between bounded groups within a given state, or resistance to cultural and political assimilation, it is something more fundamental. It concerns deciding on the content of a given nationalism – the central signs that give meaning and passion to the bonds of solidarity which hold nations together. But given the diversity of peoples within a given nation, irrespective of gender, class, age and ethnicity, there will always be more than one meaning of nation. There will always be multiple accounts and differentiated narratives. For any given meaning or narrative to have durability – it must be convincing to enough people for them to desire that account to be the basis upon which national solidarity rests. Some forms of nationalism will have more power than others, usually aided by the force and resources of the state, and political power, but these are rarely exlusive and cannot prevent the possibility of other nationalisms emerging.

By focusing on the multiple possibilities of nationalism within a nation state, this work has also sought to challenge and move beyond the ethnic and civic dichotomy. The distinction between ethnic and civic, political and cultural and Eastern and Western forms of nationalisms has long been a cornerstone within nationalism studies.[14] The dichotomy emerged both as an historical interpretation of the development of different types of nationalism and an analytical binary with which to compare forms of nationalism across cases. As an analytical category, this is not the first study, nor will it be the last, which will complicate the dichotomy or seek to go beyond it. The application of the ethnic-civic binary as a heuristic device has been criticised for being a myth in relation to how it applies to specific regions of the world,[15] and the extent to which any nation can be considered civic.[16] Yet, when it comes to the study of the politics of nationalities in Kazakhstan, the ethnic-civic dichotomy has been an assumed given.[17] It is possible to observe ethnic and civic narratives, but we can also see the religious and socio-economic constructions of Kazakh nationhood. This book builds on work in other regions of the world that also demonstrates the complicating of the ethnic-civic dichotomy, such as Lisa Wedeen's work on Yemen, which explores the relationship between theology and nationalism – and the combination of both which became the basis of statehood in the country.[18] Likewise, as noted in the Introduction, scholarship on Ukraine has also pointed towards the multiple nature of Ukrainian identity beyond the simple ethnic-civic dichotomy, illustrating its heterogenous and polyphonic nature.[19] The existence of multiple narratives regarding nationhood in Kazakh cinema illustrates that we need to continue to think beyond the boundaries of the ethnic-civic binary to better capture the multiple and contentious nature of constructions of nationhood and identity within nation states, and especially within titular national groups.

Dissent and Contentious Politics in Cinema

This book has made the argument that cinema can be a site of dissent and political contention in non-democratic systems. As the preceding chapters sought to illustrate, the form of dissent takes is not static and is variable across time. In the case of the Soviet period, Kazakh cinema was not a site of outright dissent from the regime, far from it. Directors such as Shaken Aimanov were fully paid-up Party members and celebrated comrades. Nonetheless, the depiction of the ethnic Kazakh world in films such as a *Land of the Fathers*, *My Name is Kozha* and *Kyz-Zhibek*, with their references to Kazakh language, tradition and religion, was a form of indirect contention with the Soviet conception of an all-union identity. Differently put, these films did represent a degree of deviation from the Soviet norm of prescription to an all-Soviet identity as well as from an interpretation of ethnic identity that went further than those permitted by state authorities within Soviet nationalities policy. The ability of film directors to offer up a freer and slightly contentious interpretation of Kazakh national identity and nationhood was largely a consequence of the political and cinematic thaw that loosened ideological control following Khrushchev's 'secret speech' of 1956.[20] It was also indicative of a much larger trend for aesthetic freedom across the USSR in this period. Films of the thaw period focused on the lives of ordinary people, featured ambivalent heroes, and explored critical icons and mythologies such as Lenin, the Civil War and the Great Patriotic War from new angles and perspectives.[21] The films sought to both follow official policy as well as defy official strictures.[22] As Chapter 3 highlighted, Kazakh cinema offered a more tangible form of political contention in the late-Soviet period. The 'Kazakh New Wave' provided a far more critical reading of Soviet authority. In its revisiting of the silences of Kazakh history, especially the processes of collectivisation and sedentarisation, its negation of Soviet authority through the creation of new romantic heroes and disruption of time, and in its depiction of the everyday lives of Kazakh villagers, the films of the 'Kazakh New Wave' represented a dissenting and disrupting force in tune with the broader context of *perestroika* and *glasnost*. In Kazakhstan, at least, cinema became a space where the nature and authority of the Soviet system was challenged.

In the contemporary period, despite cinema being used as a tool of the authorities in Kazakhstan for the dispatch of its ideological preferences with respect to nationhood, identity and the legitimation of Nazarbayev's rule, it does appear to be a forum whereby political dissent is observable. However, the type of dissent and political contention is again, however, variable. On the one hand, in the case of Adilkhan Yerzhanov, his films are a statement on the very nature of the political system — and the corrupt and obstinate bureaucracy. On the other hand, other directors inscribe into their work a subtle form of critique courtesy of the social commentary they offer, as in the case of *Tulpan* or the work of Zhanna Isabayeva. On another level, we can observe a more esoteric and philosophic critique of modern Kazakhstan in the films of Yermek Tursunov, especially *Kelin* and *Shal*. Contemporary cinema in Kazakhstan shows us that dissent and political contention takes varying forms, sometimes concrete and deliberately antagonistic, while other times more subtle and mild. But we should be in no doubt that in this case cinema provides a space for dissent from the authoritarian regime that formal political institutions do not offer. In this instance, political contention shifts from the formal area of institutional politics, from political parties, trade unions, the judiciary, to the arena of culture and art.

Culture and art has long been considered a forum for political dissent in the US and Europe. In the post-World War II period, art was seen to engage with social and political movements and was 'explicit in its combative stance, or in its tone of political dissent, and did not shrink from making direct reference to social problems and issues'.[23] Of course, art and culture as a site of dissent in Western established democracies is demonstrative of the importance of pluralism and freedom of expression to democratic politics. This was evidenced by the New-Left and protest art of the 1960s,[24] especially in relation to the Vietnam War,[25] or in the work of the situationists and the notion of the *spectacle*.[26] However, at the same time, we should not negate the extent to which art as a site of political contention was also subject to marginalisation and repressive practices in Western democracies, and particularly the US in the 1960s, but it should be acknowledged that such pressures are not as widespread or intense as in authoritarian regimes.

The role of art and culture as a platform for political contention in authoritarian systems has not been extensively explored in scholarly literature. This is perhaps because the commonly held view is 'that authoritarianism, by definition wanting of freedom of expression and abound with censorship and self-censorship, is inimical to art'.[27] Nevertheless, even a brief survey of examples would perhaps suggest that this is an assumption built on a questionable terrain. Indeed, we can observe many instances where art and culture provide a space for political contention in non-democratic regimes, and as in the case of Kazakh cinema, the form dissent or political contention takes in authoritarian environments can be variable. By way of an example, at one end of the spectrum there is culture and art in totalitarian systems. We might typically assume that within regimes such as Hitler's Nazi Germany or in Mussolini's fascist Italy, culture is only there to serve the ideological interests of the regime. Yet, in the case of cinema in the totalitarian regimes of the 1930s and 1940s, scholars have challenged such assumptions. Steven Ricci's work on fascist Italy unpacks cinema's ambivalent nature, to the extent that films in that period were neither openly fascist nor propagandistic.[28] Furthermore, even Nazi cinema has been interpreted as possessing a diverse range of themes, approaches and techniques beyond 'a definitive categorisation as either "art" or "propaganda"'.[29] This is not to suggest that any of this pertains to a deliberate challenging of totalitarian authority, rather that even in such closed political systems cultural space can allow for ambivalence when it comes to the meaning of the political and its relationship to ideology and power. In less closed regimes, there is evidence that art and artists can play an important role in political resistance. For example, Claudia Calirman's work on art under dictatorship in Brazil demonstrates how, despite repression, artists were able to deploy various creative strategies that resisted the curtailing of critical thought.[30] In Egypt in the 1980s and 1990s, films were argued to engender varied public spaces which speculate on a variety of political possibilities, which 'express a heterogeneity of involvements, signalled by the markers of resistance, habituation and interference.'[31] In other words, cinema in Egypt provided space, through its speculative nature of meaning, for various political possibilities outside those expressed by the regime. Similarly, we can point towards the Chinese artist Ai Weiwei, who again, despite the best efforts of the Chinese authorities to repress and censor, has continued to produce art which criticises the nature of communist rule in the country and the extensive corruption that underpins the system. Furthermore, in the post-Soviet space, scholars have pointed towards the role of humour, aided by the development of digital technologies, as a means of mobilising dissent in Azerbaijan.[32]

The point here is not to conflate cinema with other forms of art, but only to conject that these varied types of artistic endeavours offer a public site for differentiated forms of political contention in non-democratic regimes, and that perhaps culture and art has been too often overlooked as a scholarly site for investigating resistance within authoritarian regimes. Nevertheless, we are left with the question of how it is possible that an art form like cinema can emerge as space for political contention and dissent. Why is it the case that cinema in Kazakhstan, especially through the Tengrist and socio-economic narratives, deliver forms of political contention that are not possible through conventional political institutional means? Given the perceived control of Kazakhstan's Ministry of Culture has on the direction of cinematic output of Kazakhfilm Studios, we would assume films produced by the Studios would not be critical of the political system or offer a social critique of the country. However, that is exactly what we see in various cases. All Yermek Tursunov's films have been produced by Kazakhfilm Studios. While he does not offer any formal political or social critique of the political system, he does provide a very different account of Kazakh nationhood and identity to that of the regime. Similarly, Yerzhanov's films *Realtors* and *The Owners* were produced by Kazakhfilm Studios, and the latter was an especially critical portrait of the modern political and social condition of Kazakhstan. So how and why did such films get past censors?

There are perhaps two potential answers to that question. It might be the case that in such instances an authoritarian regime allows the representation of social and political critique within cinematic works as a low-cost way of releasing political tension which would otherwise build up into more active and violent forms of dissent. The suppression of pluralism creates a pressure cooker environment that has the potential to boil over, and authoritarian elites recognising this might utilise less obvious political sites, such as art and cinema, as a space in which some of that steam can be released. This could be because culture might be viewed as apolitical and therefore a less obvious forum in which broader and more tangible political dissent might coalesce.

Nonetheless, at the same time, that cinema, art and culture can provide spaces where political contention can emerge in non-democratic systems is perhaps also indicative of the fact that authoritarian regimes do not possess total control over their societies. Kazakhstan is not a totalitarian state where all aspects of society are closely monitored, controlled and suppressed. To assume that the authorities in Kazakhstan are complete masters of the social and public space would perhaps ascribe too much power and agency to political elites. It is true that formal institutions that can potentially provide forums of contention and pluralism are perhaps easier to manage through legislation and institutional configuration of the political system (something Nazarbayev has been very successful in achieving in post-Soviet Kazakhstan, especially in relation to managing institutional threats to his power), [33] but on the other hand, culture and art, and cinema especially, are more porous social constructions, which are difficult to secure and control. Simply put, this is because the meaning of art is polysemic.

Any piece of art or film is open to an interpretation of meaning. It is not possible for any government to control all the multiple meanings that can be ascribed to a film or piece of art. Kazakhfilm Studios is not a homogeneous organisation. It is made up of individual directors, producers, actors, writers, editors and artists who have agency within their writing and producing of cinema. Even if the Ministry of Culture or Presidential Administration attempts to shape the themes of specific cinematic projects, those actively involved in the production of such films have the agency to subscribe their meaning and interpretation, thus rendering a straightforward relationship between the regime and film production deeply problematic. This also goes someway to explaining why we have seen fluidity across the four narratives discussed in the second half of this book. A director such as Akan Satayev has made films that have been understood to be regime-sponsored (*Zhauzhurek Myn Bala* and *The Road to Mother*) and fit within the ethnic and civic narratives, while also producing work which provides a critical and moral interpretation of the state of post-Soviet society in Kazakhstan (*Racketeer* and *Strayed*) and are situated within the socio-economic narrative. As a director, Satayev possesses his own artistic agency, which cannot be simply controlled and leveraged by the Ministry of Culture. Satayev will take money to produce big-budget ideological movies from the Ministry of Culture in as much as it allows him to follow his own artistic spirit in other projects that might, but not always, offer a portrait of contemporary Kazakhstan that is at odds with a cinematic depiction of what the Ministry of Culture or Presidential Administration would prefer. This is not to say that forms of censorship do not exist within Kazakhfilm Studios or the film industry at large. Self-censorship prevails rather than active state censorship in that people may censor themselves in producing work that might touch too close to the political bone. But nonetheless, cinema can be observed as a site of political and social contention in Kazakhstan not because of the deliberate effort of the regime to offer some space for social critique to avoid more active and obvious areas of political dissent, but rather because it is unable to control the polysemic nature of cinema. In this way, cinema, and art more broadly, demonstrates the limits of the authoritarian state.

Film and Nation-building

If film can be a site for dissent and political contention in authoritarian regimes, then it is important to consider how influential such films might be in terms of their social reach. In the case of this study, it is the question of whether the multiple narratives pertaining to Kazakh nationhood and identity that can be observed in contemporary cinema play any role in informing peoples' view of their national identity. The truth is that there is no determinate answer to that question. As noted in the Introduction, the domestic audience for Kazakh cinema is limited. Focus groups and a survey of the kino.kz comments section provided a flavour of whether specific films and/or narratives had some purchase with self-selecting cinema audiences in the country. From the findings of Chapters 4 to 7 the picture is mixed. There were sections of the audience who responded positively to the different prescriptions (especially the ethnic and civic narratives of nationhood) and saw them as patriotic representations of national history and life. At the same time, sections of the audience were sceptical of such narratives but recognised the portrayal of hardship and national divisions present in the socio-economic portrayal of nationhood. What is noticeable is that the audience and reception of films in the socio-economic narrative are largely variable. The work of Adilkhan Yerzhanov and Zhanna Isabayeva possess less of a domestic audience because of their lack of domestic distribution and arguably because of their art-house aesthetic. These are directors whose work is at the sharper and more explicit end of dissent. On the other hand, more commercially minded films, such as the work of Akan Satayev, Nurtas Adambayev or Kairzhan Orynbekov, do have a larger reach because of their commerciality and use of Hollywood form. The extent to which these directors' films offer prominent sites of contention and dissent is muted. They do provide a soft-lens critique of contemporary Kazakh society, but it is not overtly political. Therefore, assessing audience reception to these narratives is not easy and largely inconclusive. An analysis of television perhaps could provide more insight into the way government sponsored or other narratives related to nationhood and identity have a role in shaping identity formation.[34] Domestically produced television programmes do have a larger audience than domestically produced films and thus research into this area could potentially prove more conclusive regarding audience reception.

Ultimately, this indeterminate answer of the extent to which film shapes audiences' understanding of nation, identity and belonging is unsatisfactory. We engage with cinema at an emotional and irrational level – it allows us to suspend belief in our immediate reality – allowing us to conceive of our existence in alternative realities.[35] Cinema is also a shared experience, perhaps making efforts of signifying a shared belonging of nationhood on screen even more powerful. The stories and narratives of film (and other texts) give meaning to our existence and this perhaps explains its allure as a nation-building tool for both elites and those wishing to challenge authority. However, it can also be transitory. Emotional responses may dissolve after watching a film or they may last, only to be re-written by other emotional responses. In this way, film is not necessarily a practical nation-building tool. Indeed, large-scale state-led ideological cinematic projects often tend to falter in the longer-term.

Nevertheless, that the Kazakh government (and many governments around the world) continue to persist in financing and producing films that offer ideological representations of nationhood and national histories demonstrates the continued importance of film as a platform for the dissemination of national and ideological narratives. Cinema, therefore, is important to understanding the narratives that the Kazakh government wishes to convey in terms of their conception of its nationhood, but in investigating these narratives it is also possible for us to see the contentious nature of nationalism.

Cinema, as this book has demonstrated, is a useful analytical lens to reveal the political and contentious nature of nation-building. Whether the narratives of nationalism that appear in Kazakh cinema, and in broader policy and intellectual discourse, are representative of other cases has not been as aspect of this research inquiry. Other cinemas are likely to possess their own readings regarding nationhood and identity. Moreover, the broader discourse with regards to the film industry in other cases is likely to be different. There may be greater or lesser influence of the regime and the state in terms of cinematic production, more investment in the domestic industry and a larger or smaller domestic audience. In other words, the broader cinematic context (understood as the concept of national cinema), including the global cinematic industry, is likely to vary from case-to-case, and therefore will impact on the form and type of nationalist narratives which emerge. In each case, the context will be different and the signs which make up distinct narratives could also be dissimilar. What is important is the way in which cinema can be utilised as an analytical lens to open-up both the multivalent possibilities of drawing the boundaries of what constitutes nationhood and identity, specifically in terms of the the heterogeneity of nationalism within the titular national majority, and the extent to which cinema can be a site for varying intensities of dissent, contention and critique. The latter is especially important. This work has not sought to suggest that cinema, art and culture will lead to the inevitable collapse of authoritarianism in Kazakhstan, or any other non-democratic state for that matter. Instead, like how the flourishing of arts during the 'thaw' in the Soviet Union in the 1960s led Hannah Arendt to see the de-totalitarianisation of Soviet society, cinema as an analytical lens allows us to observe the shared and marginal public spaces that are often obscured by authoritarian politics.[36] It provides us with some collective insight into the possibilities of pluralism in otherwise culturally closed societies and for the emergence of a potentially more imaginative and active civil society.

NOTES

Introduction

1. There is an important political difference between the terms 'Kazakh' and 'Kazakhstani'. 'Kazakh' relates to the ethnic group that identifies as Kazakh, while 'Kazakhstani' refers to those who are citizens of the Republic of Kazakhstan, which features many different ethnic groups. This is a distinction that is central to two of the narratives discussed in this work (ethnic and civic). However, to ensure clarity in terms of this distinction within these two cinematic narratives, and a general ease of reading, the term 'Kazakh' will be used when referring to generalities associated with Kazakhstan such as 'Kazakh cinema' and 'the Kazakh government'. This does not mean to disenfranchise those who are not of Kazakh ethnicity but reside in Kazakhstan, nor to obfuscate the complexity of identity in Kazakhstan (given this is the argument of the book).
2. For a sample of this literature see: Andrew Higson, The Concept of National Cinema, *Screen*, 30 (4), 1989, pp. 36–47; John Hill, The issue of national cinema and national film production, in D. Petrie (ed.), *New Questions of British Cinema*. London: BFI, 1992, pp. 10–21; Wimal Dissanayake, *Colonialism and Nationalism in Asian Cinema*. Bloomington and Indianapolis: Indiana University Press, 1994; Andrew Higson, *Waving the Flag: Constructing a National Cinema in Britain*. Oxford: Oxford University Press, 1995; Mette Hjort and Scott Mackenzie (eds), *Cinema and Nation*. London and New York, Routledge, 2000; Hans Joachim Meurer, *Cinema and National Identity in a Divided Germany, 1979–1989: The Split Screen*. Lewinston, New York, Queenston, Ontario and Lampeter, Wales: Edwin Mellen Press, 2000; Alan Williams, *Film and Nationalism*, New Brunswick, NJ and London: Rutgers University Press, 2002; Valentina Vitali and Paul Willemen (eds), *Theorising National Cinema*. London: British Film Institute, Palgrave MacMillan, 2006; Chris Berry and Mary Farquhar, *China on Screen: Cinema*

and Nation. New York: Colombia University Press, 2006; Zakir Hossain Raju, *Bangladesh Cinema and National Identity: In Search of the Modern?* London and New York: Routledge, 2015.
3. Dissanayake, *Colonialism and Nationalism in Asian Cinema*, p. xi.
4. The commonplace understanding of the 'nation' is that of a modern interpretation in which a nation is congruent with a political state, often referred to as the nation state. On the one hand, this book takes as a point of departure Kazakhstan as a modern nation in this political sense, understanding it as a recent social phenomenon dating back to its political construction by the Soviets in the 1920s and 1930s. However, nations can be understood as not being limited to this political definition. Nations can exist without a recognised political state such as in the case of the Kurdish or Tuareg nations. Moreover, a further contention of this work is that there can exist the possibility of multiple constructed nations within any given nation and beyond cultural exclusivist and politically inclusive conceptualisations of nations and nationalism. This does not mean, however, that there are no limits to what constitutes a nation. There requires a critical mass among a given group as to what constitutes the boundaries of a construction of a nation (i.e., ethnicity, religion, language, political etc.) and the claims being made in relation to nationhood (shared myths, history and memory etc.). This is not something that can be quantified, but instead it must be based on the reasonability and feasibility of such claims of nationhood even if not accepted by all actors internal to the nation (or nation state) or external (such as international recognition of nationhood). This explains why nations (whether contrived in political or cultural terms) are inherently contentious entities.
5. Accounts of nations and nationalism as products of modernity are vast and ubiquitous. Some of the key texts are: Ernest Gellner, *Nations and Nationalism* 2nd Edition. Malden, MA: Blackwell Publishing, 2006, pp. 1–2; Tom Nairn, *The Break-up of Britain: Crisis and Neo-Nationalism*. Melbourne: Common Ground Publishing, 1977; Karl W. Deutsch, *Nationalism and Social Communication*, 2nd Edition. Cambridge, MA: MIT Press, 1953.
6. Eric J. Hobsbawm, *Nations and Nationalism since 1780: Programme, Myth, reality*, Cambridge: Cambridge University Press, 1990, p. 94; Michael Hechter, *Internal Colonialism: the Celtic Fringe in British National Development, 1536–1966*, London and Henley: Routledge & Kegan Paul, 1975.
7. Benedict Anderson, *Imagined Communities: Reflections on the Origin and Spread of Nationalism*, London: Verso, 1983.
8. In the twenty-first century, new forms of media beyond print capitalism exist to promote representations of specifically defined national, cultural and group boundaries. See David Morely and Kevin Robins, *Spaces of Identity: Global Media, Electronic Landscapes and Cultural Boundaries*. London and New York: Routledge, 1995; Deborah Wheeler, 'New Media, Globalization and Kuwaiti National Identity', *Middle East Journal*, 54 (3), 2000, pp. 432–44; Clay Shirky, 'The Political Power of Social Media: Technology, the Public Sphere,

and Political Change', *Foreign Affairs*, 90 (1), 2011 pp. 28–41; Shani Orgad, *Media Representation and the Global Imagination*. Cambridge: Polity Press, 2012.
9. Sally N. Cummings, 'Soviet Rule, Nation and Film: the Kyrgyz wonder years', *Nations and Nationalism*, 15 (4), 2009, pp. 636–57.
10. Dissanayake, *Colonialism and Nationalism in Asian Cinema*, p. x.
11. Walter Benjamin understood homogeneous empty time as our ordinary conception of time that was a product of capitalist development. Time is measured in discrete calendrical units (seconds, hours, days, months and years etc.). Time passes in a similar repetitive fashion with the old replicating the new in a progressive linear way. Anderson uses Benjamin's conceptualisation of empty homogeneous time to theorise the way in which individuals who have never met can share simultaneous attachments to a social organism as it allows for a confidence in their steady, anonymous and simultaneous activity. Benjamin was more interested in revolutionary disruptions to empty homogeneous time or what he also termed 'hell of the present'. The concept of empty homogenous time is revisited in Chapter Three when the argument is put forward that the emergence of the 'Kazakh New Wave' cinema acted as a disruptive force to Soviet empty homogeneous time in Kazakhstan. For more on the concept see Walter Benjamin, *Illuminations*, New York: Schocken Books, 2007 [1968].
12. Anderson, *Imagined Communities*, p. 58.
13. Gellner, *Nations and Nationalism*, p. 34.
14. Ibid., p. 1.
15. Hobsbawm, *Nations and Nationalism since 1780*, p. 10.
16. Paul Brass, 'Elite Groups, Symbol Manipulation and Ethnic Identity among Muslims of South Asia' in D. Taylor and M. Yapp (eds), *Political Identity in South Asia*. London: Curzon Press, 1979, pp. 35–68.
17. Ernest Gellner, *Thought and Change*. London: Weidenfeld and Nicolson, 1964, pp. 155–7.
18. Anderson, *Imagined Communities*, p. 7.
19. When explaining why a general pan-Latin American nationalism did not emerge, Anderson gives the example of Mexican creoles who might learn some months later of developments in Buenos Aires, but through Mexican newspapers, not those of the Rio de la Plata. Anderson, *Imagined Communities*, p. 63.
20. Anderson, *Imagined Communities*, pp. 61–5.
21. Michael Billig, *Banal Nationalism*. Thousand Oaks, CA: Sage Publications, 1995, p. 93.
22. Michael Skey, 'The national in everyday life: A critical engagement with Michael Billig's thesis of Banal Nationalism', *The Sociological Review*, 57 (2), 2009, p. 337.
23. Vera Slavtcheva-Petkova, 'Rethinking Banal Nationalism: Banal Americanism, Europeanism, and the Missing Link between Media Representations and Identities', *International Journal of Communication*, 8, 2014, pp. 43–61.

24. Rogers Brubaker, *Ethnicity Without Groups*. Cambridge, MA: Harvard University Press, 2004.
25. Brubaker, *Ethnicity Without Groups*, p. 3.
26. Rogers Brubaker, 'Ethnicity Without Groups', *European Journal of Sociology*, 3 (2), 2002, p. 166.
27. Hobsbawm, *Nations and Nationalism since 1780*, pp. 33–34.
28. Ibid., pp. 91–2.
29. Ibid., p. 93.
30. Karl W. Deutsch and William J. Foltz (eds), *Nation-Building in Comparative Contexts*. New Brunswick, NJ: Transaction Publishers, 1966.
31. Nation-building is understood in this work as the process by which actors (both elite and non-elite) attempt to establish and convince a group of people that they belong and share the social, economic and cultural interests of a circumscribed social world. Nation-building can be undertaken by a variety of tools and mechanisms across the political, cultural and economic fields. However, nation-building cannot involve all kinds of social actions and interactions. A line must be drawn. It must be a conscious decision driven by specific human agency and intention. Therefore, even if it might seem that an instance of nation-building is a product of an unintended consequence – what some scholars have referred to as 'spontaneous' nation-building – it cannot be considered nation-building if there was no specific agency or intention on the part of either elites or non-elites. This is not to rule out the possibility that in instances where nation-building is an accidental product of a process or event, elites and non-elites can then display agency and intention to take advantage of this 'spontaneous' form of nation-building to make it 'actual'.
32. Jonathan Hearn, *Re-thinking Nationalism: A Critical Introduction*. Houndsmill, Basingstoke: Palgrave Macmillan, 2006, p. 11.
33. Charles Tilly and Sidney Tarrow, *Contentious Politics*. Oxford: Oxford University Press, 2015, p. 7.
34. For an overview of these three approaches see Douglas McAdam, Sidney Tarrow and Charles Tilly, 'Comparative Perspectives on Contentious Politics', in Mark Irving Lichbach and Alan S. Zuckerman (eds), *Comparative Politics: Rationality, Culture and Structure*. Cambridge: Cambridge University Press, 2009, pp. 268–73.
35. While this work takes the construction of claims of contentious politics as a point of departure, it is not the intention of this work to rule out or not take account of the other two approaches. Throughout the book in fact there is reference to how the structural context gives rise to the contentious politics of national representation, especially in the *perestroika* period in Soviet Kazakhstan, in which broader structural and political changes provided a space for a group of young Kazakh directors to emerge that challenged the prevailing orthodoxy not just of Soviet cinema-making, but also of the Soviet ideological edifice (see Chapter 2). Similarly, in the post-Soviet era,

the issue of resource mobilisation conditions the ability of directors to find financing to produce movies that may represent an anathema to the regime-led production of national narratives (see Chapter 7). Moreover, the broader economic context of the film industry, both globally and domestically, shapes the ability of directors and production companies to get films made and financed – in which they might conceivably make claims regarding the representation of Kazakh nationhood and identity.

36. Homi Bhabha, *Nation and Narration*. London: Routledge, 1990, p. 1.
37. Philip Spencer and Howard Woolman, *Nationalism: A Critical Introduction*. London: Sage Publications, 2002, p. 50.
38. Etienne Balibar, 'The Nation Form: history and ideology' in Etienne Balibar and Immanuel Wallerstein (eds), *Race, Nation, Class: ambiguous identities*. London: Verso, 1991, p. 93.
39. Annette Bohr, 'The Central Asian States as Nationalising Regimes' in G. Smith (ed.), *Nation-Building in post-Soviet Borderlands: The Politics of National Identities*. Cambridge: Cambridge University Press, 1998, pp. 139–66.
40. Michele Commercio, 'The "Pugachev Rebellion" in the Context of Post-Soviet Kazakh Nationalisation', *Nationalities Papers*, 32 (1), 2004, pp. 87–113; Azamat Sarsembayev, 'Imagined Communities: Kazak nationalism and Kazakification in the 1990s', *Central Asian Survey*, 18 (3), 1999, pp. 319–46; Sally N. Cummings, 'Legitimation and Identification in Kazakhstan', *Nationalism and Ethnic Politics*, 12 (2), 2006, pp. 177–204.
41. Sarsembayev, 'Imagined Communities', p. 99; Cengiz Surucu, 'Modernity, Nationalism and Resistance: Identity Politics in Post-Soviet Kazakhstan', *Central Asian Survey*, 21 (4), 2002, pp. 385–402; Donnacha Ó'Beacháin and Robert Kevlihan, 'Threading a needle: Kazakhstan between civic and ethno-nationalist state-building', *Nations and Nationalism*, 19 (2), pp. 337–56.
42. Özgecan Kesici, 'The Dilemma in the Nation-Building Process: The Kazakh or Kazakhstani Nation?' *Journal on Ethnopolitics and Minority Issues in Europe*, 10 (1), 2011; pp. 31–58; Surucu, 'Modernity, Nationalism and Resistance'; Ó'Beacháin and Kevlihan, 'Threading a needle'.
43. Charles Tilly, Louise Tilly and Richard Tilly, *The Rebellious Century*. Cambridge, MA: Harvard University Press, 1975; James C. Scott, *The Moral Economy of the Peasant: Rebellion and Subsistence in Southeast Asia*. New Haven, CT and London: Yale University Press, 1976.
44. James C. Scott, *Weapons of the Weak. Everyday Forms of Peasant Resistance*. New Haven, CT: Yale University Press, 1985.
45. Hobsbawm, *Nations and Nationalism Since 1780*, p. 10.
46. Rima Wilkes and Michael Kehl, 'One image, multiple nationalisms: Face to Face and the Siege at Kanehsatà:ke', *Nations and Nationalism*, 20 (3), 2014, pp. 481–502.
47. Karina Korestelina identifies five different conceptualisations of Ukrainian national identity. Karina Korestelina, 'Mapping national identity narratives in Ukraine', *Nationalities Papers*, 41 (2), 2013, pp. 293–315.

48. Oxana Shevel, in her analysis of Ukrainian diaspora laws illustrates how the civic-ethnic dichotomy does not provide an adequate conceptual framing for the complex tensions between different variants of ethnic nationalism. Oxana Shevel, 'The Post-Communist Diaspora Laws: Beyond the "Good Civic versus Bad Ethnic" Nationalism Dichotomy', *East European Politics & Societies*, 24 (1), 2010, pp. 159–87.
49. Peter Rodgers, 'Understanding regionalism and the politics of identity in Ukraine's Eastern Borderlands', *Nationalities Papers*, 34 (2), 2006, pp. 154–74.
50. Tanya Zaharchenko, 'Polyphonic dichotomies: Memory and Identity in Today's Ukraine', *Demokratizatsiya*, 21 (2), 2013, pp. 241–69.
51. Oxana Shevel, 'Russian Nation-building from Yel'tsin to Medvedev: Ethnic, Civic or Purposefully Ambiguous?' *Europe-Asia Studies*, 63 (2), 2011, pp. 179–202.
52. Taras Kuzio, 'The myth of the civic state: a critical survey of Hans Kohn's framework for understanding nationalism', *Ethnic and Racial Studies*, 25 (1), 2002, pp. 20–39; Stephen Schulman, 'Sources of Civic and Ethnic Nationalism in Ukraine', *Journal of Communist Studies and Transition Politics* 18(4), 2002, pp. 1–30; Petr Panov, 'Nation-building in post-Soviet Russia: What kind of nationalism is produced by the Kremlin?' *Journal of Eurasian Studies*, 1 (2), 2010, pp. 85–94; Dagikhudo Dagiev, *Regime Transition in Central Asia: Stateness, Nationalism and Political Change in Tajikistan and Uzbekistan*. London and New York: Routledge, 2014; Rico Isaacs and Abel Polese, 'Nation-Building in the Post-Soviet Space: Old, New and Changing Tools' in Rico Isaacs and Abel Polese (eds), *Nation-Building and Identity in the Post-Soviet Space: New Tools and Approaches*. London and New York: Routledge, 2016, pp. 1–23.
53. Rogers Brubaker, 'National Minorities, Nationalizing States, and External National Homelands – in the New Europe', *Daedalus*, 124 (2), 1995, p. 116.
54. Mariya Y. Omelicheva, 'Islam in Kazakhstan: A Survey of Contemporary Trends and Sources of Securitization', *Central Asia Survey*, 30 (2), 2011, pp. 243–56; Azade-Ayse Rorlich, 'Islam, Identity and Politics: Kazakhstan 1990–2000', *Nationalities Papers*, 31 (2), 2003, pp. 159–76.
55. Saulesh Yessenova, '"Routes and Roots" of Kazakh Identity: Urban Migration in Post-socialist Kazakhstan', *The Russian Review*, 64, 2005, pp. 661–79; Nurbolat Masanov et al., *Istoriya Kazakhstana: Narody i kul'tury*, Almaty: Daik Press, 2001.
56. Marlene Laruelle, 'The Three Discursive Paradigms of State Identity in Kazakhstan: Kazakhness, Kazakhstaness and Transnationalism' in Mariya Y. Omelicheva (ed.), *Nationalism and Identity Construction in Central Asia: Dimensions, Dynamics, Directions*, Layland, MD: Lexington Books, 2015, pp. 1–20.
57. Rico Isaacs, 'Nomads, Warriors and Bureaucrats: Nation-Building and Film in post-Soviet Kazakhstan', *Nationalities Papers*, 43 (3), 2015, pp. 399–416;

Scott Radnitz, 'Networks, localism and mobilization in Aksy, Kyrgyzstan', *Central Asian Survey*, 24 (4), 2005 pp. 405–24.
58. Philip Schlesinger, 'The Sociological Scope of "national cinema" in Mette Hjort and Scott Mackenzie (eds), *Cinema and Nation*. London and New York: Routledge 2000, pp. 20–22.
59. Billig, *Banal Nationalism*, pp. 6–7.
60. Williams, *Film and Nationalism*, p. 4.
61. Dissanayake, *Colonialism and Nationalism in Asian Cinema*, p. xvii.
62. Peter Kenez, *Cinema and Soviet Society*, Cambridge: Cambridge University Press, 1992, p. 29.
63. Kenez, *Cinema and Soviet Society*, p. 78.
64. Richard Taylor, *Film Propaganda: Soviet Russia and Nazi Germany*, London and New York: I.B.Tauris, 1998, pp. 7–8.
65. Denise Youngblood, *Movies for the Masses: Popular Cinema and Soviet Society in the 1920s*. Cambridge: Cambridge University Press, 1992; Richard Taylor, *The Politics of Soviet Cinema*. Cambridge: Cambridge University Press, 1979; David Gillespie, *Early Soviet Cinema: Innovation, Ideology and Propaganda*. London: Wallflower Publications, 2000.
66. Kenez, *Cinema and Soviet Society*, p. 2.
67. Roland Barthes, *Image, Music, Text*. London: Fontana Press, 1977.
68. Higson, 'The Concept of National Cinema', p. 37.
69. Stephen Crofts, 'Concepts of National Cinema' in John Hill and Pamela Church Gibson (eds), *The Oxford Guide Film Studies*. Oxford: Oxford University Press, 1998, p. 386.
70. Hill, 'British Cinema and National Cinema', p. 110.
71. Dissanayake, *Colonialism and Nationalism in Asian Cinema*, p. xxvi.
72. Anderson, *Imagined Communities*.
73. Ed. S. Tan, *Emotion and the Structure of Narrative Film: Film as an emotion machine*. New York and London: Routledge, 1995.
74. See Chapter 1 for more detail on the role of local elites in the process of Kazakh and broader Soviet nation-building. Three of the key works on this include Arne Haugen, *The Establishment of National Republics in Soviet Central Asia*. Houndsmill, Basingstoke: Palgrave Macmillan, 2003; Adrienne Lynn Edgar, *Tribal Nation: The Making of Soviet Turkmenistan*. Princeton, NJ: Princeton University Press, 2004; Francine Hirsch, *Empire of Nations: Ethnographic knowledge and the making of the Soviet Union*, Cornell, NY: Cornell University Press, 2005.
75. Nursultan Nazarbayev, *Without Right and Left*, London: Class Publishing, 1992.
76. The Kazakh government funded a modernisation program of the film studios in 2006 and provided a budget of $70 million for the studio over three-year periods. This does not include the money it provides to fund specific films.
77. David Stern, 'Building Kazakhstan One Film at a Time', *The New York Times*, 4 December 2008. Accessed 9 January 2013: http://www.nytimes.

com/2008/02/24/world/asia/24iht-kazakh.4.10338362.html?_r=0; Kate Springer, 'Kazakhstan's Growing Film Industry Aims to Counter Borat Image', *Time Magazine*, 29 January 2012. Accessed 7 January 2013: http://newsfeed.time.com/2012/01/29/kazakhstans-growing-film-industry-aims-to-counter-borat-image.
78. Fredrik Barth, *Ethnic Groups and Boundaries*. Bergen-Oslo: Universitets Forlaget/London: George Allen & Unwin, 1969, pp. 11–12.
79. Kazakhstan fits Juan Linz's definition of authoritarianism, which is that of 'political systems with limited [...] political pluralism, without elaborate and guiding ideology, but with distinctive mentalities, without extensive mobilisation [...] and in which a leader [...] exercises power within formally ill-defined limits but actually quite predictable ones'. Linz cited in Juan Linz, *Totalitarian and Authoritarian Regimes*. Boulder, CO: Lynne Rienner, 2000, p. 159. Kazakhstan has developed a form of post-Soviet authoritarianism centred on the personalistic leadership of its first and only president, Nursultan Nazarbayev. Despite regular elections, a formal division of powers and ostensibly the rule of law, parliament is subservient to the president, political opposition is restricted, the judiciary is acquiescent to the executive, civil society is weak and problems persist with regards to human rights violations. The political system corresponds to a form of neopatrimonialism whereby Nazarbayev arbitrates the political and economic interests of competing informal elite networks.
80. David Welch, *Propaganda and the German Cinema 1933–1945*. London and New York: I.B.Tauris, 2001; Patricia Lee Masters, 'Warring Bodies: Most Nationalistic Selves' in Wimal Dissanayake (ed.), *Colonialism and Nationalism in Asian Cinema*. Bloomington, IN: Indiana University Press, 1994, pp. 1–10.
81. Stuart Hall, 'Introduction' in Stuart Hall (ed.), *Representation: Cultural Representations and Signifying Practices*. London: Sage Publications, p. 6.
82. Ferdinand de Saussure, *Course in General Linguistics (trans. Roy Harris)*. London: Duckworth, 1983 [1916].
83. Stuart Hall, 'The Work of Representations' in Stuart Hall (ed.), *Representation: Cultural Representations and Signifying Practices*. London: Sage Publications, p. 31.
84. Hall, 'The Work of Representations', p. 31.
85. Orgad, *Media Representation*, p. 4.
86. Ibid.
87. Slavtcheva-Petkova, 'Rethinking Banal Nationalism'.
88. Steve Fenton, 'Indifference towards national identity: what young adults think about being English and British', *Nations and Nationalism* 13 (2), 2007, p. 321.
89. Hall, 'Introduction', p. 6.
90. Ibid.
91. Michel Foucault, 'The Subject and Power', *Critical Inquiry*, 8 (4) (Summer, 1982), p. 778.

92. Orgad, *Media Representation*, p. 25.
93. Barthes, *Image, Music, Text*, pp. 33–36.
94. Ibid., p. 39.
95. Ibid.
96. Ibid., pp. 39–41.
97. Ibid., p. 40.
98. Orgad, *Media Representation*, p. 4.
99. Ibid., pp. 4–5; John B. Thompson, 'The New Visibility', *Theory, Culture and Society*, 22 (6), 2005, p. 31.
100. See, for example, Pierre Sorlin, *Italian National Cinema*. London and New York: Routledge, 1996; Sabine Hake, *German National Cinema*. London and New York: Routledge, 2000; Brian Marshall, *Quebec National Cinema*. Montreal and Kingston: McGill Queens University Press, 2001; Tom O'Regan, *Australian National Cinema*. London and New York: Routledge, 1996.
101. Crofts, 'Concepts of National Cinema', p. 386.
102. Higson, 'The Concept of National Cinema', pp. 36–46.
103. These varieties include: United States cinema, Asian commercial successes, other entertainment cinemas, totalitarian cinemas, art cinemas, international co-productions, third cinemas and sub-state cinemas. See Crofts, 'Concepts of National Cinema', pp. 389–91.
104. Valentina Vitali and Paul Willemen, 'Introduction' in Valentina Vitali and Paul Willemen (eds), *Theorising National Cinema*. London: British Film Institute, Palgrave McMillan, 2006, p. 7.
105. Will Higbee and Song Hwee Lim, 'Concepts of transnational cinema: towards a critical transnationalism in film studies', *Transnational Cinemas*, 1 (1), 2010, p. 7.
106. Higbee and Lim, 'Concepts of transnational cinema', p. 10.
107. Higson, *The Concept of National Cinema*, p. 36.
108. Crofts, 'Concepts of National Cinema', p. 387.
109. This last point is something not adequately addressed in Crofts' analytical categorisation nor in other work on national cinema. See Crofts, 'Concepts of National Cinema', pp. 388–9.

Chapter 1   Kazakh Khanate to Kazakh Eli: Nation-building in Kazakhstan in Historical and Political Context

1. Martha Brill Olcott, *The Kazakhs*. Stanford, CA: The Hoover Institution Press, 1987; Sanjar Dzhafarovich Asfendiarov, *Istoriya Kazakhstana*. Kazakh University: Almaty, 1993; M Tynshoaev, A. C. Takenov and B. Baigaliev, *Istoriya Kazakhskogo Naroda*. Sanat: Almaty, 2009.
2. Vasili Barthold, *Four Studies of the History of Central Asia*, cited in Geoffrey Wheeler, *The Modern History of Soviet Central Asia*. London: Weidenfeld and Nicolson, pp. 11–12.
3. Martha Brill Olcott, *The Kazakhs*, p. 4.

4. Alun Thomas, *Kazakh Nomads and the New Soviet State, 1919–1934*, PhD thesis, Sheffield, 2015.
5. Much of this has focused on Russian colonisation or the silences within the Soviet history of Kazakhstan, such as the settlement of the nomads in the 1930s and the subsequent famine, rather than the ethno-genesis of the Kazakh people and nation.
6. See Nurbolat Masanov et al., *Istoriya Kazakhstana: Narody i kul'tury*. Almaty, Daik Press, 2001; Nurbolat Masanov, Zhulduzbek Abylkhozhin and Irina Yerofeyeva, *Nauchnoe znaanie i mifotvorchestvo istoriografii Kazakhstana*. Almaty, Daik Press, 2007.
7. The primary source that references the migration of Zhanybek and Kerey Khan and their associated tribes from the rule of Abu'l-Khayr Khan (Khan of the Uzbeks) is that of the work of Turko-Mongol military general Mirza Muhammad Haidar Dughlat. The origin and formation of the Kazakh Khanate can be found in chapter 33 of Dughlat's *The Tarikh i Rashidi*. London: Forgotten Books, 2013 [1895], pp. 272–4.
8. Olcott, *The Kazakhs*, p. 10.
9. Karl Baipankov and Bulat E. Kumekov, 'The Kazakhs', in I. Chaahyaradlehabib and K.M. Baipakov (eds), *History of Civilizations of Central Asia Vol V, Development in contrast: From the Sixteenth to the Mid-Nineteenth Century*. Paris: UNESCO Publishing.
10. Baipankov and Kumekov, 'The Kazakhs', pp. 94–7.
11. Ibid., p. 90.
12. Nurlan Amrekulov, 'Zhuzy v sotsial'no-politicheskoi zhizni Kazakhstana', *Tsentral'naia Aziya i Kavkaz*, 3 (9), 2000.
13. Masanov et al., *Istoriya Kazakhstana: narody i kul'tury*.
14. Wheeler, *The Modern History of Soviet Central Asia*, p. 32.
15. Amrekulov, 'Zhuzy v sotsial'no-politicheskoi zhizni Kazakhstana', p. 4.
16. Olcott, *The Kazakhs*, p. 11.
17. There is a famous note on this from British explorer Anthony Jenkinson in his letters from this time where he writes of the Kazakhs along with the Kygryz as 'two barbarous Nations . . . of great force, living in the fields without House or Towne'. See Richard Hakluyt, *Voyages and Discoveries*. London, Penguin Books, 1972, p. 71.
18. Baipankov and Kumekov, 'The Kazakhs'.
19. For example, see official state website dedicated to the 550th anniversary: http://550kazakhan.kz/?page_id=6&lang=ru. For the TV series see Jo Lillis, 'Kazakhstan creates its own Game of Thrones to defy Putin and Borat', *Guardian*, 27 January 2016. Accessed 27 January 2016: http://www.theguardian.com/world/2016/jan/27/kazakhstan-game-of-thrones-putin-and-borat.
20. Ian Traynor, 'Kazakhstan is latest Russian neighbour to feel Putin's chilly nationalist rhetoric', *Guardian*, 1 September 2014. Accessed 13 July 2016: https://www.theguardian.com/world/2014/sep/01/kazakhstan-russian-neighbour-putin-chilly-nationalist-rhetoric.

21. Anthony D. Smith, *The Ethnic Origins of Nations*. Oxford: Oxford University Press, 1986.
22. Ilyas Yessenberlin, *Kochevniki: trilogiya*. Almaty: The Fund of I. Yesenberlina, 1971.
23. Charles Weller, *Rethinking Kazakh and Central Asian Nationhood*, Los Angeles: Asia Research Associates, 2006.
24. Michael Hancock-Parmer, *From Qazaqs to Kazakhs: The Study of Eighteenth-Century Qazaqs by Nineteenth Century Russophone Scholars*, paper given at Central Eurasian Studies Conference, 17 October 2015, George Washington University, Washington, DC.
25. Hancock-Parmer, *From Qazaqs to Kazakhs*.
26. Baipankov and Kumekov, 'The Kazakhs', p. 91.
27. Shirin Akiner, *The Formation of Kazakh Identity: from Tribe to Nation-State*. Former Soviet State Papers, London: Royal Institute of International Affairs, 1995.
28. Saulesh Yessenova, 'Soviet Nationality, Identity, and Ethnicity in Central Asia: Historic Narratives and Kazakh Ethnic Identity', *Journal of Muslim Minority Affairs*, 22 (1), 2002, pp. 11–38.
29. Hancock-Parmer, *From Qazaqs to Kazakhs*.
30. Gavin Hambly, *Central Asia*. New York: Delacorte Press, 1969, pp. 143–4.
31. Steven Sabol, 'Kazak Resistance to Russian Colonization: interpreting the Kenesary Kasymov revolt, 1837–1847', *Central Asian Survey*, 22 (3), 2003, p. 239.
32. Baipankov and Kumekov, 'The Kazakhs', pp. 98–9.
33. Michael Hancock-Parmer, 'The Soviet Study of the Barefooted Flight of the Kazakhs', *Central Asian Survey* 34 (3), 2015, p. 281.
34. Michael Hancock-Parmer, *Historiography of the Bare-Footed Flight: Dynamics of a National History*, Dissertation, Central Eurasian Studies, Indiana University, 2011, pp. 76–77.
35. Peter Rottier, *Creating the Kazakh nation: the intelligentsia's quest for acceptance in the Russian Empire, 1905–1920*, PhD Dissertation. Madison, WI: University of Wisconsin-Madison, 2005, pp. 35–6.
36. Olcott, *The Kazakhs*, pp. 31–4.
37. Rottier, *Creating the Kazakh nation*; Brill Oclott, *The Kazakhs*.
38. Sabol, 'Kazak Resistance to Russian Colonization', p. 235.
39. Wheeler, *The Modern History of Soviet Central Asia*, p. 49.
40. Ibid.
41. See Sabol, 'Kazak Resistance to Russian Colonization', for a good overview of the Russian colonisation process during this period.
42. Virginia Martin, *Law and Custom in the Steppe: The Kazakhs of the Middle Horde and Russian Colonialism in the Nineteenth Century*. Richmond: Curzon Press, 2001.
43. Michael Rouland, 'A New Kazakhstan: Four Books Reconceptualise the History of the Kazak Steppe', *Nationalities Papers*, 32 (1), 2004, p. 235.

44. Sabol, 'Kazak Resistance to Russian Colonization', pp. 240–1.
45. Ibid., p. 243.
46. Ibid., p. 241.
47. Ibid., p. 244.
48. Harun Yilmaz, *National Identities in Soviet Historiography: The Rise of Nations Under Stalin*. London and New York: Routledge, p. 88.
49. The name Alash is derived from a legend that all Kazakhs are descended from Alash Khan who ruled 3000–2000 BC and that it was he who conceived the three Kazakh *zhuz*. Hence the common Kazakh phrase 'we are the children of Alash.'
50. An example of this is the education of founder and leader of Alash Orda, Alikhan Bukeikhanov, who graduated from the Omsk Technical Institute and the Saint Petersburg Forestry Institute Faculty of Economics in 1894.
51. Ernest Gellner, *Nations and Nationalism 2nd Edition*. Malden, MA: Blackwell Publishing, 2006, pp. 1–2.
52. Peter Rottier, 'Legitimizing the Ata Meken: The Kazakh Intelligentsia Write a History of their Homeland', *Ab Imperio* 1, 2004, p. 467.
53. Gulnar Kendirbaeva, '"We are Children of Alash ... ": The Kazakh Intelligentsia at the Beginning of the 20th Century in Search of National Identity and Prospects of the Cultural Survival of the Kazakh people', *Central Asian Survey*, 18 (1), 1999, p. 8.
54. Kendirbaeva, 'We are Children of Alash ... ', pp. 5–36.
55. Ibid., p. 6.
56. Yessenova, 'Soviet Nationality, Identity, and Ethnicity in Central Asia', pp. 13–14.
57. Lyn R. Fisher, *Qazaqjylyq: Nationalism and revolution in Kazakhstan, 1900–1920*. Theses, Dissertations, Professional Papers. Paper 3337, Montana: University of Montana, 1989.
58. Graham Smith (ed.), *The Nationalities Question in the Post-Soviet States*, London and New York: Longman, 1996, pp. 4–5; Ian Bremmer, 'Post-Soviet Nationalities Theory: past, present and future' in Ian Bremer and Ray Taras (eds), *New States New Politics: Building post-Soviet nations*, Cambridge: Cambridge University Press. Bremmer, 1997, p. 7.
59. Hugh Seton-Watson, 'Soviet Nationality Policy', *Russian Review*, 15 (1), 1956, p. 3.
60. Joseph Stalin, 'The Nation in Marxism and the National Question' in Bruce Franklin (ed.), *The Essential Stalin: Major Theoretical Writings 1905–1952*. London: Croom Helm, 1973, p. 57.
61. Yaccov Ro'i, 'The Soviet and Russian context of the development of nationalism in Soviet Central Asia', *Cahiers du monde russe et soviétique*, 32 (1), 1991, pp. 124–5.
62. Smith, *The Nationalities Question*; Rogers Brubaker, *Nationalism Reframed: Nationhood and the national question in the New Europe*, Cambridge: Cambridge University Press, 1996 p. 23.

63. Ronald G. Suny, *The Revenge of the Past: Nationalism, Revolution and the Collapse of the Soviet Union*. Stanford, CA: Stanford University Press, 1993; Smith, *The Nationalities Question*; Brubaker, *Nationalism Reframed*; Ahmed Rashid, *The Resurgence of Central Asia: Islam or Nationalism?* London: Zed Books, 1994; Sharam Akbarzadeh, 'Why Did Nationalism Fail in Tajikistan?' *Europe-Asia Studies*, 48 (7), 1996, pp. 1105–29; Shirin Akiner, *Central Asia: New Arc of Crisis?* Whitehall Papers, Royal United Services Institute for Defence Studies, London, 1993; 'Shirin Akiner, Melting Pot, Salad Bowl – Cauldron? Manipulation and Mobilisation of Ethnic and Religious Identities in Central Asia', *Ethnic and Racial Studies*, 20 (2), 1997, pp. 362–98; Astrid S. Tumienz, 'Nationalism, Ethnic Pressures, and the Breakup of the Soviet Union', *Journal of Cold War Studies*, 5 (4), 2003, pp. 81–136.
64. Yuri Slezkine, 'The USSR as a Communal Apartment, or How a Socialist State Promoted Ethnic Particularism', *Slavic Review*, 53 (2), 1994, p. 415.
65. Ivan Kurganov, 'The Problem of Nationality in Soviet Russia', *Russian Review*, 10 (4), 1951, p. 259.
66. Dimity Gorenburg, 'Soviet Nationalities Policy and Assimilation' in Dominique Arel and Blair A. Ruble (eds), *Rebounding Identities: The Politics of Identity in Russia and Ukraine*. Baltimore, John Hopkins University Press, 2006, pp. 273–303.
67. Gorenburg, 'Soviet Nationalities Policy and Assimilation', p. 274.
68. Paul Bergne, *The Birth of Tajikistan: National Identity and the Origins of the Republic*. London: I.B.Tauris, 2007, p. 2; Rogers Brubaker, 'Nationhood and the National Question in the Soviet Union and post-Soviet Eurasia: an institutionalist account', *Theory and Society*, 23, 1994, 47–78; Olivier Roy, *The New Central Asia: The Creation of Nations*. London: I.B.Tauris, 2000; Ro'i, *The Soviet and Russian context*; Slezkine, 'The USSR as a Communal Apartment'.
69. Boris Rumer, 'A Gathering Storm', *Orbis*, 37, 1993, pp. 89–105; Ronald G. Suny, *Looking toward Ararat: Armenia in Modern History*. Bloomington, IN: Indiana University Press, 1993; Rashid, *The Resurgence of Central Asia*; Shirin Akiner, 'Central Asia: New Arc of Crisis?'; Shirin Akiner, 'Melting Pot, Salad Bowl – Cauldron? Manipulation and Mobilisation of Ethnic and Religious Identities in Central Asia', *Ethnic and Racial Studies*, 20 (2), 1997, pp. 362–98. However, all these predictions have proven inaccurate.
70. Sally N. Cummings, *Understanding Central Asia: politics and contested transformations*. New York: Routledge, 2012, pp. 44–5; Douglass Northrop, *Veiled Empire: Gender and power in Stalinist Central Asia*. Ithaca, NY: Cornell University Press, 2004, p. 21; Roy, *The Creation of Nations*, pp. 50–84; Seton-Watson, 'Soviet Nationality Policy'.
71. Stephen Sabol, 'The Creation of Central Asia: The 1924 National Delimitation', *Central Asian Survey*, 14 (2), 1995, pp. 225–41.
72. Paul Georg Geiss, *Pre-Tsarist and Tsarist Central Asia: Communal Commitment and Political Order in Change*. London, Routledge, 2003, pp. 239–40.

73. Roy, *The Creation of Nations*; Kolstø, *Political Construction Sites*.
74. Geoffrey Wheeler, *The Modern History of Soviet Central Asia*. London: Weidenfeld and Nicolson, 1964; Alexandre Bennigsen and Marie Broxup, *The Islamic Threat to the Soviet State*. London: Croom Helm, 1983.
75. Arne Haugen, *The Establishment of National Republics in Soviet Central Asia*. Houndsmill, Basingstoke: Palgrave MacMillian, 2003; Adrienne Lynn Edgar, *Tribal Nation: The Making of Soviet Turkmenistan*. Princeton, NJ: Princeton University Press, 2004; Francine Hirsch, *Empire of Nations: Ethnographic knowledge and the making of the Soviet Union*. Cornell, New York: Cornell University Press, 2005; Bergne, *The Birth of Tajikistan*.
76. Grigol Ubiria, *Soviet Nation-Building in Central Asia: The Making of the Kazakh and Uzbek Nation*. London: Routledge, 2015.
77. Diana T. Kudaibergenova, '"Imagining community" in Soviet Kazakhstan. An historical analysis of narrative on nationalism in Kazakh-Soviet literature', *Nationalities Papers*, 45 (5), 2013, pp. 839–54.
78. Olcott, *The Kazakhs*, p. 180.
79. Alfrid K. Bustanov, *Soviet Orientalism and the Creation of Central Asian Nations*. Abingdon: Routledge, 2015, p. 45.
80. Ts. Baatar, 'Present Situation of Kazakh-Mongolian Community', *The Mongolian Journal of International Affairs* (Ulaanbaatar), nos 8–9, 2002, pp. 90–2.
81. Sharad K. Soni, 'Kazakhs in post-Socialist Mongolia', *Himalayan and Central Asian Studies*, 7 (2), April–June 2003, p. 106.
82. Eva-Marie Dubuisson and Anna Genina, 'Claiming an Ancestral Homeland: Kazakh Pilgrimage and Migration in Inner Asia, in Madeleine Reeves (ed.), *Movement, Power and Place in Central Asia and Beyond: Contested Trajectories*. New York: Routledge, 2012, pp. 118–19.
83. Isabelle Ohayon, *The Kazakh Famine: The Beginnings of Sedentarization, Online Encyclopedia of Mass Violence* [online], published on 28 September 2013, accessed 22 April 2016: http://www.massviolence.org/The-Kazakh-Famine-The-Beginnings, ISSN 1961–9898; Niccoló Painciola, 'The Collectivization Famine in Kazakhstan, 1931–1933', *Harvard Ukrainian Studies*, 25 (3/4), p. 237.
84. M.K. Kozybaev, Zh.B. Abylkhozhin, and K.S. Aldazhumanov, *Kollektivizatsiya v Kazakhstane: tragediya krest'ianstva*. Alma-Ata: Ministerstvo narodnogo obrazovaniya Respubliki Kazakhstan, 1992. Talas Omarbekov, *Golomodor v Kazakhstane: prichiny, masshtaby i itogi, 1930–1931*. Almaty: Kazakhskii Natsional'nyi Universitet im. Al'-Farabi, 2009.
85. Sarah Cameron, 'The Hungry Steppe: Soviet Kazakhstan and the Kazakh Famine 1921–1934', PhD dissertation, Yale University, 2011.
86. Cameron, 'The Hungry Steppe'.
87. Ohayon, *The Kazakh Famine*.
88. Michaela Pohl, 'It cannot be that our graves will be here: the survival of Chechen and Ingush deportees in Kazakhstan', 1944–1957, *Journal of Genocide Research*, 4 (3), 2002, p. 401.

89. Gregory Gleason, 'Fealty and Loyalty: Informal Authority Structures in Soviet Asia', *Soviet Studies*, 43 (4), 1991, pp. 613–28; James Critchlow, 'Corruption, Nationalism, and the Native Elites in Central Asia', *Journal of Communist Studies*, 4 (2), 1988, pp. 143–61; Kathleen Collins, *Clan Politics and Regime Transition in Central Asia*, Cambridge: Cambridge University Press, 2006.
90. Suny, *The Revenge of the Past*; Ian Bremmer and Cory Welt, 'The Trouble with Democracy in Kazakhstan', *Central Asian Survey*, 15 (2), 1996, pp. 179–99; Akiner, Melting Pot, Salad Bowl – Cauldron?; Olivier Roy, *The New Central Asia*.
91. Azamat Sarsembayev, 'Imagined Communities: Kazak nationalism and Kazakification in the 1990s', *Central Asian Survey*, 18 (3): 319–46.
92. Bhavna Dave, *Kazakhstan, Ethnicity, Language and Power*. London: Routledge, 2007; Martha Brill Olcott, *Kazakhstan: Unfulfilled Promise*. Washington, DC: Carnegie Endowment for International Peace, 2002.
93. Annette Bohr, 'The Central Asian States as Nationalising Regimes' in Graham Smith et al., *Nation-Building in the post-Soviet Borderlands: The Politics of National Identities*. Cambridge: Cambridge University Press, p. 139.
94. Erlan Karin and Andrei Chebotarev, 'The Policy of Kazakhization in State and Government Institutions in Kazakhstan' in N. Oka (ed.), *The Nationalities Question in Post-Soviet Kazakhstan*. Chiba: Institute of Developing Economics. Chiba: Institute of Developing Economies; Annette Bohr, 'The Central Asian States as Nationalising Regimes', p. 140.
95. Özgecan Kesici, 'The Dilemma in the Nation-Building Process: The Kazakh or Kazakhstani Nation?' *Journal of Ethnopolitics and Minority Issues in Europe*, 10 (1), 2011, p. 45.
96. Kesici, 'The Dilemma in the Nation-Building Process', p. 45.
97. Sarsembayev, 'Imagined Communities', p. 334.
98. Pål Kolstø, 'Anticipating Demographic Superiority: Kazakh Thinking on Integration and Nation Building', *Europe-Asia Studies*, 50 (1), 1998, p. 58; Sarsembayev, 'Imagined Communities', p. 334.
99. Marlene Laruelle, 'The Three Discursive Paradigms of State Identity in Kazakhstan: Kazakhness, Kazakhstanness and Transnationalism', in Mariya Omelicheva (ed.), *Nationalism and Identity Construction in Central Asia: Dimensions, Dynamics, and Directions*. Lanham, MD: Lexington Books, 2015, pp. 1–20.
100. Martha Brill Olcott, 'Emerging Political Elites' in Ali Banuazizi and Myron Weiner (eds), *The New Geopolitics of Central Asia and its Borderlands*. Bloomington, IN: Indiana University Press, p. 59.
101. Megan Rancier, 'Resurrecting the Nomads: Historical nostalgia and Modern Nationalism in Contemporary Kazakh Popular Music Videos', *Popular Music and Society*, 32 (1), 2009, pp. 387–405; Marlene Laruelle, 'In Search of Kazakhness: The Televisual Landscape and Screening of Nation in

Kazakhstan', *Demokratizatsiya*, 23 (2), 2015, pp. 321–40; Kudaibergenova, 'Imagining Community in Soviet Kazakhstan'.
102. Karin and Chebotarev, 'The Policy of Kazakhization in State and Government Institutions in Kazakhstan'.
103. Sébastien Peyrouse, 'Nationhood and the Minority Question in Central Asia. The Russians in Kazakhstan', *Europe-Asia Studies*, 59 (3), 2007, p. 482.
104. Sarsembayev, 'Imagined Communities', p. 335; Richard L. Wolfel, 'North to Astana: Nationalistic Motives for the Movement of the Kazakh(stani) Capital', *Nationalities Papers*, 30 (3), 2002, pp. 485–506.
105. Sébastien Peyrouse, 'The "Imperial Minority": An Interpretative Framework of the Russians in Kazakhstan in the 1990s', *Nationalities Papers*, 36 (1), 2008, p. 106.
106. Aziz Burkhanov and Dina Sharipova, 'Kazakhstan's Civic Identity: Ambiguous Policies and Points of Resistance' in Mariya Omelicheva (ed.), *Nationalism and Identity Construction in Central Asia: Dimensions, Dynamics, and Directions*. Lanham, MD: Lexington Books, p. 30.
107. Serik Zholdasbayev, 'Seichas ne vremya perekhodit' na latinitsu – Dos Kushim', *365info*, 16 February 2016. Accessed 28 April 2016: http://365info.kz/2016/02/dos-kushim-sejchas-ne-vremya-perehodit-na-latinitsu/.
108. However, for the most part, Russian remains de-facto the language of business and government.
109. Juldyz Smagulova, 'Kazakhstan: Language, Identity and Conflict', *Innovation*, 19 (3/4), 2006, p. 311.
110. Smagulova, 'Kazakhstan: Language, Identity and Conflict', p. 311.
111. Cengiz Surucu, 'Modernity, Nationalism, Resistance: Identity Politics in Post-Soviet Kazakhstan', *Central Asian Survey*, 21 (4), 2002, p. 391.
112. Rustem Kadyrzhanov, 'Natsional'naya ideya i natsional'naya politika v sovremennom Kazakhstane', *Kazakhstan Institute for Strategic Studies*, 29 June 2007. Accessed 24 September 2012: http://kisi.kz/ru/categories/politicheskaya-modernizaciya/posts/nacional-naya-ideya-i-nacional-naya-politika-v-sovremen.
113. Burkhanov and Sharipova, 'Kazakhstan's Civic Identity', p. 24.
114. Ibid., pp. 25–6.
115. Peyrouse, 'The "Imperial Minority"', p. 108.
116. Asel Sataeva, 'Kazakhstantsy – natsiya edinogo budushchego', *Tengrinews*, 11 March 2015. Accessed 28 April 2016: https://tengrinews.kz/kazakhstan_news/glava-gosudarstva-kazahstantsyi-natsiya-edinogo-buduschego-271423/.
117. Burkhanov and Sharipova, 'Kazakhstan's Civic Identity', p. 29.
118. Joanna Lillis, 'Astana Follows Thorny Path toward National Unity', *Eurasianet*, 29 April 2010. Accessed 25 April 2016: http://www.eurasianet.org/node/60952.
119. Burkhanov and Sharipova, 'Kazakhstan's Civic Identity', p. 29.
120. Donnacha Ó'Beacháin and Robert Kevlihan, 'Threading a needle: Kazakhstan between civic and ethno-nationalist state-building', *Nations and Nationalism*, 19 (2), p. 345.

121. Surucu, 'Modernity, Nationalism, Resistance', p. 396.
122. Taras Kuzio, '"Nationalizing states" or "Nation-Building"? A critical review of the theoretical literature and empirical evidence', *Nations and Nationalism*, 7 (2), 2001, pp. 135–54.
123. Azade-Ayse Rorlich, 'Islam, Identity and Politics: Kazakhstan, 1990–2000', *Nationalities Papers*, 31 (2), 2003, pp. 158–9.
124. Rorlich, 'Islam, Identity and Politics', p. 173; Mariya Omelicheva, 'Islam in Kazakhstan: a Survey of Contemporary Trends and Sources of Securitizaion', *Central Asian Survey*, 30 (2), p. 244.
125. Omelicheva, 'Islam in Kazakhstan', p. 244.
126. Golam Mostafa, 'The concept of "Eurasia": Kazakhstan's Eurasian policy and its implications', *Journal of Eurasian Studies*, 4 (2), pp. 161–3; Laruelle, 'The Three Discursive Paradigms of State Identity in Kazakhstan', p. 14.
127. Jacob M. Landau. *Pan-Turkism: From Irredentism to Cooperation*. Bloomington, IN: University of Indiana Press, 1995, p. 1.
128. A. Sharafutdinova, 'Tengrianstvo, ego satellichestvo i depaganizatsiya v novykh i novesishikh religiyakh', *Izvestiya Rossiskogo gosudarstvennoogo pedagogicheskogo universiteta im. A. I Gertsena*, No. 151, 2012, pp. 154–64.
129. Marléne Laruelle, 'Religious revival, nationalism and the "invention of tradition": political Tengrism in Central Asia and Tatarstan', *Central Asia Survey*, 26 (2), 2007, p. 204.
130. Laruelle, 'Religious revival', p. 203.
131. Charles Weller, 'Religious-Cultural Revivalism as Historiographical Debate: Contending Claims in the post-Soviet Kazakh Context', *Journal of Islamic Studies*, 25 (2), 2014, pp. 138–77.
132. Nurbolat Masanov, 'Perceptions of Ethnic and All-National Identity in Kazakhstan' in N. Oka (ed.), *The Nationalities Question in Post-Soviet Kazakhstan*, Chiba: Institute of Developing Economics.
133. Saulesh Yessenova, 'Routes and Roots of Kazakh Identity: Urban Migration and Post-Socialist Kazakhstan', *The Russian Review*, 64 (4), 2005, p. 661.
134. Yessenova, 'Routes and Roots of Kazakh Identity', p. 662.
135. Ibid.; Rustem Kadyrzhanov, 'Anatomiya Kazakhskogo natsionalizma', *Central Asia Monitor*, 9 October 2014. Accessed 16 January 2015: http://camonitor.kz/13726-anatomiya-kazahskogo-nacionalizma.html.
136. Radik Temirgaliev, 'Kazakhskii natsionalism i ego perspektivy', *Zonakz*, 20 December 2010. Accessed 16 January 2015: http://zonakz.net/articles/32371.
137. Kadyrzhanov, 'Anatomiya Kazakhskogo natsionalizma'.
138. Yessenova, 'Routes and Roots of Kazakh Identity', p. 662.

Chapter 2 Between Two Worlds: Kazakh Film and Nation-building in the Soviet Era

1. Kabish Siranov, *Kinoiskusstvo Sovetskogo Kazakhstana*. Almaty: Kazakhstan, 1966; Svyatoslav Antonov, 'Starye kinoteatry Alma-Aty', *Voxpopuli*, 22 May 2014. Accessed 10 May 2016: http://www.voxpopuli.kz/history/2020-starye-kinoteatry-alma-aty.html.
2. Gulnar Kendirbaeva, 'We are Children of Alash . . . : The Kazakh Intelligentsia at the Beginning of the 20th Century in Search of National Identity and Prospects of the Cultural Survival of the Kazakh people', *Central Asian Survey* 18 (1), 1999, p. 13.
3. Richard Taylor, *The Politics of the Soviet Cinema 1917–1929*. Cambridge: Cambridge University Press, 1979, p. 26.
4. John Haynes, *New Soviet Man: Gender and Masculinity in Stalinist Soviet Cinema*. Manchester: Manchester University Press, 2003.
5. Anna Lawton, *Kinoglasnost: Soviet Cinema in Our Time*. Cambridge: Cambridge University Press, p. 11.
6. Jamie Miller, 'Soviet Cinema, 1929–41: The Development of Industry and Infrastructure', *Europe-Asia Studies*, 58 (1), 2008, p. 103.
7. Richard Taylor, *Film Propaganda: Soviet Russia and Nazi Germany*. London & New York: I.B.Tauris, p. 31.
8. Peter Kenez, *Cinema and Soviet Society*, Cambridge: Cambridge University Press, 1992, p. 33.
9. Kenez, *Cinema and Soviet Society*, p. 31.
10. Natalie Ryabchikova, 'When Was Soviet Cinema Born? The Institutionalisation of Soviet Film Studies and Problems of Periodization' in Malte Hagener (ed.), *The Emergence of Film Culture: Knowledge Production, Institution*. New York & Oxford: Berghahn Books, 2014, p. 120; Kenez *Cinema and Soviet Society*, p. 33.
11. Kristin Thompson, 'Government Polices and Practical Necessities in the Soviet Cinema of the 1920s', in Anna Lawton (ed.), *The Red Screen: Politics, Society, Art in Soviet Cinema*. London & New York: Routledge, 1992.
12. Kenez, *Cinema and Soviet Society*, p. 37.
13. Denise J. Youngblood, *Soviet Cinema in the Silent Era 1918–1935*. Austin: University of Texas Press, 1991, pp. 2–3; Thompson, 'Government Polices and Practical Necessities in the Soviet Cinema of the 1920s', pp. 23–4.
14. Taylor, *Film Propaganda*, p. 35; Kenez, *Cinema and Soviet Society*, p. 34.
15. Kenez, *Cinema and Soviet Society*, p. 34.
16. Thompson, 'Government Polices and Practical Necessities in the Soviet Cinema of the 1920s', p. 35.
17. Sovkino was then re-constituted in 1930 as Soyuzkino.
18. Youngblood, *Soviet Cinema in the Silent Era 1918–1935*, p. 3.
19. Steven Hill, 'A Quantitative View of Soviet Cinema', *Cinema Journal*, 11 (2), 1972, p. 21.

20. Kenez, *Cinema and Soviet Society*, p. 50.
21. Jamie Miller, 'Soviet Cinema, 1929–41: The Development of Industry and Infrastructure', *Europe-Asia Studies*, 58 (1), 2006, pp. 103–24.
22. Yu. Drobnis, 'Vostok-Kino', *Sovetskii Ekran*, no. 52, 27 December 1927, p. 1.
23. Drobnis, 'Vostok-Kino', *Sovetskii Ekran*, p. 1.
24. Michael Rouland, 'An Historical Introduction' in Michael Rouland, Gulnara Abikeyeva and Birgit Beumers (eds), *Cinema in Central Asia: Rewriting Cultural Histories*. London & New York: I.B.Tauris, p. 3.
25. Gabrielle Chomentowski, 'Vostokkino and the Foundation of Central Asian Cinema' in Michael Rouland, Gulnara Abikeyeva and Birgit Beumers (eds), *Cinema in Central Asia: Rewriting Cultural Histories*. London & New York: I.B.Tauris, p. 33.
26. Chomentowski, 'Vostokkino and the Foundation of Central Asian Cinema', p. 33.
27. Ibid., pp. 38–9; Y. Drobnis, 'Vostok-Kino', *Sovetskii Ekran*, pp. 1–2.
28. Gabrielle Chomentowski, 'Vostokkino and the Foundation of Central Asian Cinema', pp. 38–39.
29. Baurzhan Nogerbek, 'The Various Births of Kazakh Cinema', in Michael Rouland, Gulnara Abikeyeva and Birgit Beumers (eds), *Cinema in Central Asia: Rewriting Cultural Histories*. London & New York: I.B.Tauris.
30. Drobnis, 'Vostok-Kino', *Sovetskii Ekran*, p. 2.
31. Ibid.
32. Siranov, *Kinoiskusstvo Sovetskogo Kazakhstana*.
33. Nogerbek, 'The Various Births of Kazakh Cinema', p. 58.
34. Siranov, *Kinoiskusstvo Sovetskogo Kazakhstana*.
35. Matthew Payne, 'Viktor Turin's Turksib (1929) and Soviet Orientalism', *Historical Journal of Film, Radio and Television*, 21 (1), 2001, pp. 37–38.
36. Payne, 'Viktor Turin's Turksib (1929) and Soviet Orientalism', pp. 55–56.
37. S.I. Yutkevich, S. Afanasiev, V.E. Baskakov, I.V. Vaysfel', *Kino: Entsiklopedicheskii slovar*. Moscow: Soviet Encyclopedia, 1986, p. 96.
38. Nogerbek, 'The Various Births of Kazakh Cinema', p. 67.
39. Ibid., pp. 66–7.
40. S.I. Yutkevich, S. Afanasiev, V.E. Baskakov, I.V. Vaysfel'd et al., *Kino: Entsiklopedicheskii slovar*', p. 96.
41. Nogerbek, The Various Births of Kazakh, p. 59.
42. Birgit Beumers, *Directory of World Cinema: RUSSIA 2*. Bristol and Chicago: Intellect, 2015, p. 39.
43. Fedor Razzakov, *Gibel' Sovetskogo Kino: intrigi i spory 1918–1972*. Moscow: Eksmo, 2009, p. 53.
44. Harun Yilmaz, *National Identities in Soviet Historiography: The Rise of Nations Under Stalin*. London and New York: Routledge, p. 87.
45. Arne Haugen, *The Establishment of National Republics in Soviet Central Asia*. Houndsmill, Basingstoke: Palgrave Macmillian, 2003; Adrienne Lynn Edgar,

Tribal Nation: The Making of Soviet Turkmenistan, Princeton, NJ: Princeton University Press, 2004; Francine Hirsch, *Empire of Nations: Ethnographic knowledge and the making of the Soviet Union*. Cornell, NY: Cornell University Press, 2005.
46. Nogerbek, 'The Various Births of Kazakh Cinema', p. 59.
47. Asylkhan Mamashuly, 'Vosstaniyu Kazakhov v 1916 godu predshestvoval raskol schitannoi intelligentsia', *Radio Azattyk*, 24 June 2011. Accessed 21 May 2012: http://rus.azattyq.org/a/kazakh_uprising_1916/24245068.html.
48. Film studios from other major centres were also evacuated to the Central Asian region. Soyuzdetfilm was relocated from Moscow to Stalinabad in Tajikistan, while Kiev Studio moved from Kiev to Tashkent and Ashkhabad, see Jay Leyda, *Kino: A History of the Russian and Soviet Film*. Princeton, NJ: Princeton University Press, 1960, p. 369.
49. Siranov, *Kinoiskusstvo Sovetskogo Kazakhstana*.
50. Peter Rollberg, *Historical Dictionary of Russian and Soviet Cinema*. Lanham, MD: Scarecrow Press, 2009, p. 330.
51. Jay Leyda, *Kino: A History of the Russian and Soviet Film*, p. 403.
52. Rollberg, *Historical Dictionary of Russian and Soviet Cinema*, p. 330.
53. Zholtay Zhumat, 'Kazakhskoe Kino: Kak ono razvivaetsya? (Mysli o kino)', *Gazeta Turkestan*, 15 October 2010. Accessed 6 May 2016: http://www.altynorda.kz/kazaxskoe-kino-kak-ono-razvivaetsya-mysli-o-kino/.
54. Zhumat, 'Kazakhskoe Kino: Kak ono razvivaetsya? (Mysli o kino)'.
55. Rollberg, *Historical Dictionary of Russian and Soviet Cinema*, p. 330.
56. S. Ylanovskii, 'Shaken Aimanov', *Sovetskii Ekran*, 10, 1957, p. 16.
57. Shaken Aimanov – velikii rezhisser iz stepi, *Yvision*, 19 March 2015. Accessed 26 May 2016: http://yvision.kz/post/482926.
58. S.A. Kibal'nik, 'Mif o Dzhambule po materialiam sovremennoi Kazakhstanskoi pechati', *Izvestiya Ural'skogo Federal'nogo universiteta*, 2 (139), p. 89.
59. Kibal'nik, 'Mif o Dzhambule po materialiam sovremennoi Kazakhstanskoi pechati', p. 90.
60. Ibid., p. 98.
61. Nogerbek, 'The Various Births of Kazakh Cinema', p. 67.
62. 'Rozhdenie Kazakhsogo kinoiskusstva, Sankt-Peterburgskii Gumanitarnyi universitet profsoyuzov', 17 April 2015. Accessed 6 May 2016: http://www.studfiles.ru/preview/3196002/page:2/.
63. Gulnara Abikeyeva, *Natsiostroitel'stvo v Kazakhstane i drugikh stranakh Tsentral'noi Azii i kak etot protsess otrazhaetsya v kinematografe*, Almaty: 'TSTSAK', pp. 64–5.
64. Yevgeniy Minchenko, 'Kazakhstanskii film 'Menya Zovut Kozha' v etom godu otmechaet svoe 50-letie', *Altay News*, 27 February 2013. Accessed 31 May 2016: http://altaynews.kz/12249-kazahstanskiy-film-menya-zovut-kozha-v-etom-godu-otmechaet-svoe-50-letie.html.

65. Author's interview Darezhan Omirbayev, 21 August 2014, Almaty, Kazakhstan.
66. Abikeyeva, *Natsiostroitel'stvo v Kazakhstane*.
67. Ibid.
68. Alexey Azarov, 'Ekzotika fil'ma Menya Zovut Kozha', *RadioAzattyk*, 18 November 2013. Accessed 11 May 2016: http://rus.azattyq.org/a/menya-zovut-kozha-50-letie/25171647.html.
69. Tatyana Sokolova, 'Film Menya Zovut Kozha priznali tvorcheskoi udachei kollektiva', *Komsomolskaya Pravda Kazakhstan*, 22 May 2014. Accessed 31 May 2016: http://kp.kz/node/4850.
70. Sokolova, 'Film Menya Zovut Kozha priznali tvorcheskoi udachei kollektiva'.
71. Rollberg, *Historical Dictionary of Russian and Soviet Cinema*, p. 355.
72. Galya Galkina, 'Ego Zovut Kozha, *Novoe Pokolenie*', 28 November 2013. Accessed 3 June 2016: http://www.np.kz/2013/11/28/ego_zovut_kozha.html.
73. Herbert Marshall, 'The New Wave in Soviet Cinema' in Anna Lawton (ed.), *The Red Screen: Politics, Society, Art in Soviet Cinema*. London and New York: Routledge, p. 176.
74. Marshall, 'The New Wave in Soviet Cinema', p. 176.
75. Ibid., p. 177.
76. Gulnara Abikeyeva points to five characteristics of the thaw within Central Asian cinema. These include the emergence of a national staff of artists and writers; an understanding of national history, heroes and myths; recreation of traditional ways of life, customs and practices; the attempt to create modern heroes; and the attempt to conduct a dispute with official Soviet ideology. Abikeyeva, *Natsiostroitel'stvo v Kazakhstane*.
77. Suleimenov went onto to have a well-established career as a literary figure in Kazakhstan and headed up Goskino in Kazakhstan in the early 1980s. As we will see in the next chapter he played a pivotal role in the emergence of the 'Kazakh New Wave'. He also entered politics in the late Soviet period as the leader of the Nevada-Semipalatinsk Anti-Nuclear Movement. His passion for the land and the extent to which this is something that Kazakhs should hold dear was a central motif of *Land of the Fathers*. He also set up the Peoples' Congress Party in 1991, which was one of the main political parties in the early post-Soviet period. Suleimenov also considered running for president in 1995, but to steer him away from challenging his grip on power, Nazarbayev appointed Suleimenov Kazakhstan's ambassador to Rome, a post he held until 2002.
78. L. Yagunkova, 'Zakanchivayutsya s"emki', *Sovetskii Ekran*, No. 23, 1965, p. 13.
79. Stephen Norris, 'Landscape and Loss: World War II in Central Asian Cinema' in Michael Rouland, Gulnara Abikeyeva and Birgit Beumers (eds), *Cinema in Central Asia: Rewriting Cultural Histories*. London & New York: I.B.Tauris, pp. 78–81.

80. Abikeyeva, *Natsiostroitel'stvo v Kazakhstane*, p. 88.
81. Ibid., p. 89.
82. L. Yagunkova, 'Zakanchivayutsya s'emki'.
83. A Rudenko, 'Razdum'ya Veselogo Obmanshchika', *Sovetskii Erkan*, No. 1, 1966, p. 6.
84. Rudenko, 'Razdum'ya Veselogo Obmanshchika', p. 7.
85. Ibid.
86. Author's interview with Sabit Kurmanbekov, 3 November 2014, Almaty, Kazakhstan.
87. Gabit Musrepov, 'Legenda o Kyz-Zhibek', *Sovetskii Ekran*, 3, 1969, pp. 10–11.
88. Kabish Siranov, *Ocherki i istorii Kazakhskogo kino*. Alma-Ata: Nauka, 1980.
89. Baurzhan Nogerbek, 'Folklore Traditions in Kazakh Cinematography', *Art Sanat Iskusstvo: Journal of the Academy of Arts of Uzbekistan*, Issue 1, 2010. Accessed 6 June 2016: http://sanat.orexca.com/2010/2010-1/bauryrjan_nogerbek-2/.
90. Author's interview with Sergei Azimov, 3 November 2014, Almaty, Kazakhstan.
91. Aigul Tuyakbaeva, 'Dukhovnyi mir Kazakhskogo naroda v kinokartine Kyz-Zhibek', *Mysl'*, 17 November 2014. Accessed 13 May 2016: http://mysl.kazgazeta.kz/?p=4368.
92. Tuyakbaeva, 'Dukhovnyi mir Kazakhskogo naroda v kinokartine'.
93. Diana T. Kudaibergenova, '"Imagining community" in Soviet Kazakhstan. An historical analysis of narrative on nationalism in Kazakh-Soviet literature', *Nationalities Papers*, 41 (5), 2013, pp. 839–54.
94. Maral Zhantaykyzy, 'Kazakh Cinema Remembers a Famous Father', *Astana Times*, 27 March 2013. Accessed 6 June 2016: http://astanatimes.com/2013/03/kazakh-cinema-remembers-a-famous-father/.
95. 'Kyz-Zhibek' (1970), *Kazkino.info*, 24 January 2016. Accessed 14 July: http://www.kazkino.info/kazakhfilm/kizjibek/.
96. Alexey Azarov, 'Za plenku na kul'tovyi fil'm rezhisser otdal svoyu Gospremiyu', *RadioAzattyk*, 13 March 2013. Accessed 6 June 2013: http://rus.azattyq.org/a/film-director-khodzhikov-anniversary/24927093.html.
97. Birgit Beumers, 'The End of Ataman', *Directory of World Cinema*. Russia, edited by Birgit Beumers, p. 224.
98. Most directors when interviewed as part of this research noted that they were not influenced by Kazakh Soviet cinema. Some, such as Adilkhan Yerzhanov and Serik Abishev, argue that Kazakh Soviet cinema is not Kazakh cinema as it adopts Soviet cinematic language and is not distinctly national. Others, such as Zhanna Isabayeva, reject any influence of Kazakh Soviet cinema, but as we will see in the following chapter, do speak of the influence of the 'Kazakh New Wave'. Directors committed to producing commercial cinema in Kazakhstan, such as Akan Satayev and Kairzhan Orynbekov, tend to situate their influences in Hollywood cinema with directors such as Quentin Tarantino or Ridley Scott. However, when pushed Akan Satayev spoke of appreciating the work of

Shaken Aimanov and films such as *Our Dear Doctor* (1957) and *Angel in Tyubeteika* (1968). One of the leading directors of the 'Kazakh New Wave', Darezhan Omirbayev, mentioned he liked Aimanov's work, but felt it was too theatrical, although noted that was inevitable given Aimanov's background in the theatre. Nonetheless, what is clear is that the influence of Soviet cinema of this period on contemporary directors in Kazakhstan is rather ambiguous.

99. Author's interview with Adilkhan Yerzhanov, 30 July 2014, Almaty, Kazakhstan; Author's interview with Serik Abishev, 26 July 2014, Almaty, Kazakhstan.
100. Author's interview with Serik Abishev, 26 July 2014, Almaty, Kazakhstan.

Chapter 3 The Disruption of Time: The 'Kazakh New Wave' 1985–95

1. Anna Lawton, *Kinoglast: Soviet Cinema in our Time*. Cambridge: Cambridge University Press, 1992, p. 1.
2. Anna Lawton's volume *Kinoglast*, published in 1992, provides an overview this period of the Soviet film industry providing a detailed context to the production of films during this time. Her work, however, is largely silent on developments in Kazakhstan except for four pages that focus mostly on Rashid Nugmanov's film *The Needle*, pp. 184–187.
3. Andrew Horton and Michael Brashinsky, *The Zero Hour: Glasnost and Soviet Cinema in Transition*. Princeton, NJ: Princeton University Press, 1992, p. 238.
4. Inna Smailova, 'Kazakhskaya 'Novaya Volna': Izobrazitel'noe reshenie fil'mov'', *Prostor*, 2010, No. 5, pp. 165–168.
5. Andrei Plakov, 'Uroki Frantsuzskogo', *Iskusstvo Kino*, 3, 1992, pp. 154–8.
6. Lawton, *Kinoglastnost*, p. 9.
7. There was also the trend in aesthetic auteur cinema epitomised by Andrei Tarkovskiy, but this was not necessarily 'popular' nor commercial. Tarkovskiy's work was typically seen by fewer people within the USSR, but was lauded by film critics and festivals in the Soviet Union and the West. See Lawton, *Kinoglast*, p. 10.
8. Lawton, *Kinoglastnost*, p. 11.
9. Andrey Shcherbenok, 'Everything was over before it was no more: Decaying Civilization in Late Stagnation Cinema' in Dina Fainberg and Artemy M. Kalinovsky (eds), *Reconsidering Stagnation in the Brezhnev Era: Ideology and Exchange*. Lanham, MD: Lexington Books, 2016, pp. 77–84.
10. Shcherbenok, 'Everything was over before it was no more', p. 79.
11. Lawton, *Kinoglastnost*, p. 11.
12. Ibid., p. 14.
13. Ibid., p. 53.
14. Ludmila Zebrina Pruner, 'The New Wave in Kazakh Cinema', *Slavic Review*, 51 (4), 1992, p. 792.

15. Author's interview with Sabit Kurmanbekov. Almaty, Kazakhstan, 3 November 2014.
16. Gulnara Abikeyeva, *Natsiostroitel'stvo v Kazakhstane i drugikh stranakh Tsentral'noi Azii i kak etot protsess otrazhaetsya v kinematografe*, Almaty: 'TSTSAK', p. 105.
17. Yevgeniya Smirre, 'Rezhisser Solov'ev – o Kazakhskom kinematografe 'Anne Kareninoi' i o krizise obshchestva', *Karavan*, 19 September 2014. Accessed 4 July 2016: http://www.caravan.kz/art/rezhisser-solovev-o-kazakhskom-kinematografe-anne-kareninojj-i-o-krizise-obshhestva-19365/.
18. Abikeyeva, *Natsiostroitel'stvo v Kazakhstane*, p. 106.
19. Lawton, *Kinoglastnost*, p. 185.
20. Author's interview with Rashid Nugmanov, 16 August 2014, Almaty, Kazakhstan.
21. Birgit Beumers, 'Waves, Old and New, in Kazakh Cinema', *Studies in Russian and Soviet Cinema*, 4 (2), 2010, pp. 203–9.
22. Azade-Ayse Rolich, 'Identities in the Flux: The Mirror of Popular Culture. Kazakh Cinema at the End of the Twentieth Century' in Gabriele Rasuly-Paleczek and Julia Katschnig (eds), *Central Asia on Display: Proceedings of the VII Conference on European Society for Central Asian Studies*. Vienna: Wiener Zentralasien Studien, 2004, p. 262.
23. Smailova, Kazakhskaya 'Novaya Volna', p. 166.
24. Author's interview with Rashid Nugmanov.
25. Nalia Galieva, 'Novaya Volna Kazakhstanskogo Kinematografa', *Literature Portal*, 18 March 2015. Accessed 4 July 2016: http://adebiportal.kz/novaya-volna-kazakhstanskogo-kinematografa.page/?lang=ru.
26. It should be noted, however, that both Manabayev and Shinarbayev both graduated from VGIK IN 1978 and 1982 respectively.
27. Pruner, 'The New Wave in Kazakh Cinema', pp. 796–7.
28. Abikeyeva, *Natsiostroitel'stvo v Kazakhstane*, p. 106.
29. Author's interview with Darezhan Omirbayev, 21 August 2014, Almaty, Kazakhstan.
30. See Horton and Brashinsky, *The Zero Hour: Glasnost and Soviet Cinema in Transition*, pp. 184–186; Lawton, *Kinoglastnost*, p. 187; and Marina Drozdova, 'Dendi perioda postpunka', *Iskusstvo Kino*, 1989, 3, p. 75.
31. Walter Benjamin, *Illuminations*, New York: Schocken Books, 2007 [1968], pp. 261–262.
32. Benedict Anderson, *Imagined Communities*. London and New York: Verso, 1991 [1983], p. 26.
33. John D. Kelly, 'Time and the Global: Against the Homogenous, Empty Communities in Contemporary Social Theory', *Development and Change*, 29 (4), pp. 839–871.
34. Benjamin, *Illuminations*, p. 262.
35. Author's interview with Rustem Abdrashev, 5 November 2014, Almaty, Kazakhstan.

36. Svat Soucek, *A History of Inner Asia*. Cambridge: Cambridge University Press, 2000, p. 106.
37. Christopher I. Beckwith, *Empires of the Silk Road: A History of Central Eurasia from the Bronze Age to the Present*. Princeton and Oxford: Princeton University Press, 2009, pp. 187–188.
38. Soucek, *A History of Inner Asia*, p. 106.
39. Jared Rapfogel, 'Central Asian Films', *Senses of Cinema*, issue 27, July 2003.
40. Diana T. Kudaibergenova, '"Imagining community" in Soviet Kazakhstan. An historical analysis of narrative on nationalism in Kazakh-Soviet literature', *Nationalities Papers*, 41 (5), 2013, pp. 846–847.
41. Zemfira Yerzhan, 'Gibel' Otrara Ardaka Amirkulova', *Almaty Art*, 1 (6), 2003. Accessed 16 July 2016: http://kieli7su.kz/arterzhanmenu/popkinomenu/52-gibel-otrara-ardaka-amirkulova.
42. Gulnara Abikeyeva, 'Ardak Amirkulov: Ya chelovek somnevayushchiisya', *Iskusstvo Kino*, 3, 1992, p. 151.
43. Yerzhan, 'Gibel' Otrara'.
44. Gönül Dönmez-Colin, *Cinemas of the Other: A Personal Journey with Film-Makers from Central Asia. 2nd Edition*. Bristol and Chicago: Intellect, p. 15.
45. Abikeyeva, 'Ardak Amirkulov', pp. 150–153.
46. Yerzhan, 'Gibel' Otrara'.
47. Dimitry Neroznik, 'Film Gibel Otrara: Trudno byt' bogom 1.5', *Fliker Kinoblog*, 8 July 2015. Accessed 16 July 2016: http://blog.flicker.org.ru/2015/07/4958/.
48. Abikeyeva, 'Ardak Amirkulov', p. 153.
49. Ibid.
50. Rapfogel, 'Central Asian Films'; Abikeyeva, 'Ardak Amirkulov', p. 152.
51. Abikeyeva, 'Ardak Amirkulov', p. 152.
52. Rapfogel, 'Central Asian Films'.
53. Ibid.
54. Dönmez-Colin, *Cinemas of the Other*, p. 15.
55. Author's interview with Damir Manabayev, Almaty, Kazakhstan, 21 August 2014.
56. Author's interview with Damir Manabayev.
57. Sarah Cameron, 'The Hungry Steppe: Soviet Kazakhstan and the Kazakh Famine 1921–1934', PhD dissertation, Yale University, 2011.
58. Abikeyeva, *Natsiostroitel'stvo v Kazakhstane*, p. 157.
59. Ibid., p. 159.
60. Georgii Afonin, 'Damir Manabayev: Lyubov' obshchestvennost' strast", *Literaturnaya Gazeta Kazakhstana*, 24 September 2008. Accessed 13 August 2014: http://www.litgazeta-kz.com/index.php?option=view&id=181&PHPSESSID=25ef4e91ec36748d83149d70c654e973.
61. Daniyar Kenzhibaev, 'Konets prekrasnoi epokhi', *Brodvei*, 16 March 2016. Accessed 18 March 2016: http://brod.kz/articles/konec-prekrasnoj-epohi/.

62. Gulnara Abikeyeva, 'Filmy 'Balkon' Kalykbeka Salykova 25 let', *yvision*, 2 June 2013. Accessed 5 July 2016: http://yvision.kz/post/351429.
63. Ol'ga Khrabryk, 'Balkon' 20 let spustya', *Ekspress K*, 6 February 2009. Accessed 5 July 2016: http://old.express-k.kz/show_article.php?art_id=24072.
64. Kenzhibaev, 'Konets prekrasnoi epokhi'.
65. Nailya Galeeva, 'Artkhaus v Kazakhstanskom kinematografe: Balkon Kalykbeka Zelkova', *Literation Portal*, 18 March 2015. Accessed 14 June 2016: http://adebiportal.kz/artkhaus-v-kazakhstanskom-kinematografe-balkon-kalykbeka-salykova-.page/?lang=ru.
66. Abikeyeva, 'Filmu 'Balkon' Kalykbeka Salykova 25 let'.
67. Ibid.
68. Galeeva, 'Artkhaus v Kazakhstanskom kinematografe'.
69. Kenzhibaev, 'Konets prekrasnoi epokhi'.
70. Ibid.
71. Abikeyeva, *Natsiostroitel'stvo v Kazakhstane*, p. 114.
72. The programme of Kazakh films organised by Nugmanov and Temenov in Moscow in 1989 was so successful that they took the programme of ten films to the Sundance festival in 1990.
73. Interview with Rashid Nugmanov. However, others have suggested 9 million tickets were sold for the film. See Dönmez-Colin, *Cinemas of the Other*, p. 15. Nevertheless, this is a substantial number for a Kazakh film.
74. Ron Holloway, 'Interview with Rashid Nugmanov', *Cinemaya, The Asian Film Quarterly*, No. 54–5, 2002, pp. 13–19.
75. Nugmanov has also spoken of being influenced by the working methods taught by Anatoly Vasiliev at VGIK specifically for *Ya-Ha*. Author's interview with Rashid Nugmanov; Holloway, 'Interview with Rashid Nugmanov'.
76. Pruner, 'The New Wave in Kazakh Cinema', p. 797.
77. Holloway, 'Interview with Rashid Nugmanov', p. 14.
78. Author's interview with Rashid Nugmanov.
79. Andrew Horton, 'Nomad from Kazakhstan: An Interview with Rashid Nugmanov', *Film Criticism*, 14 (2), 1990, p. 34.
80. Lawton, *Kinoglast*, p. 186.
81. Marina Drozdova, 'Dendi perioda postpank ili 'proshchai, Amerika, o', *Iskusstvo Kino*, 3, 1989, pp. 76–77.
82. Lawton, *Kinoglastnost*, p. 185.
83. Sergei Sholkhov, 'Igla v stogu sena', *Sovetskii Ekran*, No. 8, 1990, pp. 6–7.
84. Sholokhov, 'Igla v stogu sena', p. 7.
85. Abikeyeva, *Natsiostroitel'stvo v Kazakhstane*, p. 115.
86. Pruner, 'The New Wave in Kazakh Cinema', p. 800.
87. Alla Gerber, 'Ostanovit' Begushchego!', *Sovetskii Ekran*, No. 2, 1989, pp. 10–11.
88. Pruner, 'The New Wave in Kazakh Cinema', p. 796.
89. It is important to note, however, that as outside observers we do not imagine that this represents a blank slate and *tabula rasa* for Kazakh identity and

nation-building. Rather, that in cinematic terms the 'Kazakh New Wave', afforded an opportunity to re-write and re-inscribe an understanding of nationhood via the silver screen.
90. Sholokhov, 'Igla v stogu sena', p. 7.
91. Abikeyeva, *Natsiostroitel'stvo v Kazakhstane*, p. 115.
92. Horton, 'Nomad from Kazakhstan', p. 37.
93. Ibid.
94. Zebrina Pruner, 'The New Wave in Kazakh Cinema', p. 799.
95. Horton, 'Interview with Rashid Nugmanov'.
96. Abikeyeva, *Natsiostroitel'stvo v Kazakhstane*, p. 115.
97. Smailova, 'Kazakhskaya "Novaya Volna"', p. 165.
98. Author's interview with Gulnara Abikeyeva, Almaty, Kazakhstan, 16 August 2014.
99. Aleksandr Shpagin, 'V Kontse, v nachale ili nigde?' *Iskusstvo Kino*, No. 9, 1990, p. 65.
100. Viktor Demin, 'Grystnyi no chestnyi realism', *Sovetskii Ekran*, No. 6, 1990, p. 18.
101. Dönmez-Colin, *Cinemas of the Other*, p. 34.
102. Ibid., p. 35.
103. Shpagin, 'V Kontse, v nachale ili nigde?' p. 66.
104. Gulnara Abikeyeva, 'Naperekor mifu', *Iskusstvo Kino*, No. 9, 1990, p. 70.
105. Dönmez-Colin, *Cinemas of the Other*, p. 35.
106. Alla Gerber, 'Abai Karpykov, Prishlo novoe pokolenie ...', *Iskusstvo Kino*, No. 9, 1990, p. 80.
107. Gerber, 'Abai Karpykov, Prishlo novoe pokolenie ...' p. 80.
108. Nina Zarkhi, 'Durgoe kino', *Iskusstvo Kino*, No. 9, 1990, p. 72.
109. Gerber, 'Abai Karpykov, Prishlo novoe pokolenie ...' p. 79.
110. Rapfogel, 'Central Asian Films'.
111. Ibid.
112. Author's interview with Darezhan Omirbayev.
113. Kent Jones, 'The Art of Seeing with One's Own Eyes', *Film Comment*, May–June 2008, pp. 42–5.
114. Shamshad Abdullaev, 'Rannie fil'm'y Darezhana Omirbayeva', *Seans*, 18 December 2013. Accessed 29 July 2016: http://seance.ru/blog/chtenie/abdullaev_omirbaev/#text-1.
115. Author's interview with Darezhan Omirbayev.
116. Andrei Plakov, 'Uroki Frantsuzskogo', *Iskusstvo Kino*, 3, 1992, pp. 154–8.
117. *Kairat* won awards at festivals in Ashgabat, Locarno, Strasbourg, Nantes and Almaty. *Cardiogram* won awards at festivals in Venice, Nantes and Singapore, while *The Killer* won the prestigious Un Certain Regard award for best film in Cannes in 1998 along with other awards in Nantes and Tehran.
118. Elena Stishova, 'Ekh, dorogi ...', *Iskusstvo Kino*, No. 10, 2001.
119. Bauryzhan Nogerbek, 'Kazakhskoe Kino pered vyborom svoego puti', *Goethe Institute*, 2014. Accessed 12 August 2014: http://www.goethe.de/ins/kz/ru/alm/kul/mag/kiz/7672639.html.

120. Beumers, 'Waves, Old and New in Kazakh Cinema'.
121. Alua Karpykova, 'Kazakhstanskii kinematograf: proshloe, nastoyqshchee, budushchee?', Zonakz, 18 September 2001. Accessed 20 June 2014: https://zonakz.net/articles/11511.
122. Saida Suleeva, 'Nashe kino opustilos' do edinitsy', Kontinent, 22 (35), 15–29 November, 2001. Accessed 24 June 2014: http://www.continent.kz/2000/22/27.html.
123. Gulnara Abikeyeva, 'Staraya lyubov' ne rzhaveet', Iskusstvo Kino, No. 4, 2010. Accessed online 26 August 2014: http://kinoart.ru/archive/2010/04/n4-article19.
124. Beumers, 'Waves, Old and New, in Kazakh Cinema'.
125. Olga Malakhova, 'Novaya volna, dvadtsat' let spustya', Kazakhstanskaya Pravda, 8 August 2008, p. 12.

Chapter 4 Naked in the Mirror: The Ethno-centric Narrative of Kazakh Nationhood

1. Gulnara Abikeyeva, *Natsiostroitel'stvo v Kazakhstane i drugikh stranakh Tsentral'noi Azii i kak etot protsess otrazhaetsya v kinematografe*, Almaty: 'TSTSAK', 2006.
2. Michele Commercio, 'The "Pugachev Rebellion" in the Context of Post-Soviet Kazakh Nationalisation', *Nationalities Papers*, 32 (1), 2004, pp. 87–113; Azmat Sarsembayev, 'Imagined Communities: Kazak nationalism and Kazakification in the 1990s', *Central Asian Survey*, 18 (3), 1999, pp. 319–46; Sally N. Cummings, Legitimation and Identification in Kazakhstan, *Nationalism and Ethnic Politics*, 12 (2), 2006, pp. 177–204.
3. Author's interview with Adilkhan Yerzhanov, Almaty, Kazakhstan, 5 November 2012.
4. In the films analysed in this chapter the term 'Dzhungar' is used to describe the Mongolian *Oirat* tribes. Dzhungar refers to the collective identity of three western Mongolian *Oirat* tribes (Oöled, Dörvöd and Khoit). This work, however, prefers to use the term *Oirat* as Dzhungar is Russian-centric. It was utilised by Russian and Soviet historians and ethnographers and neglects to recognise that historically western Mongolians referred to themselves as either *Oriats* or by their respective tribal names.
5. Saida Suleeva, 'Nashe kino opustilos' do edinitsy', *Kontinent*, 22 (35), 15–29 November, 2001. Accessed 24 June 2014 http://www.continent.kz/2000/22/27.html.
6. Richard Pomfret, 'Kazakhstan's Economy since Independence: Does the Oil Boom Offer a Second Chance for Sustainable Development?' *Europe-Asia Studies*, 57 (6), 2005, pp. 859–76.
7. Suleeva, 'Nashe kino opustilos' do edinitsy'.

8. 'Postanovlenie pravitel'stva Respubliki Kazakhstan ot 6 iyunya 2005 goda no. 563, o nekotorykh voprosakh respublikanskikh gosudarstvennykh predpriyatii'. Accessed 10 August 2016: http://online.zakon.kz/Document/?doc_id= 30013221.
9. Michelle Witte, 'Kazakhfilm Supports Young Filmmakers, National Image', *The Astana Times*, 12 January 2015. Accessed 10 August 2016: http://astanatimes.com/2015/01/kazakhfilm-supports-young-filmmakers-national-image/.
10. Author's interview with Yermek Tursunov, Almaty, Kazakhstan, 9 November 2012.
11. Ibid.
12. Author's interview with anonymous official in the film industry.
13. Author's interview with Baurzhan Shukenov, director of Arman Cinema, Almaty, Kazakhstan, 3 July 2014.
14. Author's interview with Darezhan Omirbayev, Almaty, Kazakhstan, 21 August 2014.
15. Author's interview with anonymous official in the film industry.
16. Olga Vlasenko, 'Po volnam Kazakhskogo kinematografa', *Expert Kazakhstan*, 46 (148), 10 December, 2007. Accessed 15 August 2008: http://expert.ru/kazakhstan/2007/46/kazahstanskoe_kino/.
17. Nurtai Mustafayev, 'Kazakhstanskoe kino v otryve', *Zonakz*, 8 June 2011. Accessed 18 August 2013: https://zonakz.net/articles/35040.
18. Vladislav Yuritsyn, 'Sergei Azimov: 'V osnovnom eto kino dlya debilov i pro deblov', *Zonakz*, 27 May 2011. Accessed 14 November 2012: http://www.zonakz.net/articles/34825.
19. Valeriya Gorelova, 'Novyi Kazakhskii brend', *Rossiskaia Gazeta*, 9 August 2008.
20. Baurzhan Nogerbek, 'Kochevnniki – Nomad – fil'm dlya tineidzherov', *Vremya – Kinoman*, No. 6, August 2005, pp. 10–17.
21. Alua Karpykova, 'Kazakhstanskii kinematograf: proshloe, nastoyashchee, budushchee? . . .' *Zonakz*, 18 September 2001. Accessed 24 July 2014: https://zonakz.net/articles/11511.
22. Baurzhan Nogerbek, 'Kazakhskoe Kino pered vyborom cvoego puti', *Goethe Institute*, 2014. Accessed 12 August 2014: http://www.goethe.de/ins/kz/ru/alm/kul/mag/kiz/7672639.html.
23. Karpykova, 'Kazakhstanskii kinematograf'.
24. Nogerbek, 'Kazakhskoe Kino pered vyborom svoego puti'.
25. Author's interview with Adilkhan Yerzhanov, Almaty Kazakhstan, 30 July 2014.
26. Author's interview with Slambek Tauyekel, Almaty, Kazakhstan, 6 November 2012.
27. Peter Savodnik, 'Lights, Camera, Kazakhstan!' *Bloomberg Businessweek*, 4–10 July 2011, p. 11.
28. Galymzhan Mukanov, 'O privoznykh khanakh i vyvoznykh detyah, ili nekotorye soobrazheniya kasatel'no otechestvennogo patriotizma', *Zonakz*, 21 June 2005. Accessed 14 August 2013: https://zonakz.net/articles/9324.

29. Author's interview with Baurzhan Shukenov.
30. Nogerbek, 'Kochevniki – Nomad – fil'm dlya tineidzherov'.
31. Author's interview with Akan Satayev, Almaty, Kazakhstan, 25 February 2016.
32. Harun Yilmaz, *National Identities in Soviet Historiography: The Rise of Nations Under Stalin*. London and New York: Routledge, 2015.
33. Rico Isaacs, "'Papa' – Nursultan Nazarbayev and the Discourse of Charismatic Leadership and Nation-Building in Post-Soviet Kazakhstan', *Studies in Ethnicities and Nationalism*, 10 (3), 2010, pp. 435–52.
34. Author's interview with Nur Otan Deputy, Almaty, Kazakhstan, 22 August 2007.
35. Gulnara Abikeyeva, 'Staraya lyubov' ne rzhaveet', *Iskusstvo Kino*, No. 4, April 2010. Accessed online 27 July 2014: http://kinoart.ru/archive/2010/04/n4-article19.
36. Abikeyeva, 'Staraya lyubov' ne rzhaveet'.
37. Nogerbek, 'Kochevnniki – Nomad – fil'm dlya tineidzherov'.
38. Nogerbek, 'Kazakhskoe Kino pered vyborom svoego puti'.
39. Saule Amirbekova, 'Saga o Sardare', *Expert Kazakhstan*, 10 May 2004. Accessed 13 August 2016: http://expertonline.kz/a9954/.
40. Tat'yana Chernousova, 'Sardar – ne dlya Kitaya', *Novoe Pokolenie*, 28 June 2006. Accessed 16 August 2014: http://www.np.kz/old/2006/30/rkino.html.
41. Andrew Lednov, 'Kino: nastoyashchee i pridumannoe', *Zonakz*, 14 July 2005. Accessed 2 August 2014: https://zonakz.net/articles/9271.
42. Abikeyeva, 'Staraya lyubov' ne rzhaveet'.
43. Author's interview Oleg Boretskiy, film critic, Almaty, Kazakhstan, 8 November 2012.
44. Aygul Doshanova, 'V Almaty sostoyalsya press-pokaz istoricheskogo ekshn-fil'ma Zhauzhurek Myn Bala', *Kursiv*, 26 April 2012. Accessed 16 August 2016: http://www.kursiv.kz/news/kultura/v-almaty-sostoyalsya-press-pokaz-istoricheskogo-yekshn-filma-zhauzhurek-myn-bala/.
45. Author's interview with Akan Satayev.
46. Leonid Pavlyuchik, 'Rustam Ibragimbekov: Nashego "Kochevnika" uvidit ves' mir', *Trud*, 14 July 2005.
47. Pavlyuchik, 'Rustam Ibragimbekov'.
48. Kokpar is a Kazakh game played on horseback in which two teams compete to carry a headless goat carcass over the goal line. Again, however, Kokpar is played widely across the broader Central Asia region in varying formats and under different names, for example, 'Buzkashi' in Afghanistan.
49. Vlasenko, 'Po volnam Kazakhskogo kinematografa'.
50. Stephen M. Norris, 'Nomadic Nationhood: cinema, nationhood and remembrance in post-Soviet Kazakhstan', *Ab Imperio*, 2, 2012, pp. 378–402.
51. Michael Hancock-Parmer, 'The Soviet Study of the Barefooted Flight of the Kazakhs', *Central Asian Survey* 34 (3), 2015, p. 281.

52. Author's interview with Adilkhan Yerzhanov, Almaty Kazakhstan, 5 November 2012.
53. Stephen Dalton, 'Zhauzhurek Myn Bala: Warriors of the Steppe: Doha Tribeca Film Festival Review', *Hollywood Reporter*, 21 November 2012. Accessed 23 August 2016: http://www.hollywoodreporter.com/review/myn-bala-warriors-steppe-doha-393672; and Mark Allen, 'Warriors of the Steppe: Zhauzhurek Zhauzhurek Myn Bala Review', *Nerdly*, 15 April 2013. Accessed 23 August 2016: http://www.nerdly.co.uk/2013/04/15/warriors-of-the-steppe-myn-bala-review/.
54. Author's interview with Akhat Ibrayev, Almaty, Kazakhstan, 29 July 2014.
55. Author's interview with Akan Satayev.
56. Johann Gottlieb Fichte, *Address to the German Nation*, ed. George Armstrong Kelly. New York and Evanston: Harper & Row Publishers, 1968, pp. 92–129.
57. Karl W. Deutsch, *Nationalism and Social Communication*. Cambridge, MA: MIT Press, 1966, p. 96.
58. Author's interview with Baurzhan Shukenov; author's interview with Sabit Kurmanbekov, Almaty, Kazakhstan, 3 November 2014; and author's interview with Gulnara Abikeyeva, Almaty, Kazakhstan, 16 August 2014.
59. Author's interview with Baurzhan Shukenov.
60. Ibid.
61. Author's interview with Zhanna Isabayeva, Almaty, Kazakhstan, 18 August 2014.
62. Gulnara Abikeyeva, 'The Nomad is Coming ...', *Kinokultura*, No. 14, 2006. Accessed 14 November 2012: http://www.kinokultura.com/2006/issue14.shtml.
63. Saulesh Yessenova. 'Nomad for Export, Not for Domestic Consumption: Kazakhstan's Arrested Development to "Put the Country on the Map"', *Studies in Russian and Soviet Cinema*, 5 (2), 2011, pp. 181–203.
64. Joanna Lillis, 'Astana Harnesses Soft Power of Silver Screen', *Eurasianet*, 8 July. Accessed 9 July 2011: http://www.eurasianet.org/node/63836.
65. Galymzhan Mukanov, 'O privoznykh khanakh i vyvoznykh detyakh, ili nekotorye soobrazheniya kasatel'no otechestvennogo patriotisma', *Zonakz*, 21 June 2005. Accessed 14 August 2013: https://zonakz.net/articles/9324
66. Nogerbek, 'Kochevnniki – Nomad – fil'm dlya tineidzherov'.
67. Mukanov, 'O privoznykh khanakh i vyvoznykh detyakh, ili nekotorye soobrazheniya kasatel'no otechestvennogo patriotisma'.
68. Yessenova, 'Nomad for Export'.
69. Pavlyuchik, 'Rustam Ibragimbekov'.
70. Nogerbek, 'Kochevnniki – Nomad – fil'm dlya tineidzherov'.
71. Amirbekova, 'Saga o Sardare'.
72. Chernousova, 'Sardar – ne dlya Kitaya'.
73. Karim Kadyrbaev, 'Zhauzhurek Myn Bala vs. Kurmanjan Datca', *Gonzo*, 16 October 2014. Accessed 12 August 2016: http://gonzo.kz/blog/2620-jaujurek_myin_bala_vs_kurmanjan_datka.

Notes to Pages 141–146

74. Dalton, 'Zhauzhurek Myn Bala: Warriors of the Steppe'.
75. Allen, 'Warriors of the Steppe: Zhauzhurek Myn Bala' Review'.
76. David West, 'Warriors Of The Steppe – Zhauzhurek Myn Bala', *Neomagazine*, 27 July 2013. Accessed 13 August 2016: http://www.neomag.co.uk/art/asianfilm/review/1640/warriors-of-the-steppe-myn-bala.
77. Adolf Artsishevskii, 'Kinokritik Oleg Boretskiy o fil'makh Shal Zhauzhurek Myn Bala', *Central Asia Monitor*, 9 June 2012. Accessed 3 February 2016: http://www.altyn-orda.kz/adolf-arcishevskij-kinokritik-oleg-boreckij-o-filmax-shal-i-zhauzhurek-myn-bala/.
78. Doszhanova, 'V Almaty sostoyalsya press-pokaz istoricheskogo ekshin-film Zhauzhurek Myn Bala'.
79. Karim Kadyrbaev, 'Mif o kassovykh sborakh', *Vlast*, 4 December 2014. Accessed 24 August 2016: https://vlast.kz/avtory/mif_o_kassovyh_sborah-8642.html.
80. Emma Pritchard Jones, 'Kazakhstan strikes back with 'the real Borat story', *Independent*, 13 January 2012. Accessed 24 February 2014: http://www.independent.co.uk/arts-entertainment/films/features/kazakhstan-strikes-back-with-the-real-borat-story-6288579.html.
81. Yessenova, 'Nomad for Export', p. 190.
82. Ibid.
83. Shaun Walker, 'Kazakh leader puts own name in lights with film of his childhood', *Independent*, 16 April. Accessed 12 November 2011: http://www.independent.co.uk/news/world/asia/kazakh-leader-puts-own-name-in-lights-with-film-of-his-childhood-2268638.html.
84. Author's interview with Rustem Abdrashev, 5 November 2014, Almaty, Kazakhstan.
85. Ibid.
86. The bird of prey is a symbolic animal for Kazakhs, and it becomes a central motif across the series linking the past and the present and solidifying Nazarbayev's position as a hero. The eagle makes periodic appearances throughout the films – appearing at the beginning of *River of Fire* and at the end of *Iron Mountain*.
87. Joshua First, 'The Sky of My Childhood Review', *Kinokultura*, 36, 2012. Accessed 14 September 2012: http://www.kinokultura.com/2012/36r-nebodetstvo.shtml.
88. Joshua First, 'The Sky of My Childhood Review'.
89. Joanna Lillis, 'Movie of Nazarbayev's Childhood Offers Cinematic Surprises', *Eurasianet*, 14 April 2011. Accessed 16 April 2011: http://www.eurasianet.org/node/63292.
90. Damir Baimanov, 'Ognennaya reka i Zheleznaya Gora Nursultana Nazarbayeva, *Kazinform*, 1 December 2013. Accessed 23 August 2016: http://www.madenimura.kz/ru/materials/news/stream-fire-iron-mountain/.
91. Aleksei Azarov, 'Tri chasa po puti Nazarbayeva', *Radio Azattyk*, 13 December 2013. Accessed 14 January 2014: http://rus.azattyq.org/a/kino-o-nursultanenazarbaeve/25199563.html.

92. Author's interview with Rustem Abdrashev.
93. Bayterk is the Turkic symbol for the tree of life in which a huge bird's nest is situated at the very top of the tree, in which the mythical bird Samruk was said to have laid its egg. The Bayterek monument and observation tower constructed in Astana is a visual and structural representation of this myth, and again illustrates the appropriation of myths shared with Turkic peoples and states across the wider Central Asian region as symbols to represent Kazakh national identity.
94. Joshua First, 'The Sky of My Childhood Review'.
95. Ibid.
96. *Nomad* features 24 pages of reviews on kino.kz, while *Zhauzhurek Myn Bala* has 52, the highest for any Kazakh film. *Sardar* by comparison has just three comments.
97. Focus group with Kazakh cinema audience, 9 November 2014, Almaty, Kazakhstan.
98. Focus group with Kazakh cinema audience, 8 November 2014, Almaty, Kazakhstan.
99. Comment taken from the kino.kz website: http://www.kino.kz/notice/notice.asp?id=3906.
100. Focus group with Kazakh cinema audience, 9 November 2014, Almaty, Kazakhstan.
101. Focus group with Kazakh cinema audience, 6 November 2014, Almaty, Kazakhstan.
102. Comment taken from the kino.kz website: http://www.kino.kz/notice/notice.asp?id=1680.
103. Focus group with Kazakh cinema audience, 6 November 2014, Almaty, Kazakhstan.
104. Comment taken from the kino.kz website: http://www.kino.kz/notice/notice.asp?id=129.
105. Comment taken from the kino.kz website: http://www.kino.kz/notice/notice.asp?id=1680.
106. Comment taken from the kino.kz website: http://www.kino.kz/notice/notice.asp?id=1296&page=2.
107. Comment taken from the kino.kz website: http://www.kino.kz/notice/notice.asp?id=1680.
108. Focus group with Kazakh cinema audience, 9 November 2014, Almaty, Kazakhstan.
109. Comment taken from the kino.kz website: http://www.kino.kz/notice/notice.asp?id=1296&page=3.
110. Comment taken from the kino.kz website: http://www.kino.kz/notice/notice.asp?id=3906&page=35.
111. Comment taken from the kino.kz website: http://www.kino.kz/notice/notice.asp?id=3906&page=9.

112. This was perhaps because of the self-selecting nature of the focus groups. It tended to attract audience members more interested in art-house movies than the big historical blockbusters. Thus, there was a tendency for focus group members to be more sceptical of films such as *Nomad* and *Zhauzhurek Myn Bala*.
113. Focus group with Kazakh cinema audience, 8 November 2014, Almaty, Kazakhstan.
114. Focus group with Kazakh cinema audience, 8 November 2014, Almaty, Kazakhstan.
115. Focus group with Kazakh cinema audience, 8 November 2014, Almaty, Kazakhstan.
116. Focus group with Kazakh cinema audience, 8 November 2014, Almaty, Kazakhstan.
117. Comments taken from the kino.kz website: http://www.kino.kz/notice/notice.asp?id=4720&page=0.
118. Comments taken from the kino.kz website: http://www.kino.kz/notice/notice.asp?id=4720&page=1.
119. Focus group with Kazakh cinema audience, 8 November 2014, Almaty, Kazakhstan.
120. Comments taken from the kino.kz website: http://www.kino.kz/notice/notice.asp?id=3493&page=1.
121. Comments taken from the kino.kz website: http://www.kino.kz/notice/notice.asp?id=3493.
122. Comments taken from the kino.kz website: http://www.kino.kz/notice/notice.asp?id=3493&page=1.

Chapter 5 May the Grass Never Grow at Your Door: The Civic Conception of Nationhood in Kazakh Cinema

1. Nursultan Nazarbayev, *Without Right and Left*. London: Class Publishing, 1992.
2. Michele Commercio, 'The "Pugachev Rebellion" in the Context of Post-Soviet Kazakh Nationalisation', *Nationalities Papers*, 32 (1), 2004, pp. 87–113; Azmat Sarsembayev, 'Imagined Communities: Kazak nationalism and Kazakification in the 1990s', *Central Asian Survey*, 18 (3), 1999, pp. 319–46; Cengiz Surucu, 'Modernity, Nationalism and Resistance: Identity Politics in Post-Soviet Kazakhstan', *Central Asian Survey*, 21 (4), 2002, pp. 385–402; Donnacha Ó'Beacháin and Robert Kevlihan, 'Threading a needle: Kazakhstan between civic and ethno-nationalist state-building', *Nations and Nationalism*, 19 (2), pp. 337–56.
3. Michaela Pohl, '"It cannot be that our graves will be here": the survival of Chechen and Ingush deportees in Kazakhstan', 1944–1957, *Journal of Genocide Research*, 4 (3), 2002, pp. 401–30.

4. Joshua First, 'The Sky of My Childhood Review', *Kinokultura*, 36, 2012. Accessed 15 July 2014: http://www.kinokultura.com/2012/36r-nebodetstvo.shtml.
5. Nursultan Nazarbayev, 'Kazakhstan Nash obshchii dom!' *Nurinsk Raion*. Accessed 23 September 2016: http://nurinsk.gov.kz/ru/news/id/874.
6. Aziz Burkhanov and Dina Sharipova, 'Kazakhstan's Civic Identity: Ambiguous Policies and Points of Resistance' in Mariya Omelicheva (ed.), *Nationalism and Identity Construction in Central Asia: Dimensions, Dynamics, and Directions*. Lanham, MD: Lexington Books, p. 29.
7. Nursultan Nazarbayev, *The Kazakhstan Way*. London: Stacey International, 2008, p. 45.
8. Nursultan Nazarbayev, 'Uchastie v torzhestvennom sobranii, posvyashchennom Dnyu Nezavisimosti Respubliki Kazakhstan', *Akorda*, 14 December 2013. Accessed 23 September 2016: http://www.akorda.kz/ru/events/astana_kazakhstan/participation_in_events/uchastie-v-torzhestvennom-sobranii-posvyashchennom-dnyu-nezavisimosti-respubliki-kazahstan.
9. Author's interview with Galiaskar Dunaev Nur Otan's Political Council's Representative in Almaty, 22 August 2007, Almaty, Kazakhstan.
10. Author's interview with Kenzhegali Sagadiev, ex-Nur Otan Mazhilis Deputy, 22 August 2007, Almaty.
11. Erlan Seitimov, 'Oleg Boretskiy: "Ideologiya Ameriki kuetsya v Gollivyde"' *Zonakz.net*, 12 July 2010. Accessed 14 March 2013: https://zonakz.net/articles/30201.
12. Yuliya Milen'kaya, 'Lavrentii Son: Nuzhno prosto byt' Kazakhom', *Liter*, 24 May 2011. Accessed 17 September 2016: http://www.altyn-orda.kz/lavrentij-son-nuzhno-prosto-byt-kazaxom/.
13. Gulnara Abikeyeva, *The Heart of the World: Films from Central Asia*. Almaty: Shaken Aimanov, Kazakhfilm National Company/SKIF/Kino firm, 2003, p. 90.
14. Abikeyeva, *The Heart of the World: Films from Central Asia*, p. 105.
15. Yelena Lyubimova, 'Podarok Stalinu', *Timeout*, 17 October 2008. Accessed 22 February 2013: http://www.timeout.ru/msk/artwork/129245.
16. Yaroslav Razymov, 'Fil'm Podarok Stalinu uzhe vyzval spory', *Karavan*, 16 September 2008. Accessed 2 March 2013: http://www.caravan.kz/articles/film-podarok-stalinu-uzhe-vyzval-spory-370985/.
17. Lyubimova, 'Podarok Stalinu'.
18. Nursultan Nazarbayev, *Osnovopolzhnik Kazakhstanskoi modeli mezhetnicheskogo i mezhkonfessional'nogo soglasiya*. Almaty: Instiutut filosofii i politologii, 2010.
19. Lauren Wissot, 'The Gift to Stalin', *Slant Magazine*, 13 March 2011. Accessed 28 September 2016: http://www.slantmagazine.com/film/review/the-gift-to-stalin.

20. Raushan Shulembaeva, 'Zemlya Obetovannaya', *Kazakhstanskaya Pravda*, 27 February 2015. Accessed 17 September 2016: http://www.kazpravda.kz/fresh/view/zemlya-obetovannaya/.
21. Author's interview with Rustem Abdrashev, 5 November 2014, Almaty, Kazakhstan.
22. Author's interview with an official at Kazakhfilm Studios, 12 April 2012, Almaty, Kazakhstan.
23. Author's interview with Slambek Tauyekel, Kazakh Film Director, Almaty, Kazakhstan, 6 November 2012.
24. Author's interview with Satybaldy Narymbetov, Almaty, Kazakhstan, 6 November 2012.
25. Author's interview with Slambek Tauyekel.
26. Milen'kaya, 'Lavrentii Son: Nuzhno prosto byt' Kazakhom'.
27. Jamie Miller, 'A Gift to Stalin', *KinoKultura*, 24, 2009. Accessed 30 September 2012: http://www.kinokultura.com/2009/24r-podarok.shtml.
28. Jordana Horn, 'The Kid from Kazakhstan', *Forward*, 9 March 2011. Accessed 28 September 2016: http://forward.com/culture/135974/the-kid-from-kazakhstan/.
29. Maggie Lee, 'The Gift to Stalin', *The Hollywood Reporter*, 2 October 2008. Accessed 28 September 2016: http://www.hollywoodreporter.com/news/film-review-gift-stalin-120242.
30. Svetlana Stepnova, 'Stantsiya Pamyat'', *Ruskino*, 15 December 2008. Accessed 18 September 2016: http://ruskino.ru/review/262.
31. Stepnova, 'Stantsiya Pamyat''.
32. Author's interview with Rustem Abdrashev.
33. Taras Kuzio, 'The myth of the civic state: a critical survey of Hans Kohn's framework for understanding nationalism', *Ethnic and Racial Studies*, 25 (1), 2002, pp. 20–39.
34. Philip Spencer and Howard Woolman, *Nationalism: A Critical Introduction*. London: Sage Publications. 2002, pp. 105–106.
35. Lyubimova, 'Podarok Stalinu; Stepnova, Stantsiya Pamyat''.
36. Author's interview with Slambek Tauyekel.
37. Stepnova, 'Stantsiya Pamyat''.
38. Miller, 'A Gift to Stalin'.
39. Sarah Cameron, 'The Hungry Steppe: Soviet Kazakhstan and the Kazakh Famine 1921–1934', PhD dissertation, Yale University, 2011; Isabelle Ohayon, *The Kazakh Famine: The Beginnings of Sedentarization, Online Encyclopedia of Mass Violence* [online], published on 28 September 2013, accessed 22 April 2016: http://www.massviolence.org/The-Kazakh-Famine-The-Beginnings, ISSN 1961–9898; Niccoló Painciola, 'The Collectivization Famine in Kazakhstan', 1931–1933, *Harvard Ukrainian Studies*, 25 (3/4), p. 237.
40. Stepnova, 'Stantsiya Pamyat''.
41. Inna Smailova, *Spor Kino Kritika c Kino Vredinoi*. Astana: Dizain-kontsept i maket, p. 53.

42. 'Kazakhfilm prezentoval Tsikl animatsionnykh fil'mov 'Kazakhstan bizding ortaq shangyrghymyz', *Kazkahfilm*, 21 April 2015. Accessed 17 September 2016: http://kazakhfilmstudios.kz/press/news/8094/.
43. Mariya Gareeva, 'Kazakhfil'm presentoval tsikl mul'tfil'mov po motivam skazok narodov Kazakhstana', *Informbyuro*, 20 April 2015. Accessed 17 September 2016: https://informburo.kz/novosti/kazahfilm-prezentoval-tsikl-multfilmov-po-motivam-skazok-narodov-kazahstana-3082.html.
44. Gareeva, 'Kazakhfil'm presentoval tsikl mul'tfil'mov po motivam skazok narodov Kazakhstana'.
45. Desyat' 'fil'mov za kotorye Kazakhstanu ne stydno', *Nur.kz*, 22 October 2014. Accessed 14 January 2016: https://www.nur.kz/336862-desyat-filmov-za-kotorye-kazahstanu-ne-stydno-foto.html.
46. Focus group with Kazakh cinema audience, 9 November 2014, Almaty, Kazakhstan.
47. Comment taken from the kino.kz website: http://www.kino.kz/notice/notice.asp?id=2542.
48. Comment taken from the kino.kz website: http://www.kino.kz/notice/notice.asp?id=3546.
49. Comment taken from the kino.kz website: http://www.kino.kz/notice/notice.asp?id=3546&page=1.
50. In fact, there was not a single negative review for *The Promised Land* on kino.kz, but a good portion of negative reviews for *The Gift to Stalin*, although the majority of comments were positive.
51. See http://www.kino.kz/notice/notice.asp?id=2542.
52. Focus group with Kazakh cinema audience, 6 November 2014, Almaty, Kazakhstan.
53. Comment taken from the kino.kz website: http://www.kino.kz/notice/notice.asp?id=2542&page=5.
54. Comment taken from the kino.kz website: http://www.kino.kz/notice/notice.asp?id=2542&page=5.
55. Comment taken from the kino.kz website: http://www.kino.kz/notice/notice.asp?id=2542&page=5.
56. Comment taken from the kino.kz website: http://www.kino.kz/notice/notice.asp?id=3546.
57. Comment taken from the kino.kz website: http://www.kino.kz/notice/notice.asp?id=3546.
58. Comment taken from the kino.kz website: http://www.kino.kz/notice/notice.asp?id=3546&page=1.
59. Comment taken from the kino.kz website: http://www.kino.kz/notice/notice.asp?id=2542&page=4.
60. Comment taken from the kino.kz website: http://www.kino.kz/notice/notice.asp?id=2542&page=2.
61. Comment taken from the kino.kz website: http://www.kino.kz/notice/notice.asp?id=3546&page=1.

Chapter 6 'Hymn to Mother': Tengrism, Motherhood and Nationhood

1. Yves Bonnefoy, *Asian mythologies*. Chicago, IL: University of Chicago Press, 1993, p. 331; Marléne Laruelle, 'Religious revival, nationalism and the 'invention of tradition': political Tengrism in Central Asia and Tatarstan', *Central Asia Survey*, 26 (2), 2007, p. 204.
2. Réka Szilárdi, 'Neo-paganism in Hungary: under the spell of roots' in Kaarina Aitamurto and Scott Simpson (eds), *Modern Pagan and Native Faith Movements in Central and Eastern Europe*. Abingdon and New York: Routledge, 2014, pp. 230–248.
3. The claim of a connection between Tengrism of the Turkic-Mongols and ancient Sumerians is based on the potential, but disputed, linguistic connection between the word Tengri, which means sky god in Turkic, and the Sumerian Dingir, which in its cuneiform is a star and is understood to mean the supreme father of gods and the sky. See Olzhas Suleimenov, *Az i ya*, Alma-Ata: Zhasushy 1975; Troy Kynard, *The Esoteric Codex: Mesopotamian Deities*, first edition, Lulu.com, 2015, p. 23; H.B. Paksoy, *Tengri in Eurasia*, 8 August 2008, accessed online 19 January 2016: http://historicaltextarchive. com/sections.php?action=read&artid=783. The connection between Sumerian and Turkic language is rooted in theories regarding the migration of the Semitic population to the Central Asian region after the Akkadian Empire consolidated Sumerian and Semite speakers. See George Aaron Barton, *Semitic and Hamitic origins: Social and Religious*. Philadelphia: University of Pennsylvania Press, 1934, pp. 60–9.
4. Rein Müllerson, *A Chessboard and Player in the New Great Game*. Abingdon and New York: Routledge, 2013.
5. Rafael Bezertinov, Tengrianstvo – religiya turkov i mongolov, Naberezhnye. Chelny: Tatarstan, Russian Federation, 2000, p. 72.
6. According to Rafael Bezertinov, Turkic groups believed there to be 17 and Mongols 99. See Bezertinov, Tengrianstvo, p. 71.
7. Saira Shamakhay, 'Manifa Sarkulova, Gulnar Adayeva and Aigul Tursunbaeva, Image of a Man and the Universe in Kazakh and Mongol Myths', *Procedia Social and Behavioural Sciences*, 159 (2014) p. 382.
8. Shamakhay et al., 'Image of Man', p. 382.
9. S.A. Kaskabassov, *Kazakhskaya vol'shebnaya skazka*, Alma-Ata: Nauka, 1972.
10. *Drevnyaya etnicheskaya kult'ura Kazakhstana*, accessed online 27 January 2016: www.ethnicskazakhstan.wordpress.com/тенгрианство---древняя-религия-тюрко
11. B. Kh. Ismagulova and A.S. Bazarbayeva, *Mindset and Mentality of the Kazakh Ethnos*. Accessed online 14 December 2015: http://portal.kazntu.kz/files/publicate/2014-12-15-2020.pdf
12. A. Kodar cited in Shamakhay et al., p. 382.

13. Danuta Penkala-Gawęcka, 'The Way of the Shaman and the Revival of Spiritual Healing in post-Soviet Kazakhstan and Kyrgyzstan', *Shaman*, 22 (1–2) Spring/Autumn 2012, p. 37.
14. Charles Weller, 'Religious-Cultural Revivalism as Historiographical Debate: Contending Claims in the post-Soviet Kazakh Context', *Journal of Islamic Studies*, 25 (2), 2014, p. 139.
15. Devin DeWeese cited in James Thrower, *The Religious History of Central Asia from the Earliest Times to the Present Day*. Lewiston, New York: Edwin Mellon Press, 2004, p. 55.
16. Thrower, *The Religious History of Central Asia*, p. 56.
17. A.K. Yegenisova and A.R. Yerubaeva, 'Psikhologicheskie osobennosti natsional'nogo mentalieta Kazakhskogo naroda', *Mezhdunarodnyi zhurnal eksperimental'nogo obrazovaniya*, 2015, No. 4, pp. 371–376.
18. Yegenisova and Yerubaeva, 'Psikhologicheskie osobennosti natsional'nogo mentaliteta Kazakhskogo naroda', p. 375.
19. G.A. Adaeva and A.T. Makulbekov, 'Obraz zhenshchin v turkoyazychnoi kul'ture', *Nauka I Mir: Mezhunarodnyi Nauchnyi Zhurnal*, 2 (6), 2014, pp. 215–217.
20. Adaevaand Makulbekov, 'Obraz zhenshchin', p. 216.
21. Ibid.
22. Lev Gumilyev, *Drevnie Tyurki*. Moscow: Airis press, 2013 [1964], pp. 73–4.
23. Floya Anthias and Nira Yual-Davis, *Women and the Nation-State*. Basingstoke: Palgrave Macmillian, 1989, pp. 1–15.
24. Thrower, *The Religious History of Central Asia*.
25. Mehradad Hagheyeghi, *Islam and Politics in Central Asia*. London: Palgrave MacMillan. 1995, p. 73.
26. Olivier Roy, *The New Central Asia: the Creation of Nations*. London: I.B.Tauris Publishers, 2000, Chapter 1.
27. Thrower, *The Religious History of Central Asia*, pp. 49–50.
28. Hamilton Gibb, The *Arab Conquests in Central Asia*. London, The Royal Asiatic Society, 1923.
29. Hagheyeghi, *Islam and Politics*, pp. 74–5.
30. Alexandre Bennigsen and S. Enders Wimbush, *Mystics and Commissars: Sufism in the Soviet Union*, Berkley and Los Angeles, CA: University of California Press, 1985.
31. Hagheyeghi, *Islam and Politics*, p. 77. This point is also emphasised by the Kazakh cultural historian and philosopher Tursin Hafiz Gabitov who argues that the various types of religions of the Kazakh people should not be seen as replacing one after the other, rather that there was more a process of co-existence. For more on the work of Gabitov see Charles Weller's review of the religious cultural historical debate in Kazakhstan. Weller, Religious-Cultural Revivalism.
32. Olzhas Suleimenov, *Az i ya*.
33. Weller, 'Religious-Cultural Revivalism', pp. 148–54.

NOTES TO PAGES 181–186   293

34. Laruelle, 'Religious revival'.
35. Ibid., p. 213.
36. Gani Kasymov ob'yavil sebya priverzhentsem tengrianstva, *nur.kz*, 13 October 2010. Accessed 14 January 2016: http://www.nur.kz/165368-gani-kasymov-obyavil-sebya-priverzhenczem-tengrianstva.html.
37. Zhanat Saparbekovna Yergubekova, Esengeldi Auelbekovich Kerimbaev, Nagima Danabekovna Koshanova, Zhazira Isaevna Isaeva and Akylbek Kairatbekovich Meirbekov, 'About Some Research Methods of Linguistic Structure of the Concept of "Hero" in Turkic (Kazakh) Heroic Epics', *Middle East Journal of Scientific Research*, 16 (2), 2013, pp. 1714–1718.
38. Seth Graham, 'Review: Kelin', *Kinokultura*, 26. Accessed 19 July 2011: http://www.kinokultura.com/2009/26r-kelin.shtml.
39. Olga Khrabrykh, 'Strasti po Kelin', *Express K*, 20 February 2009. Accessed 19 January 2016: http://old.express-k.kz/show_article.php?art_id=24450.
40. Khrabrykh, 'Strasti po Kelin'.
41. Vadim Zel'bin, 'Baksy: Bratva, ne strelyaite v shamanov', film.ru, 3 October 2008. Accessed 31 January 2016: http://www.film.ru/articles/bratva-ne-strelyayte-v-shamanov.
42. 'Review: 'Baksy', *Variety*, 23 June 2008. Accessed 31 January 2016: http://variety.com/2008/film/reviews/baksy-1200508882/.
43. Richard Orange, 'Kazakhstan Film Industry Profile', *Daily Telegraph*, 23 March 2011. Accessed 9 June 2016: http://www.telegraph.co.uk/culture/film/film-news/8399034/Kazakhstan-film-industry-profile.html.
44. 'Kazakhstanskii film-fentezi vyidet v prokat 12.12.12.', *Tengrinews*, 30 November 2012. Accessed 27 January 2016: http://tengrinews.kz/cinema/kazahstanskiy-film-fentezi-vyiydet-v-prokat-121212-224418/
45. 'Knigu legend: Tainstvennyi les vylozhat v Internet', *Tengrinews*, 10 December 2013. Accessed 20 January 2016: http://tengrinews.kz/cinema/knigu-legend-tainstvennyiy-les-vyilojat-v-internet-224916.
46. Author's interview with Akhat Ibrayev, 24 July 2014, Almaty, Kazakhstan.
47. Interview with Akhat Ibrayev.
48. Khrabrykh, 'Strasti po Kelin'.
49. Dmitrii Mosovoi, 'V Kazakhstane snyali 'nemoi' film 'Kelin', *Karavan*, 13 February 2009, accessed 14 March 2013: http://www.centrasia.ru/newsA.php?st=1234768500
50. Khrabrykh, 'Strasti po Kelin'.
51. Anna Darmodekhina, 'Saundtrekom dlya Knigi legend: Tainstvennyi les stanet 'zhestkaya kolybel'naya', *Artparovoz*, 12 December 2012. Accessed 1 February 2016: http://www.artparovoz.com/8539.
52. It was the director of *The Needle*, Rashid Nugmanov, who suggested to the author that Tengrism is not a religion but more a philosophy. Author's interview with Rashid Nugmanov, Almaty, Kazakhstan, 9 August 2014.
53. Author's interview with Yermek Tursunov, Almaty, Kazakhstan, 9 November 2012.

54. Tat'yna Bendz', 'Ya kak byl Kazakpaem, tak i ostalsya – Yermek Tursunov', 16 June 2015. Accessed 4 February 2016: http://365info.kz/2015/06/ya-kak-byl-kazakpaem-tak-ostalsya-Yermek-tursunov/.
55. 'Yermek Tursunov: Ya tak dumayu', *Kazakh adebieti*, 18 January 2010. Accessed 14 March 2013: http://www.spik.kz/articles/kult-tur/2010-01-18/Yermek-tursunov-ya-tak-dumayu.
56. 'Yermek Tursunov: Ya tak dumayu'.
57. Author's interview with Yermek Tursunov, Almaty, Kazakhstan, 9 November 2012.
58. Focus group with Kazakh cinema audience, 9 November 2014, Almaty, Kazakhstan.
59. Author's interview with Oleg Boretskiy, film critic, Almaty, Kazakhstan, 8 November 2012.
60. Focus group with Kazakh cinema audience, 9 November 2014, Almaty, Kazakhstan.
61. Emily Schuckman Mathews, 'The Old Man (Shal)', *Kinokultura*, 40, 2013. Accessed 28 July 2014: http://www.kinokultura.com/2013/40r-shal.shtml.
62. Dariya Tsyrenzhapova, 'Capturing Kazakhstan's Character, Wrinkles and All', *Transitions Online*, 8 November 2012. Accessed 17 November 2012: http://www.tol.org/client/article/23456-kazakhstan-cinema-yYermek-tursunov.html.
63. Author's interview with Oleg Boretskiy.
64. Zarina Akhmatova, 'Khochetsya vyiti s kem-to stenka ne stenku, a stenki net', *Vlast.kz*, 7 April 2015. Accessed 18 April 2015: https://vlast.kz/persona/Yermek_tursunov_rezhisser_hochetsja_vyjti_s_kem_to_stenka_na_stenku_a_stenki_net-10440.html.
65. Carlos Aguilar, 'The Old Man (Shal)', 11 December 2013. Accessed 3 February 2016: http://blogs.indiewire.com/sydneylevine/foreign-oscar-entry-review-shal-the-old-man-kazakhstan-Yermek-tursunov-foreign-language-oscar-submissions-academy-awards-2014-international-film-business.
66. Snezhana Baymuhanova, 'Retsenziya na fil'm Shal', *Brodvei*, 21 February 2013. Accessed 3 February 2016: http://brod.kz/blogs/retsenziya_na_film_shal/.
67. Oleg Boretskiy makes this clear link between the film and values. He argued that 'if you want to know about Kazakh values then you should watch *Shal*'. Author's interview with Oleg Boretskiy.
68. 'Kinokritik Oleg Boretskiy o filmakh Shal i Zhayzhurek Myn Bala', *Camonitor*, 9 June 2012. Accessed online, 19 November 2012: http://www.altyn-orda.kz/adolf-arcishevskij-kinokritik-oleg-boreckij-o-filmax-shal-i-zhauzhurek-myn-bala/.
69. Kazakhstan is home to the Baikonur cosmodrome, which is located east of the Aral Sea north-west of Kyzylorda. It is not clear in the film whether this a discarded rocket from the cosmodrome. It does, nonetheless, confirm the tension between tradition and modernity and ways in which the

environmental impact of technology on the steppe is often forgotten in the race for technological advancement.
70. Emily Schuckman Mathews, 'The Old Man (Shal)'.
71. Author's interview with Oleg Boretskiy.
72. Author's interview with Yermek Tursunov.
73. Murat Uali, 'Retsenziya na Shal: Yermeka Tursunova', *yvision*, 4 March 2013. Accessed 3 February 2016: http://yvision.kz/post/351221.
74. Author's interview with Yermek Tursunov.
75. Focus group with Kazakh cinema audience, 9 November 2014, Almaty, Kazakhstan.
76. Author's interview with Yermek Tursunov.
77. Snezhana Baymuhanova, 'Retsenziya na film Shal'.
78. Author's interview with Oleg Boretskiy.
79. 'Uali, Retsenziya na Shal: Yermeka Tursunova'.
80. Focus group with Kazakh cinema audience, 9 November 2014, Almaty, Kazakhstan.
81. Focus group with Kazakh cinema audience, 6 November 2014, Almaty, Kazakhstan.
82. See comments on kino.kz: http://www.kino.kz/notice/notice.asp?id=3885.
83. These plot issues concerned the lacklustre abilities of the search and research operation who perhaps in real life would most likely have discovered the lost Kasym. It should also be noted that while there were some criticisms of the performances there was almost universal praise for Yerbolat Toguzakov who played Kasym. He was praised for the instinctive humanity and emotion he brought to the role. Toguzakov was a virtually unknown actor in the country. While he was often reported as a 'novice' actor, in fact he had been acting for years, but with little success. *Shal* made him a national star.
84. *Shal* was put forward for Kazakhstan's entry for the best foreign film category for the 2014 Oscars, but was not nominated.
85. See Emily Schuckman Mathews, 'The Old Man (Shal)'; Carlos Aguilar, 'The Old Man (Shal)'; Leslie Felperin, 'The Old Man (Shal) film review', *Hollywood Reporter*, 17 December 2013. Accessed 2 February 2016: http://www.hollywoodreporter.com/review/old-man-shal-film-review-665886
86. D. Nuketaeva, A. Kanagatova, I. Khan, B. Kylyshbayeva and G.Bektenova, 'Gender Component in the National Project of Kazakhstan', *International Journal of Social, Behavioural, Educational, Economic, Business and Industrial Engineering*, 6 (2), p. 1153.
87. Oleg Boretskiy, 'Dva yavleniya v Kazakhstanskom kino'. Accessed online 10 August 2014: http://www.goethe.de/ins/kz/ru/alm/kul/mag/kiz/7672815.html.
88. Boretskiy, 'Dva yavleniya v Kazakhstnskom kino'.
89. 'Shedevr kororyi nel'zya ne uvidet", *Karavan*, 12 October 2012. Accessed 24 January 2016: http://art.caravan.kz/news/shedevr-kotoryjj-nelzya-ne-uvidet-newsID14272.html.

90. Svetlana Shakirova, 'Kelin, Karoi i drugie semeinye sagi (kinematograf Kazakhstana v poiskakh ideala materi/natsii)' in *Vlast, sem'ya ethnos: gendernye roli v XXI veke*. Moscow. IEA RAN, 2014, pp. 170–172.
91. 'Yermek Tursunov: Ya tak dumayu'.
92. Pierre van den Berghe, 'Race and Ethnicity: a Socio-biological Perspective', *Ethnic and Racial Studies*, 1 (4) pp. 401–411.
93. 'Khrabrykh, Strasti po Kelin'.
94. Megan A. Ginn, *A Comparative Study: Women's Rights in Kazakhstan, Uzbekistan, and Tajikistan*. Honors in the Major Theses. Paper 67, 2016.
95. Ainagul Bekeeva 'Parlamentarii nedovol'ny moral'nym oblikom Kazakhskoi zhenshchiny v kino i reklame', *Zonakz.net*, 1 April 2010: http://www.zonakz.net/articles/28792; Shakirova, 'Kelin, Karoi i drugie semeinye sagi; Khrabrykh, Strasti po Kelin'.
96. Focus group with Kazakh cinema audience, 6 November 2014, Almaty, Kazakhstan.
97. 'Khrabrykh, Strasti po Kelin'.
98. Mostovoi, 'V Kazakhstane snyali "nemoi" film 'Kelin'.
99. Focus group with Kazakh cinema audience, 6 November 2014, Almaty, Kazakhstan.
100. Vladislav Yuritsya, 'Yermek Tursunov: 'Zanimayus' kontrprogrammirovaniem kul'tury', *Zonakz*, 20 December 2009. Accessed 14 August 2013: https://zonakz.net:8443/articles/27611.
101. Zarina Akhmatova, 'Khochetsya vyiti s kem-to stenka na stenku, a stenki net'.
102. Of course, the cinema audiences who participated in the focus groups were self-selecting, so there may be some legitimacy to Tursunov's claims about the size of his audience.
103. Focus group with Kazakh cinema audience, 8 November 2014, Almaty, Kazakhstan.
104. *Kelin* only features four pages of feedback and comments from people who had seen the film on kino.kz, while *Shal* has 24 pages. For Kelin see http://www.kino.kz/notice/notice.asp?id=2791 and *Shal* http://www.kino.kz/notice/notice.asp?id=3885.
105. For all comments see see http://www.kino.kz/notice/notice.asp?id=2791.
106. Mostovoi, 'V Kazakhstane snyali "nemoi" film 'Kelin'.
107. Khrabrykh, 'Strasti po Kelin'.
108. Bolat Ryskozha, 'Rezhisser Yermek Tursunov podvergsya izbieniyu v razgar skandala vokrug fil'ma 'Kelin', *Radio Azattyk*, 19 February 2009. Accessed 3 February 2016: http://rus.azattyq.org/a/Yermek_tursunov_kelin_movie/1495309.html.
109. Yuritsya, 'Yermek Tursunov: 'Zanimayus' kontrprogrammirovaniem kul'tury'.
110. Akhmatova, 'Khochetsya vyiti s kem-to stenka na stenku, a stenki net.

Chapter 7 The Steppe, Disorientation, Division and Corruption: Social and Economic Visions of Modern Nationhood

1. Dina Sabirova, 'Budushchee Kazakhstansogo kino', *Zakon*, 2 May 2013. Accessed 14 July 2013: http://www.zakon.kz/4554947-budushhee-kazakhstanskogo-kino.html.
2. Ksenia Leontyeva, 'Valeriy Kustov, Svetlana Mudrova and Oleg Berezin, Kazakh Film Market', *Neva Film Research*, 2014. Accessed 16 November 2015: www.nevafilm.ru/english/reports/... film-market/_.../Kazakhstan_eng.pdf; Karim Kadyrbaev, 'Kakie fil'my pokazhut na marafone Kazakhstankogo kino', *Vlast*, 4 February 2015. Accessed 22 March 2016: https://vlast.kz/avtory/kakie_filmy_pokazhut_na_marafone_kazahstanskogo_kino-9456.html.
3. Sayan Baigaliev and Maxim Shatrov, 'Industriya Kino', *Vox Populi*, 29 March 2013. Accessed 6 May 2016: http://www.voxpopuli.kz/business/1040-industriya-kino.html.
4. Svetlana Umyraleeva, 'Akan Sataev: 'Besplatno skachivaya fil'my s torrentov, kazakhstantsy prakticheski zanimayutsya vorovstvom', *Atameken Business Channel*, 1 February 2017. Accessed 21 May 2017: http://abctv.kz/ru/news/akan-sataev-«besplatno-skachivaya-filmy-s-torrentov-kazahs.
5. Leontyeva, 'Kustov Mudrova and Berezin, Kazakh Film Market'.
6. The other two which Narymbetov points to are: physiognomy and cinematic language.
7. Sergei Anashkin, 'Sergei Dvortsevoy 'V stepi chuvstvuyu sebya komfortnee, chem v gorakh ili lesu', *Chastnyi Korrespondent*, 16 October 2010. Accessed 20 February 2016: http://www.chaskor.ru/article/sergej_dvortsevoj_v_stepi_chuvstvuyu_sebya_komfortnee_chem_v_gorah_ili_v_lesu_20491.
8. A.O. Scott, 'A Hapless Romantic, Smitten on the Steppe', *New York Times*, 31 March 2009. Accessed 17 August 2014: http://www.nytimes.com/2009/04/01/movies/01tulp.html?_r=1.
9. Peter Hames, 'On Sergei Dvortsevoy's Tulpan', *Kinokultura*, 22, 2008.
10. Zygmunt Dzieciolowski and Sergei Dvortsevoy, 'Sergei Dvortsevoy, Talented Ripple Master', *Open Democracy*, 26 July 2013. Accessed online 20 February 2016: https://www.opendemocracy.net/od-russia/zygmunt-dzieciolowski-Sergei-dvortsevoy/Sergei-dvortsevoy-talented-ripple-master.
11. Pawel Pawlikowski, 'Sergei Dvortsevoy: the man who films goats', *Guardian*, 5 November 2009. Accessed 20 February 2016: http://www.theguardian.com/film/2009/nov/05/segei-dvortsevoy-pawel-pawlikowski.
12. Dzieciolowski and Dvortsevoy, 'Sergei Dvortsevoy, Talented Ripple Master'.
13. Oleg Boretskiy, *Tyul'pan – yavlenie v Kazakhstankom kino*, *?yulpan*, March 2010. Accessed 10 August 2014: http://www.goethe.de/ins/ru/lp/prj/drj/top/wtt/010/kik/ru5762198.htm.

14. Peter Bradshaw, 'Tulpan Review', *Guardian*, 13 November 2009. Accessed 22 February 2016: http://www.theguardian.com/film/2009/nov/13/tulpan-review.
15. Oleg Boretskiy, '*Tyul'pan* – yavlenie v Kazakhstanskom kino, *Tyulpan*'.
16. Comments taken from the kino.kz website: http://www.kino.kz/notice/notice.asp?id=2578&page=2
17. Focus group with Kazakh cinema audience, 8 November 2014, Almaty, Kazakhstan.
18. Anashkin, 'Sergei Dvortsevoy 'V stepi chuvstvuyu sebya komfortnee'.
19. *Tulpan* was the winner of the Prix Un Certain Regard at the 2008 Cannes Festival, best feature film at the 2008 Montreal Festival and Asia-Pacific Screen awards, winner of the Golden Puffin at the 2008 Reykjavik International Film Festival, and was Kazakhstan's entry for best foreign film at the 2009 Oscars.
20. Oleg Boretskiy, 'God Tyul'pana', March 2010. Accessed 14 June 2012: http://www.kino.kz/club/tulpan.asp
21. Vita Ramm, 'Krupnyi chinovnik v Astane Skazal chto "Tyul'pan" vrednee chem. 'Borat', *Izvestiya*, November 20, 2008. Accessed 14 August 2013: http://izvestia.ru/news/342931.
22. Gulnara Abikeyeva, 'Staraya lyubov' ne rzhaveet', *Iskusstvo Kino*, No. 4, April 2010.
23. Author's interview with Adilkhan Yerzhanov, 5 November 2012, Almaty, Kazakhstan.
24. We learn the husband killed his wife and son and had consumed the drugs he was supposed to deliver. See A. Hättic, Akan Sataev's Strayed review, *Kinokultura*, 30, 2010.
25. Zh. Sekerbaeva, 'Adilkhan Yerzhanov: Vse zavisit ot rakursa vashikh polusharii', *Biznes & Vlast'*, 14 October 2011. Accessed 1 November 2012: http://www.and.kz/stil-zhizni/382-adilhan-erzhanov-vse-zavisit-ot-rakursa-vashih-polushariy.html
26. Katerina Tarhanova, 'Voyazh k otecheskim grobam. "Rieltor" rezhisser Adilkhan Yerzhanov', *Iskusstvo Kino*, No. 11, November 2011.
27. Baubek Nogerbek and Alma Aidarova, 'Two Culture's Characters in Contemporary Kazakh Cinema', *International Journal of Social Management Economics and Business Engineering*, 6 (8), pp. 314–317.
28. *Beshbarmak* is widely considered the Kazakh national dish, although there are variations among many Turkic populations. It consists of boiled meat (typically mutton) and noodles in a spicy onion sauce.
29. The film was an extension of a popular TV character that had featured on the comedy sketch show *Kzlandiya*.
30. Rosa Esenkulova, '300 tysyach dollarov potratili na film 'Kelinka Sabina', *Tengri News*, 25 November 2014. Accessed 2 March 2016: http://tengrinews.kz/cinema/300-tyisyach-dollarov-potratili-na-film-kelinka-sabina-265820/

31. Rosa Esenkulova, '11 millionov tenge sobral film 'Kelinka Sabina za 5 dnei prokata, 112', *Tengri News*, 2 December 2014. Accessed online 2 March 2016: http://tengrinews.kz/cinema/112-millionov-tenge-sobral-film-kelinka-sabina-5-dney-266203/.
32. 'Shala Kazakh' is a derogatory term aimed at people who speak Kazakh with an accent and implies they are not real Kazakhs.
33. Mark Selbiev, 'Kelinka Sabina – ne ugodila 'chistym kazakham – obsor kazakhskoi pressy ot radiotochki', *Radiotochka*, 11 December 2014. Accessed 2 March 2016: http://radiotochka.kz/6316-kelinka-sabina-ne-ugodila-chistym-kazaham-obzor-kazahskoy-pressy-ot-radiotochki.html.
34. Tatyana Bakina, 'Farkhat Sharipov, Tale of the Pink Bunny', *KinoKultura*, 30, 2010.
35. Bakina, 'Farkhat Sharipov, Tale of the Pink Bunny'.
36. Alex Walters, 'Pink Bunny – Timeless Tale Set Among Modern Kazakh Youth', *Kazakhstan Edge*, 2011. Accessed 17 March 2013: http://www.edgekz.com/pink-bunny-timeless-tale-set-among-modern-kazakh-youth.html.
37. Bakina, 'Farkhat Sharipov, Tale of the Pink Bunny'.
38. Author's interview with Farkhat Sharipov, 2 November 2014, Almaty, Kazakhstan.
39. *Beshbarmak* translates as 'five fingers' as it was always traditionally eaten with hands.
40. Joe Crescente's review of the film in *KinoKultura* has a good overview of this scene. See Joe Crescente, 'Zhanna Isabaeva: My Dear Children (Oipyrmai 2009)', *KinoKultura*, 26, 2009.
41. Author's interview with Darezhan Omirbayev, 5 August 2014, Almaty, Kazakhstan.
42. The director of *My Dear Children*, Zhanna Isabayeva, self-describes as an art-house director. Her other films, *Karoy* and *Nagima*, certainly have the austere and cinematic form of art-house. Nevertheless, with *My Dear Children* she chose to use comedy as the cinematic form which alongside the evident 'national' content of it gave the film a much greater audience than those of her other movies. Despite its comic form – the film is quite a serious social drama.
43. Comments taken from the kino.kz website: http://www.kino.kz/notice/notice.asp?id=5260&page=1.
44. Focus group with Kazakh cinema audience, 6 November 2014, Almaty, Kazakhstan.
45. Adilkhan Yerzhanov, profile, accessed 9 March 2016: http://brod.kz/persons/adilhan_erjanov.
46. Author's interview with Adilkhan Yerzhanov, Almaty, Kazakhstan, 5 November 2012.
47. Olga Khrabrykh, 'Adilkhan Yerzhanov – Kazakhstanskoe kino stalo burzhuaznym', *Ekspress K*, 31 March 2014. Accessed 15 August 2014: http://old.express-k.kz/show_article.php?art_id=95757.

48. Gulnara Abikeyeva, "Stroiteli' Adilkhana Yerzhanova, Stroiteli', *yvision*, 26 October 2013. Accessed 25 February 2016: http://yvision.kz/post/381683.
49. Abikeyeva, 'Stroiteli' Adilkhana Yerzhanova'.
50. Stephen Dalton, 'The Owners – Cannes Review', *Hollywood Reporter*, 17 May 2014. Accessed 18 May 2014: http://www.hollywoodreporter.com/review/owners-cannes-review-705234#.
51. Galina Ryzhkina, 'My posmotreli film Adilkhana Yerzhanova Khozyaeva', *Buro247*, 9 November 2014. Accessed 25 February 2016.
52. Author's interview with Adilkhan Yerzhanov, 30 July 2014, Almaty Kazakhstan.
53. Cameron Gray, 'From folk to fantasy: five new east films to look out for in 2016', *The Calvert Journal*, 3 February 2016. Accessed 9 March 2016: http://calvertjournal.com/articles/show/5396/new-east-films-2016.
54. 'Kazakhfilm polozhil 'Khozyaev' na polku', *Esquire*, 3 June 2014. Accessed 10 June 2014: http://thenews.kz/2014/06/03/1601991.html.
55. Aizhan Tugelbaeva, 'Adilkhan Yerzhanov snimaet satiricheskii film o molodom akime', *Tengri News*, 11 August 2015. Accessed 25 February 2016: http://tengrinews.kz/cinema/adilhan-erjanov-snimaet-satiricheskiy-film-o-molodom-akime-279090/
56. Cameron Gray, 'From folk to fantasy'.
57. The film can be seen on YouTube: http://www.youtube.com/watch?v=MR6b0qwr3hEv
58. The film can be seen on YouTube: http://www.youtube.com/watch?v=kL8d3NXajeo
59. Jane Knox-Voina, 'Young Kazakh Filmmakers: New "New Wave" on the Road', *Kinokultura*, 27, 2010. Accessed 20 June 2013: http://www.kinokultura.com/2010/27-knoxvoina.shtml
60. Author's interview with Serik Abishev, 26 July 2014, Almaty, Kazakhstan.
61. Jane Knox-Voina, 'Young Kazakh Filmmakers: New "New Wave" on the Road'.
62. Yerzhanov and Abishev work closely together. They co-own a production company called The Short Brothers and Abishev, while working on his own films, has worked as a producer on Yerzhanov's major feature films.
63. Author's interview with Adilkhan Yerzhanov, 30 July 2014, Almaty Kazakhstan.
64. Galiya Baizhanova, 'Adilkhan Yerzhanov – ya ne snimayu blokbastery ori inoplanetyani i kovboev', *Ekspress K*, 2 February 2013. Accessed 14 April 2013: http://old.express-k.kz/show_article.php?art_id=78609
65. Among the awards the film won included the White Chameleon Award at the IFF SINDI in South Korea, the Grand Prix for the best feature film at the IFF 'Kinolikbez' in Russia, the Grand Prix in the category of 'young Cinema' at the International Film Festival 'Shaken's stars' in Kazakhstan, as well as the special jury prize Film at the 'Film Shock' Festival in Russia.
66. Author's interview with Adilkhan Yerzhanov, 30 July 2014, Almaty Kazakhstan.

67. 'Kazakhfilm polozhil 'Khozyaev' na polku'.
68. Like *Realtors, The Owners* was also the recipient of several international awards. It was nominated for the special program of the 67th Cannes Film Festival, it won the Prize from best film at the NETPAC Asian Film Festival, was awarded best film at the Grand Prix at the Lebanon International Film Festival and at the 21st Minsk International Film Festival. See Adilkhan Yerzhanov's *Brodvei* profile: http://brod.kz/persons/adilhan_erjanov/.
69. 'Britanskii kritik vklyuchil Kazakhstanskii film v top-10 Kannnskogo kinofestivalya', *Tengri News*, 28 May 2014. Accessed 1 June 2014: http://tengrinews.kz/cinema/britanskiy-kritik-vklyuchil-kazahstanskiy-film-top-10-256108/.
70. 'Kazakhfilm polozhil 'Khozyaev' na polku.
71. 'V Kazakhstane kinematograf stanovitsya ruchnym – Yerzhanov', *Karavan*, 29 December 2015. Accessed 14 January 2016: http://m.caravan.kz/gazeta/v-kazakhstane-kinematograf-stanovitsya-ruchnym–erzhanov-article117710.
72. 'Alexei Azarov, 'Shlagbaum na perekpestke nepokhozhikh sudeb', *Radio Azattyk*, 10 July 2015. Accessed 10 March 2016: http://rus.azattyq.org/content/film-shlagbaum-zhasulan-poshanov/27292434.html.
73. However, given that during the production of the film the Kazakh Tenge devalued to the tune of 50 per cent against the dollar the real budget was just $3000.
74. Katerina Tarkhanova, 'Aul krepchal: Chuma v aule Karatas rezhisser Adilkhan Yerzhanov', *Iskusstvo Kino*, No. 9, September 2016. Accessed 2 December 2016: http://kinoart.ru/archive/2016/09/aul-krepchal-chuma-v-aule-karatas-rezhisser-adilkhan-erzhanov.
75. Altai Sandybayev, 'Spisok pozoryashchikh Kazakhstan fil'mov udivil kinokritikov, *Radio Azattyk*, 10 June 2015. Accessed 12 October 2015: http://rus.azattyq.org/content/zayavlenie-ministra-o-filmakh-uroki-garmonii-khozyaeva-rieltor/27064556.html.
76. Svetlana Glushkova, 'Film 'Khozyaeva' nazvali provokatsionnym', *Radio Azattyk*, 18 March 2015. Accessed 10 March 2016: http://rus.azattyq.org/content/film-erzhanova-hozyayeva-astana/26907213.html.
77. Sandybayev, 'Spisok pozoryashchikh Kazakhstan fil'mov udivil kinokritikov.
78. 'V Kazakhstane kinematograf stanovitsya ruchnym – Yerzhanov'.
79. Comment taken from the kino.kz website: http://www.kino.kz/notice/notice.asp?id=5262.
80. Focus group with Kazakh cinema audience, 8 November 2014, Almaty, Kazakhstan.
81. Ibid.
82. Focus group with Kazakh cinema audience, 9 November 2014, Almaty, Kazakhstan.
83. Ibid.

84. Focus group with Kazakh cinema audience, 8 November 2014, Almaty, Kazakhstan.
85. Ibid.
86. Author's conversation with Serik Abishev, 7 November 2014, Almaty, Kazakhstan.
87. 'Nash orogod zarpos sornyakami i nuzhno ego vozdelyvat – Adilkhan Yerzhanov', *Dixienews*, 20 November 2014. Accessed 24 November 2011: http://dixinews.kz/articles/filmy/11744/.
88. 'V Kazakhstane kinematograf stanovitsya ruchnym – Yerzhanov'.
89. Ibid.
90. To date there have been two official screenings of *The Owners* and none of *Constructors* or *Realtors*.
91. Khrabrykh, 'Adilkhan Yerzhanov – Kazakhstanskoe kino stalo burzhuaznym'.
92. Author's interview with AdilkhanYerzhanov, Almaty, Kazakhstan, 5 November 2012.
93. Focus group with Kazakh cinema audience, 8 November 2014, Almaty, Kazakhstan.
94. 'Nash orogod zarpos sornyakami i nuzhno ego vozdelyvat – Adilkhan Yerzhanov'.
95. Author's interview Zhanna Isabayeva, 18 August 2014, Almaty, Kazakhstan.
96. Kseniya Yedokimenko, 'Zhanna Isabayeva kinorezhisser – Kommercheskoe knio – eto rabstvo', *Vremya*, 21 October 2007. Accessed 14 March 2016: http://www.time.kz/redirect_to_article/1473.
97. Baurzhan Nogerbek, *Kino v Kazakhstane: Art-Khaus i narodnoe kino*, March 2010. Accessed 11 August 2014: http://www.goethe.de/ins/ru/lp/prj/drj/top/wtt/010/kik/ru5755168.htm.
98. Aigerim Beisenbayeva, 'Ne Zhenskoe delo', *Novoe Pokolenie*, 28 September 2007. Accessed 14 March 2016: http://www.np.kz/old/2007/38/rkino.html.
99. Film 'Nagima Zhanny Isabayevoi shokiroval publiku na Berlinale', *Tengri News*, 13 February 2014. Accessed 15 March 2016: http://tengrinews.kz/cinema/film-nagima-jannyi-isabavoy-shokiroval-publiku-na-berlinale-250367/.
100. Zarina Ismailova, 'Chem Kazakhstanskii fil'm 'Nagima' Voskhitil Berlin?' *Comode*, 9 August 2014. Accessed 15 March 2016: http://comode.kz/post/novosti/chem-kazahstanskij-film-nagima-voshitil-berlin/.
101. In an interview with the author Isabayeva noted that she 'was inspired by the Kazakh New Wave'. Author's interview with Zhanna Isabayeva, 18 August 2014, Almaty, Kazakhstan.
102. Author's interview with Zhanna Isabayeva, 18 August 2014, Almaty, Kazakhstan.
103. Comment taken from the kino.kz website: http://www.kino.kz/notice/notice.asp?id=2786&page=2.
104. Focus group with Kazakh cinema audience, 8 November 2014, Almaty, Kazakhstan.

105. Comment taken from the kino.kz website: http://www.kino.kz/notice/notice. asp?id=2786&page=2.
106. This aspect of the film was also picked up by audience members' comments in both the kino.kz forum and focus groups.
107. Crescente, 'Zhanna Isabayeva'.
108. Author's interview with Baurzhan Shukenov, Director of Arman Cinema, 30 July 2014, Almaty, Kazakhstan.
109. Author's interview with Zhanna Isabayeva, 18 August 2014, Almaty, Kazakhstan.
110. *Losing Virginity in Almaty* was a highly controversial film by Isabayeva, which was released in 2011. The film featured 13 different stories about first sexual encounters. The film featured some explicit sex scenes and was removed from several cinemas in Almaty as well as inciting a reaction from the Minister of Culture who suggested 'the film would corrupt the already degrading youth'. See Makpal Mukhankyzy, 'Spory Vokrug filma 'Teryaya nevinnost v Almaty vozbudili k neu interes', *Radio Azattyk*, 12 April 2012. Accessed 16 March 2016: http://rus.azattyq.org/content/losing_innocence_in_almaty_cinema/24545749.html.
111. *Nagima* won a series of awards including the Grand Prix of Asian films at the Deauville Asian Film Festival and International Film Festival in Morocco, as well as the best feature film at the International Film Festival in El Salvador.
112. Many comments on kino.kz refer to having watched the films on DVD.
113. Comments taken from the kino.kz website: http://www.kino.kz/notice/notice. asp?id=2055&page=0.
114. Comment taken from the kino.kz website: http://www.kino.kz/notice/notice. asp?id=5277.
115. Author's interview with Kairzhan Orynbekov, 18 August 2014, Almaty, Kazakhstan.
116. Author's interview Darezhan Omirbayev, 21 August 2014, Almaty, Kazakhstan.
117. For example, in an interview with the Vremya newspaper in 2013, while his film was in production, Orynbekov talked of the need to enter the Russian market as a way to overcome the problem of limited cinemas and distribution prospects in Kazakhstan. See Tulegen Baitukenkov, Derzhi v mordy, *Vremya*, 10 January 2013. Accessed 16 March 2016: http://www.time.kz/redirect_to_article/31187.
118. 'Syn Bulata Utemuratova cnimaet 'Orgablenie po-kazakhski', *Tengri News*, 9 October 2013. Accessed 17 March 2016: http://tengrinews.kz/cinema/syin-bulata-utemuratova-snimaet-ograblenie-po-kazahski-243218/.
119. Author's interview with Kairzhan Orynbekov, 18 August 2014, Almaty, Kazakhstan.
120. Ibid.
121. Joe Crescente, 'Racketeer', *KinoKultura*, 22, 2008. Accessed 25 July 2012: http://www.kinokultura.com/2008/issue22.shtml.

122. Dmitrii Mostovoi, Chas rasplaty, *Karavan*, 23 October 2009. Accessed 7 March 2016.
123. Author's interview with Akan Satayev, 15 February 2016, Almaty, Kazakhstan.
124. Author's interview with Akan Satayev.
125. Satayev's *Strayed* was an explicit attempt to make a film that combined commercialism with the art-house genre. See 'Akan Satayev: Ne nado byt' Tarkovskim, shtoby delat' kachestvennoe kino', *Vision.kz*, 10 May 2010. Accessed 23 October 2016: http://yvision.kz/post/44716.
126. Comments taken from the kino.kz website: http://www.kino.kz/notice/notice.asp?id = 2904&page = 7.
127. Comments taken from the kino.kz website: http://www.kino.kz/notice/notice.asp?id = 2904&page = 7.
128. Comments taken from the kino.kz website: http://www.kino.kz/notice/notice.asp?id = 2203&page = 0.
129. Focus group with Kazakh cinema audience, 9 November 2014, Almaty, Kazakhstan.
130. Walters, 'Pink Bunny – Timeless Tale Set Among Modern Kazakh Youth'.
131. Nadezhda Plyaskina, 'Kokteil' dlya naroda', *Vremya*, 15 January 2011. Accessed 24 March 2016: http://www.time.kz/news/archive/2011/01/15/19664.
132. 'Kokteil dlya zvezdy', *Voxpopuli*, 8 December 2010. Accessed 24 March 2016: http://www.voxpopuli.kz/main/204-kokteyl-dlya-zvezdy-.html.
133. Focus group with Kazakh cinema audience, 8 November 2014, Almaty, Kazakhstan.
134. Author's interview with Akan Satayev.
135. 'Reiting: Potentsial'nye preemniki Nursultan Nazarbayeva', *Regnum*, 31 October 2014. Accessed 3 November 2014: http://www.regnum.ru/news/1862198.html.
136. 'Prem'era filma, Pryzhok afaliny' startovala v minuvshii uik-end', *Novoe Pokolenie*, 28 September 2009. Accessed 22 March 2016: https://www.nur.kz/133722-premera-filma-pryzhok-afaliny-startovala-v-minuvshij-uik-end.html.
137. Sergei Sakharov, 'Zagovor Oberona – udar patriotizom v mozg i yxo', *Today.kz*, 19 November 2014. Accessed 23 March 2016: http://today.kz/news/stati/2014-11-19/588847-zagovor-oberona-udar-patriotizmom-v-mozg-i-uxo/.
138. 'Prem'era filma, Pryzhok afaliny' startovala v minuvshii uik-end'.
139. Irina Boricheva, 'Kazakhstan pokazal 'Pryzhok Afaliny' i 'Drugoi Bereg', *Kinoshock*, 16 September 2009. Accessed 22 March 2014: http://www.kinoshock.ru/rus/press_centre/publication/?id = 736.
140. Author's interview with Gulnara Abikeyeva, Almaty, Kazakhstan, 5 November 2012.
141. Irina Kovaleva, 'B glavnoi roli – Astana!' *Novoe Pokolenie*, July 15 2010. Accessed 26 April 2012: http://www.np.kz/last/6161-v_glavnojj_roli__astana.html.
142. 'Kovaleva, B glavnoi roli – Astana!'.

143. Serik Mukashev, 'Rezhisser Yermek Shinarbayev o kinopoekte – Astana – lyubov moya!' *Zonakz*, 13 July 2010. Accessed 2 November 2014: https://zonakz.net:8443/articles/30228.
144. Author's interview with Yermek Shinarbayev, Almaty, Kazakhstan 7 November 2014.
145. Author's interview with Adilkhan Yerzhanov, 30 July 2014, Almaty, Kazakhstan.
146. Paul Bartlett, 'New Mini-Series Highlights Love for Astana', *Eurasianet*, 30 June 2010. Accessed 5 November 2014: http://www.eurasianet.org/node/61444.
147. Peter Rollberg, 'Small Screen Nation Building: Astana – My Love', *Demokratizatsiya*, 23 (3), 2015, p. 349.
148. Rollberg, 'Small Screen Nation Building', pp. 348–52.
149. Ibid., pp. 355–6.
150. Gulnara Abikeyeva, 'Serdtse Moe Astana', *yvision*, 27 February 2012. Accessed 23 March 2016: http://yvision.kz/post/229036.
151. Abikeyeva, 'Serdtse Moe Astana'.
152. Author's interview with Baurzhan Shukenov.
153. Comments taken from the kino.kz website: http://www.kino.kz/notice/notice.asp?id=2921&page=0.
154. Comments taken from the kino.kz website: http://www.kino.kz/notice/notice.asp?id=5251&page=1.
155. Comments taken from the kino.kz website: http://www.kino.kz/movie.asp?id=3829.

Conclusion

1. Ernest Renan, 'Qu'est-ce qu'une nation?' In John Hutchinson and Anthony Smith (eds), *Nationalism*. Oxford: Oxford University Press, 1994, p. 17.
2. Renan, 'Qu'est-ce qu'une nation?', p. 17.
3. Benedict Anderson, *Imagined Communities: Reflections on the Origin and Spread of Nationalism*. London, Verso, 1983; Eric Hobsbawm & Terence Ranger (eds), *The Invention of Tradition*. Cambridge: Cambridge University Press, 1983.
4. Craig Calhoun, *Nations Matter: Culture, History and the Cosmopolitan Dream*. Abingdon: Routledge, 2007, p. 27.
5. Anthony D. Smith, 'Gastronomy or geology? The role of nationalism in the reconstruction of nations'. *Nations and Nationalism*, 1 (1), 1994, p. 19.
6. Rima Wilkes and Michael Kehl, 'One image, multiple nationalisms: Face to Face and the Siege at Kanehsatà:ke', *Nations and Nationalism*, 20 (3), 2014, pp. 481–502.
7. Paul Brass, 'Elite Groups, Symbol Manipulation and Ethnic Identity among Muslims of South Asia' in D. Taylor and M. Yapp (eds), *Political Identity in South Asia*. London: Curzon Press, 1979, pp. 35–68 and John Breuilly, *Nationalism and the State*, 2nd Edition. Manchester: Manchester University Press, 1993.

8. Breuilly, *Nationalism and the State*. p. 1.
9. Smith, 'Gastronomy or geology?'.
10. Hobsbawm and Ranger, *The Invention of Tradition*.
11. Homi Bhabha *Nation and Narration*. London: Routledge, 1990. This is not to suggest the subjucation and oppression of colonial peoples is equivalent to an authoritarian government's repression of political rights and freedoms.
12. Bohdan Y. Nebesio, 'Questionable Foundations for a National Cinema: Ukrainian Poetic Cinema of the 1960s', *Canadian Slavonic Papers / Revue Canadienne des Slavistes*, 4 (1/2), pp. 35–46.
13. Rico Isaacs and Abel Polese (eds), *Nation-Building in the post-Soviet Space: New Tools and Approaches*. Abingdon: Routledge, 2016.
14. Hans Kohn, *The Idea of Nationalism: A Study of Its Origins and Background*. New York: The Macmillan Company, 1944; Anthony D. Smith, *The Ethnic Origins of Nations*. Oxford: Blackwell, 1986; Ernest Gellner, *Nations and Nationalism*. Oxford: Blackwell Publishers, 1983; John Plamenatz, 'Two types of Nationalism' in Eugene Kamenka (ed.), *Nationalism: The nature and evolution of an idea*. Canberra: Australian National University Press, 1975.
15. Stephen Shulman, 'Challenging the civic/ethnic and West/East dichotomies in the study of nationalism', *Comparative Political Studies*, 35 (5), 2002, pp. 554–85.
16. Taras Kuzio, 'The myth of the civic state. A critical survey of Hans Kohn's framework for understanding nationalism', *Ethnic and Racial Studies*, 25, 1, 2002, pp. 20–39; Bernard Yack, 'The myth of the civic nation', *Critical Review*, 10, 2, 1996, pp. 193–211; Fredika Björklund, 'The East European "ethnic nation" – myth or reality?', *European Journal of Political Research*, 45 (1), 2006, pp. 93–121.
17. Azamat Sarsembayev, 'Imagined Communities: Kazak nationalism and Kazakification in the 1990s', *Central Asian Survey*, 18 (3), pp. 319–46.
18. Lisa Wedeen, *Peripheral Visions: Publics, Power and Performance in Yemen*. Chicago: Chicago University Press, 2008, pp. 10–12.
19. Oxana Shevel, 'The Post-Communist Diaspora Laws: Beyond the "Good Civic versus Bad Ethnic" Nationalism Dichotomy', *East European Politics & Societies*, 24 (1), 2010, pp. 159–87; Tanya Zaharchenko, 'Polyphonic dichotomies: Memory and Identity in Today's Ukraine', *Demokratizatsiya*, 21 (2), 2013, pp. 241–69; Peter Rodgers, 'Understanding regionalism and the politics of identity in Ukraine's Eastern Borderlands', *Nationalities Papers*, 34 (2), 2006, pp. 154–74.
20. Alexander Prokhorov, 'The Unknown New Wave: Soviet Cinema of the 1960s', in Alexander Prokhorov (ed.), *Springtime for Soviet Cinema: Re/viewing the 1960s*. Pittsburgh: Pittsburgh Russian Film Symposium, 2000, p. 8.
21. Josephine Woll, *Real Images: Soviet Cinemas and the Thaw*. London and New York: I.B.Tauris, 2000, p. xiii.
22. Woll, *Real Images: Soviet Cinemas and the Thaw*. p. xiii.
23. Claudia Mesch, *Art and Politics: A Small History of Art for Social Change since 1945*. New York and London: I.B.Tauris, 2013, p. 1.

24. Francis Frascina, *Art, politics and dissent Aspects of the Art Left in Sixties America*. Manchester: Manchester University Press, 1999.
25. Julia Bryan-wilson, *Art Workers: Radical Practice in the Vietnam War Era*. Berkeley, CA: University of California Press, 2009; Matthew Israel, *Kill for Peace: American Artists Against the Vietnam War*. Austin, Texas: University of Texas Press, 2013.
26. Guy Debord, *The Society of the Spectacle*. New York: Zone Books, 1992.
27. Chun Peng, 'Chunwan, Art and Authoritarianism', *The Diplomat*, 19 February 2016. Accessed 11 November 2016: http://thediplomat.com/2016/02/chunwan-art-and-authoritarianism/.
28. Steven Ricci, *Cinema and Fascism: Italian Film and Society, 1922–1943*. Berkeley, CA: University of California Press, 2008.
29. Aristotle A. Kallis, *Cinema and Totalitarian Propaganda: 'Information' and 'Leisure' in NS Germany, 1939–45*. Houndsmill, Basingstoke: Palgrave Macmillan, 2005, p. 185.
30. Claudia Calirman, *Brazilian Art Under Dictatorship: Antonio Manuel, Artur Barrio, and Cildo Meireles*. Durham and London: Duke University Press, 2012.
31. Raymond Baker, 'Combative Cultural Politics: Film Art and Political Spaces in Egypt', *Alif: Journal of Comparative Poetics*, No. 15, Arab Cinematics: Toward the New and the Alternative, 1995, pp. 33–4.
32. Katy Pearce and Adnan Hajizada, 'No Laughing Matter: Humor as a Means of Dissent in the Digital Era: The case of Authoritarian Azerbaiijan', *Demokratizatsiya*, 22 (1), 2014, pp. 67–85.
33. Rico Isaacs, *Party System Formation in Kazakhstan: Between Formal and Informal Politics*. Abingdon: Routledge, 2011, see Chapter 4.
34. Aziz Burkhanov, *Nation-Building in Kazakhstan: Identity Formation in the Popular Culture, Media and Television*, Paper presented at the ASN World Convention Columbia University, 14–16 April 2016.
35. Ed. S. Tan, *Emotion and the Structure of Narrative Film: Film as an emotion machine*. New York and London: Routledge.
36. Seyla Benhabib, *The Reluctant Modernism of Hannah Arendt*. New Edition. Oxford: Rowman and Littlefield Publishers, 2003, p. 74.

FILMOGRAPHY

This is a selected list of the main films that are analysed in the book. It does not include those films that are mentioned only in passing. Reference to those films in the text can be found in the Index.

Aldar Kose (*Besborodyi obmanshchik*, Kazakhfilm, 1964) director: Shaken Aimanov; scriptwriters: Shaken Aimanov, Lev Varshavskii; cast: Shaken Aimanov, Yelubai Umurzakov.

Amangeldy (*Amangel'dy*, Lenfilm, 1939) director: Moisei Levin; scriptwriters: Vsevolod Ivanov, Beimbet Mailin, Gabit Musrepov; cast: Yelubai Umurzakov, Serke Kozhamkulov, Kurmanbek Dzhandarbekov.

ASSA (Mosfilm: Studio Krug, 1987) director: Sergei Solov'ev; scriptwriters: Sergei Livnev, Sergei Solov'ev, Natan Eidel'man; cast: Tat'iana Drubich, Stanislav Govorukhin, Sergei Bugaev.

Astana – My Love (*Astana – lyubov' moya*, Kazakhfilm, Turkish Radio and Television Corporation, 2010) director: Yermek Shinarbayev; scriptwriters: Leila Ahinzhanova, Eugene Nikishov, Valery Fedorovich, Irina Nakaryakova; cast: Adil Akhmetov, Bakhar Akcha, Bibigul' Suyunshalina.

Baksy (*Baksy – Native Dancer*, Kazakhfilm, Les Petites Lumieres, Kinofabrika, Kinokompaniya CTB, 2008) director: Guka Omarova; scriptwriters: Sergei Bodrov, Guka Omarova; cast: Nesipkul' Umarbekova, Farkhat Amankulov, Almaty Ayanov, Tolepbergen Baisakalov.

Balcony, The (*Balkon*, Kazakhfilm, 1987) director: Kalykbek Salykov; scriptwriters: Shakhimarden Khusaniov, Olzhas Suleimenov; cast: Ismail Igil'manov, Yurii Goroshevskii, Karina Zibagul.

Book of Legends: The Mysterious Forest, The (*Kniga legend: tainstvennyi les*, Kazakhfilm, 2012) director: Akhat Ibrayev; screenwriter: Akhat Ibrayev; cast: Alisher Khairov, Kuan Lekerov, Farkhad Abdraimov, Dinmukhammed Akhimov, Ainur Niyazova.

Botagoz (Alma-Ata Studio, 1957) director: Yefim Aron; screenwriters: A. Filippov, Mukhametkali Khasenov; cast: Gul'fairus Ismailova, Asanali Ashimov, Nina Grebeshkova.

Breaking the Vicious Circle (*Put' lidera. Razryvaya zamknutyi krug*, Kazakhfilm, 2015) director: Rustem Abdrashev; screenwriters: Shakimarden Khusainov, Rustem Abdrashev, Gennadii Zemel'; cast: Nurlan Alimzhanov, Madina Yesmanova, Valentin Gaft, Sergei Shakurov, Islyam Nurtazin.

Butter (*Maslo – Mai*, Kazakfilm, 2008) director: Serik Abishev; screenwriters: Serik Abishev, Adilkhan Yerzhanov; cast: Dauren Kasenov.

Cardiogram (*Kardiogramma*, Kazakhfilm, 1995) director: Darezhan Omirbayev; scriptwriter: Darezhan Omirbayev; cast: Zhasulan Asauov Gulnara Dusmatova, Ilyas Kalymbetov, Saule Toktybayeva.

Cocktail for a Star (*Kokteil' dlya zvezdy*, Kazakhstan Telekanal, 2010) director: Askar Uzakbayev; scriptwriters: Daniyar Kumisbayev, Askar Uzakbayev; cast: Bayan Yesentayeva. Mol'dir Auel'bekova, Nurtas Adambai, Meirambek Bespayev, Aigul Imanbayeva.

Conspiracy of Oberon (*Zagovor Oberona*, Kazakhfilm, 2014) director: Aidar Batalov; screenwriter: Adil'bek Zhaksybekov; cast: Erik Zholzhaksynov, Yerdos Tulegenov, Ainur Niyazova, Saltanat Nauruz.

Constructors (*Stroiteli*, Short Brothers, 2013) director: Adilkhan Yerzhanov; scriptwriter: Adilkhan Yerzhanov; cast: Rauf Khabibllin, Yerbolat Yerzhanov.

Dolphin's Jump (*Pryzhok Afaliny*, Kazakhfilm, 2009) director: Eldor Urazbayev; scriptwriter: Adil'bek Zhaksybekov; cast: Farkhad Amankulov, Aziz Beishenailev, Dariya Moroz, Konstantin Milovanov, Erik Zholzhaksynov.

Fall of Otrar, The (*Gibel' Otrar* (*Otrardyn kuyreyi*), Kazakhfilm, 1991) director: Ardak Amirkulov; scriptwriters: Aleksei German, Svetlana Karmalita; cast: Shukur Burkhanov, Shukhrat Iragshev, Roman Khomiatov.

Gift to Stalin, The (*Podarok Stalinu*, Aldongar Profuctions, 2008) director: Rustem Abdrashev; scriptwriters: Pavel Finn, Rustem Ibragimbekov, Viktor Markin; cast: Nurmzuman Ikhtymbayev, Dalen Shantemirov, Yekaterina Rednikova.

Harmony Lessons (*Uroki garmonii*, Kazakhfilm, 2013) director: Emir Baigazin; scriptwriter: Emir Baigazin; cast: Timur Aidarbekov, Aslan Anarbayev, Mukhtar Andasov.

Iron Mountain (*Zheleznaya gora*, Kazakhfilm, 2013) director: Rustem Abdrashev; scriptwriters: Shakhimarden Khusainov, Rustem Abdrashev; cast: Nurlan Alimzhanov, Nurzhuman Ikhymbayev, Natal'ya Arinbasarova.

Kairat (Kazakhfilm, 1991) director: Darezhan Omirbayev; scriptwriter: Darezhan Omirbayev; cast: Kairat Makhmedov, Indira Zheksembayeva.

Karoy (Sun Production, 2007) director: Zhanna Isabayeva; scriptwriter: Zhanna Isabayeva; cast: Yerzhan Tusupov, Rymkesh Omarkhanova, Aiman Aimagambetova.

Kazakh Robbery, The (*Ograblenie po-kazakhski*, Moviq, 2014) director: Kairzhan Orynbekov; scriptwriters: Fuad Ibragimbekov, Kairzhan Orynbekov; cast: Zhandos Aibasov, Aryzhan Dzhazil'bekova, Igor Shin, Aleksei Yegorov, Tolepbergen Baisakalov.

Kelin (*Nevestka*, Kazakhfilm, 2009) director: Yermek Tursunov; scriptwriter: Yermek Tursunov; cast: Gulsharat Zhubayeva, Turakhan Sadykov, Yerzhan Nurymbet.

Kelinka Sabina (*The Bride Sabina*, Nurtas Production/Sedmoi Kanal, 2014) director: Nurtas Adambayev; scriptwriter: Nurtas Adambayev; cast: Nurtas Adambayev, Ainur Ilyasova, Yerlan Kasymzhanuly, Zhan Izbasar

Kyz-Zhibek (*The Silk Maiden*, Kazakhfilm, 1969–70) director: Sultan Khodzhikov; scriptwriters: Gabit Musrepov; cast: Meruert Utekesheva, Kuman Tastanbekov, Asanali Ashimov.

Land of the Fathers (*Zemlya Ottsov*, Kazakhfilm, 1966) director: Shaken Aimanov; scriptwriter: Olzhas Suleimenov; cast: Yelubei Umirzakov, Murat Akhmadiev, Yuri Pomerantsev.

Last Stop, The (*Konechnaya ostanovka*, Kazakhfilm, 1989) director: Serik Aprymov; scriptwriter: Serik Aprimov; cast: Sabit Kurmanbekov, Bakhitzhan Alpeisov, Murat Akhmetov.

Leila's Prayer (*Molitva Leily*, Kazakhfilm, 2002) director: Satybaldy Narymbetov; scriptwriter: Roza Mukanova; cast: Azhanat Yesmagambetova, Baadur Tsuladze, Yuri Kapustin.

Little Fish in Love (*Blyublennaya rybka*, Kazakhfilm, 1989) director: Abai Karpykov; scriptwriter: Abai Karpykov, Boris Ryakhovskii; cast: Bopesh Zhandayev, Galina Shatenova, Natal'ya Novikova, Satar Dikambayev.

Little People (*Malen'kie lyudi*, Kazakhfilm, 2003) director: Nariman Turebayev; scriptwriter: Nariman Turebayev; cast: Yerzhan Bekmuratov, Oleg Kerimov, Mira Abdulina, Lyazat Dautova.

Mongol (Andreevski Flag/Kinokompaniya CTB/X-Filme Creative Pool, 2007) director: Sergei Bodrov; scriptwriters: Arif Aliyev, Sergei Bodrov; cast: Tadanobu Asano, Sun Honglei, Chuluuny Khulan, Amadu Mamadakov.

My Dear Children (*Oipyrmai ili dorogie moi deti*, Cosmos Art, 2009) director: Zhanna Isabayeva; scriptwriter: Zhanna Isabayeva; cast: Alikhan Idrisheva, Yerbolat Tolegenov, Aikyn Kalykov, Raya Adyganova, Tolepbergen Baisakalov.

My Name is Kozha (*Menya zovut Kozha*, Kazakhfilm, 1963) director: Abdullah Karsakbayev; scriptwriters: Berdybek Sokpakbayev, Nisson Zeleranskii; cast: Nurlan Segizbayev, M. Kokenov, Gul'nar Kurabayeva, E. Kurmashev.

Nagima (Sun Production, 2014) director: Zhanna Isabayeva; scriptwriter: Zhanna Isabayeva; cast: aidar Mukhametzhanov, Galina P'yanova, Dina Tukbayeva, Nazar Sultanbayev.

Needle, The (*Igla*, Kazakhfilm, 1988) director: Rashid Nugmanov; scriptwriters: Aleksandr Baranov, Bakhyt Kilibayev; cast: Viktor Tsoi, Marina Smirnova, Petr Mamonov, Aleksandr Bashirov.

Nomad (*Kochevnik/Köshpendiler*, Ibrus/Kazakhfilm/True Story Production/Wild Bunch, 2005), directors: Sergei Bodrov, Ivan Passer and Talgat Temenov; scriptwriter: Rustam Ibragimbekov; cast: Jay Hernandez, Dilnaz Akhmadiyeva, Kuno Becker, Mark Dacascos, Jason Scott Lee.

Owners, The (*Khozyaeva/Ukkili kamshat*, Kazakhfilm, 2014) director: Adilkhan Yerzhanov; scriptwriters: Adilkhan Yerzhanov, Rolaf Yan Minneboo; cast: Yerbolat Yerzhanov, Aidyn Sakhman, Aliya Zainalova, Bauyrzhan Kaptagai.

Plague in the Village of Karatas, The (*Chuma v aule Karatas*, Partizanskogo Kino, 2016) director: Adilkhan Yerzhanov; scriptwriter: Adilkhan Yerzhanov; cast: Aibek, Kudabayev, Nurbek Mukushev, Tolganay Talgat, Konstantin Kozlov.

Poem about Love (*Poema o lyubvi*, Kazakhfilm, 1954) directors: Shaken Aimanov and Karl Gakkel'; scriptwriter: Gabit Musperov; cast: Sholpan Dzhandarbekova, Nurmukhan Zhanturin, Serke Kozhamkulov.

Promised Land, The (*Zemlya obetovannaya/Zheruik*, Kazakhfilm, 2011) director: Slambek Tauyekel; scriptwriters: Lavrentii Son, Slambek Tauekel; cast: Bolat Abdil'manov, Raikhan Aitkozhanova, Nazgul' Karabalina, Yerzhan Nurymbet.

Racketeer (*Reketir*, Sataifilm, 2007) director: Akan Satayev; scriptwriter: Timur Zhaksylykov; cast: Sayat Isembayev, Vladimir Vdovichenkov, Zhan Baizhanbayev, Tolepbergen Baisakalov.

Realtors (*Rieltor*, Kazakhfilm, 2011) director: Adilkhan Yerzhanov; scriptwriter: Adilkhan Yerzhanov; Dauren Kasenov, Baurzhan Ishpanov, Akerke Kaltai, Aidyn Sakhamanov.

Renaissance Island (*Ostrov Vozrozhdeniya*, Kazakhfilm, 2004) director: Rustem Abdrashev; scriptwriters: Rustem Abdrashev, Galia Yeltai, Gaziz Nasyrov; cast: Temirzhan Daniyarov, Zhanel' Makazhanova, Sayat Merekenov, Nurzhuman Ikhtymbayev.

River of Fire (*Ognennaya reka*, Kazakhfilm, 2013) director: Rustem Abdrashev; scriptwriters: Shakhimarden Khusainov, Rustem Abdrashev; cast: Nurzhuman Ikhtymbayev, Natal'ya Arinbasarova, Nurlan Alimzhanov.

Road to Mother, The (*Doroga k materi*, Kazakhfilm/Sataifilm, 2016) director: Akan Satayev; scriptwriter: Timur Zhaksylykov; cast: Altynai Nogerbek, Adil Akhmetov, Aruzhan Dzhazil'bekova, Berik Aitzhanov, Bolat Abdil'manov.

Sardar (Kazakhfilm, 2003) director: Bolat Kalymbetov; Odel'sha Agishev, Bolat Kalymbetov; cast: Kuandyk Kystykbayev, Sana Shandybayeva, Yerzhan Nurymbet, Tungyshbai Dzhamankulov.

Shal (*Starik*/*The Old Man*, Kazakhfilm, 2012) director: Yermek Tursunov; scriptwriter: Yermek Tursunov; cast: Yerbolat Toguzakov, Isbek Abil'mazhinov.

Sky of My Childhood (*Nebo moego detstva*, Kazakhfilm, 2012) director: Rustem Abdrashev; scriptwriters: Shakhimarden Khusainov, Rustem Abdrashev; cast: Nurlan Alimzhanov, Nurzhuman Ikhtymbayev, Bibigul' Tulegenova, Asylkhan Tolepov.

Story of Kazakh Cinema, The (*Istoriya Kazakhstanskogo kino*, documentary, KBS Busan, 2016) director: Adilkhan Yerzhanov.

Strayed (*Zabludivshisya*, Sataifilm, 2009) director: Akan Satayev; scriptwriter: Timur Zhaksylykov; cast: Andrei Merzlikin, Tung'shbai Zhamankulov, Almagul' Rulas, Il'yas Sadyrov.

Surzhekey – the Angel of Death (*Surzhekei – Angel smerti*, Katarsis, 1991) director: Damir Manabayev; scriptwriters: Smagul Yelubayev, Damir Manabayev; cast: Nurmukhan Zhanturin, Meirman Nurekeyev, Zhanas Iskakov.

Tale of the Pink Bunny (*Skaz o rozovom zaitse*, Kazakhfilm, 2010) director: Farkhat Sharipov; scriptwriter: Farkhat Sharipov; cast: Anuar Nurpeisov, Maksim Akbarov, Karlygash Mukhamedzhanova, Farkhat Abdraimov.

Tulpan (*Tyul'pan*/*Tulip*, Pallas Film/Pandora/CTB Film Company/ Eurasia Film, 2008) director: Sergei Dvortsevoy; scriptwriters: Gennadii Ostrovskii, Sergei Dvortsevoy; cast: Askhat Kuchincherkov, Samal Yeslyamova, Ondasyn Besikbasov, Tolepbergen Baisakalov.

Turksib (documentary, Vostokkino, 1929) director: Viktor Turin.

Ya-Ha (*Ya-khkha*, short, VGIK, 1986) director: Rashid Nugmanov; scriptwriter: Rashid Nugmanov; cast: Boris Grebenshchchikov, Maik Naumenko, Viktor Tsoi, Konstantin Kinchev.

Zhambyl (*Dzhambyl*, Kazakhfilm, 1952) director: Efim Dzigan; scriptwriters: Nikolai Pogodin, Abdil'da Tazhibayev; cast: Shaken Aimanov, Kurmanbek Zhandarbekov, German Khovanov, Nurmukhan Zhanturin.

Zhauzhurek Myn Bala (*Voisko Myn Bala/Myn Bala: Warriors of the Steppe*, Kazakhfilm/Sataifilm, 2011) director: Akan Satayev; scriptwriters: Timur Zhaksylykov, Zhayk Syzdykov, Mukhamedzhan Mamyrbekov; cast: Asylkhan Tolypov, Ayan Utepbergen, Kuralai Anabekova, Tlektes Meiramov.

SELECTED BIBLIOGRAPHY

Abikeyeva, Gulnara, *The Heart of the World: Films from Central Asia*. Almaty: Shaken Aimanov, Kazakhfilm National Company/SKIF/Kino firm (Almaty, 2003).
———, *Natsiostroitel'stvo v Kazakhstane i drugikh stranakh Tsentral'noi Azii i kak etot protsess otrazhaetsya v kinematografe*, 'TSTSAK' (Almaty, 2004).
Adaeva, G.A. and Makulbekov, A.T., 'Obraz zhenshchin v turkoyazychnoi kul'ture', *Nauka I Mir: Mezhunarodnyi Nauchnyi Zhurnal*, 2 (6), 2014, pp. 215–217.
Akbarzadeh, Sharam, 'Why Did Nationalism Fail in Tajikistan?' *Europe-Asia Studies*, 48 (7), 1996, pp. 1105–29.
Akiner, Shirin, *Central Asia: New Arc of Crisis?* Whitehall Papers, Royal United Services Institute for Defence Studies (London, 1993).
———, *The Formation of Kazakh Identity: from Tribe to Nation-State*. Former Soviet State Papers, Royal Institute of International Affairs (London, 1995).
———, 'Melting Pot, Salad Bowl – Cauldron? Manipulation and Mobilisation of Ethnic and Religious Identities in Central Asia', *Ethnic and Racial Studies*, 20 (2), 1997, pp. 362–98.
Amrekulov, Nurlan, 'Zhuzy v sotsial'no-politicheskoi zhizni Kazakhstana', *Tsentral'naia Aziia i Kavkaz*, 3 (9), 2000.
Anderson, Benedict, *Imagined Communities: Reflections on the Origin and Spread of Nationalism*, Verso (London, 1983).
Anthias, Floya and Yual-Davis, Nira, *Women and the Nation-State*, Palgrave Macmillan (Basingstoke, 1989).
Asfendiarov, Sanjar Dzhafarovich, *Istoriya Kazakhstana*, Kazakh University (Almaty, 1993).
Baatar, T.S., 'Present Situation of Kazakh-Mongolian Community', *The Mongolian Journal of International Affair*s (Ulaanbaatar), nos 8–9, 2002.
Baipankov, Karl and Kumekov, Bulat E., 'The Kazakhs', in I. Chaahyaradlehabib and K.M. Baipakov (eds), *History of Civilizations of Central Asia Vol V, Development in contrast: From the Sixteenth to the Mid-Nineteenth Century*, UNESCO Publishing (Paris, 1998).
Baker, Raymond, 'Combative Cultural Politics: Film Art and Political Spaces in Egypt', *Alif: Journal of Comparative Poetics*, 15, Arab Cinematics: Toward the New and the Alternative, 1995.

Balibar, Etienne, 'The Nation Form: history and ideology', in Etienne Balibar and Immanuel Wallerstein (eds), *Race, Nation, Class: ambiguous identities*, Verso (London, 1991).
Barth, Fredrik, *Ethnic Groups and Boundaries*, George Allen & Unwin (Bergen-Oslo and London: Universitets Forlaget, 1969).
Barthes, Roland, *Image, Music, Text*. Fontana Press, (London, 1977).
Barton, George Aaron, *Semitic and Hamitic origins: Social and Religious*, University of Pennsylvania Press (Philadelphia, 1934).
Beckwith, Christopher I., *Empires of the Silk Road: A History of Central Eurasia from the Bronze Age to the Present*, Princeton University Press (Princeton and Oxford, 2009).
Benhabib, Seyla, *The Reluctant Modernism of Hannah Arendt*, New Edition, Rowman and Littlefield (Oxford, 2003).
Benjamin, Walter, *Illuminations*, Schocken Books (New York, 2007 [1968]).
Bennigsen, Alexandre and Broxup, Marie, *The Islamic Threat to the Soviet State*, Croom Helm (London, 1983).
Bennigsen, Alexandre and Wimbush, S. Enders, *Mystics and Commissars: Sufism in the Soviet Union*, University of California Press (Berkeley and Los Angeles, CA, 1985).
Bergne, Paul, *The Birth of Tajikistan: National Identity and the Origins of the Republic*, I.B.Tauris (London, 2007).
Berry, Chris and Farquhar, Mary, *China on Screen: Cinema and Nation*, Colombia University Press (New York, 2006).
Beumers, Birgit, 'Waves, Old and New, in Kazakh Cinema', *Studies in Russian and Soviet Cinema*, 4 (2), 2010, pp. 203–9.
———, *Directory of World Cinema: RUSSIA 2*. Intellect (Bristol and Chicago, 2015).
Bezertinov, Rafael, *Tengrianstvo – religiya turkov i mongolov, Naberezhnye*, Chelny (Tatarstan, Russian Federation, 2000).
Bhabha, Homi, *Nation and Narration*, Routledge (London, 1990).
Billig, Michael, *Banal Nationalism*, Sage Publications (Thousand Oaks, CA, 1995).
Björklund, Fredika, 'The East European "ethnic nation" – myth or reality?', *European Journal of Political Research*, 45 (1), 2006, pp. 93–121.
Bohr, Annette, 'The Central Asian States as Nationalising Regimes', in G. Smith (ed.), *Nation-Building in post-Soviet Borderlands: The Politics of National Identities*, Cambridge University Press (Cambridge, 1998), pp. 139–66.
Bonnefoy, Yves, *Asian mythologies*, University of Chicago Press (Chicago, 1993).
Brass, Paul, 'Elite Groups, Symbol Manipulation and Ethnic Identity among Muslims of South Asia', in D. Taylor and M. Yapp (eds), *Political Identity in South Asia*, Curzon Press (London, 1979), pp. 35–68.
Bremer, Ian and Taras, Ray (eds), *New States New Politics: Building post-Soviet nations*, Cambridge University Press (Cambridge, 1997).
Bremmer, Ian and Welt, Cory, 'The Trouble with Democracy in Kazakhstan', *Central Asian Survey*, 15 (2), 1996, pp. 179–99.
Breuilly, John, *Nationalism and the State*, 2nd Edition, Manchester University Press (Manchester, 1993).
Brubaker, Rogers, 'Nationhood and the National Question in the Soviet Union and post-Soviet Eurasia: an institutionalist account', *Theory and Society*, 23, 1994, pp. 23–47.

———, 'National Minorities, Nationalizing States, and External National Homelands in the New Europe', *Daedalus*, 124 (2), 1995.
———, *Nationalism Reframed: Nationhood and the national question in the New Europe*, Cambridge University Press (Cambridge, 1996).
———, 'Ethnicity Without Groups', *European Journal of Sociology*, 3 (2), 2002.
———, *Ethnicity Without Groups*, Harvard University Press (Cambridge, MA, 2004).
Bryan-Wilson, Julia, *Art Workers: Radical Practice in the Vietnam War Era*, University of California Press (Berkeley, CA, 2009).
Burkhanov, Aziz, *Nation-Building in Kazakhstan: Identity Formation in the Popular Culture, Media and Television*, paper presented at the ASN World Convention Columbia University, 14–16 April 2016.
Burkhanov, Aziz and Sharipova, Dina, 'Kazakhstan's Civic Identity: Ambiguous Policies and Points of Resistance', in Mariya Omelicheva (ed.), *Nationalism and Identity Construction in Central Asia: Dimensions, Dynamics, and Directions*, Lexington Books (Lanham, MD, 2014) pp. 21–36.
Bustanov, Alfrid K., *Soviet Orientalism and the Creation of Central Asian Nations*, Routledge (Abingdon, 2015).
Calhoun, Craig, *Nations Matter: Culture, History and the Cosmopolitan Dream*, Routledge (Abingdon, 2007).
Calirman, Claudia, *Brazilian Art Under Dictatorship: Antonio Manuel, Artur Barrio, and Cildo Meireles*, Duke University Press (Durham and London, 2012).
Cameron, Sarah, *The Hungry Steppe: Soviet Kazakhstan and the Kazakh Famine 1921–1934*, PhD dissertation, Yale University, 2011.
Collins, Kathleen, *Clan Politics and Regime Transition in Central Asia*, Cambridge University Press (Cambridge, 2006).
Commercio, Michele, 'The "Pugachev Rebellion" in the Context of Post-Soviet Kazakh Nationalisation', *Nationalities Papers*, 32 (1), 2004, pp. 87–113.
Critichlow, James, 'Corruption, Nationalism, and the Native Elites in Central Asia', *Journal of Communist Studies*, 4 (2), 1988, pp. 143–61.
Crofts, Stephen, 'Concepts of National Cinema', in John Hill and Pamela Church Gibson (eds), *The Oxford Guide to Film Studies*, Oxford University Press (Oxford, 1998).
Cummings, Sally N., 'Legitimation and Identification in Kazakhstan', *Nationalism and Ethnic Politics*, 12 (2), 2006, pp. 177–204.
———, 'Soviet Rule, Nation and Film: the Kyrgyz wonder years', *Nations and Nationalism*, 15 (4), 2009, pp. 636–57.
———, *Understanding Central Asia: politics and contested transformations*, Routledge (New York, 2012).
Dagiev, Dagikhudo, *Regime Transition in Central Asia: Stateness, Nationalism and Political Change in Tajikistan and Uzbekistan*, Routledge (London and New York, 2014).
Dave, Bhavna, *Kazakhstan, Ethnicity, Language and Power*, Routledge (London, 2007).
Debord, Guy, *The Society of the Spectacle*, Zone Books (New York, 1992).
de Saussure, Ferdinand, *Course in General Linguistics (trans. Roy Harris)*, Duckworth (London: 1983 [1916]).
Deutsch, Karl W., *Nationalism and Social Communication*, 2nd Edition, MIT Press (Cambridge, MA, 1953).

Deutsch, Karl W. and Foltz, William J. (eds), *Nation-Building in Comparative Contexts*, Transaction Publishers (New Brunswick, NJ, 1966).

Dissanayake, Wimal, *Colonialism and Nationalism in Asian Cinema*, Indiana University Press (Bloomington, IN, 1994).

Dönmez-Colin, Gönül, *Cinemas of the Other: A Personal Journey with Film-Makers from Central Asia*, 2nd Edition, Intellect (Bristol and Chicago, 2012).

Dubuisson, Eva-Marie and Genina, Anna, 'Claiming an Ancestral Homeland: Kazakh Pilgrimage and Migration in Inner Asia', in Madeleine Reeves (ed.), *Movement, Power and Place in Central Asia and Beyond: Contested Trajectories*, Routledge (New York, 2012) pp. 111–28.

Dughlat, Mirza Muhammad Haidar, *The Tarikh i Rashidi*, Forgotten Books (London, 2013 [1895]).

Fenton, Steve, 'Indifference towards national identity: what young adults think about being English and British', *Nations and Nationalism* 13 (2), 2007, pp. 321–39.

Fichte, Johann Gottlieb (ed.), *Address to the German Nation*, George Armstrong Kelly, Harper & Row Publishers (New York and Evanston, 1968).

Fisher, Lyn R., *Qazaqjylyq: Nationalism and revolution in Kazakhstan, 1900–1920*, Theses, Dissertations, Professional Papers. Paper 3337, University of Montana (Montana, 1989).

Foucault, Michel, 'The Subject and Power', *Critical Inquiry*, 8 (4) (Summer, 1982), pp. 777–95.

Franklin, Bruce (ed.), *The Essential Stalin: Major Theoretical Writings 1905–1952*, Croom Helm (London, 1973).

Frascina, Francis, *Art, Politics and Dissent: Aspects of the Art Left in Sixties America*, Manchester University Press (Manchester, 1999).

Gellner, Ernest, *Thought and Change*, Weidenfeld and Nicolson (London, 1964).

———, *Nations and Nationalism*, 2nd Edition, Blackwell Publishing (Malden, MA, 2006).

Georg Geiss, Paul, *Pre-Tsarist and Tsarist Central Asia: Communal Commitment and Political Order in Change*, Routledge (London, 2003).

Gibb, Hamilton, *The Arab Conquests in Central Asia*, The Royal Asiatic Society (London, 1923).

Gillespie, David, *Early Soviet Cinema: Innovation, Ideology and Propaganda*, Wallflower Publications (London, 2000).

Ginn, Megan A., *A Comparative Study: Women's Rights in Kazakhstan, Uzbekistan, and Tajikistan*, Honors in the Major Theses. Paper 67, 2016.

Gleason, Gregory, 'Fealty and Loyalty: Informal Authority Structures in Soviet Asia', *Soviet Studies*, 43 (4), 1991, pp. 613–28.

Gorenburg, Dimity, 'Soviet Nationalities Policy and Assimilation' in Dominique Arel and Blair A. Ruble (eds), *Rebounding Identities: The Politics of Identity in Russia and Ukraine*, Johns Hopkins University Press (Baltimore, 2006), pp. 273–303.

Gumilyev, Lev, *Drevnie Tyurki*, Airis press (Moscow, 2013 [1964]).

Hagheyeghi, Mehradad, *Islam and Politics in Central Asia*, Palgrave MacMillan (London, 1995).

Hake, Sabine, *German National Cinema*, Routledge (London and New York, 2000).

Hall, Stuart, 'Introduction', in Stuart Hall (ed.), *Representation: Cultural Representations and Signifying Practices*, Sage Publications (London, 1997), pp. 1–13.

———, 'The Work of Representations', in Stuart Hall (ed.), *Representation: Cultural Representations and Signifying Practices*, Sage Publications (London, 1997), pp. 13–74.

Hambly, Gavin, *Central Asia*, Delacorte Press (New York, 1969).

Hancock-Parmer, Michael, *Historiography of the Bare-Footed Flight: Dynamics of a National History*, Dissertation, Central Eurasian Studies, Indiana University, 2011.

———, *From Qazaqs to Kazakhs: The Study of Eighteenth-Century Qazaqs by Nineteenth Century Russophone Scholars*, paper given at Central Eurasian Studies Conference, 17 October 2015, George Washington University, Washington, DC.

———, 'The Soviet Study of the Barefooted Flight of the Kazakhs', *Central Asian Survey* 34 (3), 2015, pp. 281–95.

Haugen, Arne, *The Establishment of National Republics in Soviet Central Asia*, Palgrave Macmillan (Houndsmill, Basingstoke, 2003).

Haynes, John, *New Soviet Man: Gender and Masculinity in Stalinist Soviet Cinema*, Manchester University Press (Manchester, 2003).

Hearn, Jonathan, *Re-thinking Nationalism: A Critical Introduction*, Palgrave Macmillan (Houndsmill, Basingstoke, 2006).

Hechter, Michael, *Internal Colonialism: the Celtic Fringe in British National Development, 1536–1966*, Routledge & Kegan Paul (London and Henley, 1975).

Higbee, Will and Hwee Lim, Song, 'Concepts of transnational cinema: towards a critical transnationalism in film studies', *Transnational Cinemas*, 1 (1), 2010, pp. 7–21.

Higson, Andrew, 'The Concept of National Cinema', *Screen*, 30 (4), 1989, pp. 36–47.

———, *Waving the Flag: Constructing a National Cinema in Britain*, Oxford University Press (Oxford, 1995).

Hill, John, 'The issue of national cinema and national film production', in D. Petrie (ed.), *New Questions of British Cinema*, London: BFI, 1992, pp. 10–21.

Hill, Steven, 'A Quantitative View of Soviet Cinema', *Cinema Journal*, 11 (2), 1972, pp. 18–25.

Hirsch, Francine, *Empire of Nations: Ethnographic knowledge and the making of the Soviet Union*, Cornell University Press (New York, 2005).

Hjort, Mette and Mackenzie, Scott (eds), *Cinema and Nation*, Routledge (London and New York, 2000).

Hobsbawm, Eric J., *Nations and Nationalism since 1780: Programme, Myth, reality*, Cambridge University Press (Cambridge, 1990).

Hobsbawm, Eric J. and Ranger, Terence (eds), *The Invention of Tradition*, Cambridge University Press (Cambridge, 1983).

Holloway, Ron, 'Interview with Rashid Nugmanov', *Cinemaya, The Asian Film Quarterly*, No. 54–55, 2002, pp. 13–19.

Horton, Andrew, 'Nomad from Kazakhstan: An Interview with Rashid Nugmanov', *Film Criticism*, 14 (2), 1990, pp. 33–8.

Horton, Andrew and Brashinsky, Michael, *The Zero Hour: Glasnost and Soviet Cinema in Transition*, Princeton University Press (Princeton, NJ, 1992).

Hossain Raju, Zakir, *Bangladesh Cinema and National Identity: In Search of the Modern?* Routledge (London and New York, 2015).

Isaacs, Rico, '"Papa" – Nursultan Nazarbayev and the Discourse of Charismatic Leadership and Nation-Building in Post-Soviet Kazakhstan', *Studies in Ethnicities and Nationalism*, 10 (3), 2010, pp. 435–52.

———, *Party System Formation in Kazakhstan: Between Formal and Informal Politics*, Routledge (Abingdon, 2011).

———, 'Nomads, Warriors and Bureaucrats: Nation-Building and Film in post-Soviet Kazakhstan', *Nationalities Papers*, 43 (3), 2015, pp. 399–416.

Isaacs, Rico and Polese, Abel, 'Nation-Building in the Post-Soviet Space: Old, New and Changing Tools' in Rico Isaacs and Abel Polese (eds), *Nation-Building and Identity in the Post-Soviet Space: New Tools and Approaches*, Routledge (London and New York, 2016), pp. 1–23.

Israel, Matthew, *Kill for Peace: American Artists Against the Vietnam War*, University of Texas Press (Austin, TX, 2013).

Kadyrzhanov, Rustem, 'Natsional'naya ideya i natsional'naya politika v sovremennom Kazakhstane', *Kazakhstan Institute for Strategic Studies*, 29 June 2007. Available at http://kisi.kz/ru/categories/politicheskaya-modernizaciya/posts/nacional-naya-ideya-i-nacional-naya-politika-v-sovremen (accessed 24 September 2012).

Kallis, Aristotle A., *Cinema and Totalitarian Propaganda: 'Information' and 'Leisure' in NS Germany, 1939–45*, Palgrave Macmillan (Basingstoke, 2005).

Karin Erlan and Chebotarev, Andrei, 'The Policy of Kazakhization in State and Government Institutions in Kazakhstan', in N. Oka (ed.), *The Nationalities Question in Post-Soviet Kazakhstan*, Institute of Developing Economics (Chiba, 2000).

Kaskabassov, S.A., *Kazakhskaya vol'shebnaya skazka*, Nauka (Alma-Ata, 1972).

Kelly, John, D., 'Time and the Global: Against the Homogenous, Empty Communities in Contemporary Social Theory', *Development and Change*, 29 (4), pp. 839–71.

Kendirbaeva, Gulnar, '"We are Children of Alash . . .": The Kazakh Intelligentsia at the Beginning of the 20th Century in Search of National Identity and Prospects of the Cultural Survival of the Kazakh people', *Central Asian Survey*, 18 (1), 1999, pp. 5–36.

Kenez, Peter, *Cinema and Soviet Society*, Cambridge University Press (Cambridge, 1992).

Kesici, Özgecan, 'The Dilemma in the Nation-Building Process: The Kazakh or Kazakhstani Nation?' *Journal on Ethnopolitics and Minority Issues in Europe*, 10 (1), 2011, pp. 31–58.

Kohn, Hans, *The Idea of Nationalism: A Study of Its Origins and Background*, Macmillan Company (New York, 1944).

Kolstø, Pål, 'Anticipating Demographic Superiority: Kazakh Thinking on Integration and Nation Building', *Europe-Asia Studies*, 50 (1), 1998, pp. 51–96.

Korestelina, Karina, 'Mapping national identity narratives in Ukraine', *Nationalities Papers*, 41 (2), 2013, pp. 293–315.

Kozybaev, M.K., Abylkhozhin, Zh. B. and Aldazhumanov, K.S., *Kollektivizatsiia v Kazakhstane: tragediia krest'ianstva*, Alma-Ata: Ministerstvo narodnogo obrazovaniia Respubliki Kazakhstan, 1992.

Kudaibergenova, Diana T., '"Imagining community" in Soviet Kazakhstan. An historical analysis of narrative on nationalism in Kazakh-Soviet literature', *Nationalities Papers*, 45 (5), 2013, pp. 839–54.

Kurganov, Ivan, 'The Problem of Nationality in Soviet Russia', *Russian Review*, 10 (4), 1951.

Kuzio, Taras, '"Nationalizing states" or "Nation-Building"? A critical review of the theoretical literature and empirical evidence', *Nations and Nationalism*, 7 (2), 2001, pp. 135–54.

———, 'The myth of the civic state: a critical survey of Hans Kohn's framework for understanding nationalism', *Ethnic and Racial Studies*, 25 (1), 2002, pp. 20–39.

Landau, Jacob M., *Pan-Turkism: From Irredentism to Cooperation*, University of Indiana Press (Bloomington, IN, 1995).

Laruelle, Marléne, 'Religious revival, nationalism and the "invention of tradition": political Tengrism in Central Asia and Tatarstan', *Central Asia Survey*, 26 (2), 2007, pp. 203–16.

———, 'In Search of Kazakhness: The Televisual Landscape and Screening of Nation in Kazakhstan', *Demokratizatsiya*, 23 (2), 2015, pp. 321–40.

———, 'The Three Discursive Paradigms of State Identity in Kazakhstan: Kazakhness, Kazakhstaness and Transnationalism', in Mariya Y. Omelicheva (ed.), *Nationalism and Identity Construction in Central Asia: Dimensions, Dynamics, Directions*, Lexington Books (Layland, MD, 2015) pp. 1–20.

Lawton, Anna, *Kinoglasnost: Soviet Cinema in Our Time*, Cambridge University Press (Cambridge, 1992).

Leyda, Jay, *Kino: A History of the Russian and Soviet Film*, Princeton University Press (Princeton, 1960).

Linz, Juan, *Totalitarian and Authoritarian Regimes*, Lynne Rienner (Boulder, CO, 2000).

Lynn Edgar, Adrienne, *Tribal Nation: The Making of Soviet Turkmenistan*, Princeton University Press (Princeton, NJ, 2004).

Marshall, Brian, *Quebec National Cinema*, McGill Queens University Press (Montreal and Kingston, 2001).

Marshall, Herbert, 'The New Wave in Soviet Cinema', in Anna Lawton (ed.), *The Red Screen: Politics, Society, Art in Soviet Cinema*, Routledge (London and New York, 1992), pp. 175–92.

Martin, Virginia, *Law and Custom in the Steppe: The Kazakhs of the Middle Horde and Russian Colonialism in the Nineteenth Century*, Curzon Press (Richmond, 2001).

Masanov, Nurbolat, 'Perceptions of Ethnic and All-National Identity in Kazakhstan', in N. Oka (ed.), *The Nationalities Question in Post-Soviet Kazakhstan*, Institute of Developing Economics (Chiba, 2000).

———, Abylkhozhin, Zhulduzbek and Yerofeyev, Irina, *Nauchnoe znaanie i mifotvorchestvo isto riografii Kazakhstana*, Daik Press (Almaty, 2007).

Masanov, Nurbolat et al., *Istoriia Kazakhstana: Narody i kul'tury*, Daik Press (Almaty, 2001).

Masters, Patricia Lee, 'Warring Bodies: Most Nationalistic Selves', in Wimal Dissanayake (ed.), *Colonialism and Nationalism in Asian Cinema*, Indiana University Press (Bloomington, IN, 1994), pp. 1–10.

McAdam, Douglas, Tarrow, Sidney and Tilly, Charles, 'Comparative Perspectives on Contentious Politics', in Mark Irving Lichbach and Alan S. Zuckerman (eds), *Comparative Politics: Rationality, Culture and Structure*, Cambridge University Press (Cambridge, 2009), pp. 268–73.

Mesch, Claudia, *Art and Politics: A Small History of Art for Social Change since 1945*, I.B.Tauris (New York and London, 2013).

Meurer, Hans Joachim, *Cinema and National Identity in a Divided Germany, 1979–1989: The Split Screen*, Edwin Mellen Press (Lewinston, NY, Queenston, ON and Lampeter, Wales, 2000).

Miller, Jamie, 'Soviet Cinema, 1929–41: The Development of Industry and Infrastructure', *Europe-Asia Studies*, 58 (1), 2008, pp. 103–24.

Morely, David and Robins, Kevin, *Spaces of Identity: Global Media, Electronic Landscapes and Cultural Boundaries*, Routledge (London and New York, 1995).

Mostafa, Golam, 'The concept of "Eurasia": Kazakhstan's Eurasian policy and its implications', *Journal of Eurasian Studies*, 4 (2), pp. 160–70.

Müllerson, Rein, *A Chessboard and Player in the New Great Game*, Routledge (Abingdon and New York, 2013).

Nairn, Tom, *The Break-up of Britain: Crisis and Neo-Nationalism*, Common Ground Publishing (Melbourne, 1977).

Nazarbayev, Nursultan, *Without Right and Left*, Class Publishing (London, 1992).

Nebesio, Bohdan Y., 'Questionable Foundations for a National Cinema: Ukrainian Poetic Cinema of the 1960s', *Canadian Slavonic Papers/Revue Canadienne des Slavistes*, 4 (1/2), pp. 35–46.

Norris, Stephen M., 'Nomadic Nationhood: cinema, nationhood and remembrance in post-Soviet Kazakhstan', *Ab Imperio*, 2, 2012, pp. 378–402.

Northrop, Douglass, *Veiled Empire: Gender and power in Stalinist Central Asia*, Cornell University Press (Ithaca, NY, 2004).

Ó'Beacháin, Donnacha and Kevlihan, Robert, 'Threading a needle: Kazakhstan between civic and ethno-nationalist state-building', *Nations and Nationalism*, 19 (2), pp. 337–56.

O'Regan, Tom, *Australian National Cinema*, Routledge (London and New York, 1996).

Ohayon, Isabelle, *The Kazakh Famine: The Beginnings of Sedentarization, Online Encyclopedia of Mass Violence* [online], 28 September 2013. Available at http://www.massviolence.org/The-Kazakh-Famine-The-Beginnings, ISSN 1961-9898 (accessed 22 April 2016).

Olcott, Martha Brill, *The Kazakhs*. Stanford, The Hoover Institution Press (California, 1987).

———, 'Emerging Political Elites', in Ali Banuazizi and Myron Weiner (eds), *The New Geopolitics of Central Asia and its Borderlands*, Indiana University Press (Bloomington, IN, 1994), pp. 44–67.

———, *Kazakhstan: Unfulfilled Promise*, Carnegie Endowment for International Peace (Washington, DC, 2002).

Omarbekov, Talas, *Golomodor v Kazakhstane: prichiny, masshtaby i itogi, 1930–1931*, Kazakhskii Natsional'nyi Universitet im Al'-Farabi (Almaty, 2009).

Omelicheva, Mariya Y., 'Islam in Kazakhstan: A Survey of Contemporary Trends and Sources of Securitization', *Central Asia Survey*, 30 (2), 2011, pp. 243–56.

Orgad, Shani, *Media Representation and the Global Imagination*, Polity Press (Cambridge, 2012).

Painciola, Niccoló, *The Collectivization Famine in Kazakhstan, 1931–1933*, *Harvard Ukrainian Studies*, 25 (3/4).

Panov, Petr, 'Nation-building in post-Soviet Russia: What kind of nationalism is produced by the Kremlin?' *Journal of Eurasian Studies*, 1 (2), 2010, pp. 85–94.

Payne, Matthew, 'Viktor Turin's Turksib (1929) and Soviet Orientalism', *Historical Journal of Film, Radio and Television*, 21 (1), 2001, pp. 37–62.

Pearce, Katy and Hajizada, Adnan, 'No Laughing Matter: Humor as a Means of Dissent in the digital era: The case of Authoritarian Azerbaiijan', *Demokratizatsiya*, 22 (1), 2014, pp. 67–85.

Penkala-Gawęcka, Danuta, 'The Way of the Shaman and the Revival of Spiritual Healing in post-Soviet Kazakhstan and Kyrgyzstan', *Shaman*, 22 (1–2) Spring/Autumn 2012.
Peyrouse, Sébastien, 'Nationhood and the Minority Question in Central Asia. The Russians in Kazakhstan', *Europe-Asia Studies*, 59 (3), 2007, pp. 481–501.
———, 'The "Imperial Minority: An Interpretative Framework of the Russians in Kazakhstan in the 1990s', *Nationalities Papers*, 36 (1), 2008, pp. 105–23.
Plamenatz, John, 'Two types of Nationalism', in Eugene Kamenka (ed.), *Nationalism: The nature and evolution of an idea*, Australian National University Press (Canberra, 1975).
Pohl, Michaela, 'It cannot be that our graves will be here: the survival of Chechen and Ingush deportees in Kazakhstan', 1944–1957, *Journal of Genocide Research*, 4 (3), 2002, pp. 401–30.
Pomfret, Richard, 'Kazakhstan's Economy since Independence: Does the Oil Boom Offer a Second Chance for Sustainable Development?' *Europe-Asia Studies*, 57 (6), 2005, pp. 859–76.
Prokhorov, Alexander, 'The Unknown New Wave: Soviet Cinema of the 1960s', in Alexander Prokhorov (ed.), *Springtime for Soviet Cinema: Re/viewing the 1960s*, Pittsburgh Russian Film Symposium (Pittsburgh, 2000).
Radnitz, Scott, 'Networks, localism and mobilization in Aksy, Kyrgyzstan', *Central Asian Survey*, 24 (4), 2005, pp. 405–24.
Rancier, Megan, 'Resurrecting the Nomads: Historical nostalgia and Modern Nationalism in Contemporary Kazakh Popular Music Videos', *Popular Music and Society*, 32 (1), 2009, pp. 387–405.
Rapfogel, Jared, 'Central Asian Films', *Senses of Cinema*, 27 July 2003.
Rashid, Ahmed, *The Resurgence of Central Asia: Islam or Nationalism?* Zed Books (London, 1994).
Razzakov, Fedor, *Gibel' Sovetskogo Kino: intrigi i spory 1918–1972*, Eksmo (Moscow, 2009).
Renan, Ernest, 'Qu'est-ce qu'une nation?' In John Hutchinson and Anthony Smith (eds), *Nationalism*, Oxford University Press (Oxford, 1994).
Ricci, Steven, *Cinema and Fascism: Italian Film and Society, 1922–1943*, University of California Press (Berkeley, CA, 2008).
Rodgers, Peter, 'Understanding regionalism and the politics of identity in Ukraine's Eastern Borderlands', *Nationalities Papers*, 34 (2), 2006, pp. 154–74.
Ro'i, Yaccov, 'The Soviet and Russian context of the development of nationalism in Soviet Central Asia', *Cahiers du monde russe et soviétique*, 32 (1), 1991, pp. 123–41.
Rolich, Azade-Ayse, 'Islam, Identity and Politics: Kazakhstan 1990–2000', *Nationalities Papers*, 31 (2), 2003, pp. 159–76.
———, 'Identities in the Flux: The Mirror of Popular Culture. Kazakh Cinema at the End of the Twentieth Century', in Gabriele Rasuly-Paleczek and Julia Katschnig (eds), *Central Asia on Display: Proceedings of the VII Conference on European Society for Central Asian Studies*, Wiener Zentralasien Studien (Vienna, 2004).
Rollberg, Peter, *Historical Dictionary of Russian and Soviet Cinema*, Scarecrow Press (Lanham, MD, 2009).
———, 'Small Screen Nation Building: Astana – My Love', *Demokratizatsiya*, 23 (3), 2015, pp. 341–58.

Rottier, Peter, 'Legitimizing the Ata Meken: The Kazakh Intelligentsia Write a History of their Homeland', *Ab Imperio* 1, 2004, pp. 467–86.

——, *Creating the Kazakh nation: the intelligentsia's quest for acceptance in the Russian Empire, 1905–1920*, PhD Dissertation, University of Wisconsin-Madison (Madison, WI, 2005).

Rouland, Michael, 'A New Kazakhstan: Four Books Reconceptualise the History of the Kazak Steppe', *Nationalities Papers*, 32 (1), 2004, pp. 233–43.

Rouland, Michael, Abikeyeva, Gulnara and Beumers, Birgit (eds), *Cinema in Central Asia: Rewriting Cultural Histories*, I.B.Tauris (London and New York, 2016).

Roy, Olivier, *The New Central Asia: The Creation of Nations*, I.B.Tauris (London, 2000).

Rumer, Boris, 'A Gathering Storm', *Orbis*, 37, 1993, pp. 89–105.

Ryabchikova, Natalie, 'When Was Soviet Cinema Born? The Institutionalisation of Soviet Film Studies and Problems of Periodization', in Malte Hagener (ed.), *The Emergence of Film Culture: Knowledge Production, Institution*, Berghahn Books (New York and Oxford, 2014), pp. 118–42.

Sabol, Steven, 'The Creation of Central Asia: The 1924 National Delimitation', *Central Asian Survey*, 14 (2), 1995, pp. 225–41.

——, 'Kazak Resistance to Russian Colonization: interpreting the Kenesary Kasymov revolt, 1837–1847', *Central Asian Survey*, 22 (3), 2003, pp. 231–52.

Sarsembayev, Azmat, 'Imagined Communities: Kazak nationalism and Kazakification in the 1990s', *Central Asian Survey*, 18, (3), 1999, pp. 319–46.

Schlesinger, Philip, 'The Sociological Scope of "national cinema"', in Mette Hjort and Scott Mackenzie (eds), *Cinema and Nation*, Routledge (London and New York, 2000), pp. 19–31.

Scott, James C., *The Moral Economy of the Peasant: Rebellion and Subsistence in Southeast Asia*, Yale University Press (New Haven, CT and London, 1976).

——, *Weapons of the Weak. Everyday Forms of Peasant Resistance*, Yale University Press (New Haven, CT, 1985).

Seton-Watson, Hugh, 'Soviet Nationality Policy', *Russian Review*, 15 (1), 1956, pp. 3–13.

Shakirova, Svetlana, 'Kelin, Karoi i drugie semeinye sagi (kinematograf Kazakhstana v poiskakh ideala materi/natsii)' in *Vlast, sem'ya ethnos: gendernye roli v XXI veke*. IEA RAN (Moscow, 2014) pp. 170–2.

Sharafutdinova, A., 'Tengrianstvo, ego satellichestvo i depaganizatsiya v novykh i novesishikh religiyakh', *Izvestiya Rossiskogo gosudarstvennoogo pedagogicheskogo universiteta im. A. I Gertsena*, No. 151, 2012, pp. 154–64.

Shcherbenok, Andrey, 'Everything was over before it was no more: Decaying Civilization in Late Stagnation Cinema', in Dina Fainberg and Artemy M. Kalinovsky (eds), *Reconsidering Stagnation in the Brezhnev Era: Ideology and Exchange*, Lexington Books (Lanham, MD, 2016), pp. 77–84.

Shevel, Oxana, 'The Post-Communist Diaspora Laws: Beyond the "Good Civic versus Bad Ethnic" Nationalism Dichotomy', *East European Politics & Societies*, 24 (1), 2010, pp. 159–87.

——, 'Russian Nation-building from Yel'tsin to Medvedev: Ethnic, Civic or Purposefully Ambiguous?' *Europe-Asia Studies*, 63 (2), 2011, pp. 179–202.

Shirky, Clay, 'The Political Power of Social Media: Technology, the Public Sphere, and Political Change', *Foreign Affairs*, 90 (1), 2011, pp. 28–41.

Shulman, Stephen, 'Challenging the civic/ethnic and West/East dichotomies in the study of nationalism', *Comparative Political Studies*, 35 (5), 2002, pp. 554–85.

———, 'Sources of Civic and Ethnic Nationalism in Ukraine', *Journal of Communist Studies and Transition Politics* 18 (4), 2002, pp. 1–30.

Siranov, Kabish, *Kinoiskusstvo Sovetskogo Kazakhstana* (Almaty, Kazakhstan, 1966).

Skey, Michael, 'The national in everyday life: A critical engagement with Michael Billig's thesis of Banal Nationalism', *The Sociological Review*, 57 (2), 2009.

Slavtcheva-Petkova, Vera, 'Rethinking Banal Nationalism: Banal Americanism, Europeanism, and the Missing Link between Media Representations and Identities', *International Journal of Communication*, 8, 2014, pp. 43–61.

Slezkine, Yuri, 'The USSR as a Communal Apartment, or How a Socialist State Promoted Ethnic Particularism', *Slavic Review*, 53 (2), 1994.

Smagulova, Juldyz, 'Kazakhstan: Language, Identity and Conflict', *Innovation*, 19 (3/4), 2006, pp. 302–20.

Smailova, Inna, 'Kazakhskaya "Novaya Volna": Izobrazitel'noe reshenie fil'mov', *Prostor*, 2010, 5, pp. 165–8.

———, *Spor Kino Kritika c Kino Vredinoi*. Dizain-kontsept i maket (Astana, 2014).

Smith, Anthony D., *The Ethnic Origins of Nations*, Oxford University Press (Oxford, 1986).

———, 'Gastronomy or geology? The role of nationalism in the reconstruction of nations', *Nations and Nationalism*, 1 (1), 1994, pp. 3–23.

Smith, Graham (ed.), *The Nationalities Question in the Post-Soviet States*, Longman (London and New York, 1996).

Soni, Sharad K., 'Kazakhs in post-Socialist Mongolia', *Himalayan and Central Asian Studies*, 7 (2), April–June 2003.

Sorlin, Pierre, *Italian National Cinema*, Routledge (London and New York, 1996).

Soucek, Svat, *A History of Inner Asia*, Cambridge University Press (Cambridge, 2000).

Spencer, Philip and Woolman, Howard, *Nationalism: A Critical Introduction*, Sage Publications (London, 2002).

Suleimenov, Olzhas, *Az i ya*, Zhasushy (Alma-Ata, 1975).

Suny, Ronald G., *The Revenge of the Past: Nationalism, Revolution and the Collapse of the Soviet Union*, Stanford University Press (Stanford, CA, 1993).

———, *Looking toward Ararat: Armenia in Modern History*, Indiana University Press (Bloomington, IN, 1993).

Surucu, Cengiz, 'Modernity, Nationalism and Resistance: Identity Politics in Post-Soviet Kazakhstan', *Central Asian Survey*, 21 (4), 2002, pp. 385–402.

Szilárdi, Réka, 'Neo-paganism in Hungary: under the spell of roots', in Kaarina Aitamurto and Scott Simpson (eds), *Modern Pagan and Native Faith Movements in Central and Eastern Europe*, Routledge (Abingdon and New York, 2014) pp. 230–48.

Tan, Ed S., *Emotion and the Structure of Narrative Film: Film as an emotion machine*, Routledge (New York and London, 1995).

Taylor, Richard, *The Politics of Soviet Cinema*, Cambridge University Press (Cambridge, 1979).

———, *Film Propaganda: Soviet Russia and Nazi Germany*, I.B.Tauris (London and New York, 1998).

Thomas, Alun, *Kazakh Nomads and the New Soviet State, 1919–1934*, PhD thesis (Sheffield, 2015).

Thompson, John B., 'The New Visibility', *Theory, Culture and Society*, 22 (6), 2005, pp. 31–51.
Thompson, Kristin, 'Government Polices and Practical Necessities in the Soviet Cinema of the 1920s', in Anna Lawton (ed.), *The Red Screen: Politics, Society, Art in Soviet Cinema*, Routledge (London and New York, 1992) pp. 19–41.
Thrower, James, *The Religious History of Central Asia from the Earliest Times to the Present Day*, Edwin Mellon Press (Lewiston, NY, 2004).
Tilly, Charles, Tilly, Louise and Tilly, Richard, *The Rebellious Century*, Harvard University Press (Cambridge, MA, 1975).
Tilly, Charles and Tarrow, Sidney, *Contentious Politics*, Oxford University Press (Oxford, 2015).
Tumienz, Astrid S., 'Nationalism, Ethnic Pressures, and the Breakup of the Soviet Union', *Journal of Cold War Studies*, 5 (4), 2003, pp. 81–136.
Tynshoaev, M., Takenov, A.C. and Baigaliev, B., *Istoriya Kazakhskogo Naroda*, Sanat (Almaty, 2009).
Ubiria, Grigol, *Soviet Nation-Building in Central Asia: The Making of the Kazakh and Uzbek Nation*, Routledge (London, 2015).
van den Berghe, Pierre, 'Race and Ethnicity: a Socio-biological Perspective', *Ethnic and Racial Studies*, 1 (4), pp. 401–11.
Vitali, Valentina and Willemen, Paul (eds), *Theorising National Cinema*, Palgrave MacMillan, British Film Institute (London, 2006).
Vitali, Valentina and Willemen, Paul, 'Introduction', in Valentina Vitali and Paul Willemen (eds), *Theorising National Cinema*, Palgrave MacMillan, British Film Institute (London, 2006), pp. 1–23.
Wedeen, Lisa, *Peripheral Visions: Publics, Power and Performance in Yemen*, Chicago University Press (Chicago, 2008).
Welch, David, *Propaganda and the German Cinema 1933–1945*, I.B.Tauris (London and New York, 2001).
Weller, Charles, *Rethinking Kazakh and Central Asian Nationhood*, Asia Research Associates (Los Angeles, CA, 2006).
———, 'Religious-Cultural Revivalism as Historiographical Debate: Contending Claims in the post-Soviet Kazakh Context', *Journal of Islamic Studies*, 25 (2), 2014, pp. 138–77.
Wheeler, Deborah, 'New Media, Globalization and Kuwaiti National Identity', *Middle East Journal*, 54 (3), 2000, pp. 432–44.
Wheeler, Geoffrey, *The Modern History of Soviet Central Asia*, Weidenfeld and Nicolson (London, 1964).
Wilkes, Rima and Kehl, Michael, 'One image, multiple nationalisms: Face to Face and the Siege at Kanehsatà:ke', *Nations and Nationalism*, 20 (3), 2014, pp. 481–502.
Williams, Alan, *Film and Nationalism*, Rutgers University Press (New Brunswick, NJ and London, 2002).
Wolfel, Richard L., 'North to Astana: Nationalistic Motives for the Movement of the Kazakh(stani) Capital', *Nationalities Papers*, 30 (3), 2002, pp. 485–506.
Woll, Josephine, *Real Images: Soviet Cinemas and the Thaw*, I.B.Tauris (London and New York, 2000).
Yack, Bernard, 'The myth of the civic nation', *Critical Review*, 10 (2), 1996, pp. 193–211.

Selected Bibliography

Yegenisova, A.K. and Yerubaeva, A.R., 'Psikhologicheskie osobennosti natsional'-nogo mentalieta Kazakhskogo naroda', *Mezhdunarodnyi zhurnal eksperimental'nogo obrazovaniya*, 2015, No. 4, pp. 371–6.

Yessenberlin, Ilyas, *Kochevniki: trilogiya*, The Fund of I. Yesenberlina (Almaty, 1971).

Yessenova, Saulesh, 'Soviet Nationality, Identity, and Ethnicity in Central Asia: Historic Narratives and Kazakh Ethnic Identity', *Journal of Muslim Minority Affairs*, 22 (1), 2002, pp. 11–38.

———, '"Routes and Roots" of Kazakh Identity: Urban Migration in Post-socialist Kazakhstan', *The Russian Review*, 64, 2005, pp. 661–79.

———, 'Nomad for Export, Not for Domestic Consumption: Kazakhstan's Arrested Development to Put the Country on the Map', *Studies in Russian and Soviet Cinema*, 5 (2), 2011, pp. 181–203.

Yilmaz, Harun, *National Identities in Soviet Historiography: The Rise of Nations Under Stalin*, Routledge (London and New York, 2015).

Youngblood, Denise, *Soviet Cinema in the Silent Era 1918–1935*, University of Texas Press (Austin, 1991).

———, *Movies for the Masses: Popular Cinema and Soviet Society in the 1920s*, Cambridge University Press (Cambridge, 1992).

Yutkevich, S.I., Afanasiev, S., Baskakov, V.E. and Vaysfel'd, I.V., *Kino: Entsiklopedicheskii slovar*, Soviet Encyclopedia (Moscow, 1986).

Zaharchenko, Tanya, 'Polyphonic dichotomies: Memory and Identity in Today's Ukraine', *Demokratizatsiya*, 21 (2), 2013, pp. 241–69.

Zebrina Pruner, Ludmila, 'The New Wave in Kazakh Cinema', *Slavic Review*, 51 (4), 1992, pp. 791–801.

INDEX

Abai, 127, 134
Abdrashev, Rustem, 99, 143, 146, 154, 156, 158–60, 165, 170, 235
Abishev, Serik, 89, 212, 216–18, 220–1, 237–8, 243
Ablai Khan, 52, 128, 132–4, 141–3, 149
Accursed Trials, 68
Adambayev, Nurtas, 201, 208, 252
Aimanov, Shaken, 64, 72–3, 75, 81–5, 87–8, 246
Akubayev, Arslan, 214
Akusat, 53
Alash Orda, 34, 40, 42–3, 47, 60, 62, 71
Aldar Kose, 83–5
All-Russian State University of Cinematography (VGIK), 72, 95–7, 110
Alma-Ata and its Surroundings, 68
Amangeldy, 63, 69–70, 73, 76, 84–5, 89, 102, 128, 132, 136, 138, 203
Amirkulov, Ardak, 92, 97, 100–3, 121, 127–8, 158, 183
Anderson, Benedict, 3–4, 98–9, 241
Anniversary of the Existence of the KASSR, The, 68
Aprymov, Serik, 53, 77, 92, 97, 115–16, 121, 127, 204, 216

Arrival of the First Train to Alma-Ata, 68
ASSA, 96, 98, 110
Assembly of Peoples of Kazakhstan, 54, 155, 172
Astana – a Dream Come True, 235
Astana Arisen, 235
Astana – My Love, 234–5
Auezov, Mukhtar, 72
Auezov, Murat, 95, 97

Baigazin, Emir, 126, 206, 212, 219, 231, 243
Baksy, 182–3, 193–5
Balcony, The, 92, 99–100, 106–9, 122, 167, 169
banal nationalism, 4, 11
Baranov, Alexandr, 127, 157
Barthold, Vasili, 35–6
Bashirov, Aleksandr, 111
Begalin, Mazhit, 72, 88–9
Benjamin, Walter, 3, 98–9
Beware of the Cow, 231
Bodrov, Sergei, 175, 183
Bonus, The, 94
Book of Legends, 184–5, 193–5
Botagoz, 75
Breaking the Vicious Circle, 124, 143, 147, 170

INDEX

Bureaucrats, 216
Butter, 216
bytovoy (slice-of-life) films, 63, 94

Cardiogram, 76, 115, 118–20, 122
Chapaev, 69
Chase in the Desert, 88
China, 132
Cocktail for a Star, 230–1
collectivisation, 34, 47–8, 60, 67, 104–5, 170, 246
Conspiracy of Oberon, 232–4, 236
Constructors, 203, 206, 208, 212–16, 220–2, 233
contentious politics, 6, 8
Cooperation in the Villages, 68
Crossroad, 234

deportations, 31, 48
doctrine of national unity, 55, 155–6
Dolphin's Jump, 232–4, 236
Dvortsevoy, Sergei, 77, 203–4, 243

Educational Program of the School, An, 68
Eisenstein, Sergei, 66, 72
empty homogenous time, 3, 98–9, 113, 122
End of Ataman, 88
ethnic-civic dichotomy, 8, 10, 18, 31, 50, 54, 167, 245
Eurasianism, 35, 57

Fall of Otrar, The, 92, 97–104, 108, 122, 156, 158, 167, 183
Farewell Gulsary, 121
Freeze, The, 68

Gellner, Ernest, 3–4, 11–12, 42
Gift to Stalin, The, 17, 56, 143, 154, 156–9, 162–73, 208, 227
Girl and the Horseman, The, 75
Golden Horn, The, 72
Goskino, 65–6, 93, 95, 120

Harmony Lessons, 126, 206, 219, 231
high culture, 11, 42
Hobsbawm, Eric, 3–5, 9, 241–2
Homewrecker, 97
Hunter, The, 116, 121

Ibragimbekov, Rustam, 136–7, 141, 149
Ibrayev, Akhat, 138, 184, 191, 201
imagined community, 4
Iron Mountain, 124, 143, 145–7, 150
Irony of Fate or Enjoy Your Bath, 94
Isabayeva, Zhanna, 139, 210, 222–6, 229, 237–8, 243, 252
Islam, 35, 147
  customary law, 42
  establishment in Central Asia, 179–80
  morality, 57
  religious practice, 49, 81
  Tengrism, 188–9
Isskustvo Kino, 29

Kairat, 93, 97–8, 115, 118, 120, 122
Kalymbetov, Bolat, 134
Karakulov, Amir, 92, 96
Karoy, 223, 225–6
Karpykov, Abai, 92, 115, 117, 157
Karsakbayev, Abdullah, 72, 75–6, 79, 88, 116, 204
Kasymbekov, Kanybek, 127
Kasymov, Kenesary, 34, 40–2
Kazakh famine, 47–8
Kazakh Khanate, 16, 34–8, 51, 59, 132, 143–4, 171, 222
Kazakh New Wave, 16–17, 28, 30, 32, 49, 64, 90, 92–3, 95, 106, 108–10, 113–15, 118, 120–6, 133, 152–3, 158, 167, 174, 200–1, 226, 234, 244, 246–7
Kazakh Robbery, The, 202, 227–8
Kazakhfilm Studios
  art-house cinema, 202
  Arts Council of Studios, 79, 87

censorship, 197–9, 251
co-productions, 234
financing, 15, 104, 201, 225
history, 71–2, 95
ideology, 129, 131
ministry of culture, 56, 124, 248, 250
official representations of Kazakh nation, 7
production, 134
regime-sponsored, 143, 146, 151, 174
relationship with Adilkhan Yerzhanov, 218, 221
re-structuring, 120–1
Kazakhstan Common Home, 172
Kelin, 18, 29, 175, 181–2, 184, 186–7, 191, 193–4, 196–8, 205, 208–9, 247
Kelinka Sabina, 208–11, 237
Kenzhe, 185–6
Khodzhikov, Sultan, 72, 84, 86–8
Killer, The, 119, 121
kino.kz, 29, 148–51, 171–3, 192, 196, 211, 220, 225–6, 229, 236, 251
Know Ours, 87
Kokand Khanate, 41
korenizatsiya, 34, 49
kul'turfil'my (cultural films), 67
Kunanbayev, Abai, 52, 73, 127
Kunayev, Dinmukhamed, 45, 49, 78, 80
Kurak Korpe, 143
Kurmanbekov, Sabit, 95
Kyrgyzstan, 45, 52, 178, 180
Kyz-Zhibek, 84–7, 89, 138, 246
Kyzyl-Asker, 68

Land of the Fathers, 75, 81–4, 243, 246
language law, Kazakhstan, 53
Last Stop, The, 53, 77, 92, 97–8, 115–16, 118, 120, 122, 204, 216

Last Transition, The, 88
Lelia's Prayer, 167
Lenfilm, 69–70, 72
Little Fish in Love, 92, 115, 117–18, 122, 157
Little People, 210
Liquidator, the, 126
Losing Virginity in Almaty, 225

Mailin, Beimbet, 70
Mamonov, Pytor, 111
Manabayev, Damir, 48, 92, 100, 103–4, 106, 212
Manchurian Version, The, 88
Mazhilis, 155, 195
Mongol, 126, 183
Mongolia, 178
Mosfilm, 69, 71
Musrepov, Gabit, 70, 72
Mutiny, 68
My Dear Children, 210–11, 224, 237
My Heart Astana, 235–6
My Name is Kozha, 75–81, 83–4, 88, 116, 136–7, 147, 204, 243, 246

Nagima, 223–6
Narymbetov, Satybaldy, 163, 167, 203
national cinema, 12–13, 20, 24–8
nationalising state, 8, 10, 50, 54, 123
Nazarbayev, Nursultan, 31–2, 48, 52, 55, 57, 86, 122, 124, 127, 132, 137, 140, 142–50, 153, 155–6, 162–3, 170, 198, 235, 247, 250
Needle, The, 92, 98–9, 109–15, 122, 127, 169, 216, 244
New Economic Policy, 65
Nomad, 1, 17, 25, 29, 31, 37, 39, 41, 53, 71, 102, 124–43, 147–9, 151, 163, 171, 203, 208, 213, 217, 222, 227, 229
Nomad (*Koshpendiler*), 37, 39, 86, 198
Nugmanov, Rashid, 92, 96–7, 109–13, 121, 158, 216
Nur Otan, 55, 156

INDEX

Oirats, 17, 37, 39–41, 124, 128–30, 132, 134, 136, 138, 154, 174, 194
Old Man, The (Shal), 18, 175, 185–98, 203, 208, 247
Omarova, Guka, 175
Omirbayev, Darezhan, 77, 81, 88, 92–3, 96–8, 100, 115, 118–21, 126, 211, 226
Orynbekov, Kairzhan, 201, 202, 226–8, 252
Our Dear Doctor, 75
Owners, The, 212–16, 218, 220–2, 233, 248

Partizanskoe Kino, 219
Plague in the Village of Karats, 212, 219–20
Poem about Love, 75
polysemic, 12, 20, 64, 75
Poshanov, Zhasulan, 219
primordialism, 58, 138, 180
print capitalism, 2
Promised Land, The, 17, 56, 154, 156–7, 159, 160, 163–73, 208
Pudovkin, Vsevolod, 66, 72
Putin, Vladimir, 37

Raikahn, 72
Racketeer, 134–5, 227–30, 237, 250
Realtors, 207, 212, 217, 221, 248
Renan, Ernest, 240–1, 243
Renaissance Island, 143, 158–9, 170
representation, 20–3
Revenge, 97
River of Fire, 124, 143, 145–7, 150
Road, The, 81, 116, 121
Road to Mother, The, 170, 250
Russia, 9, 52, 132–3, 205

Salykov, Kalykbek, 92, 106–8, 169
Sardar, 17, 37, 124, 127, 129–42, 152
Satayev, Akan, 126, 131, 134–6, 138, 170, 250–2

Secret of Kara-Tau, The, 68
sedentarisation, 34, 40, 42, 47–8, 105, 170, 246
semiotics, 20–3
'Shala Kazakhs', 59, 209
Shanghai, 157
Sharipov, Farkhat, 126, 201, 209, 227, 230, 235
Shinarbayev, Yermek, 97, 127, 234
Shuga, 119, 121
Sky of My Childhood, 124, 143–52, 154, 159, 198
Sniper, 88
So There Were Stars, 124, 143
Solov'ev, Sergei, 95–8, 110
Song of Manshuk, 88
Songs of Abai, 72–3
Sovetskii Ekran, 29, 66, 81, 83, 113
Soviet Nationalities Policy, 43–7, 66, 71, 74, 89, 246
Sovkino, 67–8
Story of Kazakh Cinema, The, 85, 203, 214
Strayed, 135, 203, 206, 208, 227, 229–30, 237, 250
Student, 119
Suleimenov, Olzhas, 81, 86, 95, 101, 107, 180
Surzhekey – the Angel of Death, 48, 92, 97, 100, 103–8, 167

Tajikistan, 45
Tale of the Pink Bunny, 126, 209–11, 227, 230
Tauyekel, Slambek, 129, 154, 159, 163, 167
Temenov, Talgat, 92, 97, 110, 141
Tengrism, 18, 31, 35, 57–8, 105–6, 174–99, 200, 206, 222, 224, 243
Toll Bar, 219
Touch, The, 97
Trans-Siberian Express, 88
Tsoy, Viktor, 97, 110–13

Tulpan, 77, 203–5, 208
Turebayev, Nariman, 210
Turkmenistan, 45
Turksib, 68, 243
Tursunov, Yermek, 18, 31, 58, 105, 175–6, 181, 185–92, 194–200, 209, 247–8
Troublesome Morning, The, 80

Ukraine, 9, 52, 245–6
Uzbekistan, 45

Vostokkino, 66–8

We Live Here, 75
White Rose, The, 72
Wild East, The, 121, 158
Wolf Cub Among Little People, A, 97

Ya-Ha, 110
Yerzhanov, Adilkhan, 85, 88–9, 124, 202, 205, 207, 212–21, 229, 234, 237–8, 243, 247, 252
Yesentaeva, Bayan, 201, 230–1
Yessenberlin, Ilyas, 37, 39, 86, 142
Young Zhambyl, The, 127, 134

Zhabayev, Zhambyl, 52, 73–5, 127, 243
Zhambyl, 73–6, 84, 89, 128, 132
Zhanybek and Kerey Khan, 9, 35–7, 144
Zhauzhurek Myn Bala, 17, 29, 31, 37, 53, 124, 127, 129–43, 147–52, 171, 198, 203, 208, 213, 217, 222, 229, 250
Zheltoksan, 49, 52, 98
Zhuz, 36, 38–41, 124, 132, 174

www.ingramcontent.com/pod-product-compliance
Lightning Source LLC
Chambersburg PA
CBHW072120290426
44111CB00012B/1726